THE DIVORCE AND DIVORCE THERAPY HANDBOOK

Edited by

Martin R. Textor

JASON ARONSON INC.
Northvale, New Jersey
London

The author gratefully acknowledges permission to reprint the following material:

"Treatment of the Remarried Family" based on "Treating the Remarried Family" by C. J. Sager, H. S. Brown, T. Engel. E. Rodstein, and L. Walker, a study conducted by the Remarried Consultation Service of the Jewish Board of Family and Children's Services, New York City, and published by Brunner/Mazel, New York, 1983.

"Treating issues related to divorce and separation," by D. H. Sprenkle in *Troubled Relationships*, ed. by E. W. Nunnally and F. M. Cox © 1988 Sage Publications, Inc., Newbury Park, CA, reprinted by permission of the author and publisher.

THE MASTER WORK SERIES

First softcover edition 1994

Library of Congress Cataloging-in-Publication Data

The divorce and divorce therapy handbook / edited by Martin R. Textor.
     p.   cm.
    Bibliography: p.
    Includes index.
    ISBN 1-56821-207-0
    1. Divorce – – United States.   2. Remarriage – – United States.
  3. Divorce therapy – – United States.   I. Textor, Martin R.
    HQ834.D53 1989
    306.8'9 – – dc19   89-30761

Manufactured in the United States of America. Jason Aronson Inc. offers books and cassettes. For information and catalog write to Jason Aronson Inc., 230 Livingston Street, Northvale, New Jersey 07647.

Dedicated to my wife Inge,
for always keeping the dialogue going

CONTENTS

v

PREFACE

This handbook is an overview of contemporary clinical work on divorce and remarriage. The different approaches of divorce therapy are outlined. Special emphasis is placed on common problems and needs of adults and children faced with family disruption and reconstitution. The divorce process is conceptualized as a continuum starting with the predivorce phase and ending with remarriage (in most cases). Psychotherapists and other mental health professionals have to deal with different problems, needs, emotions, and tasks in each of these phases.

Until the end of World War II divorce was a rare phenomenon in the United States and other nations. It was regarded as social deviance and made very difficult; divorcees were discriminated against. As many marriages ended by the premature death of one spouse, remarriages and stepfamilies were common. After World War II the number of divorces increased rapidly as barriers to divorce like religious doctrine, social stigmatization, and women's dependency on their husbands diminished. As more and more wives found employment and earned their own income, they were able to leave unhappy marriages. Until the mid-70s society continued to view divorce negatively. Psychotherapists too supported this attitude. However, due to the ever increasing divorce figures a divorce was no longer seen as deviant but as a way out of a living arrangement no longer tolerable, growth-producing, or fulfilling. This new view also led to the introduction of the no-fault and equitable divorce designed to make divorce easier and less traumatic.

Although divorce and remarriage have become common experiences and the social stigma attached to separation and divorce has diminished, family dissolution and reconstitution are still experienced as periods of great stress. In many cases adults and children develop symptoms. Due to these and other negative effects, divorce and remarriage can still be considered as social problems. Thus in the mid-70s different approaches of divorce therapy and mediation were developed to help clients suffering from family disruption. Now some years later the therapeutic needs of reconstituted families are recognized, too.

In 1986 about 1,159,000 divorces were registered in the United States. This means that 7.8 percent of all persons 18 years old and over are divorced (U.S. Department of Commerce/Bureau of the Census 1987). Approximately 1.5 percent of the U.S. population is immediately involved in a divorce each year (Lyon et al. 1985). About one-half of all first marriages formed in recent years will end in divorce, with the median duration of marriage being slightly less than seven years and with the peak period for divorce being two to five years after marriage (U.S. Department of Commerce/Bureau of the Census 1987). Three in five couples filing for divorce have at least one child under 18 years of age. Thus more than one million children are affected by divorce each year, about half as many as adults (Spanier and Thompson 1984). Approximately 16 percent of all family groups with children under 18 years of age are one-parent families caused by separation or divorce (U.S. Department of Commerce/Bureau of the Census 1987). Many of these children will experience more than one family transition, as most divorced individuals remarry within an average of slightly more than three years. Thus in 1984, one partner has been married before in 22.2 percent of all new marriages; in another 23.4 percent both spouses had been married before (see above). In the United States already one-sixth of all children live in reconstituted families; about one-third of them were under the age of 5 years at the time of remarriage (Furstenberg and Spanier 1987). As 60 percent of all second marriages end in divorce (Glick 1984), many children go through the divorce cycle twice or even more often. Thus at least one child in ten will experience three or more family transitions before the age of 18. Only about half of all children living in the United States will reach that age having lived continuously with both biological parents (Furstenberg et al. 1983)—and "only 17 percent of American families now have the formerly traditional structure of the father working and the mother at home" (Moss 1984, p. 240).

I have been most fortunate in having the participation of contributors of outstanding quality in the compiling of this *Divorce and Divorce Therapy Handbook.* Their combined efforts yield a comprehensive presentation. I wish to thank each of them for the time and work invested in writing these chapters. My sincerest thanks are extended to Joan Langs and all the editorial staff at Jason Aronson, who encouraged this project from the beginning and once again accepted some extra work due to having a German editor. Last but not least, thanks to my wife, Ingeborg Becker-Textor, who put up with all those hours I spent at the typewriter.

Dr. phil. Martin R. Textor
Munich, Germany

References

Furstenberg, F. F., Jr., Nord, C. W., Peterson, J. L., and Zill, N. (1983). The life course of children of divorce: marital disruption and parental contact. *American Sociological Review* 48:656–668.

Furstenberg, F. F., Jr., and Spanier, G. B. (1987). *Recycling the Family. Remarriage After Divorce.* Updated ed. Newburg Park: Sage.

Glick, P. C. (1984). Marriage, divorce and living arrangements. *Journal of Family Issues* 5:7–26.

Lyon, E., Silverman, M. L., Howe, G. W., Bishop, G., and Armstrong, B. (1985). Stages of divorce: implications for service delivery. *Social Casework* 66:259–267.

Moss, N. I. (1984). The stepfamily: its psychological structure and its psychotherapeutic challenge. In *Marriage and Divorce. A Contemporary Perspective,* ed. C. C. Nadelson and D. C. Polonsky, pp. 240–257. New York: Guilford.

Spanier, G. B., and Thompson, L. (1984). *Parting. The Aftermath of Separation and Divorce.* Beverly Hills: Sage.

U.S. Department of Commerce/Bureau of the Census (1987). *Statistical Abstract of the United States 1988,* 108th ed. National Data Book and Guide to Sources. Washington, D.C.: U.S. Department of Commerce/Bureau of the Census.

CONTRIBUTORS

Janine M. Bernard, Ph.D.

Associate Professor, Graduate School of Education and Allied Professions, Fairfield University, Fairfield, Connecticut

Kenneth K. Berry, Ph.D.

Professor and Director of the Doctor of Psychology Program, University of Hartford, Hartford, Connecticut

Craig A. Everett, Ph.D.

Private practice and Director, Arizona Institute of Family Therapy, Tucson, Arizona

Linda Fries, M.S.

Instructor, Vocational Options Program, Clackamas Community College, Portland, Oregon

Donald K. Granvold, Ph.D.

Associate Professor, Graduate School of Social Work, The University of Texas at Arlington, Arlington, Texas

Patricia Kain Knaub, Ph.D.

Professor, Human Development and the Family, Associate Dean, College of Home Economics, University of Nebraska—Lincoln, Lincoln, Nebraska

Judy T. Konanc, Ph.D.

Clinical Associate Professor, Department of Psychiatry, University of North Carolina at Chapel Hill, Chapel Hill, North Carolina

Lawrence A. Kurdek, Ph.D.

Professor, Department of Psychology, Wright State University, Dayton, Ohio

Carol Rotter Lowery, Ph.D.

Licensed Clinical Psychologist, Family Psychology Services, P.S.C., Lexington, Kentucky

William G. Neville, Ed.D.

Private practice, Asheville, North Carolina

William C. Nichols, Ed.D.

Executive Director, Florida Governor's Constituency for Children, Miami, Florida

L. Rebecca Propst, Ph.D.

Associate Professor, Department of Counseling Psychology, Graduate School of Professional Studies, Lewis and Clark College, Portland, Oregon

David G. Rice, Ph.D.

Professor, Department of Psychiatry, University of Wisconsin Medical School, Madison, Wisconsin

Clifford J. Sager, M.D.

Director of Family Psychiatry, Jewish Board of Family and Children's Services, Clinical Professor, New York Hospital— Cornell Medical Center, New York, New York

Connie J. Salts, Ph.D.

Associate Professor, Department of Family and Child Development, Auburn University, Auburn, Alabama

Douglas H. Sprenkle, Ph.D.

Professor, Marriage and Family Therapy Program, Purdue University, West Lafayette, Indiana

Martin R. Textor, Dr. phil.

Researcher, Department of Family Research, State Institute of Early Education and Family Research, Munich, West Germany

Sandra S. Volgy, Ph.D.

Private practice, Tucson, Arizona

Nancy J. Warren, Ph.D.

Associate Professor, Department of Psychiatry, University of North Carolina at Chapel Hill, Chapel Hill, North Carolina

David M. Young, Ph.D.

Professor, Department of Psychological Sciences, Indiana University—Purdue University at Fort Wayne, Fort Wayne, Indiana

Part I

DIVORCE

1

THE DIVORCE TRANSITION

Dr. phil. Martin R. Textor

"Separations are an integral part of our human existence. Beginning with the physical separation from our mother's body at birth, we alternate attachments with separations until our final detachment from life itself, death. This engagement and disengagement pattern touches every phase and aspect of our unfolding lives" (Dlugokinski 1977, p. 27). Divorce is one of these transitions and usually affects several individuals—all family members and many network members. Like all separations it is a dynamic and complex process of changes that has a beginning and an end. It usually starts with forebodings of the impending transition (predivorce phase) and an acute time-limited crisis (separation) during which the family structure is abruptly changed. This is followed by an extended period of disequilibrium and instability (divorce phase). The usual coping mechanisms of the family members are weakened or in disarray. Then the individuals reorientate themselves and develop a new lifestyle (postdivorce phase). If the adults remarry—as most do—a new period of disequilibrium and change follows (remarriage phase). This or similar divorce cycles are described in many publications (for example, Bohannan 1973, Crosby et al. 1983, Deissler 1982, Dlugokinski 1977, Kaslow 1981, 1984, Kessler 1975, Lyon et al. 1985, Messinger and Walker 1981, Schweitzer and Weber 1985, Shapiro 1984, Turner 1980).

In each phase of the divorce cycle an individual passes through overlapping clusters of feelings, thoughts, and behaviors. Their kind, sequence, and intensity may be different in comparison to other family members, as there is a great variance between the way any two persons experience divorce. Each individual also passes through these clusters at his or her own pace. The progression from one to the next may appear at first to be linear, yet upon closer examination the emotions, thoughts, and behaviors occur, disappear, and reoccur in a way that can best be represented in spirals. It usually takes one to three years for the experience of divorce to be worked through and left behind. However, regressions, fixations, and the like can always occur.

THE PREDIVORCE PHASE

Usually several causes lead to the deterioration of a marriage; some of them may already be present a short time after the wedding. In many cases the marital relationship is unsatisfactory and/or unstable for a long time; in other cases it deteriorates suddenly and fast. Men usually see their marriage less negatively, name fewer problems, and cite less specific complaints than women. In general, most causes for the decline of the marital relationship are contributed to the spouse (Cleek and Pearson 1985, Spanier and Thompson 1984). Often too-high expectations originating from unfulfilled needs lead to the deterioration of a marriage—the partner is supposed to be one's lover, best friend, protector, parent, and so on. As these unconscious expectations cannot be met, the disappointment with the partner is great. Moreover, earlier feelings of deprivation may be exacerbated. In other cases more realistic role expectations are not fulfilled. For example, in a study of 210 individuals separated for approximately two years (Spanier and Thompson 1984), 56 percent of the women were unsatisfied with their spouses' contribution to household tasks. For 40 percent of the women and 20 percent of the men the partner did not live up to their expectations as a parent. And many were dissatisfied with their spouse as a leisure-time companion, as someone with whom to talk things over, or as a sexual partner.

Sometimes financial and job-related problems contribute to the deterioration of the marital relationship. In the aforementioned study the following economic issues were found to be points of conflict: amount of money one had (named by 55.6 percent of the respondents), individual's or spouse's working hours (54.1 percent), time away from home because of a job (40 percent), kind of one's or spouse's job (39 percent), and one's or spouse's colleagues (34.6 percent). Some partners also enjoy the gratifications of their careers more than their family life. Especially in dual-career marriages, conflicting interests and ambitions may cause problems. In many cases negative developments are precipitated by third-party involvement. For example, in the Spanier and Thompson (1984) study more than 60 percent of the respondents had extramarital sexual relationships. However, in-laws may also have a negative influence, especially if they disapprove of the marriage—this was reported, for example, by a quarter of the 335 separated or divorced individuals studied by Burns (1984).

In many cases different values and goals cause problems. For example, some partners define the gender roles in irreconcilable ways; many women fight for emancipation and equal power in marriage; some spouses feel restricted in their strivings for self-actualization, individualism, personal satisfaction, and self-fulfillment. Sometimes living as an independent and self-sufficient individual may seem to be more rewarding than maintaining the marital relationship. Moreover, growth or change in either spouse often leads to different developments and divergent life-styles—at the end little is left in common. This divergence sometimes becomes evident during the midlife crisis, when the feeling that time is running out precipitates the reevaluation of one's marriage (Kaslow 1981, Kitson et al. 1985, Lloyd and Zick 1986).

Other causes for the deterioration of marital relationships may be lack of communication, communication difficulties, bad habits like nagging, too little sharing of feelings, or lack of interpersonal skills like empathy. Sometimes negative developments are caused by the reenactment of conflict originating in early family experience, by emotional problems, by personality disorders, by substance abuse, or by brutality. In some cases the decline of a marriage is precipitated by life transitions like the birth of a child, launching the youngest child, or the retirement of a spouse. For example, a father may not adapt to his newborn child because he sees him or her as a rival for his wife's attention, feels neglected, and turns away from his family. Moreover, crises like job loss, serious illness, sexual dysfunction, or the birth of a handicapped child may have the same negative effects as life transitions (Bloom and Hodges 1981, Burns 1984, Cleek and Pearson 1985, Kaslow 1981, 1984, Kitson et al. 1985). However, in other cases there are no such events—the marriage deteriorates in a slow and creeping process, as described in the next paragraphs.

Relational Disenchantment

Relational disenchantment is the first substage of the predivorce phase. During this time a multitude of small acts contributes to a wearing away of marital satisfaction, love, and affection. The spouses become more and more disillusioned, are disappointed with each other, and feel unvalidated. When comparing their own marriage with those of acquaintances, they arrive at negative judgments. Many spouses begin to concentrate on taking rather than on giving. As they feel that they do not get enough, they may maintain a careful vigilance to prevent one's receiving more than the other. Moreover, some begin to focus on the negative aspects of their relationship.

Many spouses start to fight with each other. At the beginning they still try to be rational and attempt to find compromises. After a while, however, they no longer look for solutions due to mounting anger, frustration, disrespect, and rejection. Instead they try to hurt each other emotionally (and sometimes physically). Some spouses avoid conflicts after a while. They deny their problems and pretend that everything is all right. They stop communicating. In other cases the spouses do not experience so many conflicts. They withdraw from each other gradually. As they feel bored in each other's presence, they develop a rationale for not being together. Instead they concentrate on work, hobbies, home computers, and separate friends. Communication with each other decreases, and they grow further apart. Sometimes this slow and subtle process is not even noticed. If it is noted and confronted by one partner, the other may deny it so that no change occurs.

In all these cases there is a loss of trust and commitment to the marital union. The spouses stop sharing with each other and often avoid physical contact. Sex becomes a battleground or is discontinued. Feelings like hurt, anger, dread, inadequacy, confusion, or indifference dominate. Often one or both spouses try to win back the partner's affection—sometimes these efforts may last for three or more years. Many spouses also seek professional help: In a study of 210 separated or divorced individuals (Spanier and Thompson 1984) 70 percent of the sample consulted one or more sources—clergymen, marriage and family counselors, physicians, psychologists, and psychiatrists (in this sequence) being visited most often. Only 19 percent indicated that these professionals were not helpful; however, in most cases the marriage could not be saved because help was sought too late or one or both spouses lacked motivation (cp. Bloom and Hodges 1981). Many spouses also discuss their problems with same-sex or opposite-sex friends. Sometimes these relationships may get closer than that with the spouse. In many cases outside relationships also develop into extramarital affairs, which frequently lead to new emotional investments and strained bonds. If the sexual affair is confessed or found out, the spouse might react with strong emotions like anger, fear, or jealousy. Often he or she tries to punish the partner with withdrawal, threats of suicide, revenge affairs, or physical abuse. Attempts at penance might be rejected. The alienation between the spouses increases and they grow further apart.

Decisional Conflict

Decisional conflict is the second substage of the predivorce phase. It begins with the first serious thoughts of divorce and is a time full of ambivalence and inner stress. One or both partners analyze their marital situation again and again, usually without talking to the partner. They compare the costs with the rewards of their relationship, analyze their feelings, and consider barriers to a possible separation, such as the presence of (small) children, financial constraints, or lack of employment. Many continue to search for a solution to their marital problems as they still see some good in their relationship and feel that they risk a major loss by a separation. Other spouses feel that they are in a double bind: They may lose if they stay or if they leave. Thus the decision to separate is a very difficult and complex one that is usually preceded by intense intrapsychic conflict, vacillation, hesitation, and feelings of uncertainty. It may take two or more years to make this decision, especially after a long marriage.

During this time the spouses often lead emotional and behavioral separate lives. Many of them are no longer sexually involved with each other or have intercourse only once a week or less (Spanier and Thompson 1984). In conflictual situations they either follow an attack or an avoidance pattern—they rarely negotiate with each other in calm and rational ways, no longer search for solutions, and have little will for compromise. One or both may continue to discount or deny marital problems. Some spouses withdraw from social interaction during this time; some establish a network with other individuals to discuss their inner conflicts. The latter generally fare better after separation, because they have their own support system. Usually both spouses suffer during this time, often developing psychosomatic symptoms. For example, in a study of 153 recently separated individuals, half reported weight changes, upset stomachs, fatigue, headaches, nervousness, inner tension and the like during the time before the separation (Bloom and Hodges 1981).

Many children know about the marital problems of their parents or are even involved in these conflicts. They may suffer from this situation and develop symptoms, especially if they fulfill pathogenic roles and functions within the family system. In other cases children are kept in the dark as their parents make an effort not to let their marital difficulties affect them. Mitchell (1985) interviewed 50 children whose parents got a divorce several years ago and reports: "Half of the children did not remember any parental conflict before separation. A majority thought their family life had been happy. Some who did describe arguments had not thought them sufficient reason for their parents to separate" (p. 113).

The predivorce phase ends with the final decision to divorce, which is often precipitated by a specific event and may be followed by feelings of relief. In most cases the spouses have discussed the possibility of divorce before—quite often for a long time. When divorce is mentioned for the first time, the partner often reacts with emotions like surprise, anger, hate, hurt, despair, apathy, fear, or panic. Afterward both may show increased rates of attack or avoidance behaviors. Sometimes one partner is abused physically or emotionally by the other out of a wish for revenge and punishment. Moreover, there may be some trial separations. In many cases, the other spouse makes desperate attempts to win back the partner's affection; however, only a few would go to almost any length to save their marriage. In other cases the first discussion of divorce coincides with the final separation or follows it. These reactions were reported, for example, by about 25 percent and by 10 percent, respectively, of the divorced individuals studied by Spanier and Thompson (1984).

THE DIVORCE PHASE

The divorce phase follows the final decision to divorce and ends with the divorce decree. Usually a couple of months pass between certainty about the end of the marriage and filing for divorce. In a few cases this period may last much longer as the spouse keeps his or her decision to divorce secret in order to prepare for the separation by asking for advice, looking for an apartment, or saving money. Housewives have to plan their divorces especially carefully. Kitson and colleagues (1985) write: "Women have informally told us about deciding to put the title for a new car in their own names or opening new joint accounts at banks or department stores so that they would have a credit record" (p. 259). Many continue their education or search for a job. Some spouses also test their sexual attractiveness. They are now future oriented and fantasize about single life.

Separation

Separation is the first substage of the divorce phase. In general, more women than men initiate separation and suggest divorce (Bloom and Hodges 1981, Spanier and Thompson 1984). Usually one spouse moves out of the family residence and lives in makeshift or temporary housing for some time. Often there are several moves until this individual settles down again. Sometimes both spouses move out and search for a new accommodation. In a few cases they also try separation under one roof. This is an extremely stressful arrangement, because there may be great tensions, daily expression of hostility, and lack of communication. If children are present, they usually suffer considerably, as they are left in between. The way in which separation occurs has a great impact on the well-being and postdivorce relationship of all individuals involved. It makes a big difference whether separation happens by mutual agreement or against the will of the partner, whether it occurs suddenly or after long discussions, whether a third party is involved or not.

Both spouses usually experience separation in idiosyncratic ways. They go through common emotional and behavioral reactions at different times and often in different sequences. If separation is a one-sided decision, the initiator may feel relief in having moved out and in having made the end of the marriage known to others. As this spouse has planned the separation, he or she accepts the resulting situation, looks forward to single life, and may even be joyful and enthusiastic. However, the initiator often suffers from strong guilt feelings and doubts.

Spouses who are suddenly confronted with separation usually react with shock and strong emotional pain and feel betrayed and abandoned. They experience this situation as a traumatic crisis and suffer from feelings of anger, fury, hurt, despair, self-pity, sadness, hopelessness, or fear. In some cases rejection by the partner (and by in-laws, mutual friends, and the like) may combine with self-rejection to cause great emotional problems. In general, emotions are stronger if these individuals have invested a lot in their marriage, if they have experienced great losses previously, or if they have internalized norms and religious doctrines that forbid divorce. In other cases, the passive spouses accept their partners' decision to divorce and attempt to negotiate the separation in a rational way. Thus they try to make arrangements regarding housing, finances, and the management of their children together. This is also the case when the separation has been a mutual decision.

According to a study of 210 divorced individuals (Spanier and Thompson 1984) a great number of them still experienced positive emotions for their spouses at the time of separation. Men were more likely to report love than women, who mostly felt a combination of love and hate. Thirty-five percent of the men and 41 percent of the women experienced relief after the separation. Twenty percent of the women and nine percent of the men seriously considered taking their life, many of them making a suicide attempt (eight percent and two percent, respectively). A third of the women and 19 percent of the men experienced substantial symptomatic distress. For example, psychosomatic symptoms, depression, excessive drinking, or substance abuse were reported. Most newly separated individuals also experience sleeplessness, tiredness, headaches, nervousness, moody spells, irritability, tension, apathy, feelings of inferiority, identity crises, and the like (cp. Dlugokinski 1977, Spanier and Thompson 1984). Sometimes emotions get so strong that they are suppressed or denied.

Usually it takes some time until the full impact of the separation hits. The spouses realize that all emotional, financial, and behavioral energies invested in their family are lost, and enter a long-lasting process of mourning and grieving. Faced with an overload of life changes and stress, they may react with panic and fear, be immobilized, or block out some of the change. They are overwhelmed by their emotions, fear not being able to cope with all future uncertainties, worry about meeting financial needs, and are afraid that they will no longer be attractive to the other sex. They feel vulnerable and insecure.

After separation many spouses maintain little contact. If they still communicate with each other, they are rarely successful in resolving issues and often end up fighting, blaming, or scapegoating each other. Some spouses, however, continue to negotiate and bargain with each other. In a study of 153 newly separated individuals (Bloom and Hodges 1981), 45 percent of the respondents reported that they talked about reconciliation with their partners. Parents more often act this way than spouses without children.

The spouses now inform their relatives and friends about the separation and impending divorce; they tend to express their own righteousness and the wrongness of their partners. As friends and relatives tend to take sides, both partners get some support but also lose sources of comfort, affection, and reassurance. For example, in a study of 210 divorced individuals (Spanier and Thompson 1984) half of the women and 35 percent of the men reported parental approval, and less than a third of the women and more than a third of the men mentioned disapproval by their parents. Friends are usually less judgmental than relatives. Both relatives and friends may try to reunite the spouses.

Financial Situation

After separation many spouses are faced with financial problems, because they have to maintain and furnish separate apartments or houses. The lowered economic status is met by a reduction in the standard of living. Today the obligation of separated or divorced husbands to support their former wives and their children is less emphasized than 10 or 20 years ago. Instead it is expected that both former spouses work and earn their living themselves. This is certainly a great challenge for housewives who have been out of the labor market for a long time and lack marketable skills. Women who have part-time jobs may face problems when searching for a full-time job guaranteeing them a similar standard of living as before the separation. Many women have to get further education and start new careers.

In general, women experience a great drop of income after separation and divorce. In 1982, for example, the median family income was $26,020 for married couples and $15,156 for divorced female heads of households (Pett and Vaughan-Cole 1986). The effects of this drop in income are especially negative in lower-income households, which may become dependent on welfare, food stamps, and so on. In 1982, 30 percent of all single-parent families headed by divorced women had an income below the poverty level. Members of lower-income households feel less economically secure, score lower in their social and emotional adjustment, and are often unable to improve their lot with time (Pett and Vaughan-Cole 1986). In middle- and higher-income households the earnings of the women, alimony, and child support play a greater role. As these women find it easier to get better-paying jobs, their situation improves with time. A drop in income certainly leads to a lower social status, which might be accompanied by a loss of self-esteem.

After separation spouses have to assume the household activities that were previously carried out by their partners; they have to take over new responsibilities and develop different routines. Transitional difficulties may be especially great if the spouses have lived in traditional marriages with a distinct division of household activities. Then they are not familiar with the tasks handled by their partners, and they have to learn new skills. Thus mothers usually struggle with the provider role and fathers with domestic or child-rearing activities. Moreover, the spouses have to learn the single life-style and find new friends because they have lost those taking their partners' side and because they may be excluded from couple-dominated groups within their network.

Child Rearing

If the spouses have children, they very often give them one-sided explanations for the separation or no explanation at all. Even teenagers are rarely kept informed about separation and divorce issues. "Parents may well be in too much emotional turmoil themselves to explain much to their own children. At the point where a child needs extra support from parents, those parents are at the center of the conflict and unavailable to help" (Mitchell 1985, pp. 79–80). Many parents also give little thought to the effects of separation on their children. They may intellectualize this highly emotional event and deny their children's sense of loss, bewilderment, and fear. As they frequently do not inform teachers about the separation, their children may find little understanding and support at school.

While marital relationships can be dissolved, parenthood is an existential reality that will never end. Some spouses manage to separate their marital and parental roles, shield their children from ongoing conflicts, and acknowledge their need for a continuing positive relationship with both parents. In other cases the children are drawn into conflicts, expected to take sides, or used as message bearers. They are seldom offered a choice of parent with whom to live and are rarely informed about planned living arrangements. In general, parents decide where the children will stay until custody and access are regulated by the courts. Parents establish ground rules regarding visiting, vacations, and the like and develop new ways of communicating about their children.

The parents also establish new patterns of relating to their children. The residential parent assumes more responsibilities and authority; the nonresidential one moves to the sidelines. As the latter forfeits daily contact with the children, he or she may fear losing their affection. Moreover, nonresidential parents often report an overpowering sense of aloneness after the loss of their children. If residential parents have to work, they usually have little time and energy left to devote to their children. Thus they may be unable to adequately care for them or may even neglect them—moreover, they are often preoccupied with financial and emotional problems. If they have not been employed before and start a new job, the situation is even more problematic as the continuity of the child's relationship to *both* parents suffers. Many young children are also placed in day-care facilities for the first time. In general, there often is an increase of problems with children and a decrease in the quality of the parent-child relationship.

Children's Reactions

When children are informed about the separation and impending divorce, they may react with disbelief, fear, panic, anger, confusion, sadness, or grief. This situation is especially shocking for children who had not been aware of the marital conflicts or thought that their family was happy (see p. 8). Children who are involved in the marital struggle and know about their parents' problems may nevertheless react similarly, because they have not expected a family breakup. The perception and understanding of separation and divorce are not only shaped by children's age and development but also by the behavior of the parents and the amount of information given them. Young children have the greatest problems in grasping the meaning of separation and divorce. They may react with denial, may feel rejected and unloved, may fear being overwhelmed by intense emotions, or may have anxiety-provoking fantasies of parental abandonment.

Many older children are also bewildered; they do not understand the causes for the family breakup and do not know whether the separation will be short or permanent. They may feel insecure and worry about the future. In general, older children are more able to understand the impending changes and to sort out their feelings themselves. They may resist being drawn into ongoing conflicts or may even distance themselves by emotional detachment and increased social activities. They are also able to form independent judgments of their parents. Both younger and older children show a desire for their parents' reunion and have reconciliation fantasies for long periods of time.

Many children do not agree with their parents' separation. They experience the absence of one parent as a great loss. Often they feel angry with the parent whom they consider responsible for the family breakup. They feel concern for the parent who has been hurt and rejected and may try to take care of him or her. Many children experience great loyalty conflicts, especially if they are asked with whom they want to stay after separation. In this situation they may choose the parent who is most upset and needs help most. Siblings, acting on their sense of justice, may elect to divide the family up, one or more going with one parent, another with the other parent. Many (younger) children also feel guilty for taking sides or even for the family breakup. For example, in a study of 126 children whose parents had been separated for a long time, 21 percent showed signs of blaming themselves (Kurdek and Siesky 1979).

After their parents' separation, many children focus all their energy into the family. They feel pressured to show empathy and to give emotional support. If parents suffer from intense negative feelings and symptoms, their children may worry about their emotional health. Thus they give less attention to academic achievement and friends, which often leads to a sudden drop in school performance and peer problems. Some children also feel isolated at school and are convinced that they are alone in having separated parents. Other common reactions of children in this substage of the divorce phase are withdrawal, self-absorption, possessiveness (clinging), restlessness, nervousness, and irritability. Some children develop symptoms and show acting-out or regressive behaviors, especially in those cases in which the children's adjustment is hindered by ongoing conflicts between the parents, alliances, moves (loss of friends, new school) being sent to boarding schools, and so on. According to Mitchell's (1985) study of 71 Scottish parents and their children, nearly two-thirds of the children had been upset by their parents' separation but less than a third of their parents noticed their distress. Thus many children did not feel understood. Mitchell also reports that for one in three children separation and the following months were the worst time in the divorce cycle.

Legal Divorce

Legal divorce is the second substage of the divorce phase. During this time custody and access provisions have to be made and the couple's property has to be divided. The substage starts with hiring a lawyer and ends with the divorce date. Usually it is characterized by adversarial proceedings; that is, because lawyers are interested only in their clients, they try to win the best deal for them and do not consider the well-being of the other side or of the whole family. In their efforts to win for their clients, they often aggravate the relations between the spouses and make it difficult for them to reconcile. However, the further deterioration of the relationship between the spouses can also be caused by their using custody provisions or the division of property as issues to hurt the partner, to humiliate, or to retaliate. According to a study of 210 separated or divorced individuals (Spanier and Thompson 1984), 26 percent of them reported that their involvement with attorneys worsened the relationship with their spouses. One-third of them had negative feelings toward their lawyers and felt unsupported, because few attorneys are able to deal with psychological aspects of divorce. Moreover, they may induce unrealistic expectations or try to prolong the process in order to earn more money. Because of these negative side effects some spouses turn to mediators for help in dividing the property or in drafting custody provisions. Mediation allows maximum participation of the clients, makes them feel responsible for their own welfare, and permits them to find their own solutions. It fits the tendency toward amicable divorce and coparenting.

The division of property is a very complicated matter, especially in mid-life divorce, as more assets—investments, homes, business holdings, savings, contributions to pension funds—have to be divided. The distribution of valued possessions is also a traumatic experience. Moreover, it may obscure the process of emotional separation. Rosenthal and Keshet (1981) write that the persons who insist on having the family silver may really be saying that they are the ones "who loved more, gave more, or put more meaning into the marriage. Financial accountings take the place of needed emotional accounting" (p. 99).

Child custody and visitation arrangements are often made by the spouses themselves, sometimes after consultation with relatives and friends or with lawyers. Spanier and Thompson (1984), for example, write in their study of 210 separated or divorced individuals: "Respondents report that custody was determined by mutual agreement in about two-thirds of the cases. Courts made the decision in about one in five cases; the children made the decision in 7 percent of the cases . . ." (p. 77). Courts usually accept custody and access agreements of parents. In these cases they are reluctant to ask for further information about the children and their welfare. In other cases—especially after long custody battles—the courts decide on custody and may specify the frequency and length of access.

Today approximately nine in ten children stay with their mothers after divorce (Furstenberg and Spanier 1987). In most cases their fathers have agreed with this arrangement, although in some cases the mothers have fought for sole custody. Tolsdorf (1981) observed: "The motivations for keeping custody varied and ranged from an attempt to maintain the parental role in order to maintain a consistent self-image on the part of one partner, all the way to attempts to retain custody as a strategy to force the spouse into making concessions on other issues" (p. 277). Other reasons for seeking sole custody are, for example: greater love for the children, stronger bonds, offer of more consistency, the attempt to force the partner into reconciliation, the wish for someone who helps to fight loneliness and who comforts, the need to retaliate, guilt for being partly responsible for the child's suffering, the inability to see the spouse as a good caretaker, power struggles, and so on. Sometimes the other partner is unable to care for the child. In a few cases the parents split the children among them (split custody) or decide on joint custody; that is, they want to share the care of their children because both are committed to their parental responsibilities. These individuals are usually able to differentiate between their marital and parental roles, are willing to cooperate, have similar child-rearing attitudes, and are able to negotiate conflicts.

In general, divorce hearings are short, as most spouses have resolved (nearly) all differences before, either by themselves or with the help of mediators or lawyers. In a few cases the legal battles are continued after divorce in order to ensure the payment of alimony or to deal with problems of custody and access. Ongoing battles about visitation rights may have especially negative effects on children, because they feel torn between their parents and have difficulties in finding a basis for continuing their relationships with both of them.

THE POSTDIVORCE PHASE

After divorce the former spouses may still suffer from feelings of hurt, self-pity, despair, anxiety, anger, self-blame, guilt, or remorse. Some have to deal with an acute sense of shame and failure, feel isolated and alienated, suffer from depression and sharp mood swings. Many fear not having the strength to cope with single life or single parenthood, are disoriented, feel helpless and insecure. Often their emotional state leads to lack of concentration and fatigue, with a resulting negative impact on their work performance. Some try to avoid facing the pain of family breakup by turning to alcohol and drugs. In the course of the postdivorce phase, however, negative feelings decrease in intensity and in many cases disappear totally. This development is facilitated by the growing acceptance of divorce: "Increased social approval of personal decisions based on need for individual fulfillment and growth has provided an ideology which allows a quick recovery from feelings of guilt and inadequacy when the marriage fails. The reduced concern with guilt and blame, both self-assumed and defensively projected, reduces some of the trauma associated with divorce" (Rosenthal and Keshet 1981, p. 97). However, many divorced individuals still experience social discrimination (Spanier and Thompson 1984).

Most former spouses work through the experiences of separation and divorce on a cognitive and emotional level. They mourn the end of their marriage and the loss of all the time and energy invested in their partnership. They also deal with memories, the ghost of the ex-spouse and their feelings (love, hate, hostility, and the like) for him or her. In the course of time, however, they accept the divorce and stop analyzing their marriage. According to a study of 210 divorced individuals (Spanier and Thompson 1984) more than 90 percent had accepted the end of their marriage within two years after separation. Only 9 percent were still angry with their former spouses. In general, it is more difficult to accept the divorce if the marriage was calm in the final months, if the spouse was highly committed to it, if the individual still loves his or her ex-partner, or if he or she has been deserted. The process of psychic divorce usually is more difficult and takes longer. It encompasses purging the former spouse from one's inner self. In order to get some help in achieving the psychic divorce and in dealing with all the feelings resulting from separation, many divorcees consult mental health professionals.

During the postdivorce phase the process of establishing two separate households and of developing a new life-style is continued: "The tempo which characterizes extricating from the former marriage and becoming involved differently in parenting, work, recreation and/or social activities, is an individual matter" (Kaslow 1984, p. 36). The former spouses develop new daily routines and new coping skills, set different goals and priorities. Men become proficient in domestic tasks, while newly employed women gain job experience and a network of colleagues; both invest less in traditional role aspects and thus become more androgynous. In a study of 30 divorced custodial parents (Wedemeyer and Johnson 1982), for example, twice as many women than men mentioned their pleasure in their achievements at work, feeling that they have demonstrated their independence and survival skills. The former spouses develop a new identity as single individuals and get accustomed to their new role at work, in the social sphere, and in relating to the other sex. They become aware of the advantages and problems of being single, integrate new experiences, and become confident in their ability to cope with their new status.

Many former spouses focus inwardly, try to learn about themselves, and discover new sides of their personality. Other divorcees try to achieve personal transformation and growth not by self-examination but by experimenting with new life-styles: "Some persons redefine themselves . . . through hairstyle, new wardrobe, type of leisure and social activity selected, new hobbies, and new ways of relating sexually" (Turner 1980, p. 163). They may change jobs, return to college, travel, or engage in creative pursuits. Some live through several different patterns out of curiosity, the realization of new choices, and a sense of freedom and autonomy.

In general, it may take from six months to four years to recover from the divorce experience, to return to normalcy, and to settle down in a new life-style. According to a study of 210 divorced individuals (Spanier and Thompson 1984), roughly 20 percent did not have a sense of well-being after two years. They had a dim view of themselves, their health, and their current life. Many of them were still attached to the former spouse, harbored strong feelings for him or her, were lonely, and had financial problems (cp. Pett and Vaughan-Cole 1986). Often an individual decides by himself or herself that the transitional period is over. After having interviewed 34 middle-aged divorcees, Cauhapé (1983) reports: "I found that passage termination appears to occur by choice. That is, termination is controlled by a person's decision that a goal is reached, and hence, no more time in passage is necessary" (p. 7).

Network Changes

After divorce the split of the family's network into two relatively unconnected subsystems continues. Usually the members of each subsystem exonerate the respective spouse from blame and join him or her in faultfinding. They create their own version of the divorce and the motives for separation. If the spouses had children, the other half of the network may interfere with visits, make threatening gestures, or try to alienate the children from their second parent. Especially in these cases the children suffer great loyalty conflicts and feel torn between the two subsystems. Quite often they become the only connecting link between both sides. Tolsdorf (1981) observes: "Communication between the subsystems, and sometimes between the parents, became all but non-existent, in which case the children became the only means of passing information from one subsystem of the network to the other" (p. 277). Sometimes the grandparents on the side of the nonresidential parent make strenuous efforts to maintain contact with their grandchildren. Via them the children may meet uncles, aunts, and cousins. In some cases the split between the two subsystems is less marked. A few spouses who do not understand the end of their marriage may even turn to their in-laws for insight into their partner's actions and motives.

Support needed during the postdivorce phase is usually mobilized within one's own subsystem of the family's network. The family of origin rallies around the divorced spouse and helps, even if family members did not approve of the separation. In general, women and divorced parents with children receive more moral and financial support, as well as more services from relatives, friends, and former in-laws than do men and divorced individuals without children (Spanier and Thompson 1984). Services needed by them are assistance in finding permanent housing, baby-sitting, advice, and help with errands, housework, repairs, or moving the household. In general, divorced spouses with a strong support network fare better. Thus Daniels-Mohring and Berger (1984) report after having studied 42 divorced individuals: "More relational needs are being met by fewer persons within the high adjustment group of subjects. In addition, the high adjustment group reports more than twice as many relationships in which emotional integration and reassurance of worth needs are being met" (p. 27). Moreover, less change in the social network was related to a more positive self-concept and a higher sense of well-being.

As most former spouses lose friends after separation and divorce, they often feel lonely. According to a study of 210 divorced individuals (Spanier and Thompson 1984) 30 percent experienced severe loneliness and 55 percent felt somewhat lonely during the two years since separation. They longed for opposite- or same-sex friends, for their former spouse and their children. Although many of them had found new friends (men reported a greater number of them than women), almost half expressed a desire for more friends two years after separation. In general, divorced individuals find more friends among singles than among couples. Some make acquaintances in self-help groups (for example, Parents Without Partners) or in church-related groups, which also offer emotional support.

Dating

The majority of former spouses start dating within six months of their final separation (Spanier and Thompson 1984). Many feel insecure about where to meet others and how to approach them, are uncertain regarding their attractiveness, are concerned about rejection, and do not want to be hurt again. These are especially problems for older divorcees and middle-aged women. In general, dating helps one to adjust to divorce, reaffirms one's worth, remedies loneliness, and facilitates role reconstruction and identity formation. Sometimes it also allows them to deny the pain of divorce. Several different dating patterns can be observed (cp. Cauhapé 1983, Kessler 1975, Rosenthal and Keshet 1981, Spanier and Thompson 1984, Turner 1980). For some individuals the postdivorce phase is a time of transitional sexual contacts and of sexual experimentation ("second adolescence"). They sometimes cohabit with changing partners or even date more than one person at a time; they try to prove their sexual appeal and prowess (men may also date considerably younger women). They may get emotionally involved if one of these dating relationships continues for a longer time. However, they may also terminate it because they do not feel ready for new commitments and dependencies. If they have children, they often do not want any interference by the new partner with the parent-child relationship.

In other cases the former spouses become overinvolved in one very close, warm, and compassionate relationship in which they seek nurturance and understanding. Some divorcees start to look for a new spouse at once after separation. This is often the case if they do not manage well alone, that is, if they lack skills or resources, have financial problems, or need someone to take care of the children. Single parents look for a partner who gets along well with their children and try to integrate him or her slowly and carefully into their family. In a few cases the former spouses remarry directly after divorce. They frequently have found a new partner before choosing to separate and may have kept him or her secret. However, most extramarital relationships do not lead to marriage and usually do not last long. A few divorcees do not date because they are afraid of the risks involved, are self-absorbed, or do not want to disturb the relationship with their children.

Relationship between Former Spouses

"The partnership between husband and wife does not end with separation. The partnership continues in memory or hope, if not in actuality" (Spanier and Thompson 1984, p. 161). Usually there is still some contact between the former spouses for long periods of time. Spanier and Thompson (1984) asked 210 individuals separated for approximately two years about any contact with their ex-partners in the past few weeks. They found out that many had spoken to their former spouses by phone (59.5 percent) or in person (49.8 percent), had heard from him or her by letter (10.2 percent), had written to him or her (7.3 percent), had gone out together (10.2 percent), or even had sex together (4.4 percent). A quarter of the respondents remained close, half tolerated some contact, and the rest preferred to have nothing to do with the ex-spouse. Many still experienced some feelings of attachment and would have liked to have more contact. Usually the relationship between the former spouses became less tense. However, 30 percent reported no change or an increase of tension during the two years since divorce. According to another study of 80 divorced couples (Ahrons and Wallisch 1987) 80 percent of the respondents reported little or no involvement in each other's life one year after divorce. Only five percent still were much involved. After another two years there was even less involvement. About 30 percent of the divorcees reported some love or feelings of friendship for the former spouse. Roughly half of them were indifferent, and a quarter experienced negative feelings (one and three years after divorce). Those who were left by the spouse were more likely to maintain strong emotions of love or hate. In general, the current relations between former partners are dependent on the quality of the final months of marriage and the circumstances of the separation.

Usually there is more contact between the former spouses if they have children. According to the aforementioned study, 21 percent of the couples had a relatively high degree of parental interaction one year after divorce; 59 percent reported a moderate amount and 21 percent a low amount. Two years later only nine percent mentioned a high degree of parental interaction. "At one year following the divorce, about 45 percent of the parents reported spending time together with their children. Two years later, only about 30 percent reported spending time together as a binuclear family. The most frequently mentioned activities participated in together were holidays and celebrations (58 percent), eating together (42 percent), and school activities (29 percent). Only about 10 percent said that they visited grandparents and other relatives together" (Ahrons and Wallisch 1987, p. 280). In these cases the nuclear family had reorganized itself in a "binuclear" structure with two households as one family unit.

Those in contact with their former spouses mostly talk about major decisions regarding the children, about their children's accomplishments and problems, about child support, daily happenings, and practical or personal problems. They avoid topics like the former marriage, causes of divorce, reconcilation, new relationships, or the children's divorce adjustment (Ahrons and Wallisch 1987, Spanier and Thompson 1984). In general, there is a higher amount of interaction in joint custody cases or if the frequency of visitation is high. According to the aforementioned study of Ahrons and Wallisch (1987), about half of the 80 former couples reported conflicts and tensions with respect to parenting issues one and three years after divorce. Often mentioned problems are unclear visitation rights, lack of flexibility in scheduling visits, lack of separation between child-rearing and partnership issues, and financial tensions.

Several relationship patterns between former spouses can be observed. A few become friends and relate in constructive ways, although they lack adequate role models and are not supported by the community. Some develop a cooperative relationship but are emotionally detached. They do not share intimate details and rarely meet socially. If they have children, they stay in regular contact with each other, with both sides initiating contact. Usually there are some coparenting and mutual support (low level of conflict). Other cases display considerable enmeshment, emotional entanglement, confusion, and conflict. The former spouses are still involved in each other's life; they may use every "reason" to contact each other, may spend some time together, and may meet each other socially. Sometimes there are conflicts on child-rearing issues. In other cases, the ex-spouses become lifelong enemies. Usually patterns of continuing conflict, unfriendliness, blaming, and little communication as established in the divorce phase are maintained and may even lead to chronic litigation. If they have children, there may be new disputes about parenting, access, and the like. Sometimes intermediaries are used for communication. Another group of former spouses disengage and have nearly no contact with each other. If members of this group have children, the noncustodial parents remove themselves from their lives or keep minimum contact.

Child-rearing Issues

Parents often have great difficulties in handling their children after divorce, as the latter may show disturbed behaviors and may be symptomatic as a result of suffering from the family transitions. Usually this situation improves with time. The parent-child relationship is normalized, and the amount of communication with children increases. Parents with sole custody acquire a new range of skills, because the single-parent role incorporates all characteristics of distinct traditional roles. They have to be providers, child nurturers and disciplinarians, homemakers, and decision makers. All these responsibilities and the need to spend more time for their children contribute to many feeling overburdened, exhausted, and stressed. They have little time for themselves, are more likely to feel lonely and isolated, and frequently experience conflicts between their child-care obligations and their career or their relationship with new partners. However, children may also be a major source of support. Sometimes the parents confide their personal problems to them and ask for advice. They may expect too much of their children and dilute generational boundaries thereby disturbing their children's development (overinvolvement). Similar problems can result from transferring the love for the lost partner to a child.

Today there is a growing number of single-parent fathers; in 1980 there were already more than one million of such households (Gladding and Huber 1984). Men usually become single-parent fathers involuntarily; that is, the mothers may have deserted their families, may abuse substances, may be sick or mentally unstable, and the like. If fathers become single parents by choice, they can often afford to employ someone to look after their children. At the beginning they usually experience stress and role strain: "The role of the single-parent father is unclear. Men who take on this responsibility undergo a major shift in their life-style and priorities. They must now try to balance their roles as provider and care giver. They are no guidelines" (Gladding and Huber 1984, p. 16). Moreover, they know less about child development. Thus they experience many problems of child guidance at the beginning. Single-parent fathers usually have a strong motivation to succeed and may define child care just as another job: "When this happens, the rewards of doing that job well and feeling competent in it begins to compete with work satisfaction, thus reducing the salience of occupational role for the men" (Rosenthal and Keshet 1981, p. 121). Many such fathers give parenting a new importance. They are willing to forego promotions or accept a drop in income by working at reduced hours, in order to have more time for their children. With time they first gain experience in meeting the practical needs of their children and then in meeting their emotional needs, too. They overcome their initial feelings of inadequacy and gain positive self-regard.

Single-parent fathers usually receive little help from their former wives, with whom they have little contact. They often see their former wives negatively and may be angry with them because their children are hurt by their mother's lack of involvement. Many single-parent fathers are anxious to remarry. They are concerned with the compatibility of woman friends with their children and may involve them in child care from the beginning. Like all single parents, they experience conflicts between work and child-care obligations and would like to have more time for their children and their social life.

The more parents are in accord about their child-rearing styles, approve of each other as parents, and are able to separate marital and parenting roles, the more likely they are to share parenting after divorce (Rosenthal and Keshet 1981). Messinger and Walker (1981) observed the following nontraditional parenting arrangements: "Some parents have reported that they take turns occupying the family household, while each retains an alternate residence. Another arrangement reported by separated parents has been to include many of the child's belongings in each parental household to enable the child to move freely between the two" (p. 434). According to a study of 181 divorced individuals (Furstenberg and Spanier 1987), however, only a tiny fraction of the parents reported that their children regularly resided in two households or had daily contact with both parents four years after separation. Moreover, the number of these rare cases declined with time. Such arrangements often are informal. They tend to be more successful if they are routinized and predictable. Some of them are based on joint custody. In most cases, however, one parent has sole custody, so the other spouse is dependent on his or her good will in sharing the parenting functions.

Two forms of nontraditional parenting arrangements can be found (Durst et al. 1985, Rosenthal and Keshet 1981): "Timesharing" parents spend equal time with their children and experience child care as a routine. They are highly committed to parenting, respect the parental rights of their former spouse, and think positively about his or her parenting skills. They usually live in close proximity and have set up their homes to include everything needed by their children, who meet there with friends, play by themselves, do their homework, watch TV, and so on. However, both parents continue to feel negatively about each other. Interactions are rare, guarded, and sometimes outright hostile. Often they avoid meeting each other by picking the children up from day-care institutions or schools. There is little discussion of child-related issues and nearly no shared activity (cp. Lyon et al. 1985). In "coparenting" the former spouses are full partners in parenting and have high regard for each other's performance as parents. They are able to separate their feelings for each other from their parenting functions, can resolve conflicts, and usually arrive at joint decisions with respect to their children. In all these cases both parents develop independent relationships with their children. Most coparenting fathers were already actively involved in child rearing before separation and divorce.

Relationship between Child and Noncustodial Parent

"For the children, the patterns of access immediately after separation clearly set the pattern for the future. . . . The sooner and the more frequently that children had access, the more likely were they to continue to keep in touch with the absent parent. Those who had no access in the beginning found difficulties first in restoring broken relationships and then in maintaining them" (Mitchell 1985, p. 141). Some children lose contact with the noncustodial parent immediately after separation. A few of them meet him or her again after divorce. According to a nationwide longitudinal study (Furstenberg et al. 1983) starting in 1976 with 1747 households (2279 children aged 7 to 11) and ending in 1981 with a remaining 1047 households (1377 children), 16.4 percent of the children from disrupted families had contact with their nonresidential fathers at least once a week, 16.7 percent between 12 and 51 times during last year, and 15.2 percent between one time and 11 times during last year. Sixteen and three-tenths percent had the last contact one to five years ago, and 35.5 percent had no contact in the last five years or did not know. Contact with nonresidential mothers was more frequent; the sample, however, encompassed only 25 cases in which the children lived with their fathers after separation and divorce.

Usually the level of contact with the nonresidential parent drops with time. According to the aforementioned study 45 percent of the parents saw their children at least once a week within the first two years after separation. After 10 years this was the case for only 10 percent; 64 percent had had no more contact with their children for at least one year. The drop in the level of contact was especially sharp after the second year and after the remarriage of one or both parents (mother's marital status had a greater effect). Moreover, there was less contact if the parents were black, if the nonresidential parent lived far away, if he or she did not provide financial support, or if there was continued conflict between the former spouses. These results show little evidence of couples who make use of nontraditional parenting patterns like timesharing and coparenting (see above). It has to be added that according to another study mentioned before (Spanier and Thompson 1984), greater contact between nonresidential parents and children was connected with more frequent disagreements about child-rearing issues between the former spouses. Four in five noncustodial fathers (interviewed two years after separation) would like to spend more time with their children. Many of them were not satisfied with the custody arrangements. They felt that the closeness to their children had dwindled since separation and experienced feelings of loss, sadness, and emptiness.

Besides timesharing and coparenting, two patterns of relationships between noncustodial parents and children can be observed (Durst et al. 1985, Rosenthal and Keshet 1981): (1) Some parents visit their children regularly, infrequently, or according to a court-ordered visitation schedule (often being unsatisfied with its rigidity). They usually act like entertainers or visitors and treat their children to an endless round of outings, trips, restaurant meals, and special treats. Their residence is not set up for children; therefore, they rarely stay at home to play with their children. (2) Some nonresidential parents who tend to see their children regularly have fitted their residence with whatever makes children feel comfortable and often involve them in typical home routines. They act like friends, offer their children a meaningful, caring, and supportive relationship, and frequently feel closer to them than they were before separation.

Usually a new type of relationship develops between nonresidential parents and their children. As the former have no responsibility for child-rearing, they may be permissive, may surrender the disciplinarian role, and may offer little socialization. They rarely help with schoolwork or projects. At the beginning noncustodial parents (fathers) may not know what to do with their children during visitation, because they lack experience in dealing with them on their own. Some rely heavily on their own parents for child-care assistance (who stay in touch with their grandchildren this way) or ask their dates for help. In other cases they reduce the contact with their children as they notice that the latter are discontented with the visits or because they feel inadequate as parents. Many noncustodial parents, however, slowly learn parenting behaviors and become self-reliant and competent in child-related issues with time. Some may also use their children as a source of reassurance and support. In general, the quality of visits is more important for the children's welfare than is their frequency.

The participation of noncustodial parents in their children's life is not clearly defined and is partly determined by the custodial parents and their attitudes. If the latter have accepted the end of their marriage, no longer harbor negative feelings for their former spouses, and recognize their parental rights, they may support the relationship between their children and the noncustodial parents. Many are even frustrated with the latter's low level of involvement in child-rearing. Moreover, access time may relieve them and give them the opportunity to relax, meet friends, have sexual relations, and so on. In other cases custodial parents see the nonresidential ones as having an unfair emotional advantage, because they are able to treat parenthood as all play. Many try to close the boundaries of their family in order to exclude the other parent from their children's affections and loyalties. McNamara and Morrison (1982) write: "A custodial parent can obstruct access because of . . . bitterness and resentment. While this may have gains for that parent in the short term, when the children are older they are likely to be critical and angry with their custodial parent for refusing to allow their contact with the other parent" (p. 117). Custodial parents may also resent access because it reminds them of their former spouse, is seen as an intrusion, or is used as a venue for having arguments. Sometimes parents compete with each other, criticize each other vis-à-vis the children, or question the children about intimate details of their former spouse's present life.

According to a study of 74 divorced custodial parents separated for an average of four years (Kurdek and Siesky 1979), children exhibited discipline problems (23.5 percent), relief (12.6 percent), withdrawal (6.7 percent), or resentment (4.2 percent) after visits with their noncustodial parents. Only 37.8 percent of the 126 children in the sample showed no reactions. Many problems result from children's experiencing different rules, values, life-styles, attitudes, and the like in both households. However, children may develop a great capacity to accommodate differences between the "binuclear" families.

Children's Reactions

At the beginning of the postdivorce phase many children still suffer from anger, self-blame, sorrow, and a sense of rejection, unlovability, neediness, and powerlessness. They mourn the multiple losses of divorce and yearn for the departed parent. The loss is especially great for children who had been in a coalition with the nonresidential parent and who may now be made scapegoats of compared with the ex-spouse, or punished by receiving less help and support. If there is still some conflict between the former spouses, their children may have to hide positive feelings for the nonresidential parent, may act as go-betweens, and may experience loyalty conflicts; they may show their distress by being hard to manage, by withdrawing or clinginess. As many residential parents still suffer from divorce, their children may fear that they will commit suicide, and therefore may stay at home to offer emotional support. Some children, especially in (early) adolescence, also have problems in coping with their parents' dating and sexual exploration. Dlugokinski (1977) summarizes the situation of children after divorce: "Their relationship with their custodial parent also changes as they share the spotlight for their parent's attention with adult suitors and new parental interests. Changing family economic status may force a change in schools, residential settings, and peer groups. Daily patterns shift as children more frequently attend child care centers because their parents are forced to work, and more frequently are asked to assume new responsibilities around the house" (p. 28). According to a study of 126 children whose parents separated roughly four years ago (Kurdek and Siesky 1979), 71.8 percent had responsibilities that children whose parents are living together do not have.

At the beginning of the postdivorce phase many children still suffer from symptoms, present regressive or antisocial behaviors, abuse substances, or are prematurely involved with the other sex. At school they are unable to concentrate, are daydreaming, preoccupied, restless, aggressive, or withdrawn. Their teachers complain about tardiness, absences, and a decline in academic achievement. All these problems, however, usually disappear with time. Wallerstein (1983) reports as a result of her ten-year study of 60 disrupted families: "By the end of the first year or year-and-a-half following the separation, most youngsters in our study were able to reestablish their earlier levels of learning and to reinvest in their other activities. They were able to regain relationships with friends whom they had driven away by their moodiness and their irritability during the period immediately following the marital separation" (p. 237). With time these children also disengage from parental conflict and distress, develop some psychological distance from their parents, remove the family crisis from the center of their inner world, and master feelings like anxiety, depression, and anger. For many years, however, they may still hope for their parents' reunion. It is especially hard for them to give up these fantasies if one parent continues to hope for reconciliation. According to a study of 126 children (Kurdek and Siesky 1979), only 88.6 percent had accepted the finality of the parents' divorce roughly four years after separation. Even five to ten years after separation the divorce may remain the central event in a child's life (Wallerstein 1983). Moreover, this issue may be reawakened in adolescence and lead to fears that loving relationships will fail.

Children's adjustment to divorce is highly related to their parents' adjustment and their own predivorce adjustment (Rohrlich et al. 1977). It is usually easier if the children understand their parents and their reasons for divorce, if they can somehow approve of their conduct, if they stay in contact with nonresidential parents, and if they are supported by siblings. Children may even become more self-reliant, independent, compassionate, patient, and mature. According to Kurdek and Siesky (1979), for example, 84 percent of 74 custodial parents thought that their children had acquired strengths as a result of divorce, had developed new competencies, and had become more confident. In some cases, however, the absence of the second socializing agent (role model) and the resulting fantasies, the disappointment because of the unreliability and disinterest of the nonresidential parent, the shattering of the kinship system, the loss of emotional support, and the like lead to continuing and new problems.

THE REMARRIAGE PHASE

After the postdivorce phase—that is, when the psychic divorce is achieved, when divorce-related feelings have disappeared, and when nearly no more time is spent thinking about the former marriage or the ex-spouse—many divorcees continue to live as singles. Some have not yet found an adequate partner; others want to stay single for the rest of their lives because of their disappointment and disillusionment with marriage. For example, in a study of 210 individuals separated for two years (Spanier and Thompson 1984), 13 percent of the men and eight percent of the women felt that they will probably never remarry. Many divorcees who live alone are also comfortable with their new life-style; they are independent and autonomous, have faith in their capacity to cope, are back in the mainstream of society, and have gained self-confidence and feelings of self-worth. They take responsibility for their own growth, actions, feelings, and difficulties. Their pattern of life is stable due to effective daily living, steady employment, a large network of friends, and a broad range of satisfying leisure activities. Other divorcees struggle with common problems of singlehood, such as loneliness. Many divorced individuals continue a pattern of short dates, while others enter long-lasting and more serious relationships that may lead to cohabitation and remarriage.

Single mothers (and divorced women in general) have to face financial problems, unemployment, or unsatisfying jobs due to their lack of qualifications. They are also limited in terms of job mobility, work hours, and promotions. Many households are dependent on alimony, child support, or welfare (see pp. 11, 12). Single parents also have less time for personal development, dating, and social relationships; therefore, they often feel trapped by their children. Many single parents feel burdened by all their responsibilities. They experience less and less support in child-rearing by noncustodial parents as the latter reduce their involvement with time (especially after remarriage—men remarry sooner than women).

Some single parents focus only on their children's needs and neglect their own. They may also be overindulgent because of guilt feelings. Many fear that children are disadvantaged by growing up in a single-parent family. However, such families also offer positive conditions for a child's development, if they are seen positively and if they are well organized. Moreover, children's responses to their status as members of a single-parent family usually reflect their parents' attitudes. Even if they cannot relate to an adult of the other sex than that of the residential parent and thus lack a role model, negative effects can be minimized by frequent contact with other adults of that sex (or regular access to the noncustodial parent). Their development, however, may be harmed if they are parentified, if they have to fill the role of an "ersatz" partner, or if they fuse with their parents in a symbiotic relationship. Sometimes problems also result from grandparents' taking over child rearing as well as the family's guidance, thereby usurping the natural parents' authority.

Life as a single or in a single-parent family can no longer be considered as part of the divorce cycle as soon as the postdivorce phase is over. This is not the case with remarriage and the formation of stepfamilies, since these events can take place directly after divorce or at some time during the postdivorce phase (or after it). Most separated and divorced individuals want to remarry, and many of them would like to have more children—in fact one-fourth of them remarry within the first year after divorce and one-half within three years. Altogether 80 percent of all divorcees remarry eventually, with lower rates for (older) women and single mothers as well as blacks (Furstenberg and Spanier 1987, Rosenthal and Keshet 1981, Spanier and Thompson 1984). Furstenberg and colleagues (1983) write with respect to children from divorced families: "Within five years, four out of seven white children have entered stepfamilies, compared to only one out of eight black children" (p. 661).

Courtship

Courtship is the first substage of the remarriage phase (cp. Moss 1984, Papernow 1984, Whiteside 1983). In general, remarriage soon after divorce is problematic because many individuals have not adequately mourned the failure of the prior marriage, have not had enough time to work through the feelings caused by separation, and often are still emotionally attached to their former spouses (no psychic divorce). But even if the divorce happened a long time ago, there may be a resurgence of feelings about the prior marriage and the separation when a person plans to remarry. In these cases it may also be hard to give up the advantages of life as a single or of single-parent families, such as independence, freedom, or strong ties with children.

Many divorced individuals use different criteria in evaluating prospective second spouses. For example, single parents, but also joint-custody parents, may be more concerned with the compatibility between their children and the contemplated partners and less with the compatibility between the latter and themselves (Rosenthal and Keshet 1981). Many divorcees have less inflated expectations than before the first marriage or minimize expectations in order to protect themselves from disillusionment. Other individuals may still harbor unrealistic expectations or negate shortcomings of the prospective spouse (perhaps out of fear of not finding another partner). If both are divorced, they often share rescue fantasies: They want to save each other from the unhappiness of the former marriage and the post-separation period. Moreover, they tend to displace all blame onto the ex-spouses. Even though the risk of a second mistake is a focal concern for most divorcees, they usually believe that they have now found the right partner and describe him or her as a more understanding, sympathetic, and trustworthy companion. They claim to enjoy better communication, to be able to solve conflicts, to arrive at important decisions together, and to allocate domestic chores more equally (Furstenberg and Spanier 1987). "The perception that things are better this time can be self-reinforcing, helping to sustain the marital dialogue. As individuals gain a sense of trust that their partner is in fact different, they can take personal risks and experiment with new conjugal styles" (see above, p. 84).

If one or both prospective spouses have children, they may have the following expectations and myths: "Adult members of step-families ruefully describe shared fantasies: rescuing children from the excesses or inadequacies of the ex-spouse, healing a broken family, stepparents adoring their stepchildren and being welcomed by them; for stepparents, marrying a nurturing parent, and for biological parents, having someone with whom to share the load" (Papernow 1984, p. 357). It is evident that many of these fantasies and expectations will cause problems, for chances are low that they will be fulfilled.

Prospective spouses with children often experience conflicts between their wish to spend time with their partners and their wish to be together with their offspring. This is especially the case if they work full time and consequently have little time for their children during the week. Moreover, they may also feel a sense of disloyalty to their children because of their emotional investment in the prospective spouses. If they let their child-care obligations take priority over their relationships with their lovers, the latter may be jealous, disappointed, or dissatisfied. If they put greater emphasis on their partnership, however, their children may feel left out. Moss (1984) emphasizes: "The time that the couple spends together before their marriage is a crucial time for them to establish the primacy of their relationship in the soon-to-be-established stepfamily. They are often under great pressure from their jealous children, possessive friends, and emotionally attached former spouses" (p. 244). Therefore, not all of them arrive at a strong partnership during courtship. The prospective spouses gradually begin to share responsibilities and household chores, especially if they cohabit before remarriage. Future stepparents also increase their participation in child care slowly. If both partners have children, they usually establish relations between them during pleasurable activities, such as outings.

Children's Reactions

If children are not reassured that the new relationships will not usurp all their parent's time and attention, they experience the courtship and the prospective remarriage as threats. Messinger and Walker (1981) write: "The children may feel threatened with losing their parent to the new adult, or that the newcomer will attempt to displace the nonresident parent in their lives. Children frequently attempt to sabotage the relationship through aggressive or defiant behavior" (p. 436). They may act out to attract their parent's attention or react with symptomatic behaviors, withdrawal, angry tantrums, and the like. Their reactions are usually stronger if they still hope for their parents' reunion or if they were parentified or treated as surrogate spouses; they may now fear loss of status and power. If they do not succeed in their fight against the new partner of their parent, they often "feel twice defeated—first for not preventing the divorce and second for not preventing the remarriage" (Skeen et al. 1985, p. 122). It has to be added that grandparents who played an important role in supporting the divorced spouse and in raising their grandchildren may also try to disrupt the new relationship because they want to keep their position. They may instill fears in their grandchildren (for example, fears based on the myth of the wicked stepparent), undermine the authority of the prospective spouse, or engage in a power struggle with him or her.

Early Marriage

There are many forms of reconstituted families as none (or both) spouses may bring children to the marriage and/or may have children living with the former spouse—children who may visit frequently (nearly being members of the household), rarely, or not at all. There may also be mutual children. Additionally, one or both partners may be divorced. Just by using these criteria one arrives at a huge number of possible combinations that do not exist in first marriages or first families of procreation. Moreover, in contrast to them there is an overlapping of individual life cycles, divorce cycles, and family cycles in reconstituted families. Therefore it is nearly impossible to recreate a biological family after remarriage, especially if children are present; and each stepfamily trying to do so will face great problems and will feel frustrated and disappointed. Thus they have to develop their own model of family life. There are nearly no role prescriptions or norms to help clarify the nature of interactions among former and new spouses, noncustodial, custodial, and stepparents as well as stepchildren, mutual, and nonresidential children. Each stepfamily evolves its relationships in unique ways. It passes through a long period of disequilibrium and transition, which may last from two to five years. If its members move too rapidly, resistances can be expected.

The complexity of life in reconstituted family systems also results from being embedded in a very large social network encompassing relatives as well as former and new in-laws (and friends). The subgroups of the network may compete or fight with each other, may try to replace each other, or may offer a great deal of (emotional) support and assistance. If there is conflict between the subsystems, many members of reconstituted families experience conflicting emotional bonds and loyalties. Children may not know where they belong. Many problems also result from family boundaries being either too loose or too rigid.

In remarriages there are usually greater age differences between the partners. The spouses face the same tasks as in all early marriages; that is, they have to establish routines, develop their own rules, set up decision-making and conflict-resolving mechanisms, and the like. They monitor the development of their relationship very closely. At the beginning, second marriages normally benefit by comparison to the first ones. However, according to a study of 181 individuals four years after separation (Furstenberg and Spanier 1987), remarried divorcees do not report a significantly higher level of well-being in comparison to those living alone or in single-parent families. Moreover, if marital problems arise, ghosts of the past may return to haunt them.

The spouses either pool their financial resources or keep their incomes separate. They sometimes experience a great financial drain if former spouses and children living with them have to be supported. Financial matters revolving around child support, alimony, and wills frequently are a matter of conflict. Especially stepfathers often believe that they shoulder an unfair burden, if one or both biological parents of the stepchildren do not contribute to child-related expenses. Sometimes the problem arises over whether the noncustodial father or the stepfather has to pay for college education.

In some cases the new spouses dampen conflicts between former partners and help them to work out problems. However, there may also be disagreements between the remarried individuals with respect to the ex-spouse. The new partner may also feel powerless to affect arrangements (e.g., with regard to custody or visitation) between the former spouses. Moreover, he or she often experiences rivalrous feelings for the ex-partner. Competitive feelings may be a great problem in the case of coparenting or timesharing, as many stepparents find it hard to accept a very close relationship between stepchildren and nonresidential parents as well as the latter's great influence (and rights) with respect to child rearing. Conflicts may arise regarding the use of words like "Mom" and "Dad." Sometimes the remarried partner subtly encourages a rivalrous relationship between the new and the former spouse. The latter may also be used as a scapegoat or recipient of displaced feelings. Certainly the former spouse often becomes jealous, too. He or she may try to interfere in the new spouses' relationship or in the stepfamily. In a few cases, conflicts even lead to new legal fights. However, according to the aforementioned research results (see pp. 24–25) the problems mentioned before seem to be rare: "Finally, we should note that national data do not support speculations that stepfamily life is afflicted by problems created by the presence of too many parents. Typically, no more than two adults remain actively involved with the children following divorce" (Furstenberg and Spanier 1987, p. 44).

After the ex-spouse's or their own remarriage, nonresidential parents usually disengage further from the life of their former spouse and their children. If noncustodial parents remarry, they often keep their new partners away from their children at the beginning, in order not to upset the delicate truce achieved with the custodial parents. Later on, they gradually introduce them during access visits. Usually the role of the new partner is carefully circumscribed. The custodial parents may resist the latter's involvement with their children and pressure them to reject the new spouse. Thus the children may have to mediate between both sides. In many cases new patterns of interaction develop which include the impact of all individuals involved.

Child Rearing

In reconstituted families one adult becomes a spouse and a parent at the same time. However, the stepparent-child relationship is different from the biological parent-child unit; there are no blood bonds, and stepparents have no legal rights or responsibilities to their stepchildren (as long as they do not adopt them). Moreover, the biological parent-child subsystem precedes the marital unit (and may even be closer, as, for example, the spouses frequently did not have the time to develop the couple-system) and is older than the stepparent-child relationship. Thus stepparents face a system with a shared history, intensified bonds, and a previously established way of operating.

Some biological parents try to preserve the centrality of their relationship with the children and are unwilling to share their love, affection, and loyalty. They do not support their new spouses' attempts at parenting, give them little parental authority, and often control their interactions with the children. Moreover, they form a coalition with the latter and take their side in conflicts. Some stepparents do not accept this situation, because they feel like outsiders. Thus they try to get full parental rights, which may lead to many conflicts. In other cases they do not object to becoming secondary parents, sometimes even choosing this role themselves. For example, they may resent parenting children who are not their own, or they may have married solely for the intimacy and companionship with their spouse (and even may be jealous of their stepchildren and resent sharing their partner's love with them). Some biological parents accept this situation; others criticize their spouses as indifferent and uncaring.

There may also be a weak marital and parental unit, if both spouses bring children to the stepfamily. They often compete with each other and take the side of his or her (biological) children in conflicts. In general, all members of reconstituted families have to deal with the problem of complex, conflicting, and ambiguous relationships. They have to redefine roles, give up old structures, and establish a parental and marital coalition. Papernow (1984) emphasizes: "Most crucial for stepfamily integration are moves which establish stepcouple boundaries: carving out time alone together, closing the bedroom door, consulting each other on child rearing and visitation issues. Boundaries around the stepparent stepchild relationship also begin to be built. The process may include the biological parent remaining in the background when stepparent and stepchild interact, especially when they are fighting, and the stepparent beginning to ally with stepchildren against their biological parent at times" (p. 360).

Some problems in reconstituted families with respect to child rearing result from the myth of the wicked stepparent and from unrealistic expectations. For example, many adults expect instant love between stepparents and stepchildren. According to a study of 181 divorcees separated for an average of four years (Furstenberg and Spanier 1987), half of them believed that stepparents can take the place of a natural parent in a child's life and that it is not harder to love a stepchild than an own child. Stepparents and stepchildren may also have higher expectations with respect to each other—what is acceptable from a natural parent or child is often not acceptable from a stepparent or stepchild.

Many spouses who have not been married before have unrealistic expectations about family life or the behavior of children. They are self-critical and frequently feel insecure due to their lack of experience. This is a great problem especially for stepmothers, who may abruptly receive the total load of child care without being prepared for it. They are exhausted and feel overburdened or even exploited at the beginning. If both parents bring children, they are experienced in child rearing. "However, this advantage may be neutralized by the complexity of rearing two separate sets of children, the relationship with the two surviving spouses, and, often, significant financial difficulties due to the pressures of multiple households requiring financial support" (Moss 1984, p. 243). In these cases many children are concerned with whether there is enough love and affection for all of them and whether all are treated fairly.

Many problems of child rearing are caused by the clashing of different rules, goals, definitions of behavior, methods of child management, and the like, which is often the case when both spouses bring children reared according to different standards. This situation is very difficult for younger children to understand. Problems may also result from parents' having little time for their children at the beginning as they are preoccupied with their new spouses and with getting to know the relatives and friends of their partners.

Stepparent-child Relationship

In many cases both stepparent and stepchildren are suddenly thrown together and have not had the opportunity to gradually develop a relationship. Mitchell (1985), who interviewed seventy-one Scottish custodial parents and fifty children aged 16 to 18 five or six years after divorce, reports: "A quarter of the new partners had been known to the children for many years, but one in seven had suddenly become part of the family" (p. 153). One-fourth of the children liked and another fourth disliked the stepparent from the beginning; one in six was indifferent. Of the rest, more came to like than dislike the stepparent after initially resenting him or her. In sum, one child in four thought that the acquisition of the stepparent had been the worst time in the divorce cycle.

As children did not choose their stepparents (or stepsiblings), they may feel rejected and unfairly treated. At the beginning many stepchildren fight against closeness, reject attempts of stepparents to establish emotional bonds, provoke them, and test their patience and goodwill. In general, older children and boys are less likely to accept stepparents (who may then have major problems in disciplining them) than younger children and girls (Skeen et al. 1985). Many children do not want the stepparent to take the place of the nonresidential parent. They wish to keep the two relationships separate. Frequently they fear to lose the absent parent's affection when they begin to like the stepparent. "The more the stepchild accepts and adjusts to the stepparent, the more this child betrays and is disloyal to his natural absent parent (and sometimes even the one who is present)" (Schulman 1981, p. 104). Noncustodial stepparents may also experience loyalty conflicts, guilt feelings, and pain when they begin to enjoy their stepchildren, as they feel that they desert their natural offspring (who reside elsewhere).

If stepparents attempt to replace the nonresidential parents or try to assimilate their role, they often experience great resistance from stepchildren. Kent (1980) writes: "What the new parent often fails to comprehend is that the children in the family may in fact have a natural or 'real' parent, and that that particular role is already occupied" (p. 150). Thus stepparents have to accept that the stepchildren are members of two households, which means sharing them with the nonresidential parents. As they cannot replace the latter, they have to find a new role. Often they try on various roles until they find one that fits, feels comfortable, and is accepted by the stepchildren. In general, it is better for the latter's well-being if stepparents have a positive or tolerant attitude toward the nonresidential parents and if the access arrangements are good (Mitchell 1985, Moss 1984). However, there may be conflicts and tensions if children are pressured to sever old ties, if family members are not allowed to discuss the previous marriage, or if only negative feelings are allowed with respect to the noncustodial parent.

Usually closeness, affection, friendship, and trust as well as more satisfying interactions between stepparents and children develop slowly. It often takes a long time for stepparents to get accepted and to gain authority. Only with time are cohesion and good cooperation achieved. Some stepparents make their children happy, let them feel secure, and are greatly loved. They may even be regarded by them as "real" parents. In other cases they become special confidantes for their stepchildren or intimate outsiders. Many stepparents, however, are not really ever accepted—which sometimes is not even noticed. Comparing the reports of remarried or cohabiting custodial parents and their children, Mitchell (1985) observed: "On the whole, the children had painted a blacker picture of the new parent figures in their homes than might have been expected from their parents' accounts" (p. 169). For example, some children reported that they did not like the stepparents while their custodial parents reported the opposite. Stepparents may become a convenient and safe recipient of negative feelings. They are also vulnerable to stepchildren's intimations that they are not adequate parents. If children do not get along with their stepparents, they are sometimes excluded from the stepfamily and sent to relatives, boarding schools, and the like.

In some reconstituted families sexual tensions develop between stepparents and stepchildren. As the incest taboo is lower, there is a greater danger of sexual abuse. Sometimes adolescents feel attracted to their stepparents and either compete for their attention with their biological parents or defend against these feelings by hostility, aggression, distancing, running away, or prematurely leaving home. "Stepchildren may also find that the inclusion of new children from another marriage creates both rivalry for parental attentions and sexual attraction. Children may handle their sexual feelings for a stepchild in the family by abreacting, and by developing intense, negative feelings toward the sibling" (Kent 1980, p. 151).

Another problem for children in reconstituted families is the birth of a half-sibling. For example, in a study of 80 pairs of divorcees and their current partners (Ahrons and Wallisch 1987), a new child was born in about 15 percent of the cases within three years after divorce. Sometimes the birth of a mutual child acts to bind the reconstituted family together. It may also be a compensation for the loss of children living with the former spouse. The birth of a new child often is a serious blow to the self-esteem of his or her half-siblings, who may feel left out and less important. They frequently see him or her as a threat to their position in the family and may react with feelings of jealousy or disturbed behaviors.

Later Marriage

Later marriage is the third substage of the remarriage phase. However, it is not really part of the divorce cycle, as matters of separation, divorce, custody, visitation, alimony, and the like usually are of no more importance. Therefore it will only be mentioned briefly. This substage begins when the reconstituted family has achieved stable relationships, patterns of interaction, and modes of operating, when roles and authority structures are defined and accepted by all family members, and when the family system has been stabilized. Many reconstituted families, however, do not reach this substage; according to estimates nearly 60 percent of all remarriages end in divorce. There even seems to be a greater willingness to terminate relationships than during first marriages. Thus many adults and children reexperience their family's breakup and pass through the divorce cycle once again (cp. Furstenberg et al. 1983, Furstenberg and Spanier 1987).

CONCLUSION

"A 'successful' divorce begins with the realization by two people that they do not have any constructive future together. That decision itself is a recognition of the emotional divorce. It proceeds through the legal channels of undoing the wedding, through the economic division of property and arrangement for alimony and support. The successful divorce involves determining ways in which children can be informed, educated in their new roles, loved, and provided for. It involves finding a new community. Finally, it involves finding your own autonomy as a person and as a personality" (Bohannan 1973, p. 488). A successful divorce also means offering children the opportunity to maintain their relationship with both natural parents. It involves not following the model of biological families in case of remarriage, not expecting instant love between stepparents and stepchildren, as well as giving them enough time to develop a relationship.

It is evident that separation, divorce, and remarriage are highly individual experiences. Thus all persons involved tell different accounts of "their" divorce and may also name different complaints, problems, and difficulties (Kitson et al. 1985). For all family members divorce and remarriage are connected with intrapsychic and interpersonal conflicts, negative feelings, and adjustment problems. Many develop symptoms, which usually disappear when the worst is over but sometimes become chronic. For many family members divorce is also a growth-producing experience.

The high figures of divorce and remarriage suggest that a very high percentage of the population passes through the divorce cycle. This means that the commonly used models of the family life cycle are not valid for these cases. For them new models should be developed that incorporate the phases of the divorce cycle. For example, one of these integrative models may have the following stages: Courtship → early marriage → family with young children → predivorce phase → separation and divorce → single-parent family phase with visiting noncustodial parent → courtship (in presence of children) → early (re-)marriage with older children → later marriage with young (mutual) children and with older half-siblings leaving home → and so on. It is evident that this family cycle is much more complex and complicated.

REFERENCES

Ahrons, C. R., and Wallisch, L. S. (1987). The relationship between former spouses. In *Intimate Relationships. Development, Dynamics, and Deterioration*, ed. D. Perlman and S. Duck, pp. 269–296. Newbury Park: Sage.

Bloom, B. L., and Hodges, W. F. (1981). The predicament of the newly separated. *Community Mental Health Journal* 17:277–293.

Bohannan, P. (1973). The six stations of divorce. In *Love, Marriage, Family: A Developmental Approach*, ed. M. E. Lasswell and T. E. Lasswell, pp. 475–489. Glenview: Scott, Foresman.

Burns, A. (1984). Perceived causes of marriage breakdown and conditions of life. *Journal of Marriage and the Family* 46:551–562.

Cauhapé, E. (1983). *Fresh Starts: Men and Women After Divorce*. New York: Basic Books.

Cleek, M. G., and Pearson, T. A. (1985). Perceived causes of divorce: an analysis of interrelationships. *Journal of Marriage and the Family* 47: 179–183.

Crosby, J. F., Gage, B. A., and Raymond, M. C. (1983). The grief resolution process in divorce. *Journal of Divorce* 7:3–18.

Daniels-Mohring, D., and Berger, M. (1984). Social network changes and the adjustment to divorce. *Journal of Divorce* 8:17–32.

Deissler, K. J. (1982). Das Kübler-Ross-Phänomen in der Bewältigung existentieller Krisen und deren Bedeutung für die Beratung in Ehekrisen. *Familiendynamik* 7:368–374.

Dlugokinski, E. (1977). A developmental approach to coping with divorce. *Journal of Clinical Child Psychology* 6:27–30.

Duffy, M. (1982). Divorce and the dynamics of the family kinship system. *Journal of Divorce* 5:3–18.

Durst, P. L., Wedemeyer, N. V., and Zurcher, L. A. (1985). Parenting partnerships after divorce: implications for practice. *Social Work* 30:423–428.

Furstenberg, F. F., Jr., Nord, C. W., Peterson, J. L., and Zill, N. (1983). The life course of children of divorce: marital disruption and parental contact. *American Sociological Review* 48:656–668.

Furstenberg, F. F., Jr., and Spanier, G. B. (1987). *Recycling the Family: Remarriage After Divorce*. Rev. ed. Newbury Park: Sage.

Gladding, S. T., and Huber, C. H. (1984). The position of the single-parent father. *Journal of Employment Counseling* 21:13–18.

Goldmeier, J. (1980). Intervention in the continuum from divorce to family reconstitution. *Social Casework* 61:39–47.

Kalter, N., and Rembar, J. (1981). The significance of a child's age at the time of parental divorce. *American Journal of Orthopsychiatry* 51: 85–100.

Kaslow, F. W. (1981). Divorce and divorce therapy. In *Handbook of Family Therapy*, ed. A. S. Gurman and D. P. Kniskern, pp. 662–696. New York: Brunner/Mazel.

————(1984). Divorce: an evolutionary process of change in the family system. *Journal of Divorce* 7:21–39.

Kent, M. O. (1980). Remarriage: a family systems perspective. *Social Casework* 61:146–153.

Kessler, S. (1975). *The American Way of Divorce: Prescriptions for Change.* Chicago: Nelson-Hall.

Kitson, G. C., Babri, K. B., and Roach, M. J. (1985). Who divorces and why. A review. *Journal of Family Issues* 6:255–293.

Kurdek, L. A., and Siesky, A. E., Jr. (1979). An interview study of parents' perceptions of their children's reactions and adjustment to divorce. *Journal of Divorce* 3:5–17.

Lloyd, S. A., and Zick, C. D. (1986). Divorce at mid and later life: does the empirical evidence support the theory? *Journal of Divorce* 9:89–102.

Lyon, E., Silverman, M. L., Howe, G. W., Bishop, G., and Armstrong, B. (1985). Stages of divorce: implications for service delivery. *Social Casework* 66:259–267.

McNamara, L., and Morrison, J. (1982). *Separation, Divorce, and After.* St. Lucia: University of Queensland Press.

Messinger, L., and Walker, K. N. (1981). From marriage breakdown to remarriage: parental tasks and therapeutic guidelines. *American Journal of Orthopsychiatry* 51:429–438.

Mills, D. M. (1984). A model for stepfamily development. *Family Relations* 33:365–372.

Mitchell, A. (1985). *Children in the Middle: Living Through Divorce.* London: Tavistock.

Moss, N. I. (1984). The stepfamily: its psychological structure and its psychotherapeutic challenge. In *Marriage and Divorce: A Contemporary Perspective*, ed. C. C. Nadelson and D. C. Polonsky, pp. 240–257. New York: Guilford.

Papernow, P. L. (1984). The stepfamily cycle: an experiential model of stepfamily development. *Family Relations* 33:355–363.

Pett, M. A., and Vaughan-Cole, B. (1986). The impact of income issues and social status on post-divorce adjustment of custodial parents. *Family Relations* 35:103–111.

Rohrlich, J. A., Ranier, R., Berg-Cross L., and Berg-Cross, G. (1977). The effects of divorce: a research review with a developmental perspective. *Journal of Clinical Child Psychology* 6:15–20.

Rosenthal, K. M., and Keshet, H. F. (1981). *Fathers Without Partners. A Study of Fathers and the Family After Marital Separation.* Totowa, NJ: Rowman and Littlefield.

Schulman, G. L. (1981). Divorce, single parenthood and stepfamilies: structural implications of these transitions. *International Journal of Family Therapy* 3:87–112.

Schweitzer, J., and Weber, G. (1985). Scheidung als Familienkrise und klinisches Problem—Ein Überblick über die neuere nordamerikanische Literatur. *Praxis der Kinderpsychologie und Kinderpsychiatrie* 34:44–49.

Shapiro, J. L. (1984). Brief outline of a chronological divorce sequence. *Family Therapy* 11:269–278.

Skeen, P., Covi, R. B., and Robinson, B. E. (1985). Stepfamilies: a review of the literature with suggestions for practitioners. *Journal of Counseling and Development* 64:121–125.

Spanier, G. B., and Thompson, L. (1984). *Parting: The Aftermath of Separation and Divorce.* Beverly Hills: Sage.

Teachman, J. D. (1983): Early marriage, premarital fertility, and marital dissolution. Results for blacks and whites. *Journal of Family Issues* 4:105–126.

Tolsdorf, C. (1981). Social networks and families of divorce: a study of structure-content interactions. *International Journal of Family Therapy* 3:275–280.

Turner, N. W. (1980). Divorce in mid-life: clinical implications and applications. In *Mid-Life: Developmental and Clinical Issues*, ed. W. H. Norman and T. J. Scaramella, pp. 149–177. New York: Brunner/Mazel.

Wallerstein, J. S. (1983). Children of divorce: the psychological tasks of the child. *American Journal of Orthopsychiatry* 53:230–243.

Wedemeyer, N. V., and Johnson, J. M. (1982). Learning the single-parent role: overcoming traditional marital-role influences. *Journal of Divorce* 5:41–53.

Weiss, R. S. (1984). The impact of marital dissolution on income and consumption in single-parent households. *Journal of Marriage and the Family* 46:115–127.

Whiteside, M. F. (1983). Families of remarriage: the weaving of many life cycle threads. In *Clinical Implications of the Family Life Cycle*, ed. J. C. Hansen and H. A. Liddle, pp. 100–119. Rockville, MD: Aspen.

2

PROBLEMS AND NEEDS OF ADULTS

L. Rebecca Propst, Ph.D.
Linda Fries, M.S.

The phenomenon of divorce is receiving increasing attention as a stressful life event. Heretofore, the vast majority of research addressing the question of adaptation to divorce has focused on the needs and problems of children. Research focusing on the needs and problems of adults is still fairly sparse. During the past decade, a few studies have begun to appear using multivariate techniques to examine the effects of a large number of potential divorce-related problems of perceived distress.

One of the earliest of these studies, Berman and Tuck (1981), suggested that the problems and stresses encountered by divorced adults fall into three major categories: pragmatic concerns, interpersonal and social problems, and family-related stresses. This chapter discusses each of these problem areas in detail and also reviews some possible associated needs, recognition of which might have proved helpful to these adults in coping with these problems. Recent research that has supported the existence of each of the problem areas will be briefly reviewed, and then material from clinical interviews of divorced adults will be presented to supplement the discussion of each of these problem areas.

Finally, a discussion of one particular phenomenon that may be particularly striking in its ability to predict stress level will be discussed in conjunction with the three problem areas—namely, whether or not the divorce has been finalized.

INTERPERSONAL CONCERNS

The interpersonal sphere is one major area of disruption for divorced individuals. A number of writers have suggested that friends of divorced persons may begin to avoid them, whereas divorced individuals themselves may fear involvements in any long-term relationships (Bohannan 1971).

Berman and Tuck (1981), in a multivariant analysis of 65 female and 25 male volunteers from chapters of Parents Without Partners and 16 female subjects obtained from court records, found this to be an important concern. In their responses to A Checklist of Problems and Concerns, interpersonal relations and loneliness both emerged as significant factors of concern. The items making up these factors focused on both intimate and casual relationships with the same and opposite sex. In a subsequent regression analysis, difficulties in interpersonal relations were most highly related to a poorer mood state. Conversely, those items that were termed most helpful by the divorcees in helping them cope with the divorce were those defined as social activities, including involvement in Parents Without Partners, developing intimate and new friendships, and getting involved in social activities with others.

Everly (1977) states that 24 percent of older divorcees and 35 percent of younger divorcees reported that the most frequently needed supports were financial and emotional. To emphasize that emotional support is indeed often as important as financial support, over 95 percent of a sample of divorced women reported that at the time of their divorce they did not know whom to call or where to go to find the kind of support they needed. Divorced females or males who are adequately coping with their lives apparently have networks of friends and relatives to draw upon. It appears that the advice, encouragement, and understanding that these people offer tends to mitigate the feeling of isolation and depression associated with divorce and maintaining a single-parent family.

Patt (1982) studied 206 divorced custodial parents in order to determine the relationship between social adjustment after divorce and predictors of such adjustment. One of the significant predictors of adjustment was the size of the respondent's social network system. The more people that the respondent thought would maintain contact if he or she were to move from the area, the more satisfactory was his or her social adjustment. Similarly, those respondents who expressed satisfaction with the number of people available to him or her in times of emergencies, the more satisfactory was his or her postdivorce adjustment.

Spanier and colleagues (1979) presented an analysis of 50 case studies which also suggested that social supports were crucial. Eighty-four percent of the interviewees stated that their friends, relatives, and other acquaintances were generally supportive during the separation process. In the few instances where friends or family were not supportive, this lack of support seemed to increase the overall difficulties in adjusting to the separation, especially the emotional adjustments. Some of the respondents also reported isolating themselves, either because they did not feel like being social, or because "they felt like a third wheel." Again, those who did not make new friends had a very difficult time adjusting.

Over half of the respondents also reported growing away from many of their close friends after the separation. This was especially true if the friends were ones they had shared with their spouse, and particularly if the friends were also couples. For those who were losing their old friends but were unable to find new ones, and for those with no real friends during or after the marriage, the process of adjustment to separation and divorce seemed much more difficult. Finally, the study found that only eight percent of those with moderate to high social activity reported serious adjustment problems, whereas 39 percent of those with low social activity reported serious problems. Increased heterosexual dating also resulted in fewer adjustment problems.

Dreyfus (1979) suggests that social needs may be especially important to men, as they have often relied on women to meet their dependency needs and to develop the friendships in the marriage relationship. Also, friends often choose sides. They often seem to divide up like community property—his and hers—so there is usually a loss of friends for both.

The problem of interpersonal relationships and loss of closeness and support is a ubiquitous problem in divorce. Thus, Vaughn's suggestion (1981)—that skills development for forming new social relationships and dating relationships can be a very important need for these individuals—has much merit.

PRACTICAL CONCERNS

A large number of problems fall into the second category of concern—practical problems. The practical problems faced by divorcing men and women have a large impact on the distress, level of life satisfaction, and ease of adjustment to divorce (Berman and Turk 1981, Pett 1982). Difficulties encountered include the legal process, property settlements, child custody, obtaining a new residence, difficulties in home repair and maintenance, applying for welfare, finding a job, child care, and finances. More generally, people experiencing divorce express a feeling of being overwhelmed by not possessing the knowledge or time to accomplish practical concerns (Berman and Turk, 1981). In Everly's (1977) study of 250 women who responded to a questionnaire, 24 percent of women aged 35–50, and 35 percent of women aged 21–35 stated that they needed two or more kinds of support, the majority being practical needs: legal, financial, health, or emotional.

Spanier and Castro (1979) found that for 20 percent of subjects the legal system presented major problems. One-third of those interviewed felt their lawyers gave them no real help and seemed to be involved solely for the money. Two-thirds of the respondents had little difficulty negotiating property settlements, but those who did experience problems had extreme problems that included much bitterness and hostility and problems that lasted a considerable length of time. Vaughn (1981) states that the legal process adds to stress by forcing a couple into adversarial positions. The legal process also has a major influence in disrupting life patterns. She contends that therapists working with divorcees should devote at least one session to discussing legal concerns. Propst and colleagues (1986) in a multivariate study of 106 single-parent mothers found that whether or not the divorce had been legally finalized was a significant predictor of anxiety and women's subjective perceptions of their own coping. This suggests the possibility that the end of the problems encountered in the legal process allows women to move forward in the adjustment process. Pett (1982) advocates that inexpensive published information detailing legal rights would be a very important method of support for divorcees and for facilitating adjustment.

The economic problems in which divorcees find themselves after divorce adds considerably to the stress of divorce adjustment (Everly 1977). Financial concerns have been found to be significantly related to lower life satisfaction. Berman and Turk (1981) found that financial concerns were one of the factors that multivariate analysis identified as contributing to a poorer mood state in divorcees. Additionally the fact that was found to account for the greatest amount of variance in current mood state was talking with one's former spouse about money matters.

Economically the majority of divorced women are downwardly mobile following divorce, while the reverse usually occurs for men (Everly 1977). The Spanier and Castro (1979) study of divorce adjustment, detailed earlier in this chapter, found economic problems the only area in which significant sex differences were found between men's and women's problems and needs. The large majority of men reported that they were as well off financially or better off since the separation. Only 23 percent of men reported that they were somewhat but not significantly worse off since the separation. Men may feel the burden of child support, yet most men also have usually held full-time jobs, have developed salable job skills, and have established stable incomes, which many women have not.

Unfortunately, Spanier and Castro (1979) found the opposite to be true for women. Thirty-nine percent of younger women married for a short period stated that they were about as well or better off economically than before the separation. Most women, however, reported that they were significantly worse off. Everly (1977) found over 40 percent of women aged 35–50 and 70 percent of females 21–35 claim they need financial support. Statistics of 1980 from the U.S. Department of Labor corroborate these findings, since the median income of female-headed families is roughly one-half that of male-headed families (Propst et al. 1986). Households headed by women account for 25 percent of those households with below-poverty-level income (Pais and White 1979).

Pett (1982) found that the source of family income and a family's economic status position were variables that were significant predictors of adjustment. The greater the proportion of income that came from welfare, the lower a person's social adjustment. The higher a custodial divorcee's socioeconomic status, the greater her social adjustment. Propst and colleagues (1986) also found that public assistance (welfare) was a significant factor in single parents who perceive themselves as coping less than optimally. Taken together, these studies suggest that the pragmatic problems, such as lack of job skills, lack of education necessary to pursue a job, unaffordable day care, and other factors that precipitate a woman's need for public support, greatly impact a woman's adjustment and self-perception.

For many women economic problems may affect their whole adjustment (Spanier and Castro 1979). Many women not working prior to the separation, or working only part time, have real difficulty getting a good job. Reasons for these difficulties are lack of education or job training, sex discrimination in hiring, promotion, salary, and retention, less extensive work experience, and the high cost of child care (Pais and White 1979). *It is inaccurate to assume that child support considerably increases the incomes of custodial divorced females, as less than 50 percent of women receive such support regularly, thus making the woman primarily financially responsible for child care* (Everly 1979, Vaughn 1981).

Everly (1979) argues that increased education for women, prior to and following marriage, would greatly offset the economic problems and adjustments faced by women especially following divorce. This is also indicated in a study by Propst and colleagues (1982), which found the level of education a significant predictor of less anxiety and a subjective predictor of more optimal coping in female single parents. It was also a marginally predictable predictor of less depression. This may be a significant factor due to the financial security increased education may bring. Berman and Turk (1981) found that learning, including going to school, taking evening courses, and learning new skills, was a very important coping strategy of post-divorce women.

The parent who receives principal custody is also faced with a myriad of practical problems. The presence of children in families of divorce has been shown to be a central component of distress (Berman and Turk 1981). Spanier and Castro (1979) found no sex differences in problems faced between fathers and mothers with custody. They found that the parents experience difficulty in finding time to be away from their children, which creates problems with work, dating, and social life. Berman and Turk also found that the practical problems of cooking meals for the family, cleaning the house, going to the market, not having enough time to get things done, and not having enough time for their children were all significant problems. Propst and colleagues (1986) found that the number and ages of children living with the custodial parent were significant predictors of coping and adjustment. Total number of children significantly predicted depression, but the greatest predictor of anxiety and depression was the number of children under age 10. The number of children under age 5 in the home was also found to be a significant predictor of depression and a marginal predictor of anxiety. It appears that the age of children is a significant predictor of coping in single parents. A single parent with young children faces extensive practical problems in the high cost and poor quality of day care, the greater physical dependence and time demand in day-to-day care or when a child becomes ill, and greater need for supervision. The number of young children also limits a person's time and financial ability to pursue an education and job training following divorce. Pais and White (1979) found other difficulties custodial parents faced were child support based on income of the spouse rather than on need, and the difficulty in collecting child support.

FAMILY CONCERNS

There are at least three major family problems that divorcees face: the relationship to one's former spouse, the relationship to one's children, and the relationship to one's parents and former in-laws. Numerous authors and researchers have reported that prolonged problems relating to one's former spouse retarded a person's emotional separation from the marriage and adjustment to divorce (Berman and Turk 1981).

Nelson (1981), in a stepwise multiple regression analysis of 15 female single-parent families with children between ages 4 and 14, separated between 5 to 25 months, sought to determine the strongest moderators of adjustment for divorced women and their children. Three self-report measures and trained interviewers were used to gather the data. The divorcee's current relationship with her ex-husband was found to be the best predictor of negative affect in the divorcee and accounted for 31 percent of the variance. The better the relationship with the ex-husband, the less negative affect reported by the women. Current positive feelings about the ex-husband were the best predictor of affect balance for the women and accounted for 58 percent of the variance regarding affect balance. The divorcee's current relationship with her ex-husband was found to be a predictor of her total negative feelings, accounting for 49 percent of the variance regarding negative feelings. The better the relationship with the ex-husband, the lower the total negative feelings score. A woman's relationship with her ex-husband was found to be the best predictor of a higher score on the Social Adjustment Scale. In summary the greater amount of problems a woman faces with her ex-husband, the poorer her adjustment; the fewer problems a woman faces with her ex-husband, the greater her adjustment.

Berman and Turk (1981) found in response to a Checklist of Problems and Concerns that former spouse contacts (for example, talking with the former spouse about the children, visitation, meeting the former spouse in social situations, and talking with former spouse about money) accounted for the greatest amount of variance in problems faced. Problematic family interactions in former spouse contacts and parent-child interactions were both found to be related to greater mood disturbance in divorcees.

The remarriage of the noncustodial parent was also found to be a negative contributor to the postdivorce adjustment of the custodial parent (Pett 1982). It may present problems to the custodial parent both emotionally in accepting the true finality of the marriage and practically in the ex-spouse's being less available to be involved with child care.

Children from divorced homes exhibit more problematic behavior than children from happy, nondivorced homes (Vaughn 1981). Conflict between mothers and sons appears to be common during the first two years following divorce, with male children becoming more resistent and less compliant. Substantial improvement, however, occurs after two years (Nelson 1981, Berman and Turk 1981).

Berman and Turk (1981) found that parent-child interactions that included: talking to a child about one's life, talking with a child about his or her life, expressing one's feelings to the children, talking with them about the divorce, and being "too independent," accounted for a large percentage of the variance of problems experienced by parents. The authors, however, did not find "keeping control of a male child" a significant problem as earlier studies indicate. They did find that the presence of a minor male child contributed significantly to greater parental mood disturbance, indicating that in general the physical presence of a male child is more predictive of distress than the problems they present for discipline. Parent-child difficulties were found to contribute significantly to current parental mood disturbance but not to be a factor in overall life satisfaction.

Nelson (1981) found that mothers experience fewer behavior problems with their children if they decide to file for divorce after their first separation rather than after subsequent separations, and also if they had experienced a high degree of overall marital happiness. These findings indicate that marital tension and discord are the best predictors of children's behavior problems following divorce, as has been consistently shown in previous studies. His study also found that having a father substitute was associated with fewer personality problems, with these children scoring significantly higher in social adjustment than parents who report greater problems (Pett 1982).

Spanier and Castro (1979) found that in every marriage with dependent children, the children were the focus of major adjustment problems. These problems were found to include worrying about the effects of the separation on the children, deciding who should have custody, and loneliness and guilt for those without custody.

Pett (1982) found that children's having contact with the noncustodial parent more than once a week was a significant negative predictor of social adjustment for the custodial parent. Continual contact with the ex-spouse may be problematic for several reasons. Conflict over child-rearing practices may continue between parents, and continuing to work with an ex-spouse over the logistics of intense ongoing contact may create an atmosphere for the relational problems of poor communication and conflict to continue.

Pett (1982) also found that relational problems between the custodial parent's relationship with his or her family and with the former spouse's family contributed significantly to the custodial parent's negative social adjustment. Practically, this is probably seen as a lack of resources available to help the family in times of illness or emergency. Spanier and Castro (1979) found 84 percent of those interviewed reported family support during the separation process. In the instances when the family was not supportive, the lack of support seemed to increase overall difficulties for the divorcee. Problems reported included family members having strong feelings against divorce in general, and parents not understanding or accepting that their adult children were divorcing.

FINALIZATION OF DIVORCE

In addition to the three main categories of problems frequently confronted by divorcees, one specific problem has shown up sufficiently frequently in the literature and in our clinical experience to merit a discussion of its own.

The finalization of the divorce was a highly significant predictor of anxiety and coping in the study by Propst and colleagues (1986). In their discriminant analysis, they found that finalization of divorce and months since separation were the most predictive demographic variables, being exceeded only by psychological style of coping as a significant predictor. Those single mothers who had finalized their divorce reported significantly less anxiety level and described themselves as coping much better. Similarly, months since separation were also a significant predictor, but it appears that the actual finalization may be a turning point for some of these women.

Bloom and Caldwell (1981) suggest that there may be a sex difference in adjustment in relationship to the actual stage of the entire process of separation and divorce. In their study they examined symptoms after separation, as well as symptoms prior to separation. They found significant sex differences in personal well-being at the time of the separation. Women consistently showed greater symptoms in the preseparation period, and decrease in symptoms following the separation. However, in the early postseparation period, men reported significantly more severe symptoms than did women.

It appears that whereas women may have a more stressful reaction to marital difficulty and divorce earlier in the process, men may have higher levels of stress later. Thus, assertions regarding women's and men's adjustment to the process of divorce, and an assessment of their problems and needs must clearly take into account and control for the point in the process at which the assessment has been made.

It may be that initially women are confronted with the stress of the bad marriage and the threat of no financial support. Spanier and Castro (1979) suggest that decreased living standards and financial problems are a real concern for women after divorce, whereas men's status generally improves. However, as the time after separation increases, women find that they can cope, and men begin to confront the reality of what they have lost. This may be especially difficult for men because men generally have relied on women for their social contacts (Dreyfus 1979) and they soon find that they are alone. Confirmation of this hypothesis, however, must await further research.

If indeed men and women have different needs at different stages of the divorce process, then the provision of services must be different. Women may need more financial support or legal support in order to obtain a fair divorce settlement. They may also need job training skills. Men, on the other hand, may need more social skills training. Also, women may need more support earlier on, whereas men may need more support later.

CLINICAL IMPRESSIONS OF NEEDS
AND PROBLEMS OF DIVORCED ADULTS

A number of clinical interviews of divorced men and women by the two authors revealed patterns of needs and problems similar to those suggested by the literature. For example, we asked a number of divorced individuals what they saw as their greatest problems following divorce.

A woman of 50 with two grown children, who had been divorced for a year and a half following a two and a half year separation, summed up her biggest problem after the divorce as cynicism. "I feel the divorce has made me more cynical, more hard-nosed. It seems unfair. I put so much into the family and not into a career and now I have nothing." She stated that it was also difficult communicating with her spouse about selling the house, sorting through mementos and pictures, and making sure she got a fair deal. "He did not feel that he owed me anything, so I felt pushed into playing the game of being sneaky in order to determine where he had hidden his financial resources. It was very difficult in the midst of the emotional turmoil to be legally and financially astute. Fortunately, I was able to get a good lawyer. I knew that it was important to make sure that I was not cheated financially at this stage of the game or I would resent it greatly later. Since my husband was a physician and I had put him through medical school, I wanted to make sure that things were fair, so I invested in a lawyer. I don't know what women would do if they were poor."

She went on to assert that she felt her greatest needs at the time of the divorce were "supportive people and a shoulder to cry on." Two resources were helpful to her: first, finding her direction by deciding to return to school, and second, establishing some diversions such as playing a musical instrument. "School gave me something to do with my mind and my empty times at a very crucial period, and I also feel I am gaining the ability to support myself."

A somewhat younger woman of 36 with two children still at home stated that her three greatest problems were her self-acceptance, her financial situation, and her identity. "I felt I was failure and life was over." This particular woman expressed a great deal of anger in speaking of the legal system and how unprotected she felt. She stated, "The legal system is hard to access and only provides for the wealthy." Unlike the first woman, she *did* feel a great deal of bitterness in not being protected financially by the legal system. Additionally, she did not know how to get legal help because of her lack of experience and lack of money.

Another woman, aged 35, separated one year, with the divorce finalized and no children, stated that her greatest problem was seeking out the emotional support that she needed, and that her greatest need was having a role model for coping.

Men seemed to express similar concerns.

A 40-year-old male, separated five years with the divorce final and no children, said that his support system was gone. "I found I had alienated my past friends and had gravitated towards my spouse's friends. Now my spouse's friends had no interest in me. I had hoped people would not take sides, but they did. My ex-wife kept a number of my own personal things, things that belonged to my mother, and that still hurts a lot. There were also financial concerns. I took on the majority of the bills, and I had to find a very small apartment and get a roommate, which was awful for me." He stated that he felt that his greatest needs were to "maintain my dignity, sanity, not let the situation overwhelm me. I also need to not lose track of my goals, and to stay out of self-pity."

In the sample we interviewed, when divorced individuals were asked to state their greatest needs and problems following divorce, we found that social support needs were usually mentioned first, followed either by financial or legal needs. When we became more specific and asked the individuals about their practical, interpersonal, and family needs and problems, we soon gained a fuller picture of the exact nature of the needs that represent those categories. One of the biggest concerns shared by the women was their difficulty in "getting through the legal process." One woman, who reported that she could not afford a good lawyer, stated, "My lawyer put no effort into the case and I ended up with a very bad settlement. Since I had recently moved from the state in which the divorce had actually happened, legal assistance in my new state of residence would not help me. Yet I could not afford to make long distance calls to the old state."

Other practical problems often included getting a job and finding affordable child care. One woman stated that when she could not find a job, she went to the welfare office. They told her, however, that she would run the risk of losing her children to her ex-husband if she applied for welfare. "They said he could petition the court that I was incapable of supporting my children. They advised me not to apply if I thought he wanted to take custody from me, which he did. My only choice was then to move in with my parents."

Women who had more education and/or were married to wealthier men stated that their greatest practical need was to get good legal help to insure that they got a good legal settlement. Those with less education and/or a less wealthy husband stated the lack of legal help and the lack of finances as a problem. Males, in our clinical experience, reported fewer difficulties with the legal system and fewer financial difficulties after separation and divorce. Most women, on the other hand, indicated that their greatest concerns were to know how to deal with the legal system, and they expressed concern that if such information had been available, the process might have been easier for them.

These financial and legal concerns are evident not only in our own clinical experience but are also suggested by the literature in its assertion that education and money are big predictors of coping with divorce for women. Given that this is the case, it seems obvious that perhaps one of the greatest needs (to ensure less painful transitions for women coping with divorce in the future) is to socialize women to get a good education so that they can be prepared to support themselves. The second greatest need is to educate them in a more effective use of the legal system.

In the area of relationship problems, both sexes reported the phenomenon of "always being an extra, not knowing where to fit in." One woman stated, "I found that after my divorce, friendships were not as strong as I had thought they were. People I thought were close friends ended up being acquaintances. They were not supportive."

Those individuals who were hesitant to seek out support or who reported that talking about their divorce with their friends was a "hands-off subject" generally were still having difficulty coping with the divorce at the time we interviewed them. Most of the individuals reported that their greatest needs in their area of relationships were validating friends and/or support groups. Talking with others about the problems was crucial. One woman reported that her greatest asset during that time was "crying with my sister for hours at a time."

Family problems for our group also match those in the literature. One woman was concerned about her grown children being in the middle of the divorce, and the difficulty the in-laws had in accepting the divorce. Those individuals who said that they were close to their in-laws reported experiencing a conflict of loyalty, and were not quite sure whom they could talk to. One woman stated that being forced to move in with her parents to survive financially led to a strained relationship with them.

For most of the individuals we interviewed, the relationship with the spouse was still strained. One woman stated, "I am not sure I want my ex-spouse to know anything about me."

The finalization of the divorce was a great relief for most of the women in our interview sample. When they were asked if there was a time when things suddenly got better, most of them said it was when things were settled legally in the final divorce decree.

One woman stated it was at that point that she finally felt that she had control of her life again. She no longer needed to consult with her husband regarding many different practical or financial concerns. She was free to make her own decisions. All expressed relief after this stage. Men's descriptions of when things got better were more varied. Often it followed their mental decision that the marriage was indeed ended.

Perhaps men were more likely to find relief early in their initial decision to divorce; they felt they *did* have more control over their destinies, since they were not financially dependent upon their wives. Women, however, because of their financial dependence, became more dependent upon the final decision of the legal system before they felt they could gain control. Certainly, this is a question for future research.

CONCLUSION

Both the literature and our own clinical experience seem to suggest that practical problems, interpersonal concerns, and family concerns are all problems for divorcing individuals. These problems may follow a slightly different pattern for men and women. One of the biggest needs for women appears to be practical legal advice for dealing with the vicissitudes of the legal system. Some were not even financially able to secure reasonable legal assistance. It may be that the development of a practical legal handbook for obtaining and using legal advice would be valuable for many women.

As one woman noted, she felt helpless until legal affairs were settled. Thus it may also be helpful to encourage women who are under stress *to attempt to finalize their divorce as soon as possible.* Such a finalization of the legal process may give them back control of their lives.

Since both sexes reported difficulties in interpersonal relations, *support and instructions for developing better social relationships may also be helpful.* Certainly support groups that stress the development of these skills could be a beginning. Those individuals who counsel a fair amount with divorcees may also find it helpful to maintain *lists of resources for social support systems for singles.* These lists could contain such information as local singles groups, Parents Without Partners, or information on cooperative child-care networks. Probably most divorce counseling should include *homework assignments focusing on encouraging the individual to make regular social contacts.* It has been our clinical experience with lonely single and/or divorced individuals that such assignments should start out slowly and in a nonthreatening manner. For example, the individual could be asked to attend a meeting of a nonthreatening same-sex group in which intimacy was not expected. Attending classes is often a nonthreatening way to begin to initiate social interactions as a newly single person.

Such homework assignments should continue on a regular basis, with the demands of the assignment gradually increasing as the individual is able to fulfill the previous assignment. The literature suggests that regular social support networks are crucial for alleviating stress in the newly divorced individual. Therefore, if such networks are not present, then the counseling must gradually institute them via graded task assignment (see Beck 1979 for a discussion of graded task assignments for depressed individuals).

The third area of concern, family problems, seems to result often from family members (children, parents, in-laws) not knowing how to respond or with whom to continue their relationships. Perhaps the divorcee could be helped by providing *information to extended family members as to how they can behave.* Here again, perhaps an instructional booklet would be helpful.

It may also be very helpful for the *counselor to set up the logistics for visits between children and the noncustodial parent.* Since this is such a source of stress for both parents, a prearranged plan designed to minimize stress as much as possible would be useful.

In all areas, it is obvious that better coping appears to result when practical problem-solving skills have been improved. This certainly confirms the results in our 1984 study (Propst et al.), which showed that problem-focused coping (coping aimed towards practical problem solving) was a better predictor of coping than emotion-focused coping (coping directed toward controlling one's emotions). This finding also agrees with the general coping literature, which suggests that a greater sense of self-efficacy and a perception that one's coping resources exceed the environmental demands lead to reduced stress.

REFERENCES

Beck, A. T., Rush, A. J., Shaw, B. F., and Emery, G. (1979). *Cognitive Therapy of Depression.* New York: Guilford.

Berman, W. W., and Turk, D. C. (1981). Adaptation to divorce: problems and coping strategies. *Journal of Marriage and the Family* 43:179–189.

Bloom, B. L., and Caldwell, R. A. (1981). Sex differences in adjustment during the process of marital separation. *Journal of Marriage and the Family* 43:693–701.

Bohannan, P. (1971). *Divorce and After: An Analysis of Emotional and Social Problems of Divorce.* New York: Doubleday.

Dreyfus, E. A. (1979). Counseling the divorced father. *Journal of Marriage and the Family* 5:79–85.

Everly, K. (1977). New directions in divorce research. *Journal of Clinical Child Psychology* 6:7–10.

Freund, J. (1974). Divorce and grief. *Journal of Family Counseling* 2:40–43.

Heritage, J. G., and Daniels, J. L. (1974). Postdivorce adjustment. *Journal of Family Counseling* 2:44–49.

Kessler, S. (1978). Building skills in divorce adjustment groups. *Journal of Divorce* 2:209–216.

Nelson, G. (1981). Moderators of women's and children's adjustment following parental divorce. *Journal of Divorce* 4:71–83.

Pais, J., and White, P. (1979). Family redefinition: a review of the literature toward a model of divorce adjustment. *Journal of Divorce* 2:271–281.

Pett, M. G. (1982). Predictors of satisfactory social adjustment of divorced single parents. *Journal of Divorce* 5:1–17.

Propst, L. R., Pardington, A., Ostrom, R., and Watkins, P. (1986). Predictors of coping in divorced single parents. *Journal of Divorce* 9:33–52.

Spanier, G. B., and Castro, R. F. (1979). Adjustment to separation and divorce. *Journal of Divorce* 2:241–253.

Vaughn, F. K. (1981). A model of divorce adjustment therapy. *Family Therapy* 8:121–128.

3

PROBLEMS AND NEEDS OF CHILDREN

William C. Nichols, Ed.D.

The needs and problems of children in divorce are related to the needs of children as human beings. What do children need in order to grow up and take their place in society and live satisfactory lives of their own? How does the divorce of their parents affect what they require in order to develop adequately?

If the children of divorcing parents are already mature adults, the question obviously is different. I was 35 when my parents divorced after thirty-seven years of marriage. At that point I experienced no difficulty in feeling that it was their decision and, in view of the fact that they had been separated for almost twelve years, it had no significant impact on my life or that of my children. Had I been 15, it would have been of more than passing interest to me. Had I been 5, it would have been perhaps the major thing in my life at the time and possibly during my entire developmental years. This illustration is deliberately stated in personal, egocentric "I" and "me" terms, because that is how children inevitably experience the divorce of their parents.

Some important background factors relating to child development and the context in which divorce is occurring in western society generally, and the United States in particular, need to be mentioned before we look more specifically at the reactions of children to divorce. The child development factors pertain to the lengthy dependence of the human infant, deep and primitive anxieties about the possibility of abandonment, and the contingent nature of the child's reactions and adaptation. The context factors are described in terms of social change factors, the marital breakup-family reorganization factor, and the "normless" situation factor.

CHILD DEVELOPMENT FACTORS

The Dependency-Independency Factor

Dependency is one of the more striking characteristics of the human young. Born totally helpless, the human infant will not survive physically unless it is cared for, protected, and nourished. This period of physical dependency on caretakers lasts for an extremely long time in comparison with the remainder of the earth's animal kingdom.

Equally important are the needs for emotional nurturance and socialization into the adaptive patterns of homo sapiens. Spitz's (1945) classic report on hospitalism and the condition of *marasmus,* or wasting away, witnessed in infants who were adequately fed, but inadequately stimulated tactilely and undernourished emotionally, illustrates all too graphically and tragically the outcome when emotional support and closeness are lacking.

Similarly, the accounts in sociological literature of "Anna" and "Isabelle" underline the need for socialization into human behaviors. School-age youngsters, who more resembled little animals than children when they were discovered in the United States in the 1930s, both had been locked up in their homes in virtual isolation and with little stimulation. One was evidently developmentally disabled as well as deprived. The other, with support and interested human contact, quickly progressed until she was able to enter school and function at grade level within a few years.

Parenting involves helping children to move from being originally helpless and totally dependent on an older generation for their very survival toward preparation for appropriate independence from their parents and into interdependent living. Whether parenting is conducted by a single parent, two parents, or by the agency of an extended family or society, the dependency needs of children require a dynamic and continuing balance between dependency and independency. It is a matter of providing enough support and not too much, of giving enough freedom and not to much, if the child is to develop adequately or, certainly, optimally.

Abandonment Anxiety

Deriving from their dependence, this deep and primitively based apprehension over the potential loss of their supports, their safety nets, is easily triggered in young children. Repeatedly one can see evidence of what may be an intuitive sense that they will not survive without "the giants." Although this anxiety, which sometimes becomes a specific fear, tends to attenuate with the attainment of age, experience, and increasing mastery and coping skills, indications of its early life effects and potency linger on in many adults, and probably appear under certain kinds of stress in all of us.

Whatever threatens breakup of the primary support and protection (that is, disruption or destruction of the dependency pattern) of a child elicits "abandonment anxiety." How severe the reaction will be and how traumatic and damaging it will be in the long run depends on a number of variables. How long does the threat last, for example? How many such threats have there been in the past, and how have they turned out? How helpful and trustworthy have been the main supports of the child?

The Contingency Factor

Children, like adults, are not reacting to a single event when they respond to divorce. Rather, they are involved in a process in which their family life is undergoing transition for several years. It is a process over which they exercise little or no control. It is a process about which they may have little comprehension. Life for children is contingent anyway; in the divorce process life become particularly contingent upon the actions and attitudes of other people.

What happens with children and what they must do in order to make the transitions between their original situation to new circumstances and roles depends on what the significant adults in their lives do and how they do it. The married adult who takes the divorce route has specific tasks to fulfill at the decision to divorce stage, the separation/divorce stage, and the postdivorce stage (Nichols 1988). How the adults handle those tasks and deal with their children in the process invariably affects the child. Some research has shown that "the quality of life relationships may be more important than life changes in moderating the outcomes of divorce and remarriage" (Hetherington et al. 1985, p. 230).

CONTEXT FACTORS

The Social Change Factor

In the long sweep of things, dealing with children of divorce is a new issue. Marital breakup is not new, although the manner in which the disruption occurs has changed drastically in this century from termination by death of one of the partners to breakup through divorce. At the turn of the twentieth century, ". . . death was the rule during the age period between twenty and fifty" (Kubie 1956). For a significant number of persons marrying in the United States in the latter part of the twentieth century, marriage is not destined to be a traditional "until death do us part" journey. Rather, it is the first stage in a process that involves marriage → marital discord → separation/divorce → single living (with or without children) → remarriage for those adults.

If there are no children, marital breakup can be a comparatively simple process. A couple who are married split apart and the matter formally ends. Property is divided; there is no longer a relationship with former in-laws or any reason to be concerned with them; the formerly married persons deal with their personal emotional reactions adequately or inadequately; life goes on.

Marital Breakup and Family Reorganization Factor

Where children are involved the situation is considerably more complex. Divorce brings about marital breakup and the continuation of the family in different forms. "Family breakup" is a misnomer (Nichols 1986); rather, the marriage ends and family reorganization occurs. Parents continue to be parents and the children continue to be the children of their parents, regardless of how satisfactorily or how poorly the parent-child relationship fares in the postseparation/divorce period.

The "Normless" Situation Factor

The large numbers of stepfamilies that result from remarriage between divorced persons is a new occurrence; historically, the majority of stepfamilies resulted from marriage after the death of a spouse of one or both of the new partners. When the divorce proceeds to the remarriage stage and the formation of stepfamilies, the newness of the contemporary stepfamily pattern (remarriage of formerly married persons after divorce) brings people into situations for which there are few established norms. What is the family? Who is in the

family? How are new relatives-by-marriage addressed and introduced? Who is the stepmother to the child, for example, and how
can this be handled (Nichols 1980)?

REACTIONS TO DIVORCE

Children's reactions to divorce are not necessarily the same as the
effects of divorce on children. We need to make this distinction, one
that I have made previously (Nichols 1984, 1986). Such a distinction
is important as we begin to learn about some of the reactions children have to both the divorce event and the divorce process in both
short-term and long-term manifestations.

Divorce is one of many disruptive experiences in the lives of
children that can cause them to become anxious or fearful about
their own well-being. Of course, it works the other way around, in
that clinging, possessive behaviors can drive others away from us.
Clinicians occasionally see spouses whose behaviors of that type set
a self-fulfilling prophecy into motion, driving the other spouse away
and bringing about that which was feared.

We do not need to limit ourselves to the psychoanalytic explanation—that there is a wish behind a fear—in order to account for
such behaviors. Living under the tension of continuing, unresolved
anxiety spurs some individuals to take actions that bring about
that which was feared. It is as if they "must do something," virtually anything, to break the tension. At the moment, even the risk of
pain and punishment or even loss may seem preferable to unmiti-
gating tension and the continuing threat of loss.

The reactions that children have to the divorce event or the divorce process are far from being automatically problematic or pathological behavior (Nichols 1984). A considerable amount of children's
disruptive and "attention-getting" behavior in divorce situations
may be an unwitting protest against continuing tension, against
uncertainty, against continuing parental discord, for example. As
such it may be a healthy response to a situation that is not conducive to good child development. When the behavior occurs and what
it is in relation to must be considered when one is assessing the
reactions of children in divorce situations.

The excellent research of Hetherington (Hetherington 1972,
1981, 1982, Hetherington et al. 1978) and Wallerstein and Kelly
(Wallerstein and Kelly 1980, Kelly and Wallerstein 1976), for example, is providing guidance to comprehending children's reactions to
the separation/divorce event and the divorce process. The recent

research focused on long-term follow-up of cohorts of children whose parents have divorced (for example, Hetherington et al. 1985 in a six-year follow-up, and Wallerstein 1984, 1985a, 1985b, in a 10-year follow-up) is particularly significant with regard to the longer-term reactions that sometimes occur.

Both Hetherington and Wallerstein have emphasized the effects of the divorce situation on children's development. A key concept for Wallerstein (1983) has been the disruption of the child's normal course of development. How well was he or she doing prior to the marital discord and separation/divorce events? How quickly did he or she get back on track? These are questions that pertain essentially to reactions to the initial separation/divorce event.

Just as adults have developmental tasks to perform in dealing with divorce, so do children have tasks to perform in coping with it. Wallerstein (1983) has described six psychological tasks that children need to master: (1) acknowledging that the divorce is real, that it is happening or has happened; (2) disengaging from the parents' conflict, so that they can get on with their own usual pursuits, such as school; (3) resolving the loss that is occurring, such as the loss of a member from daily participation in the family life and feelings of rejection; (4) resolving anger and self-blame for the divorce; (5) accepting the permanence of the divorce; and (6) achieving realistic hope regarding their own future relationships. The failure to achieve or complete these tasks results in visible disruptions in the child's daily living, such as schoolwork. Some of these pertain to the divorce event and some to the divorce process.

The reactive and adjustmental nature of what is being studied in the reactions to divorce research is illustrated in a report on a six-year follow-up by Hetherington and colleagues (1985): "In summary, children do adjust to their parents' marital rearrangements, although children who go through divorce and remarriage show at least more short-term problems than do children in nondivorced families" (p. 530). Similarly, Wallerstein and Kelly (1980) found that most of the children they studied got back on track and resumed their normal developmental progress within 18 months after the separation/divorce break occurred. There were exceptions among some of the adolescents studied, who were still manifesting signs of difficulty a few years later (Wallerstein 1983).

Postseparation/Divorce Stress

There are two major sources of postseparation/divorce stress for children, according to available research and careful clinical observation:

loss and parental discord (Nichols 1984). The loss of the father from the home and daily life has been one of the most widely cited and studied losses in the literature. When one views research historically, those children who have had limited contact or no contact with their fathers after separation/divorce appear to manifest the greatest emotional and developmental difficulty among the children of divorce who have been studied (Hetherington 1979, Wallerstein and Kelly 1980). One clinical study recently indicated that feelings about the loss of their father may not be as important for preschool children as the relationship with the residential parent, and a supportive environment (Rosenthal 1979).

Other recent research has pointed to the environmental and support losses suffered by the children and by the custodial parent—still the mother in 90 percent of the cases—that are indirect results of father-absence, as being significant (Longfellow 1979, Wallerstein 1983). Father-loss is exceedingly important, but the lowering of the family's living standard and deprivation of emotional supports for the child also are part of the loss suffered (Derdeyn 1977).

Continued conflict between the separated/divorced parents tends to affect not only the child's adjustment and ability to cope with the situation (Hetherington 1977, Kelly and Wallerstein 1976) but also in many instances to inflict damage on the child's self-esteem (Berg and Kelly 1979). Clinical observation as well as empirical research seem to support the idea that the most damaging form of parental discord is where a child is triangulated into the conflict between the parents or in alliance with one against the other or is made a scapegoat (Nichols 1984).

Fortunately for some children, not all parents engage in discord following separation/divorce. Ahrons (1979, 1980, 1981) has demonstrated in her research that a number of different relationship modes between formerly married persons are possible as they continue their parenting work. Wallerstein and Kelly (1980) have pointed to the absence or attenuation of acrimonious relations between the parents in this period as contributing to the ability of children of all ages to deal with divorce.

The point here is that the nature and extent of the losses suffered and the nature and degree of parental conflict are major sources of stress for children in the postseparation/divorce stage. Consequently, they are not only significant influences on the reactions that children can be expected to manifest but also sources of the effects that the divorce process has on children. Once again, there is a significant amount of contingency in the reactions of children to the actions of their parents in the divorce process, just as the parents begin to react to the reactions of their children in a systemic feedback fashion.

The Question of Treatment

When a child is exhibiting problematic behavior or pathological reactions, does he or she need psychological help? Is treatment needed? Perhaps so. Perhaps no. As indicated above, a number of behaviors by children of divorce may be justifiable and understandable under the circumstances in which they are living at the time of the actions. Other upsets suffered by a child or miserable behavior may be related to his or her age and the vicissitudes of coping with normal developmental tasks for that age level. Parents and sometimes others demonstrate an understandable tendency to assume that untoward behavior by a child or teenager stems from the unusual circumstance in his or her life, such as being a child of divorce or being physically handicapped. The reality often is that the behavior has no discernible relationship to the unusual circumstance but occurs because he or she is engaging in typical behavior for a 14-year-old.

Sometimes a youngster gets into trouble because of sheer bad luck.

Jack, age 13, was taken to a psychologist by his father and stepmother with whom he lived. They were concerned because Jack had been caught "mooning" in the middle-school library. Careful and sensitive questioning by the psychologist disclosed that Jack was far from being pathological. On the contrary, he was terribly embarrassed at what had happened. All indications were that he had not been alone in "mooning," that he did not seem to have any "wish to get caught," any propensity for risk-taking behavior, or other self-defeating dynamics operating, but that he simply had the misfortune to have the librarian return unexpectedly when she discovered she had forgotten something when she left the room. Jack's behavior gave no indications that it was related to "being a child whose parents divorced" or any other problem source. Rather, it appeared age-appropriate at that time, and no sillier than the exhibition of similar behavior by the young mayor of his city.

In addition to assessing the problems and strengths of a child of divorce in the context of appropriate family and social settings, his or her need for treatment should be considered in the light of: the child's developmental level, her or his experience with and response to the parents' separation and divorce, the nature and duration of the problematic behavior or pathological reactions, and the existing network of support for the child (Nichols 1984, pp. 33–34). Attention to developmental level includes noting the child's age and ability to discharge the developmental tasks accompanying that stage of the life cycle, success in coping with the psychological tasks of the child of divorce described by Wallerstein (1983), and comparison of how he or she was faring with the normal developmental tasks for the age/stage level both prior to the family discord and marital breakup and subsequently.

How he or she learned about the coming marital splitup, how the parents handled it, the child's reactions, the amount of change in his or her living arrangements, and related questions are part of what should be assessed with regard to the child's experience with and response to the separation/divorce. How severe have the problematic behaviors or pathological reactions been and how long have they lasted? Gardner (1976) has described chronicity as the main factor in determining whether or not a child needs treatment. Passive-aggressive refusals to cooperate, significant difficulties in peer relations, school misbehavior that indicates a lack of internal controls, and the presence of phobias, obsessions, compulsions, and similar symptoms are cited by Gardner (1976) as specific indications that therapy is needed. Therapy may not be required, nevertheless, if the network of support around the child is extensive and strong enough. Can the child depend on and trust parents, grandparents, teachers, siblings, friends, and other significant persons? Can they help to tide her or him over the rough spots?

Assessment of the need for treatment involves a consideration of all of these factors. Combinations of strengths in some of them may outweigh problems in other areas. A crucial question, even if the child is showing markedly the effects of the family transitions, is whether the child or children require therapy or whether the unit of treatment or other intervention should be someone else in addition to or instead of the child. Perhaps in no other family situation is the child more clearly a reflection of a family system than in divorce situations.

Different interventions are needed at different points of the divorce process (Nichols 1985), depending on what is occurring during the predivorce, divorcing, and postdivorce stages. Major stress points for children during the process are typically the separation/divorce (breakup of the nuclear family household) and the remarriage of one or both parents (Nichols 1985). Although a considerable amount of the psychological treatment provided to children of divorce has been and evidently continues to be individual psychotherapy (Gardner 1976), that is not the preferred therapy approach, in my judgment. Both transgenerational family therapy involving in some instances the child's grandparents (Nichols 1985) and, in some cases, therapeutic work with the family's sibling subsystem combined with other family interventions (Nichols 1986) typically would be the approaches of choice.

EFFECTS OF DIVORCE

The longer I observe and work with divorce situations and their outcomes, the more convinced I become that we know very little about the effects of the divorce process on children at the time the marital breakup and family reorganization are occurring. The longitudinal research that has been reported in recent years is helpful, but it is necessarily limited and incomplete. Perhaps it is impossible to know what the effects are for many years, if ever.

We can continue to make observations and do research, and we can provide treatment and other forms of helpful intervention. We also can, as psychotherapy has done historically, on occasion learn a considerable amount about normal needs from pathological reactions and outcomes. Three "good kids" who reportedly gave "no strong signals" that things were not going well provide illustrations to the point that the effects of divorce may not be evident for many years. The problems of two of them centered on specific events that they internalized as children and were consciously affected by for decades. The other could never get focused on exactly what went wrong or what was wrong, and that was the crux of her problems.

Depression and Confusion

Ann was six when her parents divorced; both quickly remarried other divorced persons with children. Within two years, both parents had children from their new marriages. The youngest in her original family, Ann soon went with her siblings, mother, stepfather, and new half-siblings and stepsiblings to live in an affluent life-style abroad, where the stepfather's high-level executive position took them for several years. Both while living in Europe and after returning permanently to the United States, Ann was able to visit annually for short periods her father, stepmother, and the stepsiblings and half-siblings in that part of her family. She "had no problems" as far as she and the family noted until she entered college. She had been particularly close to her two older sisters, one of whom was described as "kind of a second mother."

While the clinician's official diagnosis was "depressive reaction," the early clinical record also contained notations such as the following: "Major identity issues. Has no idea who she is and where she fits in, if she does." "Nurturance needs long denied." "Two older siblings have helped her cope well in the past." "Evidently her confusion about what her family is extends to who she is." Subsequent therapeutic work with Ann, as well as sessions with other family members, disclosed her feelings that she had been "ping-ponged" between her parents, whom she felt did not want her very much. Going to college reactivated the "abandonment anxiety" that had been aroused with the separation/divorce, the remarriages, and the advent of half-siblings on each side of her family and crystallized the feeling that she was unloved and too much on her own.

Threat of Abandonment

Bob's long-term fears and anxieties were symbolized by an incident when he was eight in which his mother locked him in the family automobile and threatened to leave him unless he obeyed her injunction to "behave yourself." Although "she only walked away a few feet, I really started screaming for her to come back, that I would be a good boy, and I was," he recalled. "I did everything I was supposed to do from then on, nearly." How much Bob's anxieties were fueled by the departure of his father from the home a year or so later is difficult to ascertain, but it appeared evident that seeing his mother tell his father, "If you can't stop drinking and running around, just leave!" had helped to concretize his childhood abandonment anxiety into specific fears of rejection.

Bob's abandonment concerns were not his immediate presenting problem to a therapist. Rather, he sought help because his marriage was breaking up. After a couple of years of "lying to my wife and having a couple of affairs, I know that I rubbed her face in it and did things so that she could not help but know I was running around when I was supposed to be working late. She would beg me to be different. I told her a bunch of times that if she didn't like things the way they were to do something about it, and I think that finally pushed her over the edge. This weekend, she told me that she's in love with somebody else and is filing for a divorce," he said, "and I don't want it."

Probing by the clinician brought Bob's response, "I'm scared to death," in which he gave verbal expression to what he was manifesting in his posture and mannerisms. Working through the abandonment which had finally come for Bob when his wife left him was a major therapeutic task. In his late thirties, he worked out his decades-old feelings about his mother's threats, his father's leaving, the divorce, and his own sense of worth so that eventually, after he entered a second marriage, he could relate as an adult peer rather than as an overly scared "good little boy" or a blustery macho male.

The Fear of Failure

Cindy's fears also were specific, although she never talked about them from age 14, when a "curse" was put on her, until twenty years later, when it was fulfilled. In therapy she recalled what happened, "like it was yesterday." Her parents became embroiled in a bitter divorce and a tug-of-war custody struggle. Cindy and her younger sibling were brought into the courtroom by the judge and compelled to voice a preference as to whether they went to live with their mother or their father. For reasons that seemed quite understandable and reasonable, they chose to go with their father when the judge would not heed their protestations that they did not wish to pick one parent over the other. Outside the courtroom the mother told Cindy, "You'll get married and you'll be unhappy and you'll end up with it failing, and then you'll know how I feel."

Unable to talk with anyone, including her father, about her fears, and feeling that she had to protect the younger sibling, she "forgot about them" until she got married. Then she lived with the fear of failure inside herself for twelve years. When her husband blamed her for his problems, including his premature ejaculation difficulties, she believed that it was her fault and existed with the fear that he would leave her. After a messy public exposure of his current extramarital affair by one of his angry former lovers, Cindy's husband blamed her once again and threatened to end the marriage. At that point, she finally "decided that he had already left me, a long time ago, even though he was still around physically," and sought professional help for herself.

Cindy found perhaps her greatest therapeutic help and certainly her greatest confirmation of her own worth and value, when she entered into a relationship with a kind, gentle man. Engaging in her first sexual experience with anyone other than her former husband, she quickly learned that she was "capable, competent, and *desirable* as a sex partner, as a woman." Later she could talk about "the wasted years in which I let my husband blame me for everything that didn't work and believed him, when I was so afraid I was going to be wrong that I couldn't point out the things that I see now were actually him and his problems."

These three cases are not given to prove what happens in terms of the effects of divorce. Rather, they illustrate some of the long-term effects of divorce processes and inadequate support or poor handling of children during the process. There certainly are others that show up earlier. These difficulties did not manifest themselves until new circumstances occurred that could not be handled through old coping means. Without the occurrences and dynamics of the parental divorce situations, it is not highly likely that any one of them would have ended up in a therapist's office as they did.

The major points from these cases are, however, the points that (1) "the good kids," the quiet or conforming ones who do not act out or act up in the face of situational provocations during the divorce process, probably deserve more careful attention than they generally receive; and (2) mishandling of children of divorce, including failure to provide them with an appropriate balancing of their dependency-independency needs during the divorce process, can be costly.

WHAT CHILDREN NEED—SIMPLY STATED

The needs of children in divorce situations can be stated very simply: They need whatever will provide them with continuing assistance to develop as normally as possible. At all stages of the divorce process, the prebreakup stage, the breakup stage, and the postseparation stage, the child needs a clear explanation of what is happening and what it means to her or him. The egocentric concern of the child is well-founded, because what happens to her or him is so highly contingent on what transpires with the parents.

Some specific needs are

Clear boundaries between generations in which parents continue to be adults and permit children to be children.

Adequate handling of the adult developmental tasks by the parents so that children are free to handle their own developmental tasks in relation to the divorce process and their own normal life-cycle developmental tasks.

Adequate parenting so that their age-appropriate dependency-independency needs are maintained in a reasonable state of dynamic balance.

Adequate attention and support so that predictable "abandonment anxieties" can be speedily allayed.

CONCLUSION

Considerable evidence exists to convince the observer that it is the presence of dependable and familiar adult figures upon whom the youngster can rely rather than the availability of a particular category of individual such as a mother or a father that is crucial in human development. Extended family forms in which the dependency and parenting are spread across several family members prove adequate in many societies and appear to moderate the impact of parental divorce on children.

The roles of biological parenthood and social parenthood in such settings are not combined nearly so completely as they are in the societies in which most family therapists and other professional persons live and function. Some important nurturing and socialization functions are assigned to persons other than the biological parents. Significantly, the splitting of the parents and the subtleties of their relationship frequently do not have the kind of impact on children's lives and adjustment that they have in western, complex, urban, industrialized societies.

This does not imply that adults are easily interchangeable and that children who have become attached to particular figures such as their mother or father can be shuffled off to someone else without deleterious effects. Rather, it indicates that there is nothing automatic or magical about biological parenthood and child rearing. Whatever the child has become accustomed to cannot be abruptly replaced without cost. Even in instances in which abuse or neglect lead to legal termination of parental rights, the changes require sensitivity to the reactions of the child.

REFERENCES

Ahrons, C. R. (1979). The binuclear family: two households, one family. *Alternate Lifestyles* 2:499–515.

—— (1980). Redefining the divorced family: a conceptual framework for postdivorce family system reorganization. *Social Work* 25:437–441.

—— (1981). The continuing coparental relationship between divorced spouses. *American Journal of Orthopsychiatry* 51:415–428.

Berg, B., and Kelly, R. (1979). The measured self-esteem of children from broken, rejected, and accepted families. *Journal of Divorce* 2:363–369.

Gardner, R. A. (1976). *Psychotherapy with Children of Divorce*. New York: Jason Aronson.

Hetherington, E. M. (1972). Effects of father absence on personality development in adolescent daughters. *Developmental Psychology* 7:313–426.

—— (1979). Divorce: a child's perspective. *American Psychologist* 34:815–198.

—— (1981). Children and divorce. In *Parent Child Interaction: Theory, Research, and Prospect*, ed. R. Henderson, pp. 33–58. New York: Academic Press.

—— (1982). Effects of divorce on parents and children. In *Nontraditional Families: Parenting and Child Development*, ed. E. M. Lamb, pp. 233–288. Hillsdale, NJ: Erlbaum.

Hetherington, E. M., Cox, M., and Cox, R. (1977). The aftermath of divorce. In *Mother-Child, Father-Child Relations*, ed. J. H. Stevens and M. Matthews, pp. 110–155. Washington, DC: NAEYC.

—— (1985). Long-term effects of divorce and remarriage on the adjustment of children. *Journal of the American Academy of Child Psychiatry* 24:518–530.

Kelly, J. B., and Wallerstein, J. S. (1976). The effects of parental divorce: experience of the child in early latency. *American Journal of Orthopsychiatry* 46:20–32.

Kubie, L. S. (1956). Psychoanalysis and marriage: practical and theoretical issues. In *Neurotic Interaction in Marriage*, ed. V. Eisenstein, pp. 10–43. New York: Basic Books.

Longfellow, C. (1979). Divorce in context: its impact on children. In *Divorce and Separation*, ed. G. Levinger and O. C. Moles, pp. 287–306. New York: Basic Books.

Nichols, W. C. (1980). Stepfamilies: a growing family therapy challenge. In *Group and Family Therapy 1980*, ed. L. Wolberg and M. Aronson, pp. 335–344. New York: Brunner/Mazel.

—— (1984). Therapeutic needs of children in family system reorganization. *Journal of Divorce* 7:23–34.

—— (1985). Family therapy with children of divorce. *Journal of Psychotherapy and the Family* 1:55–58.

————— (1986). Sibling subsystem therapy in family system reorganization. *Journal of Divorce* 9:13–31.

————— (1988). *Marital Therapy: An Integrative Approach.* New York: Guilford.

Spitz, R. (1945). Hospitalism: an inquiry into the genesis of psychiatric conditions in early childhood. *Psychoanalytic Study of the Child* 2: 113–117.

Wallerstein, J. S. (1983). Children of divorce: the psychological tasks of the child. *American Journal of Orthopsychiatry* 53:230–243.

————— (1984). Children of divorce: preliminary report of a ten-year follow-up of young children. *American Journal of Orthopsychiatry* 54:444–458.

————— (1985a). Children of divorce: preliminary report of a ten-year follow-up of older children and adolescents. *Journal of the American Academy of Child Psychiatry* 24:545–553.

————— (1985b). The overburdened child: some long-term consequences of divorce. *Social Work* 30:116–123.

Wallerstein, J. S., and Kelly, J. B. (1980). *Surviving the Breakup: How Children and Parents Cope with Divorce.* New York: Basic Books.

4

CHILDREN'S ADJUSTMENT

Lawrence A. Kurdek, Ph.D.

Based on current information regarding the processes that promote healthy development, there are several reasons to expect that children experiencing parental separation and divorce will be at risk for short- and long-term psychological problems.

1. Ratings of stressful life events by children have consistently indicated that parent divorce is a very stressful experience (Brown and Cowen 1988). In view of findings that negative stressful life events are moderately correlated with disorders during childhood and adolescence (Johnson and Bradlyn 1988), children experiencing parental divorce may be predisposed to experience later psychological difficulties.

2. Because divorced parents usually have a history of interpersonal discord, their children are likely to have been directly and indirectly exposed to verbal and even to physical conflict (Emery 1982). Such exposure may engender anxiety, model aggressive solutions to interpersonal difficulty, and prevent children from observing constructive methods for resolving anger (Emery 1982). The continuation of conflict between parents after the divorce might dilute any positive effects associated with continued contact with both parents (Johnston et al. 1985).

3. Because divorce usually involves one parent, typically the father, physically leaving, the child is likely to mourn this parent's absence. This is especially true if this parent has a warm

and supportive relationship with the child (Emery 1982). Given that nonresidential fathers typically reduce or even sever contact with their children (Furstenburg and Nord 1985), divorce may negatively affect the development of interpersonal trust and the resolution of gender role issues, as well as remove the father from the child's support system (Kalter 1987, Stevenson and Black 1988).

4. Divorce often results in decreased financial resources for the residential parent, typically the mother (Weiss 1984). For some children, finances may be so limited that the stresses of poverty are added to the stresses of divorce. In order to achieve solvency, residential mothers may seek employment, resulting in the child's having decreased exposure to the second parent as well.

5. Some children are not given age-appropriate explanations for why their parents are divorcing (Waldron et al. 1986). Consequently, they may construct dysfunctional beliefs about their role in the divorce decision, about what to expect from interpersonal relationships, and about how family systems function (Roehling and Robin 1986). Such dysfunctional beliefs may underlie behavioral problems (Kurdek and Berg 1987).

6. Children may experience a variety of environmental changes due, in part, to decreases in financial resources. For example, they may move to a new residence, a new school, and a new neighborhood. Such transitions may result in the loss of significant persons from the child's support system and may strain available coping resources (Wolchik et al. 1984).

7. Because of stresses associated with the divorce, parents are likely to experience drains on their own time and energy (Buehler and Langenbrunner 1987). As a result, parents may not be available to meet children's needs, to supervise their academic and social activities, and to provide structured home routines and consistent discipline (Hetherington et al. 1978).

8. Due to financial stresses and the limited availability of the residential parent, older children may be given child-care and household responsibilities that exceed their developmental level (Elkind 1981). While such responsibilities may foster a sense of maturity, they may also interfere with the successful negotiation of age-appropriate developmental tasks.

9. Although the frequency of divorce as a social-cultural phenomenon may have reduced some of the negative social stigma surrounding it, children whose family structure differs from the traditional two-parent nuclear family may still be viewed negatively (Fine 1986, Santrock and Tracy 1978). Because of this negative bias, common behavioral problems experienced by

such children may be viewed as more pathological than they really are.

10. Divorce is best regarded as a series of interrelated events and processes (Raschke 1987). The major risk for children of divorced parents may arise from the particular multivariate profile of cumulative stresses experienced and the extent to which these stresses overload existing coping capacities (Barocas et al. 1985). Cumulative stresses may be especially likely for children who experience repeated parental divorces (Brody et al. 1988).

Taken together, the above issues lead one to predict that children from divorced families would function more poorly than those living with both biological parents. The purpose of this chapter is to review empirical evidence regarding this prediction and to identify factors predictive of children's positive postdivorce functioning. A major assumption of this chapter is that a critical evaluation of the children and divorce literature can guide the design of effective intervention strategies. Studies regarding the divorce adjustment of parents (cf. Raschke 1987) and children's functioning in stepfamilies (cf. Pasley and Ihinger-Tallman 1987) will not be of direct concern. Before the review of the literature begins, the assessment of children's divorce adjustment needs to be discussed.

THE ASSESSMENT OF CHILDREN'S DIVORCE ADJUSTMENT

The assessment of children's divorce adjustment raises both conceptual and methodological issues. Conceptually, one can ask whether a child's divorce adjustment is separate from the child's general behavioral adjustment. That is, are difficulties experienced in circumscribed divorce-related domains (e.g., beliefs about the divorce) or are they pervasively manifested (e.g., self-esteem)? Methodologically, one can ask whether assessments of children's postdivorce functioning should be obtained from the children themselves, from parents, from teachers, from clinicians, or from objective trained observers.

Currently, there is no consensus on how best to assess children's postdivorce functioning, although two strategies frequently have been used. One assesses specific divorce-related issues, while the other assesses broader areas of functioning. The first strategy assumes that children's postdivorce functioning is best measured in domains that tap divorce-related content. Thus, children's own perceptions of divorce-related events have been measured by open-ended clinical interviews (Gardner 1976, Wallerstein and Kelly 1980); by structured open-ended questionnaires (Kurdek and Siesky 1980); by objective rating scales (Kurdek and Berg 1987); and by projective techniques (Warshak and Santrock 1983). Children's specific divorce functioning has also been assessed by means of ratings by parents and mental health workers (Stolberg and Ullman 1984, Wallerstein 1987).

The second strategy assumes that children's postdivorce functioning is best assessed by traditional measures of general behavioral adjustment that include children's self-reports of self-esteem, anxiety, attributional style, depression, goal-directedness, and physical and psychological symptoms (Farber et al. 1985, Guidubaldi et al. 1987, Kurdek 1987, Kurdek and Berg 1987, Kurdek and Sinclair 1988a, Pedro-Carroll and Cowen 1985); standardized parent and teacher rating scales (Forehand et al. 1987, Guidubaldi et al. 1987); and standardized tests of academic achievement (Kurdek and Sinclair 1988b).

Although the above assessment issues are not resolved, two consistent patterns of findings have relevance for the choice of assessments. First, while measures of children's divorce-specific adjustment and general behavioral adjustment tend to be positively correlated, the actual correlations are low enough to indicate that the two kinds of measures are not interchangeable (Kurdek and Berg 1983, 1987). Thus, both kinds of measures should be present in any assessment battery. Second, information from different sources (for example, child, parent, and teacher) may actually be unrelated to each other (Fulton 1979, Kurdek 1987). Consequently, whenever possible, information should be obtained from each source of information because of the unique perspective provided. Parents see children in diverse settings, and of all other sources of information probably have the most contact with the child. Teachers can evaluate children's behavior relative to that of their peers. And children themselves can provide access to thoughts and feelings that may be hidden from parents and teachers. In the review to follow, specific mention will be made of the type of measure used and the source of information from which it was derived.

COMPARATIVE STUDIES

The effects of divorce on children have been summarized in recent reviews of this literature (e.g., Emery et al. 1984, Hetherington and

Camara 1984, Kelly, in press, Kurdek 1981). These reviewers are unanimous in one conclusion: The literature concerning the impact of divorce on children is fraught with methodological and conceptual difficulties.

These difficulties include the:

1. use of small, nonrepresentative, white, middle-class, volunteer samples
2. failure to assess changes during the critical period between physical separation and the actual legal divorce
3. collection of retrospective rather than prospective data
4. lack of comparison groups necessary to attribute obtained effects to family structure differences
5. failure to assess the generalizability of findings across children of different ages and differing socioeconomic strata
6. failure to address psychometric issues such as reliability, validity, measurement bias, measurement artifacts, and situation specificity
7. absence of process-oriented measures that would explain obtained differences
8. lack of a conceptual framework for integrating complex findings

Some of these difficulties are endemic to applied research, which cannot match the methodological rigor of studies performed in a laboratory setting. Nonetheless, because information regarding the effects of divorce on children has implications for the development and implementation of clinical interventions as well as social policy (Emery et al. 1984), reliable and valid longitudinal findings are critical. Unfortunately, few longitudinal studies have been done. Consequently, the studies to be discussed in this section involve one-time comparisons or longitudinal comparisons of at least two groups: children living with both biological parents and children living with a single parent because of divorce.

Comparisons Made Only Once

The studies comparing children from differing family structures only once are summarized in Table 4-1 on the following dimensions: the age range of sample; whether or not the sample was divided into age levels (rather than having age serve as a covariate); the number of boys and girls; length of parent separation; whether or not controls were included for socioeconomic status (SES); the measures

Table 4-1 Summary of Studies Comparing Differing Family Structures:

Study	Age Range	Age Level	TP		D		SP		Separa-ration	SES
			M	F	M	F	M	F		
1. Amato (1987)	8–16	Yes	201[a]		89		54		3–7 yr	Yes
2. Amato and Ochiltree (1987)	8–16	Yes	201		89		0	0	5–7 yr	Yes
3. Ambert and Saucier (1984)[c,d]	12–19	No	1785	1762	219	239	0	0	NR	No
4. Brady et al. (1986)	2–17	Yes	270		277		156		NR	No
5. Carson et al. (1987)	13–15	No	12	12	12	12	0	0	> 1 yr	No
6. Dornbusch et al. (1985)[d]	12–17	No	2760	2444	385	413	0	0	NR	Yes
7. Fergusson et al. (1986)[d]	6	No	426	409	33	27	25	29	NR	Yes
8. Forehand et al. (1987)	11–14	No	16	14	13	15	0	0	NR	Yes
9. Ganong et al. (1981)[d]	15–17	Yes	225		48		48		NR	No
10. Kalter et al. (1984)	Grade 3–5	Yes	12	12	12	12	0	0	NR	No
11. Kurdek and Sinclair (1988a)	13	No	67	85	15	17	14	21	NR	No
12. Kurdek and Sinclair (1988b)	12–14	Yes	73	88	16	18	18	21	7.54 yr	Yes
13. Parish and Taylor (1979)	Grade 3–8	No	347		44		15		NR	No
14. Pedro-Carroll et al. (1986)	Grade 4–6	No	78		25	29	0	0	0–82 mo	No

One Assessment

Measures	Source	Pattern of Adjustment	Effect Size[b]
Family environment	Child	TP > D	0.24
Academic skills, self concept, social competence, impulse control	Child, Parent	TP > SP on academic skill and impulse control; SP > TP on everyday skills	0.21
School achievement and aspirations	Child	For boys only: TP > D	
Child behavior problems	Parent	TP > D	0.10
Current problems	Child	TP > D	0.05
Deviant behavior own decisions	Child	D > TP on own decisions	
Aggression, withdrawn behavior	Parent, Teacher	TP > D, SP	
Grades, social competence	Child, Teacher	TP > D	0.39
Positive attitudes about divorce	Child	R > D, TP	
Internal locus	Child	D > TP	0.89
Grades, achievement, school behavior	School records	TP > D, SP	0.28
Goal directedness, general maladjustment, school problems	Child	TP = D = SP	0.13
Self-concept	Child	TP > D	0.42
General maladjustment, anxiety, school maladjustment	Teacher, Child	TP > D	0.48

Table 4-1 (continued)

Study	Age Range	Age Level	TP M	TP F	D M	D F	SP MF	Separation	SES
15. Rosenthal et al. (1985)	3–6	No	18	12	13	17	0 0	>1 yr	No
16. Saucier and Ambert (1983a)[c]	12–19	No	1680	1665	195	263	0 0	NR	No
17. Saucier and Ambert (1983b)[c]	12–19	No	1579	1604	178	243	0 0	NR	No
18. Saucier and Ambert (1983c)[c]	12–19	No	1709	1744	216	274	0 0	NR	No
19. Slater et al. (1983)	16	No	52	60	16	50	0 0	NR	Yes
20. Stolberg and Anker (1984)	6–16	No	21	19	21	18	0 0	6–36 mo	No
21. Stolberg et al. (1987)	7–13	No	47		43	39	0 0	16 mo	No
22. Wyman et al. (1985)	9–12	No	170		98		0 0	<80 mo	No

Note: TP = child living with two biological parents; D = child living with single parent due to divorce; and SP = child living in stepfamily. NR = not reported.
[a]When the number of males and females is not provided, the total sample for each family structure group is given.
[b]Effect size is presented for two-group comparisons involving families with both biological parents

used; who provided the information; the general pattern across measures and sources of information of which family structure group was found to be *better* adjusted; and the effect size (see below).

The control of SES influences deserves additional comment. Ideally, comparisons between experimental groups are made with the assurance that the groups are equivalent on all but the factor of interest (e.g., family structure). With this assurance, one can conclude with reasonable certainty that any differences found on a dependent variable can be attributed to the factor of interest. In research comparing children from different family structures, groups often cannot be matched on relevant background variables, so statistical techniques (like analysis of covariance or partial correlations)

Measures	Source	Pattern of Adjustment	Effect Size[b]
Home environment	Observer	TP > D on variety	0.55
Physical health	Child	For boys: TP > D	
Mental health	Child	TP > D	
Health risks	Child	TP > D	
Self-concept, family conflict	Child	Boys: D > TP; Girls: TP > D	0.17
Child behavior problems	Parent	TP > D	0.32
Self-concept, social competence	Child, Parent	TP > D	0.22
Anxiety, self-concept, social support	Child	TP > D	0.31

and families with a divorced single parent. When relevant, effect sizes were averaged across multiple dependent variables in a single study.
[c]This study included a group of children with a single parent due to the death of the other parent.
[d]An effect size could not be derived from the information provided in this study.

are used to accomplish the same goal. The problem with using these procedures in studies comparing two-parent and single-parent families is that some background characteristics, like income, are the result of the family structure differences and are not sampling artifacts (Weiss 1984). Thus, some of the studies presented in Table 4-1 which control for SES factors may report no differences between family groups when a difference, albeit one explained by SES factors, does in fact exist (Rosenthal et al. 1985).

Several features of the twenty-two studies listed in Table 4-1 warrant mention: (1) only a handful of studies have included a group of children raised in stepfamilies for comparison; (2) all but one study (Brady et al. 1986) used a nonclinic sample, so an initial pathological bias in sampling can be dismissed; (3) the ages of children in the samples range from 2 through 19, with few studies doing any developmental grouping; (4) most studies included both boys and girls in the sample; (5) most studies do not present information on length of separation, and those that do rarely cover the very early separation period; (6) most studies do not present SES information; (7) consistent with the earlier discussion of assessment issues, "adjustment" has been assessed in a variety of ways, most frequently as some type of self-reported general behavioral functioning.

Given these characteristics and limitations, what general picture emerges from these studies about the adjustment of children living with single divorced parents? Considering the ten studies that contrasted children living with both biological parents with those living with only one parent because of divorce (studies 5, 6, 8, 10, 14, 15, 19, 20, 21, and 22 in Table 4-1), the general pattern of findings indicates better functioning for children living with both parents. However, this effect is not pervasive. Of the ninety univariate comparisons reported across these studies, only forty (44 percent) were statistically significant.

In order to examine the differences between these two family structure groups more formally, effect sizes were derived by subtracting the mean of each dependent variable for the divorce group from that of the two-parent group, and then dividing this difference by the standard deviation of the two-parent group (Glass et al. 1981). This procedure gives one a numerical index of how children with divorced parents are functioning relative to children living with both parents. Because relevant data on the two family structure groups were available from five studies which included children in stepfamilies (studies 1, 2, 11, 12, and 13 in Table 4-1), these were also included.

Many studies had multiple dependent variables. In order to avoid problems with interdependent scores, a single effect size was obtained for each study by averaging the effect sizes for all dependent variables. This effect size is reported for each relevant study in the last column of Table 4-1. Studies for which effect sizes could not be derived are noted in the table. Across studies, the average mean effect size was 0.32, with an average weighted mean effect size of 0.25. This weighted mean effect differed significantly ($p < 0.05$) from 0 (Hedges and Olkin 1985, p. 113), but is not large. To put this effect in perspective, the mean adjustment score of a child from a two-parent family was one-fourth of a standard deviation higher than that of a child from a one-parent family. Put another way, the average child in the two-parent family (who surpasses 50 percent of other children in this group) surpasses only 60 percent of the children in one-parent families. On the whole, knowing a child's family structure accounts for little more than one percent of the variance in adjustment scores for all children.

Considering the thirteen studies in which children from one-parent families due to divorce are compared with children living with both biological parents, children living with a parent and a stepparent, and/or children living with a widowed parent (studies 1, 2, 3, 4, 6, 7, 9, 11, 12, 13, 16, 17, and 18 in Table 4-1) a pattern similar to that identified above emerges. When significant differences are found, they tend to favor the biological parent group. As above, however, the effects are not pervasive. Of the fifty-nine univariate comparisons performed, significant effects were obtained in only thirty instances (51 percent).

It might be argued that the family structure main effects may not be as frequently obtained as are interactions between family structure and gender or between family structure and developmental level. Previous reviews of the children and divorce literature (e.g., Hetherington and Camara 1984) indicate that boys may be more negatively affected by divorce than girls, and that developmental effects are inconsistent. Five of the studies in Table 4-1 (studies 8, 13, 20, 21, and 22) either did not include or did not report the effects of children's gender. Of the seventeen remaining studies, the interaction between family structure and gender was significant in only five (studies 3, 5, 6, 9, and 19 in the same table). Typically, the significant interactions indicated that boys' functioning was particularly poorer than girls' in divorced families.

Developmental level was included as an independent variable in only six studies, and interactions between this variable and family structure were obtained in only four out of thirty-six comparisons (11 percent). Thus, overall, the family structure effects do not seem greatly affected by either gender or developmental level.

While these findings indicate that the relatively poor functioning of children from divorced families is a reliable effect, they give little insight into relevant process mechanisms. Of all of the processes highlighted at the beginning of this chapter, none has been more frequently implicated as a pathogenic factor than interparent discord (Emery 1982). Support for the importance of this factor is obtained from a set of studies that has related children's adjustment not only to family structure but also to degree of conflict in the family (Cooper et al. 1983, Dancy and Handal 1984, Enos and Handal 1986, Long 1986, Long et al. 1987, 1988, Raschke and Raschke 1979, Slater and Haber 1984).

Table 4-2 Summary of Studies Comparing Differing Family Structures:

Study	Time 1 Age Range	Age Level	Follow-up	TP M	TP F	D M	D F	SP M	SP F	Separation	SES
Fry and Scher (1984)	10	No	5 yr	50	35	50	35	0	0	No	Yes
Guidubaldi and Perry (1985)	Grade 1, 3, 5	Yes	2 yr	180	178	185	156	0	0	6 yr	Yes
Hetherington et al. (1985)	4	No	6 yr	30	23	10	18	20	22	No	Yes
MacKinnon et al. (1986)	3–6	No	18 mo	14	14	7	7	0	0	2.5 yr	Yes
Rickel and Langner (1985)	6–18	No	5 yr	523[a]		138		71		No	Yes

Note: TP = child living with two biological parents; D = child living with single parent due to divorce; SP = child living in stepfamily.
[a]The number of males and females was not provided. Therefore, the total sample for each family structure group is given. The stepparent group was labeled a "father surrogate" group.

These studies consistently report that the variability in children's adjustment scores is related to high family conflict *regardless* of the type of family structure. That is, in studies using family structure and degree of family conflict as separate factors in the design, the main effect for family conflict is typically strong, while the main effects for family structure and the interaction effect between family conflict and family structure are typically weak or nonsignificant. Bolstering the view that family conflict has a particularly pathogenic impact on children's functioning are findings from two longitudinal studies, which indicate that frequent exposure to interparent conflict in the preschool years is related to maladjustment in adolescence (Block et al. 1986) and young adulthood (Chess et al. 1983).

Longitudinal Comparisons

Five studies have compared children from differing family structures more than once. These studies are summarized in Table 4-2 along the dimensions used earlier. In addition, information is given on the timing of the follow-up or for the study by Hetherington and col-

Measures	Source	Pattern of Adjustment
Achievement motivation, educational aspirations, ego strength, self-esteem, locus of control	Child	TP > D
Social-emotional adjustment, academic performance, physical health	Child, parent, observer	TP > D, especially boys
Internalizing problems, externalizing problems, social competence	Child, parent, teacher, peer	Boys: TP > D; TP = SP Girls: D = TP; TP > ST
Home environment, child rearing	Parent, observer	TP > D
Delinquency, social competence	Observer, parent	TP > ST > D

leagues (1985), the timing of the most recent follow-up. All studies involve nonclinic samples. Other characteristics of these studies deserve mention. The age range of the samples varies widely, as does the time interval between follow-ups; remarried families are included in two studies (actually, Rickel and Langner 1985 included a "father surrogate" group); information regarding length of separation is missing in three studies; all studies included information on SES factors which, as in the earlier set of studies, restricts findings to primarily white, middle-class samples; and adjustment measures were obtained from diverse sources that included parents, teachers, peers, observers, mental health professionals, and the children themselves.

Several trends in the findings are of note. First, family structure main effects were obtained in surprisingly few studies. Of the seventy-eight univariate comparisons involving family structure, only fourteen (18 percent) were statistically significant. Effects that were significant did indicate relatively poorer functioning for children from divorced families. Second, only one study (Hetherington et al. 1985) provides strong support for family structure differences interacting with gender. Out of twenty-four univariate interactions

tested in this study, sixteen (67 percent) were statistically significant. Typically, this effect indicated that boys were more negatively
affected than girls in divorced families, and that girls were more
negatively affected than boys in stepfather families, especially if the
mother had been remarried for two years or more. Third, it is sur-
prising that these studies have not systematically assessed changes
in children's adjustment over time (that is, have not included time of
assessment as a repeated measures factor). Longitudinal studies
focusing only on samples of nonclinic children in divorced families
have reported a general decrease in problematic functioning over
time (Hetherington et al. 1985, Kurdek 1988, Kurdek et al. 1981).
This decrease would be accepted with greater confidence if it were
shown that children living with both biological parents did not also
show decreases in adjustment difficulties.

FACTORS RELATED TO CHILDREN'S POSITIVE ADJUSTMENT TO DIVORCE

As noted above, divorce has short-term and long-term negative effects on some children's adjustment. Consequently, there has been
much interest in identifying factors predictive of children's positive
adjustment to divorce. Part of this interest stems from current concerns with factors that buffer the negative impact of stressful events
in children (Anthony and Cohler 1987).

Unfortunately, several problems have impeded our understanding of resilience in children experiencing parental divorce. First, studies have used different measures of adjustment derived from different
sources of information. Second, because of the correlational nature of
these studies, no statements regarding the causal relation between
buffering factors and adjustment can be made. Third, although adjustment is likely to be multiply determined, few studies have employed multivariate techniques. Most of the studies have used simple
bivariate correlations. Not surprisingly, the amount of variance in
adjustment accounted for by single variables has been small.

The factors purportedly related to children's positive divorce adjustment fall into two groups. The first relates to the children's own
competencies for dealing with stress. The second concerns family
interactions, especially relations with the parents (Kurdek 1981).

Children's Own Competencies

One of the most global ways to examine the relation between children's own competencies and adjustment is to examine effects re-

lated to developmental status or chronological age. Relevant findings have been inconsistent, with most studies reporting a nonsignificant relation between adjustment and children's age at the time of separation or their age at the time of the assessment of adjustment (Chess et al. 1983, Dancy and Handal 1984, Kalter and Rembar 1981, Pett 1982). Studies using a wider age range have reported weak positive relations between adjustment and children's current age (Kurdek 1987, Kurdek and Berg 1983, 1987, Kurdek et al. 1981). The major conceptual problem with analyses using age differences to define competencies is that measures of adjustment are assumed to be valid for all ages sampled. This latter point warrants further discussion.

We know that stresses associated with parental divorce (e.g., interparent conflict, parent depression, lack of social support, financial stress) have a negative impact on children whether they are infants (Cohn and Tronick 1983, Crnic et al. 1983, Vaughn et al. 1980) or young adults (Cooney et al. 1986). However, we also know that stressful events are experienced, appraised, and adapted to in qualitatively different ways across this portion of the life span (Compas 1987). Nonetheless, studies correlating age and adjustment assume the developmental validity of adjustment as a quantitative construct (e.g., a continuum of low self-esteem to high self-esteem or few behavioral problems to many behavioral problems means the same thing at different ages).

There is evidence that preschool children, school-age children, and adolescents reason about (Kurdek 1986a) and react to (Wallerstein and Kelly 1980) divorce differently. Compared with younger children, older children reason about parental divorce in terms that are inferential, abstract, and psychological. They are aware of interparent discord and provide descriptions of each parent that combine positive and negative features. Further, they can identify both positive and negative consequences of the divorce.

With regard to reactions, family disruption for preschoolers can trigger regression, fretfulness, bewilderment, aggression, and neediness. For school-age children, it can engender sadness, grieving, fear, anger, feelings of deprivation, fantasies of responsibility and reconciliation, somatic complaints, and loyalty conflicts. Finally, adolescents can react to divorce with painful feelings, concern over their own future marriage, worry over financial matters, loyalty conflicts, an accelerated individuation from parents, and a heightened awareness of parents as sexual beings.

Given these age-related effects, it is critical to consider how parental divorce impedes or facilitates the negotiation of normal age-appropriate developmental tasks (Kalter 1987, Kalter and Rembar

1981, Wallerstein 1983). Unfortunately, few studies have examined the relation between age-appropriate processes and adjustment separately for samples at different age levels or developmental periods.

While no empirical studies have examined the relation between age-appropriate buffering factors and adjustment separately at different age levels, several studies have examined this relation for total samples varying in age. The age-related variables that have been found to be positively related to children's healthy divorce adjustment include few problematic beliefs regarding the divorce (e.g., parents will reconcile, the self is to blame for the divorce) (Kurdek and Berg 1987); an internal locus of control (Kurdek et al. 1981); well-developed social cognitive skills, especially in the areas of interpersonal understanding and conflict resolution (Kurdek 1987, 1988); the use of constructive coping strategies (e.g., using personal resources and focusing on the problem rather than escaping or ventilating) (Kurdek and Sinclair 1988b); and involvement in a social support system (Kurdek, in press).

Family Factors

Compared with the child competency factors, family factors have been more widely investigated. This area of study has yielded what is arguably the most pervasive and consistent finding in the children and divorce literature: interparent discord, both in the pre- and the postseparation periods, is related to children's poor adjustment (Emery 1982). In addition, children's positive adjustment has been related to low stress and to psychological health (especially low depression) of the residential parent (Forehand et al. 1987, Kurdek 1987, 1988, Shaw and Emery 1987); authoritative parenting (Guidubaldi et al. 1987, Hetherington et al. 1982, Slater and Power 1987); and a positive relation with the residential parent (Pett 1982, Wallerstein and Kelly 1980).

The most controversial finding in this area concerns involvement of the nonresidential parent. While some studies report that children's positive adjustment is facilitated by good relationships with *both* parents (Camara and Resnick 1987, Guidubaldi et al. 1987, Kanoy et al. 1985), other studies have found weak or nonsignificant relations between dimensions of the nonresidential parent's involvement (e.g., frequency, duration, and reliability of visitation) and children's adjustment (Furstenberg et al. 1987, Hess and Camara 1979, Kurdek 1986b).

Two resolutions of the controversy seem plausible. First, in view of the powerful effect interparent discord has on children's adjustment, one might expect that contact with the nonresidential parent in conflictual settings might negatively affect adjustment (Kurdek 1986b). Thus, contact with both parents might be beneficial only when such contact occurs in harmonious settings. Second, the locus of the anticipated salubrious effect of involvement by the nonresidential parent might be misplaced. Due possibly to a reliance on nonsystemic models of family functioning, researchers have expected that involvement of the nonresidential parent would have a *direct* effect on children's adjustment. However, there is suggestive evidence that such involvement may directly affect the well-being of the *residential parent* rather than the child. Emotional and financial support by the nonresidential parent may reduce the strain experienced by the residential parent, and thereby increase his or her parenting competence. It is this parenting competence which, in turn, directly affects children's adjustment (Kurdek 1986b, 1987, Stolberg and Bush 1985).

CONCLUSION

The evidence reviewed in this chapter indicates that children living with a single parent as a result of divorce are less well adjusted than children living with both biological parents. Adjustment here is defined broadly and is assessed by reports from diverse sources of information. While the difference between these two groups of children is reliable, it is neither a pervasive nor a large difference. Clinicians should keep in mind that most children in time adjust well to their parents' divorce. Those who do not, on the average, perform only one-fourth of a standard deviation below children living with both biological parents. Given that published studies are likely to be biased in favor of studies finding differences between these two groups of children, the actual performance deficit may be even less than one-fourth of a standard deviation. Thus, knowing a child's family structure is likely to account for less than one percent of the variance in adjustment scores. Further, family structure differences do not seem greatly influenced by either children's developmental level or gender.

Available evidence also indicates that children's positive adjustment to parental divorce is related to children's own competencies for dealing with stress and to family factors. When the pieces from bivariate correlational data are put together, the following profile of the well-adjusted child emerges: He or she has few problematic beliefs regarding the divorce, tends to attribute the outcome of events to internal factors, has well-developed social-cognitive skills (especially in the areas of interpersonal understanding and conflict resolution), uses constructive coping strategies, and is embedded in a social support system. Further, this child experiences low interparent conflict, has a good relationship with a psychologically healthy residential parent, and receives authoritative parenting.

Taken together, these findings have practical implications for assessment and intervention strategies. Because the one-fourth standard deviation deficit in the functioning of children with divorced parents is an average figure, individual children will vary around it. In the absence of other information, clinicians can assume that a child with divorced parents will be functioning slightly less well than a child living with both biological parents. Assessments—of the child's own beliefs about the divorce, the child's general style for explaining the outcome of negative events, the child's social-cognitive skills, the strategies the child uses to cope with stress, the nature and density of the child's support system, the extent of interparent conflict, the psychological functioning of the residential parent, the child's relationship with this residential parent, and the kind of parenting the child receives—will enable the clinician to gain a multidimensional profile of the child's level of adjustment.

Although the causes of children's divorce adjustment remain to be documented, the correlates of adjustment listed above can serve as the targets of intervention with children or with parents. For example, children's functioning might be improved if their beliefs about divorce are rational, if they explain the divorce in terms that do not implicate their own abilities or efforts, if they understand the divorce from the point of view of each parent, and if they utilize age-appropriate coping strategies and have access to a social support system. Work with parents can reinforce gains that may be made with children in the areas just listed and may address the parents' own psychological functioning and parenting skills. Family therapy may also be effective in improving the functioning of the entire single-parent family system.

There is no question that rapid gains have been made in our understanding of how children are affected by their parents' divorce. Nonetheless, there are many gaps in our understanding, and two are highlighted here. First, more attention needs to be paid to developmental factors. As already noted, while there is ample documentation of the position that appraisals of and reactions to stressful events change with age, there are few models of children's divorce adjustment that give center stage to developmental issues. We need large-scale descriptive data on what are healthy, normative, age-appropriate responses to events occurring in the process of parent separation and divorce. With this information, children in need of clinical services can be identified, and age-appropriate interventions can be designed.

Second, multivariate, systemic process models of children's adjustment to divorce are needed. The profile of the well-adjusted child presented earlier is based largely on findings derived from bivariate correlations. Thus, the relations among the buffering factors and their relative importance are unknown. Multisource, multimethod, longitudinal studies with large representative samples are needed to justify the kinds of analyses that can ferret out patterns of direct and indirect influences on adjustment over time.

REFERENCES

Amato, P. R. (1987). Family processes in one-parent, stepparent, and intact families: the child's point of view. *Journal of Marriage and the Family* 49:327–338.

Amato, P. R., and Ochiltree, G. (1987). Child and adolescent competence in intact, one-parent, and stepfamilies: an Australian study. *Journal of Divorce* 10:75–96.

Ambert, A., and Saucier, J. (1984). Adolescents' academic success and aspirations by parent marital status. *Review of Canadian Sociology and Anthropology* 21:62–74.

Anthony, E. J., and Cohler, B. J., eds. (1987). *The Invulnerable Child*. New York: Guilford.

Barocas, R., Seifer, R., and Sameroff, A. J. (1985). Defining environmental risk: multiple dimensions of psychological vulnerability. *American Journal of Community Psychology* 13:433–447.

Block, J. H., Block, J., and Gjerde, P. F. (1986). The personality of children prior to divorce: a prospective study. *Child Development* 57:827–840.

Brady, C. P., Bray, J. H., and Zeeb, L. (1986). Behavior problems of clinic children: relation to marital status, age and sex of child. *American Journal of Orthopsychiatry* 56:399–412.

Brody, G. H., Neubaum, E., and Forehand, R. (1988). Serial marriage: a heuristic analysis of an emerging family form. *Psychological Bulletin* 103:211–222.

Brown, L. P., and Cowen, E. L. (1988). Children's judgments of event upsettingness and personal experiencing of stressful events. *American Journal of Community Psychology* 16:123–135.

Buehler, C., and Langenbrunner, M. (1987). Divorce-related stressors: occurrence, disruptiveness, and area of life change. *Journal of Divorce* 11:25–50.

Camara, K. A., and Resnick, G. (1987). The interaction between marital and parental subsystems in mother-custody, father-custody, and two-parent households: effects on children's social development. In *Advances in Family Intervention, Assessment and Theory*, vol. 4, ed. J. P. Vincent, pp. 165–196. Greenwich, CT: JAI Press.

Carson, A. D., Madison, T., and Santrock, J. W. (1987). Relationships between possible selves and self-reported problems of divorced and intact family adolescents. *Journal of Early Adolescence* 7:191–204.

Chess, S., Thomas, A., Korn, S., Mittelman, M., and Cohen, J. (1983). Early parental attitudes, divorce, and separation, and young adult outcome: findings of a longitudinal study. *Journal of the American Academy of Child Psychiatry* 22:47–51.

Cohn, J. F., and Tronick, E. Z. (1983). Three-month-old infants' reaction to simulated maternal depression. *Child Development* 54:185–193.

Compas, B. E. (1987). Coping with stress during childhood and adolescence. *Psychological Bulletin* 101:393–403.

Cooney, T. M., Smyer, M. A., Hagestad, G. O., and Klock, R. (1986). Parental divorce in young adulthood: some preliminary findings. *American Journal of Orthopsychiatry* 56:470–477.

Cooper, J. E., Holman, J., and Braithwaite, V. A. (1983). Self-esteem and family cohesion: the child's perspective and adjustment. *Journal of Marriage and the Family* 45:153–159.

Crnic, K. A., Greenberg, M. T., Ragozin, A. S., Robinson, N. M., and Basham, R. B. (1983). Effects of stress and social support on mothers and premature and full-term infants. *Child Development* 54:209–217.

Dancy, B. L., and Handal, P. J. (1984). Perceived family conflict, psychological adjustment, and peer relationship of black adolescents: a function of parental marital status or perceived family conflict? *Journal of Community Psychology* 12:222–229.

Dornbusch, S. M., Carlsmith, J. M., and Bushwall, S. J., et al. (1985). Single parents, extended households, and the control of adolescents. *Child Development* 56:326–341.

Elkind, D. (1981). *The Hurried Child*. Reading, MA: Addison-Wesley.

Emery, R. E. (1982). Interparent conflict and the children of discord and divorce. *Psychological Bulletin* 92:310–330.

Emery, R. E., Hetherington, E. M., and DiLalla, L. (1984). Divorce, children, and social policy. In *Child Development Research and Social Policy*, ed. H. W. Stevenson and A. E. Siegel, pp. 189–266. Chicago: University of Chicago Press.

Enos, D. M., and Handal, P. J. (1986). The relation of parental marital status and perceived family conflict to adjustment in white adolescents. *Journal of Consulting and Clinical Psychology* 54:820–824.

Farber, S. S., Felner, R. D., and Primavera, J. (1985). Parental separation/divorce and adolescents: an examination of factors mediating adaptation. *American Journal of Community Psychology* 13:171–185.

Fergusson, D. M., Dimond, M. E., and Horwood, L. J. (1986). Childhood family placement history and behaviour problems in 6-year-old children. *Journal of Child Psychiatry* 27:213–226.

Fine, M. A. (1986). Perceptions of stepparents: variations in stereotypes as a function of current family structure. *Journal of Marriage and the Family* 48:537–543.

Forehand, R., Fauber, R., Long, N., Brody, G., and Slotkin, J. (1987). Maternal depressive mode following divorce: an examination of predictors and adolescent adjustment from a stress model perspective. In *Advances in Family Intervention, Assessment and Theory*, vol. 4, ed. J. P. Vincent, pp. 71–98. Greenwich, CT: JAI Press.

Forehand, R., Middleton, K., and Long, N. (1987). Adolescent functioning as a consequence of recent parental divorce and the parent-adolescent relationship. *Journal of Applied Developmental Psychology* 8:305–315.

Fry, P. S., and Scher, A. (1984). The effects of father absence on children's achievement motivation, ego-strength, and locus of control orientation: a five-year longitudinal assessment. *British Journal of Developmental Psychology* 2:167–178.

Fulton, J. A. (1979). Parental reports of children's post-divorce adjustment. *Journal of Social Issues* 35:126–139.

Furstenberg, F. F., Morgan, S. P., and Allison, P. D. (1987). Paternal participation and children's well-being after marital dissolution. *American Sociological Review* 52:695–701.

Furstenberg, F. F., and Nord, C. W. (1985). Parenting apart: patterns of childrearing after marital disruption. *Journal of Marriage and the Family* 47:893–904.

Ganong, L., Coleman, M., and Brown, G. (1981). Effect of family structure on marital attitudes of adolescents. *Adolescence* 16:281–288.

Gardner, R. A. (1976). *Psychotherapy with Children of Divorce.* New York: Jason Aronson.

Glass, G. V., McGaw, B., and Smith, M. L. (1981). *Meta-analysis in Social Research.* Beverly Hills, CA: Sage.

Guidubaldi, J., and Perry, J. D. (1985). Divorce and mental health sequelae for children: a two-year follow-up of a nationwide sample. *Journal of the American Academy of Child Psychiatry* 24:531–537.

Guidubaldi, J., Perry, J. D., and Nastasi, B. K. (1987). Assessment and intervention for children of divorce: implications of the NASP-KSU nationwide study. In *Advances in Family Intervention, Assessment and Theory,* vol. 4, ed. J. P. Vincent, pp. 33–70. Greenwich, CT: JAI Press.

Hedges, L. V., and Olkin, I. (1985). *Statistical Methods for Meta-Analysis.* New York: Academic Press.

Hess, R. D., and Camara, K. A. (1979). Post-divorce family relationships as mediating factors in the consequences of divorce for children. *Journal of Social Issues* 35:79–96.

Hetherington, E. M., and Camara, K. A. (1984). Families in transition: the processes of dissolution and reconstitution. In *Review of Child Development Research,* vol. 7, ed. R. D. Parke, pp. 398–439. Chicago: University of Chicago Press.

Hetherington, E. M., Cox, M., and Cox, R. (1978). The aftermath of divorce. In *Mother-Child, Father-Child Relations,* ed. J. H. Stevens, Jr., and M. Matthews, pp. 110–155. Washington, DC: National Association for the Education of Young Children.

—— (1982). Effects of divorce on parents and children. In *Nontraditional Families: Parenting and Child Development,* ed. M. E. Lamb, pp. 233–287. Hillsdale, NJ: Erlbaum.

—— (1985). Long-term effects of divorce and remarriage on the adjustment of children. *Journal of the American Academy of Child Psychiatry* 24:518–530.

Johnson, J. H., and Bradlyn, A. S. (1988). Life events and adjustment in childhood and adolescence. In *Life Events and Psychological Functioning: Theoretical and Methodological Issues,* ed. L. H. Cohen, pp. 64–95. Beverly Hills, CA: Sage.

Johnston, J. R., Campbell, L. G., and Tall, M. C. (1985). Impasses to resolution of custody and visitation disputes. *American Journal of Orthopsychiatry* 55:112–129.

Kalter, N. (1987). Long-term effects of divorce on children: a developmental vulnerability model. *American Journal of Orthopsychiatry* 57:587–600.

Kalter, N., Alpern, D., Spence, R., and Plunkett, J. W. (1984). Locus of control in children of divorce. *Journal of Personality Assessment* 48: 410–414.

Kalter, N., and Rembar, J. (1981). The significance of a child's age at the time of parental divorce. *American Journal of Orthopsychiatry* 51:85–100.

Kanoy, K. W., Cunningham, J. L., White, P., and Adams, S. J. (1984). Is family structure that critical? Family relationships of children with divorced and married parents. *Journal of Divorce* 8:97–105.

Kelly, J. B. (in press). Longer-term adjustment in children of divorce: converging findings and implications for practice. *Journal of Family Psychology.*

Kurdek, L. A. (1981). An integrative perspective on children's divorce adjustment. *American Psychologist* 36:856–866.

——— (1986a). Children's reasoning about their parents' divorce. In *Thinking About the Family,* ed. R. D. Ashmore and D. M. Brodzinsky, pp. 233–276. Hillsdale, NJ: Erlbaum.

——— (1986b). Custodial mothers' perceptions of visitation and payment of child support by noncustodial fathers in families with low and high levels of preseparation interparent conflict. *Journal of Applied Developmental Psychology* 7:307–324.

——— (1987). Children's adjustment to parental divorce: an ecological perspective. In *Advances in Family Intervention, Assessment and Theory,* ed. J. P. Vincent, pp. 1–32. Greenwich, CT: JAI Press.

——— (1988). A one-year follow-up study of children's divorce adjustment, custodial mothers' divorce adjustment, and post-divorce parenting. *Journal of Applied Developmental Psychology* 9:315–328.

——— (in press). Social support of divorced single mothers and their children. *Journal of Divorce.*

Kurdek, L. A., and Berg, B. (1983). Correlates of children's adjustment to their parents' divorces. In *Children and Divorce,* ed. L. A. Kurdek, pp. 47–60. San Francisco: Jossey-Bass.

——— (1987). Children's beliefs about parental divorce scale: psychometric characteristics and concurrent validity. *Journal of Consulting and Clinical Psychology* 55:712–718.

Kurdek, L. A., Blisk, D., and Siesky, A. E. (1981). Correlates of children's long-term adjustment to their parents' divorce. *Developmental Psychology* 17:565–579.

Kurdek, L. A., and Siesky, A. E. (1980). Children's perceptions of their parents' divorce. *Journal of Divorce* 3:339–378.

Kurdek, L. A., and Sinclair, R. J. (1988a). Relation of eighth graders' family structure, gender, and family environment with academic performance and school behavior. *Journal of Educational Psychology* 80:90–94.

——— (1988b). Adjustment of young adolescents in two-parent nuclear, stepfather, and mother-custody families. *Journal of Consulting and Clinical Psychology* 56:91–96.

Long, B. H. (1986). Parental discord vs. family structure: effects of divorce on the self-esteem of daughters. *Journal of Youth and Adolescence* 15: 19–27.

Long, N., Forehand, R., Fauber, R., and Brody, G. H. (1987). Self-perceived and independently observed competence of young adolescents as a function of parental marital conflict and recent divorce. *Journal of Abnormal Child Psychology* 15:15–27.

Long, N., Slater, E., Forehand, R., and Fauber, R. (1988). Continued high or reduced interparental conflict following divorce: relation to young adolescents' adjustment. *Journal of Consulting and Clinical Psychology* 56: 467–469.

MacKinnon, C. E., Brody, G. H., and Stoneman, Z. (1986). The longitudinal effects of divorce and maternal employment on the home environments of preschool children. *Journal of Divorce* 9:65–78. .

Parish, T. S., and Taylor, J. C. (1979). The impact of divorce and subsequent father absence on children's and adolescents' self-concepts. *Journal of Youth and Adolescence* 8:427–432.

Pasley, K., and Ihinger-Tallman, M., ed. (1987). *Remarriage and Stepparenting: Current Research and Theory.* New York: Guilford.

Pedro-Carroll, J., and Cowen, E. L. (1985). The Children of Divorce Intervention project: an investigation of the efficacy of a school-based intervention program. *Journal of Consulting and Clinical Psychology* 53:603–611.

Pedro-Carroll, J. L., Cowen, E. L., Hightower, A. D., and Guare, J. C. (1986). Preventive intervention with latency-aged children of divorce: a replication study. *American Journal of Community Psychology* 14: 277–290.

Pett, M. G. (1982). Correlates of children's social adjustment following divorce. *Journal of Divorce* 5:25–39.

Raschke, H. J. (1987). Divorce. In *Handbook of Marriage and the Family,* ed. M. B. Sussman and S. K. Steinmetz, pp. 597–624. New York: Plenum Press.

Raschke, H. J., and Raschke, V. J. (1979). Family conflict and children's self-concepts: a comparison of intact and single-parent families. *Journal of Marriage and the Family* 41:367–374.

Rickel, A. U., and Langner, T. S. (1985). Short- and long-term effects of marital disruption on children. *American Journal of Community Psychology* 13:599–611.

Roehling, P. V., and Robin, A. L. (1986). Development and validation of the Family Beliefs Inventory: a measure of unrealistic beliefs among parents and adolescents. *Journal of Consulting and Clinical Psychology* 54: 693–697.

Rosenthal, D., Leigh, G. K., and Elardo, R. (1985). Home environment of three- to six-year old children from father-absent and two-parent families. *Journal of Divorce* 9:41–48.

Santrock, J. W., and Tracy, R. L. (1978). Effects of children's family structure status on the development of stereotypes by teachers. *Journal of Educational Psychology* 70:754–757.

Saucier, J., and Ambert, A. (1983a). Adolescents' self-perceived health and parent marital status. *Canadian Journal of Public Health* 74:396–400.

——— (1983b). Adolescents' self-reported mental health and parents' marital status. *Psychiatry* 46:363–369.

——— (1983c). Parental marital status and adolescents' health-risk behavior. *Adolescence* 18:403–411.

Shaw, D. S., and Emery, R. E. (1987). Parental conflict and other correlates of the adjustment of school-age children whose parents have separated. *Journal of Abnormal Child Psychology* 15:269–281.

Slater, E. J., and Haber, J. D. (1984). Adolescent adjustment following divorce as a function of familial conflict. *Journal of Consulting and Clinical Psychology* 52:920–921.

Slater, E. J., Stewart, K. J., and Linn, M. W. (1983). The effects of family disruption on adolescent males and females. *Adolescence* 18:931–942.

Slater, M. A., and Power, T. G. (1987). Multidimensional assessment of parenting in single-parent families. In *Advances in Family Intervention, Assessment and Theory*, ed. J. P. Vincent, pp. 197–228. Greenwich, CT: JAI Press.

Stevenson, M. R., and Black, K. N. (1988). Paternal absence and sex-role development: a meta-analysis. *Child Development* 59:793–814.

Stolberg, A. L., and Anker, J. M. (1983). Cognitive and behavioral changes in children resulting from parental divorce and consequent environmental changes. *Journal of Divorce* 7:23–41.

Stolberg, A. L., and Bush, J. P. (1985). A path analysis of factors predicting children's divorce adjustment. *Journal of Clinical Child Psychology* 14:49–54.

Stolberg, A. L., Camplair, C., Currier, K., and Wells, M. J. (1987). Individual, familial, and environmental determinants of children's post-divorce adjustment and maladjustment. *Journal of Divorce* 11:51–70.

Stolberg, A. L., and Ullman, A. J. (1984). Assessing dimensions of single parenting: The Single Parenting Questionnaire. *Journal of Divorce* 8:31–46.

Vaughn, B. E., Gove, F. L., and Egeland, B. (1980). The relationship between out-of-home care and the quality of infant-mother attachment in an economically disadvantaged population. *Child Development* 51:1203–1214.

Waldron, J. A., Ching, J. W. J., and Fair, P. H. (1986). A children's divorce clinic: analysis of 200 cases in Hawaii. *Journal of Divorce* 9:111–121.

Wallerstein, J. S. (1983). Children of divorce: the psychological tasks of the child. *American Journal of Orthopsychiatry* 53:230–243.

——— (1987). Children of divorce: report of a ten-year follow-up of early latency-age children. *American Journal of Orthopsychiatry* 57:199–211.

Wallerstein, J. S., and Kelly, J. B. (1980). *Surviving the Breakup: How Children and Parents Cope with Divorce*. New York: Basic Books.

Warshak, R. A., and Santrock, J. S. (1983). The impact of divorce in father-custody and mother-custody homes: the child's perspective. In *Children and Divorce*, ed. L. A. Kurdek, pp. 29–46. San Francisco, CA: Jossey Bass.

Weiss, R. S. (1984). The impact of marital dissolution on income and consumption in single parent households. *Journal of Marriage and the Family* 46:115–127.

Wolchik, S. A., Fogas, B. S., and Sandler, I. N. (1984). Environmental
change and children of divorce. In *Stress in Childhood,* ed. J. H. Hum-
phrey, pp. 79–96. New York: AMS Press, Inc.

Wyman, P. A., Cowen, E. L., Hightower, A. D., and Pedro-Carroll, J. L.
(1985). Perceived competence, self-esteem, and anxiety in latency-aged
children of divorce. *Journal of Clinical Child Psychology* 14:20–26.

5

MEDIATION

William G. Neville, Ed.D.

The family has been called "the school of community"—that place where children learn how, in their particular culture, they are to deal with others, with differences, with conflict, and with opportunity. The child learns by watching the adults, and usually before the child enters formal schooling, he or she has already absorbed "the way our kind of people do it."

The family has an enormously important educative and socializing function, making the family a *social* entity, but not a *legal* one. Wives, husbands, children—individuals—all have legal rights, but the family *per se* is not accorded legal status. Therefore, when a divorce occurs the legal rights of the individuals are activated, but the rights of the family are disregarded. The system, the interaction, and the dynamics that make individuals a family are ignored or left to therapists, who have no direct involvement with the legal outcome. The court system, in effect an adversarial system, defines these individuals as competitors rather than colleagues and supports the individual's rights rather than examining the impact of divorce as it leads to a family restructuring. One of the marks of a healthy family is that it restructures itself almost daily; people do not get stuck in any particular role, and the system shifts constantly as its members come and go (Neville 1984).

We rarely feel that the family unit dies as the result of the death of one of its members, but traditionally we have accepted the myth that divorce does mean the end of the family, and we wonder why there is so much residual fighting and bitterness after a divorce. Whether or not the legal system recognizes it, the family is an entity with which we must deal in divorce. Divorce does not destroy that entity, but only restructures it.

MEDIATION AS AN ALTERNATIVE
TO ADVERSARIAL DIVORCE PROCESS

In 1974 in Atlanta, Georgia, O. J. Coogler (1978), a retired attorney who had started a second career as a family therapist, was going through his third divorce with the same embittering results. This time, however, following the wisdom of Gandhi, Coogler "transmuted the energy of his anger" into starting to change the way divorces are handled. He pointed out that the industrial sector had been using mediation for years as labor and management had worked out mutually agreeable contracts, and that there was no reason why the same principles that applied to labor-management mediation would not be applicable to the field of divorce settlements.

Coogler understood the complexities of the legal system. He was also trained as a family therapist to respect the systemic implications of family members, and had studied Transactional Analysis, which provided him with an interaction model for examining such family phenomena as rebellion, compliance, freedom, judgment, and nurture. Transactional Analysis also provided a model to examine the games and interactions that occur within systems and ways to cathect ego states that were being destructive, so that the individual might behave in a more free and mature manner. In the six remaining years before his death, Coogler and his colleagues applied the principles of mediation to divorcing families with the result that the American Bar Association has blessed divorce mediation as an acceptable approach for divorce settlements. There is now a *Mediation Quarterly* with international readership, a professional organization (The Academy of Family Mediators) with international membership, and a growing global awareness that mediation is applicable in most situations of conflict around the planet.

Mediation in its purest form is a process in which parties in dispute are empowered by a neutral third party to settle their differences in a mutually agreeable fashion. Parker (1980) made a comparison of the results of mediation a year after divorces were finalized and found that with the mediation approach, the divorce process was completed in one-third the time and one-third the cost of the adversarial system; that over a year after divorce 90 percent of the parties were still satisfied with their overall settlement, and over 93 percent were satisfied with their custody and visitation arrangements. He further noted that most of the mediated clients not only spoke of their former spouses but did so caringly. On the other hand, the adversarial clients, *if they spoke of their former spouses at all*, tended to do so with hostility and bitterness. Other studies have shown that where couples have been offered the option of mediation, most of them have chosen to use the process, and of those seeking mediation approximately 85 percent have successfully completed the task (Pearson and Theonnes 1982). Every settlement has both a legal and an emotional component, and in the final analysis, compliance by both sides with the terms of the agreement is the test of any settlement's validity. Since mediated settlements come from within the disputants themselves, there is a higher likelihood that this emotional component will be both satisfying and motivational.

Looking back, we see that the history of western civilization has largely been one in which two or more people or groups came into combat with each other over some particular issue, and whoever swung the heaviest stick was declared the winner. In Deuteronomy the early Hebrews attempted to modify the destruction of that stick by decreeing *only* "an eye for an eye and a tooth for a tooth." Basically, all of our legal codes since then have done the same thing: recognizing certain rights of the individuals so that the settlement of differences did not render the participants incapable of going on—severely bruised, perhaps, but not destroyed. This basic approach to settling differences has remained the same, however, as (a) the parties have been pitted against each other; (b) the differences have been interpreted that one was right and the other was wrong; (c) the settlement has been based on which side had the biggest stick and could thereby convince the jury that their point of view was the "right" way. We have become very sophisticated in our ability to mask this approach, but the fact remains that the adversarial approach has to do with winning and not with justice, fair play, or with what makes sense—which are all subjective and culturally defined. All of the systems of our western world have supported this approach, and for years we have all bowed down to it as the most acceptable, if not the best, way to resolve differences. The carnage left on the battlefields of the world, however, testifies to the enormous waste and inefficiency of an adversarial battle—at any level.

To apply such an approach to families seems to be especially futile, benefiting only the attorneys who keep representing the unhappy clients in litigation. Court calendars are clogged, family estates are chewed up, people's lives are embittered, and society is not served well, as too often these people become functional cripples—a daily burden on society. Many studies have been done through the years showing the results of divorce to be broken homes, emotionally disabled children, former wives in the poverty class, and fathers who disappear.

It is the thesis of this chapter, however, that this chaos is more the result of *how the divorce is handled*, rather than the fact of divorce *per se*. Or, to borrow terms from stress-management: what happens to you is not as important as is what you make of it. Mediation is not a win-lose game, but a win-win approach in which power is reinterpreted not as the ability to dominate but as the opportunity to serve. "Winning," in mediation, is experienced by the family's restructuring in such a way that all of the participants are empowered to get on with the next chapter of their lives in a healthy and functional way.

As an approach to managing differences, mediation would be much more at home in the Eastern societies and religions where Buddhism teaches that peace comes from within rather than from rearranging the circumstances outside. Even the martial arts suggest using the opponent's own energy to defeat his own attack is preferable to attempting to stop or counter the thrust. Western societies, on the other hand, have tended more toward "might makes right," the extreme result of which is the nuclear standoff with its accompanying debilitating costs. In the West, the Christian faith has taught for centuries that we have the option to love rather than judge those whom we call "enemy" and to find power and strength in service rather than in retribution. Gandhi told his followers, according to Fischer (1983), "We must help the British see the wisdom of leaving India . . . [and] if blood must flow, it must not be British blood." Clearly the interdependency of the human community mandates an urgent need for us to learn to do cooperative problem solving at every level if we are literally to survive as a species.

Mediation as an approach has at least three basic premises: (1) The difference or the conflict is best resolved by the participants themselves, rather than by third-party outsiders, thereby enabling them to own or take responsibility for their own solutions. (2) The process empowers the disputants to find mutually agreeable solutions where each party goes away feeling that he or she has been heard, is respected, and is reasonably satisfied with the particular solution/decision. (3) The results can be tailor-made and sufficiently creative to deal with the particular needs of each individual, family, or person.

THE ROLE OF THE MEDIATOR

The mediator is an "enabler" or a "facilitator" rather than an arbitrator, a judge, an advocate, or a therapist. The mediator does not dictate to the couple what they should do, but helps them look at the pros and cons of the various alternatives in a cooperative way. The mediator does not pressure either party into a particular position, but rather invites both to share what they would be willing to do. The mediator is not there to assess blame or to coerce, but rather to help a family as it restructures. Sometimes the mediator is like a teacher offering alternatives and exploring options and possibilities, sometimes like a priest offering forgiveness, acknowledging grace and expressing gratitude, and sometimes like a wise friend whose caring, impartiality, and wisdom the couple in stress have decided to trust.

The mediator must be skilled in the areas of sensitivity, feelings, caring, listening, family dynamics, conflict management, economics, and the law, but the mediator is *not* there to give legal advice, to write a contract, or to do therapy on unresolved issues. The mediator is there to uncover the couple's own abilities to behave in their best interests.

Child Custody

Studies now indicate that it is in the best interest of the child to have both parents communicate and cooperate in the parenting process (Roman and Haddad 1974). To offer the parents, then, an adversarial courtroom and the advice to *not* talk to each other, but only to and through their lawyers, or even to add yet another attorney to represent the child, would be to go *against* the child's best interest, because to do so would only further fragment the family and frustrate communication. The mediator, on the other hand, can help them understand that the divorce will not end their relationship but will restructure it, and that, for better or for worse, they will still be related legally, economically, and emotionally; that both parents are important to the healthy growth and development of their child, and that both parents need time with and time away from the child. The mediator is thus helping parents explore how they will do *coparenting* (a functional term rather than a legal one), and is asking both to delineate their parenting commitment to their children rather than simply defining legal custody.

Years ago the child was viewed as the property of the father. Later the child was given to the mother as the one best suited by nature to raise the child. Then we came to see "mothering" as a functional rather than a sex-role term, and consequently the question became one of which parent could do the best mothering. Now we are seeing that *both* parents are important to a child; that each parent has a significant contribution to make to the child's ability to grow and develop. The meaning of *custody* has therefore evolved from ownership to the full complexity of child development. In such a context, the question of who has *legal* custody becomes relatively unimportant. Indeed, it is not uncommon that mediation can so free up the relationships that the children will literally wind up with the best of both parents.

This is not to say that the question of legal custody is not important; it is, for legal custody establishes who has the legal right to make the final decision regarding the child's health, education, and welfare. When needed, this is a very important right. Custody becomes an issue, however, only when the functional coparenting agreement breaks down. And under those circumstances the couple is encouraged to come back for a simple session of mediation rather than resort to the courts. Otherwise, as new and unexpected issues come up, the parents, using what they have learned in mediation, simply discuss the matter with each other. The coparenting agreement does need to be quite clear about the times and conditions under which each parent will be the "primary caregiver." If one is going to have the child, for example, from 6 P.M. Friday to 6 P.M. Sunday, the question arises, "Who is going to feed the child supper on those nights?" It is frequently those simple but unclear expectations—the assumptions—that get people into fights.

Helping to Manage Differences

A woman whose divorce I mediated two years ago told me recently that she and her former husband were talking over some decisions that needed to be made and an argument was erupting. She proudly told me how she had intervened with, "Wait a minute. It is not a matter of who's right and who's wrong; we are all important to each other, and we must make this as a family decision." And then she added to me, "You taught us to do that. We would never have known how to do that if we had gone through the adversarial system." Mediation worked for them in the beginning, and it is continuing to work as unexpected situations arise.

Couples will have different levels of ability for managing their differences. Each particular couple has usually developed its own style for handling conflict, and a good mediator must be flexible to modify his or her approach to the present situation. Ken Kressel at Rutgers University studied and labeled fight styles of couples in mediation (Kressel et al. 1980). The easiest to work with was the *direct* style; these couples give clear and direct messages, deal with issues rather than personalities, and are both patient and assertive. The *disengaged* couples have probably been separated for some time and have dealt with their emotional involvement; they have "turned loose" and now simply want to get their decisions down on paper to satisfy the court. They are quick and easy to work with, but are almost ho-hum, lacking the fun and creativity of the direct couples. The *autistic* couples sit silently expecting to be drawn out; their passive-aggressive stance is saying, "I'm here in body, but I'm not going to cooperate or take responsibility for my situation." The *enmeshed* couples are the most difficult to work with in mediation, because they still have so much emotional entanglement and such inefficient skills for cooperative problem solving. They fight badly; they blame; they are not ready to divorce, and they are still trying to get their needs met by making other people feel guilty. Each of these styles requires a different approach by the mediator, and sometimes the mediator may need to be honest and declare his or her inability or unwillingness to mediate with a particular couple. To declare the mediator's lack of ability to cut through a particular pattern shows the strength of the family unit and is preferable to making them feel wrong for being where they are. It is simply recognizing that given the complexity of the situation and the time available, not everyone is ready for mediation.

Parenting and Child Support

Mediation normally begins with an orientation session in which the mediator introduces the process and suggests behaviors that are helpful to the tasks ahead. Custody, or coparenting, is an easy area to explore first. It immediately involves the parents in discussing ways they can be cooperatively involved in the restructuring of their family. The scene is immediately shifted from "winners and losers," "good guys and bad guys," to "Hey! Both of us are important and needed, and both of us are going to be counted in!" Parents can *do* almost anything they wish with their children—short of abusing them—and the courts will have no reason to become involved. The court *will* become involved when the parents choose not to settle issues in a mutually agreeable manner and one parent then appeals to the court to render a judgment on the issue. Custody, therefore, is a natural place for the couple to have the experience of how mediation works, and it provides a natural transition to the area of money and child support.

The principles of mediation are the same whether we are dealing with child care or pension funds, whether we are dividing parenting time or real estate, whether we are establishing child support or spousal support. How is this family going to restructure so that all of its members are heard and all of its assets and liabilities are shared in some equitable fashion?

The court wants to know in a divorce settlement that no one will become a ward of the state and that property records will be maintained with accuracy and clarity. Aside from that, the court basically doesn't care what a couple does with their property. They may sell it, trade it, negotiate it, give it away, keep it and jointly own it—and the court will generally approve any division of an estate that a family offers in the name of mutual agreement. If, however, the family does not resolve these issues and asks the court to render a division for them, then they must accept whatever division the court renders or take the consequences of the court's punishment. The adversarial process is a competitive setting that has nothing to do with fairness or compassion or with motivating internal compliance, but rather is concerned with persuasion and winning.

When child support is figured, the couple needs to draw up a budget based on the financial needs of the children. The question is then raised as to the source of the money. It is not a foregone conclusion that the husband, or the "absent parent" will pay all of the support. Instead, the budgeted amount is examined in light of who has what available income, other expenses, other forms of "contribution" such as time or travel, or even extended family that can contribute to the care of the children. One husband, for example, agreed to the wife's taking the children and returning to her parents' home—about a thousand miles away—so that child care could be provided by the grandparents while their daughter returned to school at the local university. A wife agreed to continue teaching with a particular private school because of the free tuition their three children could receive as a fringe benefit for faculty. Another went to work with a particular bank because they had a policy of paying for their employees' continuing education. A handyman husband agreed to build a bedroom and bath onto the family home so that the wife's mother could come live with her and help out with child care. These are actual illustrations of ways parents have been willing to cooperate to benefit their families at the time of a divorce—cooperative solutions made possible by mediation.

Spousal Support and the Division of Assets

This same blending of budgets, cooperation, and mutuality is also important for questions around spousal support. Each is free to examine the budget of the other, and when budgets and income are placed side by side on a chalkboard, the issue then becomes "How can *we* make this work?" rather than "*You* have to give me more money. . . ." It is fairly common at this point to see a husband be willing to give considerably more than "normal" in spousal support for the first three or four years so that the wife can update her education and job skills and be better able to take care of her own needs—and perhaps even be able to share in child support or to help pay for the college education of their children.

A wife with a good work history was told by her attorney, "Go back in there and ask for $500 a month in alimony." She did. The husband, feeling sabotaged after a number of cooperative settlement decisions had been reached, was so angry he had to leave the room. While he was gone, I asked the wife what the $500 per month represented to her. It meant, she said, that she could get a master's degree in her field. I asked if she would rephrase her request and ask her husband, a college professor, if he would help her get a master's degree. When he returned, still adamantly opposed to the payment of alimony, she asked if he would help her go back to school. He immediately replied, "Oh hell, yes. I've always told you that you ought to get a master's!" One approach took the form of a one-sided demand; the other was a cooperative endeavor that would require the effort of both and would benefit both.

In another case a wife just starting a new business asked her husband for a variable amount of spousal support—to guarantee her a level of income during the shaky years of business start-up. This amount was then reduced by one dollar for every two dollars she made, thereby providing an incentive to each for her to be successful as soon as possible. The point of spousal support is not to punish one who wants out of the present arrangement but to make possible the ability of each spouse to provide for his or her own needs.

A divorce may occur at a time when it is not advantageous to sell real estate, stocks, or bonds, or to cash in certificates of deposit or individual retirement accounts or other forms of investments. Pension plan payments may vary considerably by waiting for a particular age of the divorcing client. Health and insurance can be another area for cooperation. Professional competency and job skills also need attention. For example, the spouse who has been doing the primary parenting may take a year or two of schooling or special training in order to obtain a more lucrative position, which in turn can later benefit the whole family. In another case, a couple had bought some acreage which was likely to show real profit in a few years, but at the time of the divorce there had been little gain. They agreed to continue to be joint property owners until such time as there would be a mutual agreement to sell. In the meantime they would share equally all liabilities and decisions about the acreage.

GUIDELINES FOR MEDIATION

I would encourage mediators to develop and use a set of guidelines for mediation.[1] Some of these may be hard rules, and some may be more suggestions that are important for effective mediation. Some may have to do with legal issues, and some may be more behavior oriented. One of the *rules* would be that the couple agrees to make *full disclosure* of their assets and liabilities. Either they are willing to play fair and expect to be treated fairly, or they are not. If they are not willing to make full disclosure, then we simply are not willing to mediate. If it is later discovered that someone had lied about his or her assets, that person would then have to go back to the judge who had approved the settlement and explain to the court the reason for the lie—not a very pleasant prospect.

One of my *suggestion* guidelines, for example, seeks agreement before mediation begins on what is meant by marital property. It is my recommendation, but not a rule, that "marital property" be all that property—asset or liability—acquired since the marriage began, with the exception of gifts, inheritance, bequest, or appreciation of what each had individually when they came into the marriage. This guideline can then be modified by mutual agreement to deal with any specific variations which their own meaningful histories may dictate. Generally, "marital property" is viewed by the courts as belonging equally to both spouses. What the guideline adds is the opportunity to include the feelings the parties have about the property and the meaning that the property has to each of the spouses in their understanding of what is "equitable division."

I remember a very heated exchange over a particular art object—

---

[1]There is an extensive set of guidelines in the appendix of *Structured Mediation In Divorce Settlement* (Coogler 1978). Others have developed guidelines that were more comfortable for the consumer, and some do not use any guidelines.

the husband insisting that it was not "up for grabs" because it was not "marital property"; it had been his for many years even before they had met. The wife sadly agreed that was true and that in fairness it was not marital property—but it was the one symbol of their life together that she had always loved and that was why she wanted it. The husband then gently replied, "Knowing that it means that to you, I would be happy for you to have it, and it means something to me to be able to give you something you love rather than simply seeing you take it as part of a property division." Both people had agreed to the guidelines, and yet both had been able to transcend the guidelines, or "the law," as they were willing to be human and share their innermost feelings.

To have an equitable division of property does not mean a fifty-fifty split, but it does mean taking into account a variety of factors, settling items that are loaded with meaning one by one, and then looking at the overall balance of division and feelings and wishes. One wife, married to a financial estate planner, was legally entitled to one-half of the estate—some $300,000. She knew the law and understood her entitlement, but said that she did not know what to do with so much money, so she would prefer to leave it all with him to continue to manage, if he would agree to give her a guaranteed income of $1000 per week for the rest of her life—a figure and a time period that she could more easily comprehend. That took a lot of trust on her part, but she said, "I know he is an honest man, and I know if he says it, he will do it." There were other protectionary contingencies that were added to that agreement, but the point is that people will frequently choose something other than that to which they are legally entitled.

A mediator must remember that frequently money—even a large amount of it—is not a blessing and is not perceived as such. One woman remarked to me that she was getting ready to go back to court for the seventh time. She said she wanted "more money," but when I suggested that what she really wanted was to hear her former spouse say, "You *were* a good wife, and we *did* have some good times, and I am *genuinely sorry* that our good times didn't go on," she said quietly with moist eyes, "If I could ever hear him say that, I would never bother him again."

I believe it is part of the human condition that we all want to be acknowledged. When two people have chosen each other and given the best that they have, and then one wants out of the relationship, there is a very special and important need in the other to have his or her own being affirmed, to know that his or her original choice was not all bad, to know that at least some of their history together will be remembered with tenderness. The legal adversarial system does not deal in this kind of settlement-making, and to ask it to do so would be inappropriate, but the mediator who is willing to hear and facilitate at this level will perform an enormously healing, educational, and peacemaking function for individuals, families, and society.

A guideline that is more *behavioral* is that we ask clients to take responsibility for what each says and for what each hears. Blame simply does not fit in mediation: "*You* are not responsible for my condition; *I* am responsible for my world." Kicking the other person does not give one long-term satisfaction, but learning to get our own needs met does. Mediation teaches people to ask for what they want—without having to "pad the budget"—rather than blame someone else for the circumstances of their lives. The mediator is not caught up in their emotional history, so he or she is in a good position to help them say to each other what is true, but what they have been afraid to disclose, or to ask for what they want. One wife was very resistant to asking for a precise amount of alimony. She knew her husband hated the concept of alimony, but at the same time her needs were very real. She continued to respond to our requests about her needs for some support by saying, "Well, my needs don't matter; he isn't going to pay it anyway." We continued to push for her budget, and she finally with great reluctance shared it. Her husband studied her budget for a few minutes and then looked up and said, "Okay, that seems very reasonable. . . ." Learning to take responsibility for one's own condition rather than blaming others, or doing their thinking for them, or putting them in the wrong is a key behavioral ingredient of successful mediation.

MEDIATING SKILLS

A good mediator needs special skills to be effective. One is his or her ability to reframe—to take messages of anger, jealousy, hurt, and resentment and put them in a different context verbally and emotionally so that the negative messages are reflected back in positive settings, which transform the way they are heard and experienced. To do this the mediator must be able to attribute honestly good intention to the clients even when they are behaving in a most unseemly manner. So much of our gruff exterior is hiding the little child within—who is often hurt and frightened. Reframing is this ability to stand in the face of a blustery facade and to respond with gentleness and compassion rather than getting drawn into a fight by a client's "hurt child." Anger is usually a secondary response; behind the anger is hurt, disappointment, or even fright. If the mediator will gently probe this background, he or she can frequently effect a transformation that will suddenly shift the prevailing mood from retaliation to caring.

A good mediator needs to exercise confirmation and caring. Both are closely related to "active listening"—the skill Tom Gordon describes in *Parent Effectiveness Training* (1970). These abilities enable the mediator to reach past the point the client has thus far been willing to go, and to invite that person to experience coming out of bondage into freedom. A word of caution: By doing this the mediator is saying, "You can trust me." Do not offer this invitation unless you are willing to be fully present and totally nonjudgmental with your clients in whatever they disclose.

Another dynamic for a mediator to understand thoroughly is the power of forgiveness. In most divorces there are some strong feelings that if only one or the other had been different everything would have worked out. If people are not relieved of this blame and judgment, they will have a difficult time moving with confidence into the next phase of their lives. *Forgiveness*, however, *benefits most the one who does the forgiving*. If we do not forgive, we stay stuck in the past, full of resentment and bitterness, unable to move forward or take control of our future. Forgiveness is turning loose that which is past, that which can neither be brought back nor changed. We may be wiser and more responsible for the experience, but we cannot rewrite history; we can only acknowledge it and let it go. The paradox, however, is that when A forgives B, A finds enormous freedom. Learning to help people let go is a very important mediational skill. If an older wife forgives her husband for running off with his younger secretary, for example, she not only turns loose something over which she has absolutely no control, but she becomes quite clear that he, and only he, is responsible for his behaviors, and that his behaviors are in no way a reflection or a judgment of her; they are a manifestation of him. By letting herself be drawn into anger or hurt, she takes on a contest as to who is the more powerful over *his* behaviors—the husband? the secretary? or herself?—a contest she is sure to lose, not because she is weak, but because she has absolutely no control over someone else. Acceptance is painful, perhaps, but very freeing.

Although mediation will probably be therapeutic, it is different from therapy. The mediator is not there to keep the marriage together, nor to diagnose where it went awry, nor to deal with the perceptual health of the individuals (although the process of mediation may well illumine all of these). The mediator has been hired by the couple to help the family with a particular task—restructuring in a mutually agreeable manner. The two tasks may be similar, but they are different by contract, and under normal circumstances the roles of therapist and mediator, just as those of attorney and mediator, should be kept separate. The mediator who has a background in therapy needs to know as much family law as possible and yet not try to play lawyer. The mediator who has a legal background should pay special attention to learning some of the sensitivities of a therapist and some of the games and dynamics of families. Mediation is sometimes spoken of as a first cousin to law and a first cousin to therapy, and it is neither law nor therapy. Mediation is an art that flows from an informed heart.

Ethical Issues

If a therapist-mediator or an attorney-mediator has had a professional relationship with either or both of the parties as either therapist or attorney, it would probably be best to disqualify oneself from being the mediator. Short of that, however, and perhaps due to a scarcity of mediators, the potential hazards of continuing as mediator should be acknowledged and talked about openly. Full permission should be given to the other spouse to check out the mediator's motives or behaviors at any point in the process. By such willingness to be scrutinized (and really that is simply asking for feedback) and by responding honestly, I believe the mediator can build the confidence and trust of the other spouse. But just as an attorney who has served as a mediator should not later represent either of the spouses in court, neither should social workers or other mental health professionals who have mediated later allow themselves to be called to testify for or against either of the parties in court.

Maintaining confidentiality concerning the mediation sessions is an absolute imperative. This whole process is based on trust and the willingness of each person to be open and honest with each other. It would be most detrimental to the process of mediation if someone who had served as a mediator were to disclose to a social worker, attorney, or judge any of the background that led to a particular decision. Mediators should be granted the privilege of immunity from having to testify in regard to any of the contents of a particular session. Only the final mutually agreeable decisions should become publicly shared information.

The mediator's job is multifaceted—setting the stage for trust and for full and open disclosure, refraining from judgment of either a person or a position, raising questions for clarification whenever there seems to be an imbalance, managing effectively anger or vindictive outbursts by the parties, brainstorming alternatives when people feel stuck, being comfortable with but not slavishly bound to the law, and finally being willing to be the facilitator without having to be the star. The mediator is there to serve, not to be served, and when the task is completed, it is quite appropriate for the mediator to applaud the couple for *their* courage and *their* caring, for without that, mediation simply would not have been possible. Like any good teacher, the good mediator works to put himself or herself out of business with any given client.

THE MEDIATION PROCESS

It is important for the mediator to learn early on something about the family and its history. How did this couple meet? Are parents still living? Has the possibility of divorce been discussed with them? With others? Does either have an attorney? Is the attorney aware that they are here in mediation? What are their feelings about divorce? Are there children in the family? What ages? Have they been told? How are they handling the family restructuring? Knowing that there are some things still to be worked out, what things have the couple already agreed on? Are they willing to abide by the guidelines of mediation? Have they had family therapy? Is there any possibility of reconciliation? (Even though the possibility of reconciliation is at first denied, this alternative should always be held open.)

In this process the mediator is not only gathering data, some of which will be needed later in the drawing of the agreement, but is also assessing the strengths and weaknesses of the family, the level of respect that is accorded each, their fight style, and something of an order of priorities—what can be acknowledged early as evidence of agreement and what should be left until later when more trust in the process and of their own abilities has been built. By the attention paid to each person the mediator models for his or her clients listening skills, receptivity, balance, and patience.

Mediation is normally conducted in two-hour sessions with the admonition that there will be no discussion of issues over the telephone by the mediator and either party alone. This rule not only discourages after-hours phone calls for no pay, but it also emphasizes that the mediator is just that—a mediator, not an arbitrator; that they need to talk with each other; that no deals or discussions about the issues will be held without both parties being present and privy to the same information at the same time.

Often by the end of the first session, most of the custody and visitation has already been worked out. This is an opportunity to applaud the couple for their cooperativeness over their most important "possession"—their children—to point out that this is an area over which many people go into horrendous battles in court, spending thousands of dollars; but *they* have just completed it in less than two hours! Positive stroking (again a TA term) goes a long way toward building cooperation and self-esteem, and, as is typical of the whole process, it should be honestly and genuinely shared or not given at all. In later sessions the clients will probably need and benefit from gentle reminders that cooperation does work and does work best.

Homework sheets are given out to be completed at home for use in future sessions. These may be budgets for child or spousal support, or they may be a listing of assets and liabilities, but the data are needed for future decisions. In mediation the client furnishes the necessary information; the adversarial system fosters "discovery" as one of the big and expensive ways of harassing the other party into an unwilling settlement, thereby building in irresponsibility and gameplaying ("catch me if you can") from the start. One of the tasks of an adversarial attorney is to make sure that all of the "facts" (checks, bank accounts, partnerships, investments, debts, and the like) in the case are made known. This being the responsibility of the attorney, the client is thereby given permission and even expected to be dishonest and uncooperative. Again, in TA game theory, this "Critical Parent" stance of the attorney invites the other party to get into his or her "Rebellious Child" behavior. The mediator, on the other hand, seeks to cathect the "Adult" ego state of both parties, enabling them to take responsibility for making full and open disclosure.

If they choose the adversarial route, they are playing a game of persuasion where the attorneys are permitted to lie, cheat, and steal in order to "win" for their client, and when the judge dictates "the way it shall be," they are stuck with whatever they get. A judge in Atlanta used to tell of a husband who was obviously upset with the judge's ruling, so, the judge, trying to give him an opportunity to have his say, asked if there were any comments before they were dismissed. The husband looked the judge squarely in the eye and said, "That is the worst damn decision I ever heard in my life!" The judge looked at him calmly but equally straight in the eye and replied, "Son, if you want to go make your own decisions with your family, that's fine with me. But if you turn those decisions over to me to make for you, then that's what you get."

There may be a need at some point in mediation for input from another specialist—an accountant or tax consultant may be called, real-estate appraisals may be obtained, pensions or annuity programs may need to be explained, health insurance options may need to be investigated. Many of these consultants may already be friends of the family and will frequently go the extra mile in suggesting other ways that cooperation can benefit the family in that particular area. The couple should be urged to attend these consultations together so that all their questions and responses can be explored in the presence of both. It becomes increasingly obvious how different the mediation process is from an adversarial approach, which says "don't talk to each other; talk to your attorneys, and let them work it out for you." Mediation is a process of empowering people to make their own decisions in a cooperative framework.

Once all the decisions have been made, some mediators may draw up a "memorandum of agreement," a listing of all the firm decisions that have been made, to give to the parties to take back to their own attorneys for drafting into contract form. Other mediators, myself included, prefer to have an impartial attorney, not representing either party, come to the mediation session as a legal information consultant. As the mediator reads over his or her understanding of the couple's decisions, the attorney asks clarifying questions, and once again the couple hears their agreement in full before it is drafted by this impartial attorney. That same attorney, the couple, and the mediator then meet once more to read over the draft-document, now in "legalese." Further refinements may also be made, but then, before signing it, they are urged to take this draft agreement to their own representative attorneys for another review, fine tuning, and final signing.

Margot Gebhardt-Benischke (1986) has pointed out that if someone (male or female) fears not being dealt with fairly, he or she really needs to be in mediation in order to participate responsibly in every decision that is made. The nature of the process assures that mediation is not *for* women and *against* men, nor is it *for* men and *against* women; it is for the family. Even the sex of the mediator need not be seen as a factor in the process. Some people may still be hesitant to use mediation for fear that the negotiating skills of the wife and husband may not be equally balanced. In that assumption they are absolutely correct; the negotiating skills are never balanced, and even having two attorneys creates a balance only in theory. Mediation, however, is based, not on a "balancing of negotiation skills," but rather on creating an entirely different kind of setting—one in which the wife and husband come to see and experience that even in divorce their own well-being is served by cooperation.

TRAINING FOR MEDIATORS

Given the significance of the task of mediation, the importance of thorough and skillful training of those who would be mediators should be obvious. Consensus in the field of mediation training is that at least an advanced degree in one of the behavioral sciences, at least 40 hours of training in the management of conflict, family dynamics, divorce law, skills of communication and cooperation, and role-play, plus at least five supervised mediations are the barest minimum of training standards. I would add the necessity of some introspective evaluation by the trainee as to motives for entering the field. If it is simply the latest fad or a new way to "make a buck," or simply another way of managing divorces, then I would suggest the trainee look for something else to do. The cooperative-empowering-of-the-other nature of mediation must be manifest in the motives of the mediator, or the process will quickly turn into a setting where the mediator is afraid to lose.

You can teach teachers to teach, but their *effectiveness* is that extra something they bring to the interaction; it is the same with mediation. The process can be taught, but that extra something that makes mediation effective is the respect and caring about people which refuses to judge or be drawn into judgments, that ability and willingness to stand with people in their pain and empower them to experience life beyond their pain. Underneath all of the anger and hurt and disappointment and blame and resentment and retribution that we so frequently see in those who are divorcing, there is also a lot of caring, a lot of wanting to be confirmed as a person whose contribution was appreciated and with whom life was not all bad. Mediation offers the opportunity for this compassionate element to be addressed, for a sense of completion to occur, for the family not to end but to restructure in a way that enables each member to move into the next phase of life as whole and equipped as possible.

CONCLUSION

I understand the Chinese have a symbol for "crisis" that incorporates the two elements of "danger" and "opportunity." Mediation works with the crisis of a divorce, transforming danger into opportunity for learning, a caring experience where parents and children may learn that life never goes the way one expects it to, that all of us are different, and that no matter what form it may take, the truth is that we are all inextricably bound up with each other. Our planet sorely needs the cooperation, the caring, the forgiveness that is or can be exhibited in the divorce mediation process.

REFERENCES

Coogler, O. J. (1978). *Structured Mediation In Divorce Settlement*. Lexington, MA: D. C. Heath.

Fischer, L. (1983). *The Life of Mahatma Gandhi*. New York: Harper and Row.

Gebhardt-Benischke, M. (1986) Family law, family law politics, and family politics. *Womens Studies Int. Forum* 9:25–33.

Gordon, T. (1970). *Parent Effectiveness Training*. New York: Peter H. Wyden.

Kressel, K., Jaffee, N., Tuchman, B., Watson, M., and Deutsch, M. (1980) A typology of divorcing couples: implications for mediation and the divorcing process. *Family Process* 19:101–116.

Neville, W. G. (1984). Divorce mediation for therapists and their spouses. In *Psychotherapy for Psychotherapists*, ed. F. Kaslow, pp. 103–119. New York: Haworth.

Parker, A. (1980). A comparison of divorce mediation versus lawyer adversary processes and the relationship to marital separation factors. Unpublished doctoral dissertation, University of North Carolina, Chapel Hill.

Pearson, J., and Thoennes, N. (1982). The mediation and adjudication of divorce disputes: some costs and benefits. *Family Advocate* 4:26–32.

Roman, M., and Haddad, W. (1974). *The Disposable Parent: The Case for Joint Custody*. New York: Penguin.

6

MEDIATING CHILD CUSTODY DISPUTES

Craig A. Everett, Ph.D.
Sandra S. Volgy, Ph.D.

While the number of practitioners of divorce mediation has increased dramatically over the past decade, the field itself remains in the earliest stages of professionalization and development of a professional identity. A growing body of literature has become available over the past five years, but an empirical base of data regarding mediation procedures and outcomes has not yet been established. While a few graduate programs in mediation are emerging, the majority of practitioners in divorce mediation comes from the clinical and legal professions, or even from paraprofessional fields with limited training.

In many respects, the field of divorce mediation has clearly diverged from the normally expectable stages of the professionalization of an emerging discipline. Typically, these stages include the development of a body of knowledge and data base, the development of training and educational standards, and a definition of practice and ethical principles for the field. The curious nature of the evolution of divorce mediation appears to stem from certain economic issues as well as from professional values. There is little question that some clinical and legal practitioners moved rapidly into divorce mediation as a means of expanding the economic base of their own practices. Other practitioners moved into mediation because they observed the destructive effects the adversarial legal system had on the family and believed mediation to be a viable and preferable alternative.

Thus the *practice* of divorce mediation appears to have evolved much more quickly than the normal evolution of underlying principles and foundations for the field as a profession. In fact, in many areas of the country the provision of mediation appears to exceed the demand for such services from the consumer due to lack of awareness and poor community education. This was perhaps nowhere better illustrated than in a series of events that occurred in Florida several years ago. During 1984 a bill was introduced into the Florida legislature that would have defined, regulated, and licensed divorce mediators. At that time there was little public awareness or education regarding mediation services in Florida communities. With only loose associations of practicing mediators, there were no courses related to divorce or mediation in any of the numerous private or public colleges, and no formal training programs were available except occasional weekend or week-long workshops. Yet a small group of practitioners sought prematurely to establish an as-yet undefined professional practice. That legislation was understandably defeated.

It seems clear that, at this time, the practice of divorce mediation is still in its earliest stages of development. We simply do not always know what procedures and models of intervention work most effectively with what types of family systems and disputes. The role of mediating a child-custody agreement carries the effect of defining crucial and often fragile human parameters involving child development, parenting roles and interactions, and intergenerational ties that will span future lifetimes. In fact, the divorce mediation field has still not answered even the very basic question of what training and education mediators should possess.

We believe that the mediation of child-custody disputes should be entered into with great professional care and by those who have secured education and experience in areas of child development, family systems, the divorce process, parent-child dynamics, and family law. Mediators without these backgrounds should use consultants to help them understand better how the disputed areas involve parent-child issues and what optimal outcomes are necessary to preserve and enhance parent-child functioning. As we have worked with increasing numbers of failed, formerly mediated cases, we are convinced that mediating a child-custody agreement must involve more than assisting warring, or even congenial, parents simply to find a "negotiated middle ground" in order to resolve the dispute. Responsible mediation needs to go further than managing conflict and to begin to consider the personal and developmental issues and needs of the children, parents, and family system involved.

The model that we present here and the issues that we raise have evolved from our clinical practices in divorce mediation (approximately ten years each) and our professional backgrounds (family therapy and child psychology). We will define the process of mediating child-custody disputes through several stages and identify specific tasks and issues within each.

THE MEDIATION PROCESS

Typical cases for child-custody mediation are referred by attorneys, by the court, by therapists working with some part of the family, or by the parents themselves. In the majority of cases the parents are seen initially together. This is true even when attorneys advise us that they would not recommend that we see their client with the other spouse. The exception, of course, would be in certain instances of spousal violence. We always say clearly to parents and attorneys that there is nothing magic about mediation and that if a self-determined agreement is to be reached, the parents must face each other and begin to learn to communicate and negotiate with each other.

The majority of mediation in our clinical practices is not limited to child-custody disputes but tends to cover the full range of financial and property matters. In such cases, we prefer to begin with the child-custody dispute and attempt to assist the parents in first reaching an agreement in that area. We have found through experience that once this area can be settled satisfactorily, the majority of serious disputes in subsequent financial areas can be more readily settled. *It is the issues over parenting and children that capture and focus the emotionality of the divorce process, and bring forth the latent anger and disappointments of the failed marital relationship.* Similarly, as we have reported elsewhere (Everett and Volgy 1983), it is the child-custody and access disputes that may also pull grandparents from the sidelines, further complicating and dramatizing the adversarial process. Thus the child-custody aspect of the mediation process tends to focus the drama of the dispute and often can serve as a predictor for the potential resolution of other disputed areas. Mediation practices that begin by trying to resolve financial matters before the resolution of child-custody and access issues may become hopelessly stuck.

Typically, mediation of only the child-custody areas of the dispute with amicable parents may take from three to eight hour-long sessions. This will depend, of course, on the range of the areas of dispute, the number and ages of the children, and residential and geographic issues that may complicate the decisions to be made. Mediation with angry, warring parents may take from two to four months.

Assessing Interaction and Power

The first task of the mediator in the early phases is to establish and maintain structure and control of the sessions. Here the mediator must learn to use his or her personal skills in evolving rapport, defining limits and procedures, and managing emotional volatility and communication. If the mediator cannot provide a safe and controlled setting for the parents to deal with their concerns and occasionally to vent their anger and disappointment, the parents will either lose confidence in the process itself or feel intimidated and withdraw from the mediation prematurely.

In the initial sessions, we constantly assess both the interactional patterns and use of power by each parent. We observe who speaks first and how the other responds; who presents more overt or covert anger; who uses intimidation; who responds with guilt; who feels more betrayed and aggrieved; what coping skills each has. The pattern most commonly recognized by clinicians involved with the divorce process is one where the spouse who initiated the divorce carries aspects of guilt for leaving, while the spouse who is being left carries the anger and need for revenge (see Everett and Volgy 1988, in press).

The interactional patterns that defined both the complementarity of the marital relationship as well as the dysfunctional elements of the couple's communication will continue through the divorce and mediation process, but with more intensity. Other factors involving intergenerational coalitions, economic and financial management patterns, career and educational status, and gender issues (see Ricci 1985) will define the power base between the parents. The mediator's skill in assessing these patterns will aid in the definition of structure and control for the process and in balancing the emotional intensity of the interactions.

Collecting Information and Family Data

In the initial two sessions we simultaneously shift between letting the parents explain their areas of concern and dispute and asking them to tell us something of their relationship, its history, their parenting styles, and the roles of their children. The blending of history and current issues provides a useful mechanism for defining direction in the session and defusing the escalation of conflict. We ask parents to define the disputed areas and issues, which often include the underlying anger and resentment. We allow some controlled expression of anger in these early sessions. It is foolish to deny or restrict the anger, but it must be managed for self-expression and not for threats or intimidation. Often parents primarily need to feel that someone is listening to them and validating their feelings, and that they can say, in this controlled setting, what they have been unable to say to the other spouse without the safety provided by the mediator.

We also believe that it is important for the mediator to know some limited family history. We collect this in an informal manner with the parents together. We want to know something of the developmental sequence of their marriage (for example, births, losses, geographical moves, illnesses, separation). We want to understand their respective roles in their families of origin, their continuing loyalties, and the roles of grandparents or other family members. We begin to explore each parent's respective parenting roles and resources. Then we ask for their appraisal of each child's personal characteristics, developmental patterns, and school and peer adjustments. We also begin to raise issues of how they expect the children to respond to the pending divorce. If parents are early in the divorce process, we will assist them in developing a strategy for telling the children, and perhaps even their own parents, of their decision.

We construct a three-generation genogram to aid in our assessment and to assist us in recognizing the patterns of attachment and loss in their family. For example, if one spouse has had significant losses in the past two years, such as the death of a parent, we can help him or her to realize that some of the intensity regarding the breakup of the marriage may be exacerbated by that recent loss. (A preliminary research project has identified that a significant percentage of separations and divorces occur within two years following the death of a parent [Strange 1987].) If the ending of the marriage is emotionally replicating early attachment problems for one of the spouses, this can be identified and ongoing psychotherapy can be recommended. Overall, this limited gathering of family data assists the mediator in identifying and managing areas of emotionality and occasionally in predicting the reactivity of a spouse or family of origin member.

Education

One important aspect of mediation is that it provides an educational experience for the parents. At one level we try to inform the parents about the divorce process and what to expect, as well as how to anticipate issues and decisions that they must face (see Everett and Volgy, in press). Here we try to assist them in understanding parenting during and after the divorce and provide them with explicit information regarding issues and patterns of custody and access.

At another level we assist the parents in facing the communication difficulties that have plagued the course of their marriage. Most spouses in mediation have had limited experience with their partners in talking through and actually resolving disagreements or conflicts. Now as their marriage is ending they must learn to communicate with each other as parents even after they have ceased to be spouses and lovers. The mediation process here often takes the form of assisting them in acquiring skills to facilitate communicating with each other.

The third level of education is focused directly on parenting issues after divorce. This involves helping them think through what roles they can and wish to play, how they assess their own parenting resources and skills in terms of the developmental needs of their children, what involvement and/or support they can expect from their own parents and family members, how career or educational issues will affect their parenting time, and how financial concerns and needs will influence these patterns. Then we focus specifically on the children's needs in and following the divorce process. We quote from research that suggests that children can enhance their adjustment to divorce by maximizing their time with each parent. We tell them some "horror" stories where parents have continued warring in the courts for years after the divorce and the disastrous consequences that the children have suffered. At this point we may invite or recommend that the children come in for a session so that we can give the parents feedback with regard as to how they are handling the divorce at this point and can evaluate how the children appear developmentally, so that access plans can be structured as closely to the children's needs as possible.

Involving Children in Mediation

We have been successful in involving children (typically over four years of age) in the mediation process to achieve four goals: (1) to give them an opportunity to talk about and express fears and apprehensions regarding their parents' divorce; (2) to evaluate the children's developmental stages and needs with regard to informing parents of the most effective time-sharing and access plan; (3) to utilize the evaluation data to diffuse parental disputes and unrealistic demands; (4) to allow parents to share with their children (typically over the age of 5) the results of the mediation process and their plans for parenting and access. However, we would recommend that this stage be conducted only by mediators who have prior training and experience in interviewing and evaluating children.

The involvement of children for the initial three goals should be done carefully and in separate sibling sessions without the parents present. The children's privacy should be protected and their fears regarding the divorce respected. They should never be grilled or confronted regarding parental issues or accusations, and unless they are adolescents they should *never* be asked, "Which parent do you really want to live with?" A skilled interviewer can engage the children and assess both their levels of development and differential involvement and attachment with each parent. If a child is experiencing excessive fears, anger, or depression, an individual session may be scheduled with possible referral for psychotherapy. The children may be seen in sibling groups or interviewed both individually or accompanied by siblings, depending on situational and age-specific variables.

These sessions with the children achieve the initial goal of understanding the children's responses to the divorce process and identifying developmental needs of the children. These observations can then be reflected to the parents and used to assist them in formulating a realistic access plan. Most parents value this professional assessment and are willing to incorporate it into their parenting plan. For example, one set of parents had been reading in the popular literature about joint custodial models of allowing a child to alternate weeks in each parent's household. While neither parent felt comfortable not seeing their 7-year-old for a full week, they had convinced themselves that this was what they should do. The clinical feedback to the parents, following an interview with the child, suggested that the child was somewhat immature for his age and that he was struggling with and expressing considerable fears about losing his parents after they had separated. Therefore, a plan of allowing frequent visits during each week in order to maximize contact with both parents was worked out for the first six months. This was to be increased gradually over the ensuing school year and summer.

In disputes where there are unreasonable demands regarding access to children, the feedback of child data to the parents can accomplish the third goal of breaking impasses in mediation. For example, the father of an 8-year-old daughter and 4-year-old son insisted on an equal access plan of alternating weeks with both the daughter and the young son. The mother refused such a plan because of her close relationship with the son, because she felt that he "needed her more." The father recognized that due to his career travel, he had not been as available during his son's early years and was therefore not as bonded to him. He was also aware that the son clung to the mother when he tried to take him to his own apartment following the separation.

However, he continued to maintain that the son needed a strong male image that could be achieved only by maximizing time with him. Following the interview with the child, the mediator was able to reflect with the father that the divorce was dramatizing the child's fears and increasing dependency on the mother, and that he was indeed fearful of going to his father's apartment. After some discussion, the father was able to recognize some of the child's developmental needs and agreed to a gradually increasing access time with the son over a two-year period. The mother was able to support this and agreed that the son needed to develop further bonding with the father.

The fourth goal is to invite the children to a closing session with the parents when the completed self-determined agreement regarding custody and access is completed. We need to be clear that the children are never involved personally in the actual parental mediation activities but only after it is completed. The value of this involvement is that it allows the parents, still in a controlled setting with the mediator present, to share with the children the details of their custody and access plan. The mediator can enhance the role of the parents by explaining the effort they have made to work out a plan that is best for the children. These sessions often represent both a symbolic closure on the painful aspects of separation and announcement to the children of the divorce, and can represent a sense of direction for both the children and the parents in moving through the remainder of the divorce process. The session also allows the children to observe the parents talking and working together instead of the observations of their parents typically fighting and threatening. In cases with children over 12 years of age, we often invite them to cosign the mediated agreement with their parents, again as a symbolic gesture.

Balancing Needs and Issues

The final phase of the custody mediation process involves helping the parents balance their personal needs regarding parenting and anticipating more personal issues for themselves following divorce. This is where negotiation skills are important. However, if the foregoing process has been constructive, the parents will have by now gained some confidence in communicating with each other; they may have identified and diffused some anger and resentment; they may have a clearer and more realistic understanding of their children's needs and the potential effect the divorce will have on them; they may have begun to see themselves as ongoing parents after the divorce. Thus, in many cases, the original disputed areas will not seem quite as unmanageable and, in fact, the parents will have moved closer to the potential of a mutual agreement.

This stage deals with the logistics of access, the allocating of special days and holidays, school and religious issues, grandparents, and other time-sharing factors. If the question of custody is still not agreed upon at this point, we typically leave it until last. Often after the logistics are defined and settled, the question of the custodial arrangement becomes moot. This is particularly true in jurisdictions where joint or shared custody is expected or mandated.

Many courts and mediators have been satisfied to leave the details of access loosely defined, assuming that the parents are "adult" enough to work these matters out for themselves. Our experience over the years in custody evaluations and litigated custody disputes (Everett and Volgy 1983) has convinced us that parents and children benefit from as much detail as possible in defining access patterns. A general rule of thumb is that the more conflicted and angry the parents, and the younger the children involved, the greater the necessity for defining access terms. It is always better to err on the side of too much definition than too little. One of the implicit goals of assisting parents in working out a specific access plan is that they can continue to separate emotionally and find some new direction for their lives apart from each other. Taking issues of access and scheduling out of the middle of their relationship, which means literally taking the children themselves out of the middle, helps them to begin to get on with their lives. Often, the parents who have trouble letting go of the marriage are those who will call the former spouse daily for minor complaints, to ask for more time, or to intrude into the daily decision making of the former spouse.

As we progress through balancing and negotiating these issues, we enter all agreed-upon plans into a formal custody agreement on our computer word processor. Each parent receives an up-to-date printout of the evolving agreement so that he or she can review what it means and feel that progress is being made. At the conclusion of each agreement we recommend a brief paragraph stating that should any major life events occur—remarriage, disability, unemployment, relocation, and the like—that might affect aspects of the agreement, the parents agree to seek a third-party mediator in an effort to resolve such matters prior to pursuing relitigation. The other important component that we recommend in all cases of child-custody mediation is an agreement that the access plan be reviewed by a third-party mediator or therapist within a defined period of time to determine its continuing effectiveness. This may involve just the parents, or the parents and children together. With children under the age of 7, we often recommend that this occur after the initial six months and then after the first year. With older children, we recommend that this occur between nine and twelve months following the divorce. We believe this is important in helping the parents anticipate predictable developmental changes in their young children, recognizing that an access plan developed when a child is 3 years old may be irrelevant when that child is 10. The built-in evaluation also provides the family with a sense of structure and continuity with the mediator. They often feel that if something does go wrong they can come back to discuss the problem without invoking the threat of attorneys to get the other's attention. It has been our experience that satisfactory postdivorce adjustment takes most adults two to three years to accomplish. Usually after this period the potential for conflict has lessened and they have learned how to interact more successfully with parenting concerns. Therefore, evaluations after this period are typically not necessary.

FINALIZING THE MEDIATED AGREEMENT

The word processor is an invaluable resource for mediation, because it allows the mediator to provide up-to-date progress and information to the parents. When certain issues cannot be agreed upon early, they appear on the printout as issues yet to be resolved. We do not recommend that parents review these weekly printouts with their attorneys, because the mediation process at this point is between the two parents. When we have achieved a "preliminary draft" of the agreement, prior to inviting the parents to sign the document, we discuss with the parents the importance of reviewing the draft in person with their attorney in order to clarify any concerns or questions. In fact, we send a copy of the draft with a cover memorandum to each attorney in an effort to facilitate communication and avoid sabotaging of these efforts.

At this point in finalizing the agreement, all identified disputed areas may not have been resolved. However, we may feel that we have gone as far as we can at that point. Often the entry of attorneys here can settle unrealistic expectations or identify other potential models for negotiation around a difficult issue (however, this occurs more often when the mediation involves financial and property matters than child-custody and access issues). We invite the attorneys to call us with concerns or for clarifications.

After the parents have reviewed the preliminary draft with their attorneys, the next session is scheduled to make any suggested changes or revisions. Once this is accomplished, we invite the parents to sign the document to communicate their mutual support of the custody and access plan. After the parents have signed the agreement, we schedule a final session where the children will be present and the parents will explain the plan and the goals they have for their children.

CONCLUSION

We have tried to present in this chapter an applied model of our work in child-custody mediation. We are aware that many competing strategies of mediation are available—some more narrowly defined and others more loosely defined. It is our hope and expectation that readers will take from our experiences perhaps a broader awareness and recognition of issues underlying child-custody mediation and aspects of our model that may inform and benefit their own mediation skills.

REFERENCES

Everett, C., and Volgy, S. (1983). Family assessment in child custody disputes. *Journal of Marital and Family Therapy* 9:343–353.

——— (1988). Assessment and treatment of polarizing couples. In *When One Wants Out And the Other Doesn't*, ed. J. Crosby. New York: Brunner/Mazel.

——— (in press). Treating divorce in family therapy practice. In *Handbook of Family Therapy*, rev. ed., ed. A. Gurman and D. Kniskern. New York: Brunner/Mazel.

Ricci, I. (1985). Mediator's notebook: reflections on promoting equal empowerment and entitlements for women. *Journal of Divorce* 8:49–61.

Strange, J. (1987). The intergenerational effects of death upon marital attachment and dissolution patterns in cohesive and non-cohesive family systems. Unpublished doctoral dissertation. Florida State University, Tallahassee, Florida.

7

THE MENTAL HEALTH SPECIALIST AS CHILD ADVOCATE IN COURT

Kenneth K. Berry, Ph.D.

In the last two decades, there has been increasing involvement of mental health workers in litigation relating to children. Most of this work has been around the issues of divorce, child custody, and postdivorce visitation and living arrangements. There appears to be a number of reasons for the burgeoning of this involvement. Primary factors include the increase in the divorce rate during the past 20 years, the changing gender roles in Western society, and the recognition of the significant role that mental health specialists can play in the lives of children. Perhaps a less than altruistic reason may be that of the potential financial rewards for the clinician.

All the major mental health disciplines have served as expert witnesses in making recommendations about children in divorce proceedings. The primary criterion used has been "in the best interests" of the child. However, there has been a good deal of debate in the literature regarding appropriate criteria, as well as the procedures, roles, and techniques used in performing family custody evaluations.

In Western legal systems the judge, or the court, makes the ultimate decision regarding custodial arrangements and visitation. Thus, the mental health professional can serve only the function of obtaining information to assist the court in making these important decisions. In performing custody evaluations the mental health worker gathers information in a variety of ways. Most evaluators gain information through examination of the child and family members, the use of interviews, observation of interaction between various family members, and the frequent use of standardized psychological techniques.

As a consequence of the increasing demand for evaluations, a number of ethical issues and confusions have developed. This chapter examines the role of the mental health professional involved with children whose families are undergoing divorce proceedings, the procedures used and the content of such evaluations, and ethical issues facing these practitioners.

TECHNIQUES OF CUSTODY EVALUATION

A number of techniques and approaches have been developed in the attempt to obtain information and answer questions regarding which postdivorce living arrangements are in the best interests of the child. Prior to the selection of procedures and techniques, the mental health professional must first examine the criteria involved, as well as develop some understanding of the situational variables and parental characteristics that have an impact upon the developing child. A number of professionals tend to use the legal criteria in the Uniform Marriage and Divorce Act, which was approved by the American Bar Association in 1974. The best interests criterion of this act strives to take into account family interactions and preferences of the child and parents, as well as the adjustment levels of all parties involved (Musetto 1981). However, many workers believe this criterion and its many aspects to be too vague and not sufficiently well-defined, making it of minimal use in gaining information to make recommendations regarding postdivorce living arrangements for the child. Therefore, many mental health workers have developed their own criteria of best interest. Unfortunately, a good deal of the literature indicates that a great many professionals tend to make these judgments based almost entirely upon rather vague clinical impressions and, at times, unwittingly permit their own biases and personal paradigmatic perceptions of the world to affect both their data gathering and their recommendations.

However, some clinicians have reported utilizing behavioral and psychological assessment techniques. The clinicians who tend to limit themselves to primarily clinical impressions, such as Trunnell (1976), generally develop criteria and evaluation procedures to determine the mental health of the child as well as the parent. In addition, most strive to determine the level of "psychological nurturing" ability of each parent. Beaber (1982) recommends the determination of "parental competency," which includes such factors as the ability to clothe, feed, and shelter the child, as well as the capability to provide appropriate medical care and insure regular school attendance. With his focus upon parental competency, Beaber suggested that when both parents appear to be equally "competent," then the worker should utilize his or her clinical skills in determining the more "subtle criteria of parental competence."

Other professionals have suggested the utilization of criteria involving such concepts as emotional availability, empathy skills, and the capacity of the parent to stimulate interactions with the child. Clinicians focusing upon these characteristics believe that they are important in parenting (Gardner 1982, Jackson et al. 1980). However, it would seem that many aspects of these criteria would tend to favor, perhaps unfairly, the parent who has higher verbal fluency and skill over the parent who is lower in these attributes. Since parenting is such a complex behavior, the development of parenting criteria is extremely difficult and presently there appear to be no data available that would suggest that these particular characteristics would make one a better parent than another.

In conjunction with clinical impressions, many professionals make use of standardized assessment instruments. Although one would think that psychologists would be the major mental health professionals to do so, psychiatrists also report use of such tests. Levy (1978) supports the use of the Rorschach and the Thematic Apperception Test (TAT). However, Gardner (1982), who is also a psychiatrist, believes that the practitioner should not use these particular devices, but he, himself, reports the use of "tests," including his own "Talking, Feeling, and Doing Game" (Gardner 1973), which appears to be primarily a nonstandardized "test." Gardner states that this device, along with a sentence completion instrument, hold up better under cross-examination. However, he presents no data to support these conclusions (Karras and Berry 1985).

More recently, Keilin and Bloom (1986) surveyed mental health workers concerning their activities in, experiences of, and attitudes toward custody evaluation. While their sample consisted primarily of psychologists, some psychiatrists, social workers, and nondoctoral counselors were included. The findings of this study indicated that the most prevalent assessment technique used was interviews of children and parents (99 percent and 100 percent, respectively) but that psychological assessment of parents fell at 76 percent and of children at 74 percent. The devices reported to be the most frequently used by professionals in assessing parents were the Minnesota Multiphasic Personality Inventory (MMPI), the Rorschach, the Thematic Apperception Test (TAT), and the Wechsler Adult Intelligence Scale.

A similar battery was also used with children, including the Rorschach, the TAT, and the Wechsler Intelligence Scale for Children—Revised. Thus, in the majority of cases, some forms of standardized test instruments are used in gathering information in family studies. In addition, approximately 69 percent of the sample of professionals also utilized observation of interactions between various family members.

Other relevant findings of Keilin and Bloom (1986) were that most practitioners, when given the choice, prefer to serve in an impartial capacity, for example, being appointed by the court. However, many professionals continue to be retained by only one parent, which may tend to stimulate further the adversarial attitude that many professionals are prone to develop when involved in custodial family studies (Barnard and Jenson 1984, Karras and Berry 1985, Keilin and Bloom 1986). It was noted that split custody and joint custody were not frequent recommendations made by professionals and that the majority of practitioners continued to make very specific recommendations regarding placement by what they consider to be the best interests criterion of the child. This practice presents a number of problems (Karras and Berry 1985) in that it could be regarded as usurping the province of the court in making the ultimate decision and at times may foster the development of an advocacy role, thus placing the professional in a position of at times perhaps acting counter to the wishes and best interests of the child (Melton 1987). When direct recommendations are made, the mental health professional may not actually be representing the true wishes of the child. Other than impartiality, there are a number of issues yet to be resolved in serving the child of divorce in the courtroom. The important issues revolve about the tendency of professionals to be unwittingly drawn into the adversarial role and failing to distinguish the other roles frequently involved. Lack of insight into these issues can result in a number of serious ethical pitfalls.

THE ROLE OF THE MENTAL HEALTH PROFESSIONAL IN CUSTODY DETERMINATION

The role of the custody evaluator began to become defined in the late 1970s. Even then the role varied from impartial witness to one of strong advocacy for the parent. For example, Woody (1978) and Gardner (1982) state that after determining as "impartially" as possible which parent is better suited, the evaluator should then actively and openly act as an advocate for that parent. In contrast, Ochroch (1982) expresses the belief that the child should always be considered the client and that one should serve strictly as an advocate for the child in divorce proceedings. Both of these attitudes, especially the former, may tend to result in an adversarial stance on the part of the mental health professional.

An examination of the available literature reveals that there continues to be a good deal of confusion concerning the proper legal role of the evaluator. While the majority of writers acknowledge the importance of impartiality and neutrality and many discuss the disadvantages of the adversarial approach, their terminology suggests that they do, indeed, take an adversarial stance, perhaps at times unwittingly. If one examines the articles written, one finds that many papers are sprinkled with adversarial terminology. Evaluators "examine allegations," "seek facts," strive to uncover "contradictory findings," and "weigh the evidence." Rather than submitting opinions or making predictions about possible outcomes of the various alternative postdivorce living arrangements available, they tend to make strong custodial judgments and recommendations (Karras and Berry 1985). Some (Jackson et al. 1980) utilize a procedure in which each family member is provided his or her own "evaluator" and, through what seems to be mini-courtroom situations, arguments are presented representing all sides involved in the litigation.

In contrast, Ochroch (1982) warns against submitting generalized opinions regarding life-style, morality, and sexual preferences of the parents and indicates that specific recommendations for postdivorce living arrangements should not be made, since such recommendations could possibly be construed as an unauthorized practice of law, if not an attempt to usurp the court's perogative. Other practices reported in the literature by some evaluators, such as the use of surreptitious observations of families in the waiting room (Jackson et al. 1980) and the making of unannounced home visits (McDermott et al. 1978) could pose ethical problems. Unless the family is told of the use of these techniques beforehand and their informed consent obtained, techniques such as these could be considered a breach of ethics. Ochroch (1982) suggests that many ethical pitfalls, as well as the avoidance of the adversarial stance and the role of "sleuth," could be overcome by the use of mediation whenever possible. She stresses that the direction of choice in the future should be that of mediation.

Perhaps a greater number of ethical problems have arisen because of the practitioner's failure to distinguish between the three major roles that mental health professionals can play within the legal system. These roles and their difficulties come into sharper focus when information regarding custody and visitation arrangements is gathered. The different roles are those of the *expert witness*, the *consultant*, and the *advocate*. While these roles at first glance may seem to overlap, there are significant differences among them, and the mental health professional should consider them to be mutually exclusive; that is, the mental health professional can serve in only one role at any given time or in any given situation. Professionals who attempt to assume simultaneously more than one role clearly place themselves at risk of committing ethical violations.

The Role of Expert Witness

When serving as an expert witness, a mental health professional simply presents findings, opinions, and predictions in an impartial and neutral manner. Technically speaking, an expert witness does not advocate for any parties involved, including the child (Shapiro 1984). If a professional presents himself or herself as an expert witness and is accepted as such by the court, then any form or feelings of advocacy must be placed aside. Should an expert witness succumb to any feelings of being a "rescuer" or of bias in any direction, then that professional has moved from the role of expert witness to that of advocate. In doing so, the professional runs a risk of not only decreasing his or her personal credibility, but also of affecting the credibility of the entire mental health profession within the courtroom. Many professionals may find themselves caught in a bind when they agree to serve as an expert but then feel ethically bound to rescue the child from what they perceive as an unhealthful situation (Ochroch 1982). Indeed, Barrett and colleagues (1985) believe that when an expert witness uses his or her unique role to advocate for anything other than an expert opinion, an abuse of due process and a breach of ethics occur.

The Role of Consultant

In contrast to the expert witness is the role of consultant. This is a role in which the professional is frequently invited both directly, and at times implicitly, to perform. Many attorneys engage "expert witnesses" because of their own ethical need to do their utmost for their clients, but may then attempt to engage the mental health professional in the consultant role. When serving in the role of consultant, the mental health professional's "client" is primarily the attorney and his or her legal client. In this role, the professional may be asked to examine records and previous reports, recommend expert witnesses, advise the attorney about such things as evidence presentation, provide general information regarding parenting and child development, and, perhaps, even prepare a report to answer hypothetical questions. While functioning in this role, the professional may have little, if any, contact with the actual parties involved in the litigation proceedings.

The Role of Advocate

Serving as an advocate presents, perhaps, the most challenge and probably the most danger in terms of ethical pitfalls for the mental health professional in the courtroom. It would appear that the advocacy role may best be performed in the interest of social action in increasing the self-determination of children in general (Melton 1987). When one takes an advocacy role in a specific court action, the mental health professional may have his or her own personal motives, which may or may not be directly related to the particular case. In this role the worker becomes a "team member" for a particular side or issue and has the goal of "winning" (Barrett et al. 1985).

The advocacy role on the behalf of children is one that has been carefully examined and discussed by Melton (1987). He states, "Simply helping children or 'being nice to kids' does not make one a child advocate . . ." (p. 357). He believes that advocacy should consist of attempts to "empower" children in such a way as to make it possible for them to gain access to and use of the resources of society. Professionals assuming the role of child advocate must be constantly aware of their own professional limitations as well as the limitations of the general body of knowledge in their fields. They should very clearly identify to themselves and others who the "client" is, and all parties involved should have the right to expect the rudiments of due process (Melton 1978). A good example of what *not* to do when engaging in child advocacy, as so clearly pointed out by Melton (1983), is the widely used *Beyond the Best Interest of the Child* (Goldstein et al. 1973). This work appears to provide some easy answers for what is an exceedingly complex problem. In this book the authors ignored virtually all of the available empirical data and made recommendations for the determination of custody and visitation arrangements, that most mental health workers today would view as highly questionable. Relying on a small number of single case studies drawn from a clinical population, Goldstein and colleagues made such recommendations as the elimination of child visitation with non-custodial parents and even suggested "drawing straws" when the professional is unable to determine which parent is the better "psychological parent." This would, in effect, perform a paternal "parentectomy," since in the majority of cases in Western societies, the child or children are awarded to the mother (Berry 1981a,b).

Even in the best of situations, child advocacy is filled with numerous hazards. This is particularly apparent when one is dealing with specific court cases. For example, in a case involving excessive punishment of school children, Shore (1985) found that what can be important for legal purposes may, in fact, be psychologically detrimental to the child. In the case he reported, children had been punished by being locked in a public school storage room for extended periods. As an advocate, Shore wanted to demonstrate that this punishment could be psychologically harmful to children. At the same time, in order to make the court appearance less threatening, Shore very carefully prepared the children with visits to the courtroom and through role-playing. The preparation was so successful, however, that in the courtroom during the actual hearing, they appeared to be so relaxed, confident, and well-functioning that the jury, as well as another mental health professional, concluded that they could not have experienced any harm from the long periods of isolation.

One of the basic difficulties arising when the mental health professional assumes the role of child advocate is that of conflict of interest. Melton (1987) draws an analogy between the miscarriage of child advocacy and the typical removal of power from people and the assignment of it to attorneys as it occurs in public interest litigation. He states: ". . . child advocacy can take power legitimately belonging to children and give it to psychologists and others who work with children. Child advocates act *on behalf of* children, but they do not always represent children" (p. 359).

Melton believes that the frequent confusion of whose interests are involved and the fact that child advocates may often believe that the policies they are advocating will benefit children indicates, perhaps, that the underlying values are probably highly related to the individual advocate's views, and thus may not actually *represent* the views of the children themselves. Through the use of empirical evidence, Melton (1983, 1987) makes a good case for allowing children a stronger voice in making decisions concerning themselves and their own futures.

Although the issues can never be entirely resolved, the adverse aspects can possibly be mitigated to some extent through the destruction of the myth of children as incompetent, apolitical creatures. If children are made partners in their own advocacy and are involved in the development of plans concerning them through gaining information about *their* views, then the conflict of interests could possibly be avoided (Melton 1987).

In legal custody and visitation issues, the mental health worker is taking over the child's interest whenever he or she makes a recommendation that a child should "be given" to one parent over the other because he or she believes that person to be a "better" parent. As a further example, the same situation occurs whenever a child is removed from a home without consideration of the child's wishes because a worker believes that a sexual act may have occurred with one of the parents or siblings. Of course, it should be made clear that it may not always be possible to gain the child's view in all circumstances, such as in the case of an infant or when a child, for whatever reason, cannot make an informed decision. However, Melton (1983, 1987) makes it clear that there is abundant empirical evidence that children are capable of making decisions far beyond what we thought they could in the past. An historical analogy is the treatment of women. Prior to women's suffrage, society believed that women were not capable of making decisions in their own behalf and thus fathers, husbands, and the courts assumed this responsibility. This is essentially the situation today with children.

AVOIDING ETHICAL PITFALLS IN CUSTODY EVALUATIONS

In order to avoid ethical pitfalls when performing child custody evaluations, the guidelines adopted by the Nebraska Psychological Association (1986) are recommended. These guidelines list seven major points to be considered. In a condensed version, they are the following:

1. *The child should be considered the major client.* There are three major implications stemming from this guideline (Ochroch 1982). (a) The mental health professional should make every effort to evaluate all parties involved. This may require that the evaluator contact attorneys of each party. This action alone tends to reduce the adversarial stance of the mental health professional. In the situation in which all efforts have failed and only one party will participate, the mental health worker is ethically required to emphasize the partial and incomplete nature of the results and the extreme difficulty in making *any* recommendations. In addition, the appropriate wishes of

the child should be taken into consideration in all custody evaluations. (b) The worker as an expert must maintain impartiality and neutrality, regardless of who assumes responsibility for the fee. (c) Regardless of the custody decision, the professional must acknowledge the children's continuing relationship with each parent, and these relationships should be taken into account if any recommendations or suggestions are made to the court (Wallerstein and Kelly 1980).

2. *Mediation should be considered the preferred prior intervention.* This approach (Cleveland and Irvin 1982, Koch and Lowery 1984, Musetto 1981, Ochroch 1982) seems to ameliorate the negative aspects of family litigation upon the children. If a decision can be reached either by the mental health professional or through referral to a trained mediator, then the best interest of all parties, especially the children, will be served through the avoidance of a drawn-out and ever-continuing litigation situation.

3. *The mental health professional should function as a professional expert.* This implies that the mental health professional is not a judge and, thus, his or her job is to assist the court by supplying information based insofar as possible upon empirical findings and data. The worker should strive in most cases to present descriptive data and make predictive, albeit tentative, statements regarding alternative postdivorce living arrangements rather than making firm recommendations. Given the current state of our knowledge, only in the most clear-cut cases can firm recommendations be made. It should be emphasized that the mental health professional is not a lawyer or a detective and should not attempt to serve as such.

4. *Dual relationships should be avoided.* One should not attempt to maintain two separate kinds of relationships with any party involved in litigation. For example, in a case in which the worker has served in a therapeutic role with one of the parties, he or she should not act like an unbiased expert. In this situation it might serve all parties' best interests if a referral were made to another professional for the purposes of family evaluation.

5. *Multiple avenues of data gathering are preferred.* An adequate family study should include interviews and formal assessment of all parties as well as observation of the various family interactions (Chasin and Grunebaum 1981, Gardner 1982, Heller and Derdyn 1979, McDermott et al. 1978). With appropriate consent from the family, interviews and reports from school personnel and extended family members may also be part of a thorough evaluation. Because of the complexity of such an evaluation, collaboration with colleagues from allied professions with expertise is useful. Such collaboration may contribute to the objectiv-

ity and quality of the evaluation (Duquette 1978, Jackson et al. 1980).

6. *Many factors must be considered.* A custody study is directed toward assessing the strengths and weaknesses of each possible postdivorce arrangement, including but not limited to primary residence with the father, primary residence with the mother, "splitting" of siblings, and shared parenting. The mental health of the parent is only one issue to be considered. We have virtually no empirical data that because a parent has experienced emotional difficulties, this *ipso facto* makes him or her a poor parent. Perhaps most importantly, the mental health worker must recognize that "parenting ability" is not a unitary behavior, but rather is an exceptionally complex pattern of interactions across time. The evaluator must acknowledge the great difficulty of accurately predicting specific outcomes for children, given our current state of knowledge.

7. *Quality of service should not be dictated by fees.* The evaluator must adhere to ethical practices in setting and collecting fees. The worker must render an adequate evaluation regardless of the fee agreed upon. One cannot simply perform a less than adequate assessment in order to reduce costs. The fees and collection of fees should be outlined prior to the evaluation. The mental health worker must be truthful in any communications with third-party payers, such as insurance companies. Any evaluation performed for obtaining information for the court should not be represented as an assessment for treatment planning purposes. This latter action may not only be unethical but could possibly constitute criminal fraud.

CONCLUSION

To sum up, one should always determine the role one is playing, whether it is consultant, expert witness, or advocate, and take care to avoid multiple roles. If this is done, then a great many of the ethical problems faced by mental health professionals in the courtroom can be avoided.

REFERENCES

Barnard, C., and Jenson, G. (1984). Child custody evaluations: a rational process for an emotion-laden event. *The American Journal of Family Therapy* 12:61–67.

Barrett, C., Johnson, P., and Meyer, R. (1985). Expert eyewitness, consultant, advocate: one role is enough. *Social Action and the Law* 11:56–57.

Beaber, R. (1982). Custody quagmire: some psychological dilemmas. *Journal of Psychiatry and Law* 10:309–327.

Berry, K. (1981a). The male single parent. In *Children of Separation and Divorce*, ed. I. R. Stuart and L. E. Alt, pp. 33–52. New York: Van Nostrand-Reinhold.

——— (1981b). The male single parent and his children. Paper presented at the meeting of the Royal Australian and New Zealand College of Psychiatry (Child Psychiatry Section) Queensland, Australia, May.

Chasin, R., and Grunebaum, H. (1981). A model for evaluation in child custody disputes. *American Journal of Family Therapy* 9:43–49.

Cleveland, M., and Irvin, K. (1982). Custody resolution counseling: an alternative intervention. *Journal of Marital and Family Therapy* 8:105–111.

Duquette, D. (1978). Child custody decision making: the lawyer-behavioral scientist interface. *Journal of Clinical Child Psychology* 7:192–195.

Gardner, R. (1973). *Talking, Feeling, and Doing Game.* Cresskill, NJ: Creative Therapeutics.

——— (1982). *Family Evaluations in Child Custody Litigation.* Cresskill, NJ: Creative Therapeutics.

Goldstein, J., Freud, A., and Solnit, A. (1973). *Beyond the Best Interests of the Child.* New York: Free Press.

Heller, J., and Derdyn, A. (1979). Child custody consultation in abuse and neglect: a practical guide. *Child Psychiatry and Human Development* 9:171–179.

Jackson, A., Warner, N., Hornbein, R., Nelson, N., and Fortescue, E. (1980). Beyond the best interest of the child revisited: an approach to custody evaluations. *Journal of Divorce* 3:207–222.

Karras, D., and Berry, K. (1985). Custody evaluations: a critical review. *Professional Psychology: Research and Practice* 16:76–85.

Keilin, G., and Bloom, L. (1986). Child custody evaluation practices: a survey of experienced professionals. *Professional Psychology: Research and Practice* 17:338–346.

Koch, M., and Lowery, C. (1984). Evaluation of mediation as an alternative to divorce litigation. *Professional Psychology: Research and Practice* 15:109–120.

Levy, A. (1978). Child custody determination: a proposed psychiatric methodology and its resultant case typology. *Journal of Psychiatry and Law* 6:189–214.

Melton, G. (1978). The psychologist's role in juvenile and family law. *Journal of Clinical Child Psychology* 7:189–192.

————— (1983). *Child Advocacy: Psychological Issues and Interventions.* New York: Plenum Press.

————— (1987). Children, politics, and morality: the ethics of child advocacy. *Journal of Clinical Child Psychology* 16:357–367.

McDermott, J., Tseng, W., Char, W., and Fukunga, C. (1978). Child custody decision making: the search for improvement. *American Academy of Child Psychiatry* 17:104–116.

Musetto, A. (1981). The role of the mental health professional in contested child custody: evaluator of competence or facilitator of change. *Journal of Divorce* 4:69–79.

Nebraska Psychological Association. (1986). Special focus: child custody guidelines. *NPA Forum* Summer:10–14.

Ochroch, R. (1982). Ethical pitfalls in child custody evaluations. Paper presented at the American Psychological Association, Washington, DC, August.

Shapiro, D. (1984). *Psychological Evaluation and Expert Testimony.* New York: Van Nostrand-Reinhold.

Shore, M. (1985). The clinician as advocate—interventions in court settings: opportunities, responsibilities, and hazards. *Journal of Clinical Child Psychology* 14:236–238.

Trunnell, T. (1976). Johnnie and Suzy, don't cry: Mommy and Daddy aren't that way. *Bulletin of the American Academy of Psychiatry and the Law* 4:120–126.

Wallerstein, J., and Kelly, J. (1980). *Surviving the Breakup: How Children and Parents Cope with Divorce.* New York: Basic Books.

Woody, R. (1978). *Getting Custody: Winning the Last Battle of the Marital War.* New York: Macmillan.

PART II

DIVORCE THERAPY

8

MARITAL THERAPY AND THE DIVORCING FAMILY

David G. Rice, Ph.D.

Any therapist with a general marital therapy practice is likely to see a substantial number of couples who will eventually decide to divorce. Indeed, perhaps the biggest frustration as a couples therapist is a feeling that therapy has begun too late, that is, beyond the point of maximum therapeutic effectiveness for helping the marriage. In the author's experience, most couples come to therapy with at least some hope that the therapist will be able to "save" the marriage. Even if divorce seems inevitable in both their minds, they want to make sure they have "pulled out all the stops" in attempting to stay together. By presenting the relationship to a therapist, couples attempt to reassure themselves that they have indeed tried everything. Going to a therapist may also represent a wish to reduce guilt.

When therapy begins, the probability of divorce varies from couple to couple, from partner to partner. The therapist's first question is usually: Where do I start? The initial section of the present chapter discusses this issue. Then some basic considerations for the therapist in dealing with divorcing couples are presented, followed by a review of the therapist's own issues, determinants of the decision to divorce, and how the decision is implemented. Finally, a case study illustrates issues and complications in the divorce decision-making process.

WHERE THE THERAPIST STARTS

Though it is rare, couples may enter therapy with the issue of divorce never having been raised in the marriage. In such instances, religious proscriptions against divorce may have been the predominant factor. Other couples believe they are "married for life" and truly have not considered the possibility of divorce. However, coming to therapy signifies that at least one partner is unhappy. Unless they utilize massive denial, the other spouse cannot help but react to the partner's feelings and sense a mutual marital dissatisfaction.

The literature makes clear the necessity of seeing both spouses for effective marital therapy (Gurman et al. 1986). This chapter will not deal extensively with the issue of getting a recalcitrant spouse to come to therapy. In the author's experience, pressure first by the spouse who sought therapy and, if necessary, a direct appeal from the therapist is usually sufficient to get the resistant spouse into the therapist's office. Saying that the therapist needs at least one session of "consultation" to hear the other side of the story can succeed with difficult cases.

Marital therapy that began with a couple who had never raised the issue of divorce is likely to be long and difficult once it becomes clear to the therapist and the couple that the marriage is, in all probability, not going to continue. One thing that makes the decision so painful in such situations is the strong "set" in the therapist's and the couple's mind that therapy was supposed to make the marriage last forever, not lead to its termination. In a very literal sense, the beginning phases of the long process of psychic divorce (see Kressel and Deutsch 1977) have taken place only during the period the couple has been in therapy. The shifting of goals in therapy from facilitating marital growth to helping implement a constructive divorce is not likely to be done easily. Some sense of failure and painful disappointment on the part of both therapist and clients is likely to be present.

Most couples who come to marital therapy have at least raised the issue of divorce, for example, in the context of "if things don't get better, then we may have to split." The therapist needs to inquire as part of the intake evaluation whether the question of separation or divorce has come up and, if so, what each partner's feelings were at the time. It is important to discern what the threat of separation or divorce actually means in the context of a particular marriage. The author has discussed the issue of pseudodivorce (Rice 1976), where the intent of one spouse is to communicate how desperately unhappy he or she feels in the marriage and how the other spouse has not heard or listened to such feelings, or at least has not taken them seriously. Sometimes, a period of living apart may even be necessary to get the message of dissatisfaction across; in this case, the "separation" is not necessarily seen by the initiating partner as a prelude to divorce.

Other circumstances in the marital interaction where the question of divorce is likely to be raised include: (1) if one or both spouses see symptomatic evidence that their children are being harmed by the parents' marital discord; (2) where threatening divorce is the only way left to get a resistant spouse into couples therapy; and (3) where the marriage feels stagnant and the desire is to stir up some emotional interaction in order to "heat up" the relationship (having an affair can serve a similar purpose).

It is thus quite important for the therapist to ascertain what bringing up the question of divorce in this relationship at a particular time means. Only when it is clear that the intent is truly to explore the ending of the marriage can therapy focus profitably on that issue. Couples are likely to vary in how ready they are to engage seriously with the issue of separation and/or divorce. The two spouses are likely to be at different points of certainty about whether the marriage should continue. For most couples, every attempt to keep the relationship together must be exhausted before the "last stone" of divorce can be overturned. This does not mean that the therapist will need to be part of the whole process; the couple themselves may have tried many alternative solutions prior to therapy, including one or more separations.

Other couples seek therapy at the point where the question of divorce is actually being decided. They have concluded divorce is probably inevitable but are feeling much ambivalence and uncertainty over how to begin the process. Usually the issue for spouses in this situation is whether or not to try a separation. A common therapeutic question is whether a structured separation with counseling (Toomin 1972) would be helpful. Such a procedure defines a specific time line for making a decision about the future continuance of the marriage—three months is a common recommended initial period of separation. The couple negotiates several important issues in regard to the separation, for example, how often they will see each other, who the children will be with and when, and whether they will date other people. They agree to come in for counseling, usually on a weekly basis and with individual and couple sessions interspersed. This procedure attempts to reintroduce to the relationship feelings of choice about how each partner lives his or her life. The door is kept open for the possibility of reconciliation after three months (or longer, if the couple is unable to make a decision at that point).

In other instances, an "unstructured" separation may be preferred, where one or both spouses truly want a break from the relationship. They wish to be on their own for a while without deciding definitely to divorce. One or both partners may wish to be in individual therapy; thus there is a deliberate decision not to work on the marital relationship and interaction, but each may focus on the question of whether he or she really wants to be married.

Therapists may also see couples who mutually have already decided to divorce and want help with implementing that decision. Usually the partners want help with specific focal issues, for example, how and what to tell children and families of origin, how to decide on custody/visitation, and how to negotiate a financial settlement. Divorce mediation may be the treatment of choice for dealing with such issues. In this circumstance, given that the decision has already been made, divorce therapy is appropriate. As divorce therapy is discussed in other chapters, it is not explicated here.

To summarize, couples begin therapy at various points on the divorce decision continuum. The therapist needs to set treatment goals based on how far along the couple is in considering realistically the question of divorce. Flexibility on the therapist's part is important; for example, he or she may work with both partners present initially and then move to individual therapy or to a combination of individual and couple sessions as the divorce decision is made and implemented.

BASIC CONSIDERATIONS FOR THERAPY

It is crucial to see *both* spouses when one is intervening therapeutically in the divorce decision-making process. Conjoint sessions are preferred, at least initially, since the therapist is dealing with a system and, in general, can gain greater leverage by interacting with the whole rather than the parts. Seeing just one spouse not only leads to hearing one side of the story, but also makes the therapist vulnerable to aligning or colluding with one spouse against the other (Whitaker and Miller 1969). Since separation is a time for taking sides, given the adversarial nature of the legal process of divorce, there is potential for the therapist, by seeing only one spouse, to contribute to the polarization. Proceeding in this manner is not likely to help the couple make decisions that are in the best interests of all members of the family.

The therapist should actively attempt to see both spouses. The resistant spouse who chooses to decline when given a choice to participate in therapy, at least cannot claim therapy proceeded without his or her knowledge. Deciding whether to leave a marriage is most often a difficult and psychologically painful period. Given the opportunity and, if necessary, a direct appeal by the therapist, both spouses will usually come to therapy.

A related issue concerns others intimately involved with one or both spouses, for example, if there is an ongoing affair. Such a situation is encountered quite frequently in distressed marital relationships. Ideally, the individual(s) having the affair would agree to end or at least suspend the relationship until the fate of the marriage has been decided. Some therapists insist the affair must end before marital therapy can take place (Springer 1981). Given the power of a transitional relationship, for example, in offering hope and ego enhancement, such a request usually is not very realistic. The therapist needs to acknowledge that an important part of the interactional system will be missing from the couple sessions. In those cases where the extramarital relationship consistently undermines and/or makes progress impossible, the lover can be brought into therapy for a session, and his or her current role in the marital interaction explored directly. The *suggestion* of this intervention is usually resisted by one or both spouses and may be enough to decrease the extramarital partner's outside interference with the marital treatment goals.

Another difficult issue in focusing on the divorce decision concerns concurrent individual therapies. Given the stress the spouses feel in their lives, frequently one or both have entered individual therapy. They may have been referred to couple therapy for a variety of reasons by the individual therapist, who may not feel comfortable treating the couple or may lack expertise in marital/family therapy. Or, not uncommonly, the individual therapy has led to a crisis in the marriage when the patient has discovered and/or explored deep marital dissatisfaction. The spouse not in therapy is perplexed and frightened over what is happening to the marriage and usually is angry at the therapy and therapist for threatening the marital integrity. This situation is hardly the ideal circumstance to bring the spouse into the "individual" therapy. It also makes couple therapy more difficult. The ambivalent feelings of the spouse not in therapy often generalize to the new therapist, and the resultant anger and resistance must be dealt with before couples therapy can be helpful.

To avoid the complications outlined above, the author prefers that individuals be in only one therapy at a time; at least not being in individual therapy at the same time marital therapy is being conducted (Rice 1988). Experience has shown that two therapies inevitably compete and that individual therapy, because of the more powerful patient-therapist transference, is likely to "win." The marital therapist in such a situation faces a definite handicap. The "real" therapy, where one's honest feelings are expressed, is likely to take place in the safer confines of individual therapy, where one can feel the undivided attention and support of the therapist.

Although initially they commonly resist the therapist's request, most spouses are willing to suspend individual therapy in favor of marital therapy, at least while the divorce decision-making process is taking place. Most therapists can understand the rationale for this, especially if the two therapists confer and an appeal is made based on the best interests of the client(s) and the marriage.

An alternative procedure is for the two therapists (the "marital" and the "individual") to work together in a cotherapy format. Practical considerations, such as having to pay two therapists, and the issue of whether they can work together effectively, may argue against this treatment format. Such arranged cotherapist "marriages" are usually not made in heaven.

A brief case study (altered to preserve confidentiality) illustrates some of the difficulties the marital therapist faces with concurrent individual therapy:

Rick (age 29) and Ada (age 27) were referred for marital therapy by Ada's individual therapist, whom she had been seeing for about one year. The couple had been married for a little over three years. Ada sought individual therapy because she was depressed. Over the year in therapy it became clearer that a lack of felt attention from Rick was contributing to her depression. However, Ada enjoyed her therapist's attention and concern and did not feel the desire to upset Rick by sharing her feelings of marital dissatisfaction directly with him. Denial was a prominent defense of both partners, but was shattered when Rick decided to seriously consider an attractive position in another state. Ada felt she had to choose between going with him (as he insisted) or getting a divorce in order to stay put and continue her therapy with a therapist she valued. The marriage was suddenly in crisis and Rick was anxious to see someone professionally with her. He suggested joining her "individual" therapy. Ada and the therapist both resisted this idea; however, the therapist suggested a referral to the present therapist, who was willing to see them in a time-limited arrangement focused on whether Ada would move with her husband and thus continue the marriage. Rick made it clear that he did not want to stay married if Ada did not plan to move with him. The present therapist suggested that her individual therapy be suspended until the fate of the marriage had been decided. Neither Ada nor her therapist would agree to this arrangement; both continued to believe that the individual therapy was critical to ameliorating her depression, and they both believed she would get more depressed if individual therapy stopped. The present therapist then suggested that Ada's therapist get a female cotherapist and meet for a few marital therapy sessions. Ada's therapist resisted this notion and Ada made it clear (indirectly, through her resistance to the suggestion) that she did not wish to share the attention of her therapist with another woman. Things were at a stalemate and the present therapist referred the couple to a woman therapist, who agreed to permit Ada's individual therapy to continue.

Another basic consideration in intervening therapeutically in the divorce decision-making process concerns the degree of crisis presented by the couple. Not infrequently, the marital therapist needs to intervene at a time of great stress, particularly for the spouse who has just learned that his or her partner seriously intends to leave the marriage. The therapist must actively use crisis intervention techniques to structure the situation and facilitate rational decision making (Rice and Rice 1986). One should be alert to the potential for a variety of extreme responses to such a marital situation, including suicidal and homicidal wishes (Kaslow and Schwartz 1987). A careful assessment of each partner's psychopathology is important, including any history of acting out behaviors, either self- or other-directed. In the author's experience, suicidal preoccupation at these times is seen most frequently in very dependent individuals, for whom the perceived narcissistic injury from being "left" by the spouse is overwhelming to the ego. In dealing with such crises, the therapist must feel comfortable in taking a very active stance, including being willing to work with the larger community system (attorneys, social services) to insure the safety of each partner.

A related consideration in intervening therapeutically in the divorce decision is whether the legal process has begun. Therapists vary in their willingness to work with couples once attorneys are involved (Kressel and Deutsch 1977, Kressel 1985). The necessarily adversarial nature of the legal process in divorce can lead to pressures to take sides, directly going against the therapist's desire to maintain neutrality in the therapeutic alliance with the couple.

Given the desire of each partner to protect his or her own interests, it seems likely that the legal and therapeutic processes cannot be separated. Each spouse is likely to need his or her own attorney, except in perhaps the more uncomplicated case where a *pro se* divorce may be possible between very cooperative spouses. In the author's experience, the great majority of lawyers are willing to listen to their clients and to "back off" while the couple works in therapy to try to decide if they really want to divorce.

THE THERAPIST'S OWN ISSUES

Dealing with separating and divorcing couples is the one area of marital therapy where the therapist's own problems may be as salient as the clients' problems. In part, this is related to the promarriage bias that traditionally has characterized the field of marriage counseling (Vines 1979). Most therapists wish to help marriages grow, not to preside over their demise. A similar dilemma is felt by many obstetrician-gynecologists, who enter the field to "save lives" and promote the delivery of healthy babies, yet face pressures to perform abortions.

Marital therapists should examine carefully whether they need to keep marriages together "at all costs." The author has supervised therapists who figuratively could not hear the couple's repeated statements that neither spouse thought the marriage was going to last. The therapist's response generally was to suggest one more possible task to enhance marital interaction. In the author's experience, this situation occurs usually when the therapist has not worked through the ending of a relationship in his or her own life, for example, a parental divorce or a recent, painful separation.

Most therapists work long and hard to help a marriage; however, they are also realistic and are prepared to work with the couple to end the marriage in a psychologically humane way. The therapist should be willing to refer the couple to another therapist if he or she is uncomfortable in making the transition from marital to divorce therapy.

A related issue is the therapist's own feelings of failure (Woody 1981). As noted earlier, in a general marital therapy practice many of the couples who come in initially for marital help will go on to divorce; the therapist who measures his or her success rate by how many couples stay together is likely to feel like a failure much of the time. It is important that the therapist come to terms with such feelings and realize that, indeed, helping a couple to divorce more comfortably may also be helping the individuals toward potential growth (Rice and Rice 1986). If the therapist feels like a failure because the marriage is ending, he or she is likely to compound the client's similar feelings. No one gets married without hope that the marriage will last, even though as one wag put it: "Marriage is the first step toward divorce." One does not make a large emotional investment, such as that represented by marriage, without some feeling of failure at the imminent loss of the investment. Thus, individuals are very sensitive to even subtle feelings from the therapist that they have failed because the marriage is breaking up. They look to a therapist for the strength to face difficult times, not for a verification that they have failed a task (marriage) everyone is supposed to succeed in.

Another issue for the therapist concerns the intense feelings, particularly anger, likely to be present during the divorce decision-making process. The therapist needs to be comfortable with the expression of anger in therapy, yet be able to set limits to prevent things getting out of hand and nonproductive use of the session, for example, simply as a forum for one spouse to berate the other. Anger is likely to be magnified if there is another individual involved in the decision to separate. Also, feeling that one spouse has "ganged up" with a lawyer in an unfair way can generate a good deal of hostility. In both these instances, anger is partly a response to felt narcissistic injury, along the lines of the question: "How could someone who loves (used to love) me do something like this?" The therapist often needs to walk a thin line, creating an environment for honest feelings to be expressed on the one hand, and guarding against their inappropriate expression on the other. Dumping anger and then wanting to leave the therapy prematurely is a common scenario that requires the therapist to set limits, for example, telling the spouse about to leave, "Please sit down and let's talk this over." If the therapist is anxious in response to strong, overt expressions of anger, the client(s) may become fearful of losing control and miss the opportunity to understand and work through these feelings.

Several issues for the therapist arise in conjunction with vested interests in one member of the couple. This situation can arise when the therapist has seen the couple and finds himself or herself liking or being more sympathetic to the position of one of the spouses. Although therapists espouse the goal of therapeutic neutrality (Kressel and Deutsch 1977), they are human and subject to value judgments, likes, and dislikes. For example, usually it is hard to remain neutral toward either the victim or the perpetrator when one is dealing with a marriage involving serious physical abuse. Hearing one side of the marital dispute first, from the partner willing and eager for therapy, can leave a strong impression in the therapist's mind that can carry over when he or she hears the other side of the story from a spouse who resisted coming into therapy.

Most commonly, vested interests become an issue when the therapist has worked individually with one of the spouses. For example, one partner comes to therapy initially for help with a defined "individual" problem, for example, a clinical depression that both spouses agree should be treated therapeutically. Even dyed-in-the-wool systems therapists might choose to treat this situation with at least some individual sessions, after having seen both spouses as part of an initial evaluation and being cognizant that both play a role in the depression of one spouse (Coyne 1984). Working individually with one partner in this situation can set up a vested interest in that spouse and lead to some loss of objectivity if the therapist is called on subsequently to treat the couple or the family.

The most frequent therapy occurrence in the divorce decision process where vested interests arise relates to seeing one spouse individually following a separation. In the author's experience, most divorce therapy begins initially as conjoint marital therapy. When it becomes clear that the marriage isn't going to continue, many couples opt for a separation rather than proceeding directly to divorce. When this happens, it is common for one spouse to feel like the "leaver" and the other to feel that he or she is being "left" (Weiss 1975). The "leaver" not uncommonly has another relationship to go to and may not be interested in continuing therapy. The spouse who perceives himself or herself as having been "left" is usually in pain (partly from narcissistic injury) and is more eager to remain in therapy. There are several choices for therapy at this point; the author favors making therapy (with the "marital" therapist) available to both and continuing to treat either one or both spouses individually, depending on who accepts the therapist's offer (Rice 1981). The most compelling reason for not switching therapists at this point is that it would add another loss at a time when at least one spouse is already feeling a sense of loss from the marriage breaking up. However, continuing to see only one of the spouses, as is common in this situation, does raise the issue of undue vested interest by the therapist in the spouse who continues therapy. This bias may not be troublesome to the therapy unless the other spouse wishes to return, for example, as part of an attempted reconciliation. A change in therapy format is usually necessary at this point. The easiest transition involves simply bringing the spouse in for couples sessions. Upon inquiry, the spouse who has not been in therapy may voice pleasure over the changes in the other spouse via therapy and have a positive set toward the therapist, thus helping to neutralize any perception of vested interest.

In the more common situation, it is necessary to actively reestablish the therapeutic alliance with the spouse whom the therapist has not been seeing. The therapist can offer to meet one or more times individually to "catch up" and/or provide support; following these individual sessions, conjoint marital therapy can be resumed. Another alternative is to bring in a cotherapist. Depending on client preference, the spouse who has not been a participant in the individual therapy can meet one or more times with the potential cotherapist, or the cotherapy can begin immediately with the two "new" participants. In this situation, each partner may perceive himself or herself as having a therapist "ally." Unfortunately, pragmatic concerns, such as financial cost, may prohibit use of a cotherapy format in this situation.

A related issue for the therapist in the divorce decision-making process is the pressure to take sides. This situation is usually related to what is going on in terms of legal proceedings during the period of therapeutic intervention. As noted earlier, ideally the legal process would stop and wait for the therapeutic process to take place. Such a format is not very realistic (Kressel 1985). For example, one spouse may need legal help to guarantee an adequate maintenance income during the separation.

Pressure to take sides may occur if one attorney feels the therapist has information to support his or her client's position. Needless to say, testimony supporting one of the partners against the other is likely to destroy rapport. In this situation, the therapist is fortunate if he or she has exercised good clinical judgment and has seen both spouses at some point. The lawyer can then be told that both spouses are the therapist's clients and it is unfair to force a choosing of sides. If the attorney persists, suggesting an "outside" evaluation by another mental health professional is usually an effective and appropriate response.

One of the most difficult questions for the therapist and the couple has to do with the actual decision to divorce. The parameters of this decision are discussed in the next section.

THE DECISION TO DIVORCE

Most important decisions in life are complex and multifaceted. The decision to divorce is no exception, particularly when minor children are involved. Therapists almost universally agree that the final decision must rest with the couple (Kressel and Deutsch 1977). But many couples find making the final decision very difficult; the culprit is often intense ambivalence. A common pattern in therapy is for the couple to get close to a decision and then back away from it. Each spouse wants the other to make the final decision, partly as a way of avoiding or assuaging guilt. The temptation is to let external circumstances decide, for example, one spouse refusing to leave when the other gets another job in a different town (discussed in the prior case study) or assuming that one spouse's participation in an affair is a *definite* indication that he or she no longer wants to be married. Also, it is common for couples to feel they should stay together "for the sake of the children." The author stresses that this can put too much pressure on the children. It can be helpful for spouses to know that children do worse psychologically growing up in a tension-filled home than with divorced parents who feel happy and fulfilled in their own lives (Raschke and Raschke 1979).

The issue for the therapist frequently is how long should marital therapy last when the couple can't reach a definite decision? If the therapist considers a decision to divorce as a failure of therapy, after a long period of working to help the marriage stay intact, he or she may collude with one part of the couple's ambivalence to prolong the therapy. On the other hand, the couple may come to therapy with a long history of dissatisfaction, having had one or more prior periods of therapy, and yet having been unable to decide to leave each other. In this situation, the therapist may be tempted to push for a premature decision to divorce, feeling that it is the only way he or she can help the couple, that is, by offering them something different. The author favors a position between these two extremes. It is generally useful to work for a short time with the couple, to make sure all the important conflictual issues in the marriage have been explored. The couple and their prior therapist(s) may have had "blind spots" that need to be pursued further. Once this has been done, the present therapist favors saying to the couple near the end of a session something along the following lines: "We've been working together for some time and it's probably time for a decision about your relationship, either to separate and perhaps proceed toward divorce or to really reinvest in the marriage and work very hard to make it go. You need to make the decision; I'm willing to continue working with you whatever you decide, assuming you want me to. Why don't you talk this over and let me know next time what you've decided?"

If the couple is still living together and agrees something clearly must change, but are not yet sure they wish to proceed to divorce, a structured separation with counseling can be suggested (Toomin 1972). The therapist can help the couple negotiate the important parameters of the separation, for example, how long the separation will last, whether and how often they will see each other, and whether they will date other people (Granvold and Tarrant 1983).

Once the couple has decided on separation or divorce, the therapist can help with implementation of the decision. As discussed previously, one or both individuals may wish to continue in therapy. The next section discusses how therapy can proceed once the decision has been made.

IMPLEMENTING THE DECISION

If both spouses desire a brief period of therapy to help implement their decision to end the marriage, the initial therapeutic task usually involves helping the couple to deal realistically with the marital dissolution, including setting realistic goals (Woody 1981). For example, in the haste to resolve a painful separation, one spouse may promise generous financial support or offer to give up custody of one or more children, promises that later may lead to a change of heart. The two individuals need to make decisions carefully and thoughtfully during this time; therapy can help by setting up a format (in or out of the therapy sessions) wherein this kind of decision making can be accomplished.

Issues that cannot be agreed upon by the individuals can be dealt with through mediation. As this topic is discussed in another chapter, it will not be elaborated here. However, there are some important differences between divorce therapy and divorce mediation (Kressel 1985). The therapist who worked with the couple to arrive at a decision about ending the marriage may not feel comfortable doing divorce mediation and thus should be prepared to refer to a specialist in this area.

A large part of implementing the decision to separate and/or divorce involves telling significant others. Spouses frequently request information about what and how to tell their children. The author stresses that both parents should be present when telling the children and that the parents should agree ahead of time what the children will be told. Two of the most important things children need to hear are (1) that both parents still love them and (2) that the decision to get a divorce is not the children's fault. Also stressed is that the best thing parents can do is for both to stay actively involved with their children postdivorce. It is important for both parents ultimately to convey to their children a sense of personal happiness and well-being in their own postdivorce lives. As other chapters deal with children and divorce, further elaboration of this topic will not be presented here.

Divorcing individuals may need help with the task of telling their parents and/or other relatives about the marital breakup. Preferably, each spouse should tell his or her own family. Spouses are cautioned to expect that parents will take the side of their son or daughter; blood is thicker than water. Also, they need to anticipate that news of the separation may place friends of the couple in a difficult position. Friends don't like to be the recipients of loyalty tests, being made to feel as if they must take sides. Given a choice, most individuals wish to remain potential friends of both spouses; however, they acknowledge realistically that the relationships may change, since the two couples will no longer be doing things together. Also stressed is the importance for each spouse to develop a support system appropriate to one's status as a newly single person. One facet of this is not abandoning completely individuals who have been supportive in the past.

In the final section of this chapter, a case study (altered to protect confidentiality) is presented to illustrate several of the salient points in the divorce decision-making process:

Rita (age 44) was referred for outpatient therapy after having been seen by her family physician for a variety of stress-related physical symptoms. Her husband Darrell (age 46) had served divorce papers and moved out approximately two weeks prior to the first therapy session. When Rita called the therapist for an appointment, he asked that she bring Darrell too. She replied, "He's made up his mind and he won't come in. But I'll try." Sure enough, Darrell did not come to the initial session.

Rita indicated they had been married for 24 years and had a son (age 21) and a daughter (age 18). She had felt problems in the marriage over the past 10 years, along the lines of growing apart and feeling that Darrell didn't really want to be with her. The question of divorce had come up on several occasions, with no action taken subsequently. When Rita received the divorce petition she was "stunned, because I didn't think he was serious about leaving." She began to feel a variety of somatic symptoms related to anxiety and depression. She was having trouble sleeping and had diminished appetite, with subsequent weight loss, and this led her to make an appointment with her family doctor. Compounding her felt level of stress was the fact that her mother (whom she felt very close to) had died a year ago and the anniversary of her mother's death occurred around the time she received the divorce papers.

On further questioning, Rita said she was "still getting mixed messages from Darrell about whether he really wants to end the marriage." For example, he took very few of his belongings when he moved out. The therapist took these behaviors to be signs of ambivalence on Darrell's part and encouraged Rita to try to get him to come in for the next therapy session. She was instructed to tell Darrell that it was important for the therapist to understand the other side of the story and that this would not be "marriage counseling" (attempting to keep the marriage together) unless that was what they both desired. These additional efforts were successful, and Darrell came to the next four therapy sessions.

The therapist met individually with Darrell for the first part of the second session, in order to balance things out, and to help prevent Darrell's feeling that Rita and the therapist had formed a "team" against him. He indicated that he "just had to do something. We've drifted apart. She's just not interested in me like before. There's no cooperation." Specifically, he mentioned working at his skilled labor job long hours and feeling "used" financially when Rita would spend money on herself, even though she worked part-time in retail sales and brought in a modest income. He also felt their intimacy had markedly decreased. "We just don't have any fun anymore. We used to do things together, now we don't."

When the therapist summarized his meeting with Darrell with Rita present, she became defensive and angry. She felt *he* had been the one to pull away, preferring to spend weekends with his "buddies." She was perplexed: "I just don't understand why he wanted to leave. It's not like I've been a bad wife." Indeed, by the standards of fidelity, reliability, and capable parenting, Rita had been a "good" wife. She had trouble understanding the change in the psychological aspects of marriage, that is, that mounting feelings of anger and disappointment over the years could undermine intimacy. She thought: "He must have another woman; that's why he wants out." Darrell denied that he was involved with anyone else, though Rita continued to hold onto that belief as an explanation of his behavior. She also thought: "He's having a mid-life crisis. Now that the children are grown, or almost grown, he just doesn't want any more responsibility." Rita cried easily and often in expressing her hurt at Darrell's behavior; he would typically turn away with a half-guilty/half-disgusted expression. The couple agreed at the end of the second session to get together and try to talk about the marriage and also to continue the conjoint therapy sessions. The therapist suggested a structured communication exercise aimed at enhancing listening and empathy (Rappaport 1976). They indicated a willingness to give this a try.

Darrell and Rita were seen four more times as a couple. Their between-session talks were sporadic and, not surprisingly, mutual hurt and anger made meaningful communication difficult.

Family background factors were explored in therapy: Rita came from a loving but somewhat emotionally constrained family; Darrell felt rejected by his father, who favored a younger sibling. His mother tried to make up for her husband's behavior but was only partly successful in this regard, and Darrell has continued to feel distant and emotionally alienated from his family of origin.

At the seventh session, Rita showed up alone. She said, "I don't think it's going to work. His heart isn't in it. And even the kids are beginning to take sides. My daughter is so angry and hurt about the way he's treated me." It was difficult to tell how much of Rita's feelings represented projection. The therapist suggested a family session to try to explore the children's feelings directly. Rita didn't think Darrell would come back to therapy: "He won't want to take the heat." She was wrong; he did come to the family session, where his son was somewhat supportive and his daughter was, indeed, withdrawn and angry. The therapist pointed out the split in the family (reflecting the split in the marriage) and tried to get each family member to own his or her feelings and not feel the need necessarily to be the ally or spokesperson for someone else. Darrell said he did not feel the couple's sessions were "helping us get back together" and wished to discontinue therapy. Rita wanted to still meet with the therapist; Darrell said that was fine with him.

During three subsequent individual sessions, Rita dealt with her hurt and disillusionment. She indicated after the second of these sessions that "Darrell came back and we spent the weekend together." She summarized: "We talked and tried to have fun, but it just wasn't the same. I still don't think he wants me. Given how he feels about his father, I'm not sure he can really care about anyone. I know I haven't made him feel as appreciated as he'd like, but he was gone so much. I felt sometimes like I raised those kids alone." The therapist inquired: "How were things left?" Rita said: "We both sort of knew it was finally over. I know he's seen an attorney and I need to get one too."

Rita was seen for two more individual sessions. She had established a good support system. There was less splitting in the family, and Darrell was seeing his daughter occasionally. Rita ended therapy with the following: "I know I'll survive this. I'm not sure just where I'm going, but I feel like I'll be able to handle it."

In some ways, this case typifies the divorce decision-making process:

1. There was much ambivalence, with both parties going back and forth about whether to continue the marriage or to split up.
2. The whole family felt polarized and torn.

3. The spouses were unsure why their feelings had changed over the years.

4. The decision in many ways was a process rather than a unitary event.

5. Both parties looked for explanations outside their interaction (for example, another woman, Darrell's father) as "causes" of the marital breakup.

In another way, the case was not representative: One partner (Darrell) had decided to leave the marriage before therapy started. By definition, the therapist began by doing "separation" therapy rather than "marital" therapy. Thus, as is all too common, the time had passed for optimal therapeutic input into the process of marital functioning. Therapy was necessarily remedial, although both spouses appeared to hope at times it would be curative of the marital dysfunction.

CONCLUSION

Many couples seen by the therapist are likely to be somewhere on the separation to divorce continuum. This chapter has dealt with basic considerations for the therapist in dealing with such couples, including: (1) therapeutic strategies dictated by where one intervenes in the dissolution process, (2) how to deal with the therapist's own issues and feelings, (3) how the decision to divorce is actually made by the couple/family, and (4) how the therapist can help in implementing the decision. These parameters of the separation/divorce process were illustrated with brief case studies.

REFERENCES

Coyne, J. C. (1984). Strategic therapy with depressed married persons: initial agenda, themes and interventions. *Journal of Marital and Family Therapy* 10:53–62.

Granvold, D. K., and Tarrant, R. (1983). Structured marital separation as a marital treatment method. *Journal of Marital and Family Therapy* 9: 189–198.

Gurman, A. S., Kniskern, D. P., and Pinsof, W. (1986). Research on the process and outcome of family therapy. In *Handbook of Psychotherapy and Behavior Change*, 3rd ed., ed. A. E. Bergin and S. J. Garfield, pp. 565–624. New York: Wiley.

Kaslow, F. W., and Schwartz, L. L. (1987). *The Dynamics of Divorce: A Life Cycle Perspective*. New York; Brunner/Mazel.

Kressel, K. (1985). *The Process of Divorce: How Professionals and Couples Negotiate Settlements*. New York: Basic Books.

Kressel, K., and Deutsch, M. (1977). Divorce therapy: an in-depth survey of therapists' views. *Family Process* 16:413–443.

Rappaport, A. F. (1976). Conjugal relationship enhancement program. In *Treating Relationships*, ed. D. H. L. Olson, pp. 41–66. Lake Mills, IA: Graphic Publishing Company.

Raschke, H. J., and Raschke, V. J. (1979). Family conflict and children's self-concepts: a comparison of intact and single parent families. *Journal of Marriage and the Family* 41:367–374.

Rice, D. G. (1976). "Pseudo-divorce": a factor in marital stability and growth. *Psychotherapy: Theory, Research and Practice* 13:51–53.

—— (1981). Transition from marital/family therapy to individual therapy following separation or divorce. In *Questions and Answers in the Practice of Family Therapy*, ed. A. S. Gurman, pp. 277–279. New York: Brunner/Mazel.

—— (in press). An individual psychotherapist discovers marital therapy. In *Voices in Family Psychology*, ed. F. W. Kaslow. Newbury Park, CA: Sage Publications.

Rice, J. K., and Rice, D. G. (1986). *Living Through Divorce: A Developmental Approach to Divorce Therapy*. New York: Guilford Press.

Springer, K. J. (1981). "Unsharable" secrets in sex and marital therapy. In *Questions and Answers in the Practice of Marital Therapy*, ed. A. S. Gurman, pp. 392–396. New York: Brunner/Mazel.

Toomin, M. K. (1972). Structured separation with counseling: a therapeutic approach for couples in conflict. *Family Process* 11:299–310.

Vines, N. R. (1979). Adult unfolding and marital conflict. *Journal of Marital and Family Therapy* 5:5–14.

Weiss, R. S. (1975). *Marital Separation.* New York: Basic Books.

Whitaker, C. A., and Miller, M. H. (1969). A reevaluation of "psychiatric help" when divorce impends. *American Journal of Psychiatry* 126:57–62.

Woody, J. D. (1981). Transition from marital therapy to divorce adjustment therapy. In *Questions and Answers in the Practice of Family Therapy,* ed. A. S. Gurman, p. 280–283. New York: Brunner/Mazel.

9

THE CLINICAL PRACTICE OF DIVORCE THERAPY

Douglas H. Sprenkle, Ph.D.

The field of divorce therapy has gained public and professional respectability only recently. Articles and books began to appear in the professional literature about marriage counseling in the 1930s and family therapy in the 1950s, but it was not until the mid-1970s that divorce therapy emerged as a substantive aspect of marital and family therapy (Kaslow and Schwartz 1987). Until the past decade even many professionals associated divorce with pathology and believed that divorce therapy was somehow antifamily or anti-marriage (Sprenkle 1985). Practitioners dealt with divorce under the guise of marriage therapy and viewed divorce as intervention that failed (Ahrons and Rogers 1987).

Divorce therapy developed both in response to the large increase in the number of divorces and also to an increased awareness that divorcing people need help uncoupling (Olson et al. 1980). It is striking, however, that although there are some excellent articles and book chapters on divorce therapy (Brown 1976, Kaslow 1981, Storm et al. 1985), there are still only a few general texts on divorce therapy per se (Everett 1987, Rice and Rice 1986, Sprenkle 1985). Most books have been written about special topics, such as mediation (Coogler 1978, Folberg and Milne 1988, Haynes 1981, Irving 1988) and treating postdivorce families (Hansen 1982, Sager et al. 1983, Visher and Visher 1979, 1988), or they have focused primarily on the dynamics of divorce (Ahrons and Rogers 1987, Kaslow and Schwartz 1987).

DEFINING DIVORCE THERAPY

The definition of divorce therapy is a bit "slippery," since marital and divorce therapy are not so much distinct entities as they are points along a continuum that cannot easily be demarcated.

Viewed as ideal types, marital therapy could be described as relationship treatment that focuses on maintaining, enhancing, and strengthening the marital bond. Conversely, divorce therapy could be described as relationship treatment that focuses on decreasing the function of the marital bond with the eventual goal of dissolving it (Brown 1976). However, such a clear-cut dichotomy does not often appear in clinical practice. People who present themselves for marital therapy frequently have desires and/or behave in ways that suggest they want to terminate their relationship. Likewise, divorce therapy clients are often highly ambiguous about uncoupling. Therefore, establishing and sometimes redefining therapeutic contracts are often a major aspect of this work (Sprenkle and Piercy 1986).

It is helpful to consider three interrelated continua when one is contracting with couples for therapy (see Figure 9-1). The first continuum centers on the *commitment* to the relationship. The second describes the *focus* of the therapy sessions themselves. Do in-session behaviors focus on strengthening the marital bond or terminating it? The final continuum relates to the *motivation* to use therapy to facilitate the commitment and focus described in the first two continua.

What makes contracting so complex is that the husband and the wife (and sometimes the therapist) may be at very different points on each of these continua. In its most pure form, there would be a "contract" for divorce therapy when both spouses are committed (or at least resigned) to ending the relationship and the therapist accepts this commitment as the basis for his or her own commitment to the couple. The husband, the wife, and the therapist would all engage in behaviors in the session consistent with this commitment. Finally, the husband, the wife, and the therapist would all be highly motivated to use therapy for this purpose.

Frequently, however, even when partners present themselves for "divorce therapy," one or both spouses (and even sometimes the therapist) are not committed to working toward ending the relationship. The focus of the session frequently drifts away from behaviors

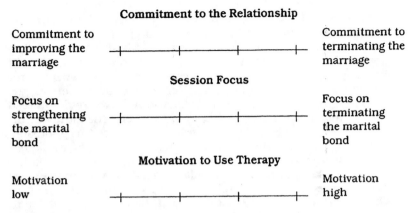

Figure 9-1. Three continua useful in defining divorce therapy.

related to terminating the marital bond. Then, too, even when a spouse truly wants a divorce, he or she may not be motivated to work on this process in therapy. Perhaps he or she wants the therapist to "take this person off my hands." Alternatively, when some clients discover the therapist cannot save the marriage (their real intention), they will abruptly terminate therapy.

These ambiguities are not necessarily bad (indeed, they are quite normal) and will be discussed in more detail later in the section Therapy Around Divorce Decision Making. The point here is to stress that the distinction between divorce therapy and marital therapy is seldom tidy. As therapy progresses and circumstances change, the therapist frequently must (in keeping with the continua in Figure 9-1): (1) clarify the commitment of the clients as well as his or her own commitment; (2) monitor the congruence of the session focus and commitment and take appropriate action; (3) recognize the level of motivation and try to enhance it when appropriate.

Jim and Susan contacted the author to mediate their divorce settlement. Although both said the decision to divorce was final, and that their purpose in coming to therapy was to avoid the deleterious effects of the adversary legal process, it became increasingly clear that Susan was not committed to ending the relationship. Telling behaviors included failing to complete assigned tasks, such as preparing lists of marital assets, and complaining about the "mechanical" nature of the mediating process. She frequently attacked Jim for leaving her and cried out that he had never given her adequate reasons for doing so. Clearly, Sue's in-session behavior was inconsistent with her stated goal. Privately (and sensitively, we hope) this author clarified with Sue that her commitment was really to convince Jim of the mistake he was making. Conjointly, the therapist shared with the couple that they appeared to have different contracts for therapy and that one of three options was possible. They could move ahead with divorce mediation (not acceptable to Sue) or refocus on preserving the marriage (not acceptable to Jim). Alternatively, we would proceed with a "marital evaluation" that would suspend the ultimate outcome. Fortunately, both parties were amenable to this approach. After four sessions, and examining the viability of their relationship, Sue was more willing to "let go," and the divorce mediation proceeded satisfactorily for awhile. Later, however, Jim became disenchanted with Sue's child support request and became convinced that he could "do better" in court; hence, his motivation to utilize therapy to facilitate ending the marriage diminished. To enhance his motivation, I showed him support tables utilized by the local judge suggesting that Sue's requests were reasonable—if not generous—to him. His motivation was enhanced, and the mediation was completed satisfactorily.

Without being sensitive to these continua, and without clarifying and reclarifying the therapy contract, therapy might well have hopelessly bogged down or prematurely terminated.

A Broader Definition

This author favors a broad definition of divorce therapy. It is helping couples and families dissolve the marital bond and restructure the family as constructively as possible through the stages of: (1) predivorce decision making; (2) divorce restructuring; and (3) postdivorce recovery.

In stage 1, the author helps couples to look at divorce as one alternative to relationship difficulties and helps them to appraise the consequences of such a major decision. The therapist also encourages nondestructive communication about the decision so that family members are better prepared for the major changes that will follow. In stage 2, the therapist helps family members make the social, emotional, legal, financial, and parental arrangements necessary for the transition from marriage to the postmarriage family. During stage 3, the therapist facilitates the growth of divorced persons as autonomous individuals with stable life-styles and helps them to develop social relationships independent of the former love relationship. Continuing difficulties related to parent-child relationships, sibling relationships, and custody/visitation issues often occupy therapists during this postdivorce stage. Preparation for remarriage and facilitating the remarriage process can also be included here, or remarriage can be considered a fourth stage, since the majority of divorcing families will experience remarriage of one or both partners (Sprenkle 1985). However, since treating families around remarriage issues is being dealt with in a separate chapter in this volume, it will not be discussed further here.

It is important to note that these stages are more heuristic than literally descriptive of all divorces, since divorces vary widely and issues cycle and recycle among the various stages. Some individuals, for example, have no time or even the option to think about the decision to divorce, since they are abruptly abandoned (Sprenkle and Cyrus 1983). Other persons, far into the second stage, reevaluate their decision and reconcile. Nonetheless, these stages are generally accurate and serve as useful benchmarks for the divorce process and for categorizing interventions. The reader should note that a number of authors have posited other stage theories that may be heuristic for therapists. Useful tables that compare the various models are found in Price-Bonham and Balswick (1980) and Salts (1979). Recently Kaslow and Schwartz (1987) have described a similar three-stage theory in which they use the terms "predivorce," "during divorce," and "postdivorce."

THE GOALS OF DIVORCE THERAPY

Based on a study of a random sample ($n = 400$) of clinical members of the American Association for Marriage and Family Therapy, Sutton and Sprenkle (1985) delineated ten criteria for the constructive, *long-term* adjustment to divorce. These authors stressed that divorce is seldom quickly growthful, creative, or freedom-producing. Almost a decade and a half ago, Robert Weiss offered the often quoted statistic that it typically requires two to four years to achieve a constructive resolution of divorce-related changes and stress (Weiss 1975). There have been no convincing data since to challenge that assumption.

The reader should remember that it is easier to delineate these criteria than help divorcees to achieve them. The criteria are for long-term adjustment, and progress is typically slow, if not plodding. Furthermore, the "graph" of divorce recovery is typically jagged rather than straight, and each forward step is likely to be matched by a retreat. Therefore, while these goals can guide the therapist's work, they do not delineate the typical process of adjustment (Sprenkle and Cyrus 1983, Sutton and Sprenkle 1985).

These criteria are not comprehensive nor exhaustive. It is not possible to cover all types of divorces; for example, second or third divorces following complex postdivorce family forms may require unique criteria.

With these caveats in mind, goals of divorce therapy include helping partners to:

1. *Accept the end of the marriage.* The cornerstone of long-term adjustment is accepting that one is not, and will no longer be, married to one's ex-spouse (Fisher 1981).

2. *Achieve a functional postdivorce relationship with the ex-spouse.* This entails "making peace" with the ex-spouse, ideally both within one's self and between one's self and one's former mate. While an ongoing relationship is unnecessary if there are no children, parents must be capable of separating parental and spousal roles.

3. *Achieve a reasonable emotional adjustment.* While divorce inevitably entails negative emotional consequences, it is important that divorcees not get stuck in long-term self-blame, guilt, or anger.

4. *Develop an understanding of their own contributions to the dysfunctional behavior that led to the failure of the marriage.* Awareness of personal responsibility, ways in which the marital struggle may be linked to family-of-origin issues, and reasons for choice of mate are issues that are fruitfully pursued.

5. *Find sources of social support.* The divorcee needs to develop formal and informal contacts with individuals and groups who provide emotional or material resources while escaping the temptation to deny stress by developing another (premature) intimate relationship.

6. *Feel competent and comfortable in postdivorce parenting roles.* Parents need to be concerned and attentive without becoming overly emotionally dependent on their children.

7. *Help their children adjust to the loss without triangulating them or nourishing unrealistic expectations.* Teaching partners the "do's" and "don'ts" of child management at this time is among the therapist's most important roles.

8. *Use the "crisis" of divorce as an opportunity for learning and personal growth.* Divorce often "shakes up the system" and forces people to clarify values and revise priorities. Establishing a new identity for oneself, setting new goals, or developing new roles or activities may be entailed.

9. *Negotiate the legal process in a way both feel is reasonably equitable.* It is most constructive when divorcees believe they

neither gave nor took too much and are satisfied with the terms of custody and visitation (Sutton and Sprenkle 1985).

10. *Develop physical, health, and personal habits consistent with adjustment for anyone.* This includes issues related to dealing with alcohol and drugs, sleep, eating habits, hygiene and grooming, decision making, job performance, and financial management.

In their very insightful book on divorce therapy, Rice and Rice (1986), present a more parsimonious view of the goals of divorce therapy. They believe it is the task of the divorce therapist to help individuals cope with two major losses: (1) object loss (which results in narcissistic injury) and (2) role loss (which results in disorientation). These losses result in major challenges to the clients' self-esteem, identity, and the capacity to be intimate. Ultimately, the therapist must help the individual get to the point where he or she can say, "I love myself without the love of that other" and "I can love myself without being the spouse of that other" (Rice and Rice 1986, p. 108).

GENERAL GUIDELINES FOR INTERVENING

There is certainly no one way to do divorce therapy. In fact, Gurman and Kniskern have written ". . . there is little that is strategically or technically unique to divorce therapy itself" (1981, p. 694). As this author has reviewed the literature, proponents of most of the major marital and family therapy theories have described divorce intervention from these perspectives. Unique to divorce therapy are its goals and content. Gurman and Kniskern (1981) also note that ". . . specialized knowledge of the common patterns in the divorce process does seem central to clinical work in this area" (p. 694). For this reason, therapists are wise to be familiar with a number of recent books that focus on the dynamics and process of divorce (Ahrons and Rogers 1987, Isaacs et al. 1986, Everett 1987, Kaslow and Schwartz 1987).

The following general guidelines are offered for professionals commencing work in this area:

1. It is crucial that one understand both the nature of the divorce process and the criteria for constructive divorce (such as those just outlined).
2. Effective divorce therapy tends to have a strong didactic component. People going through divorce and experiencing its typical

symptomology frequently think they are "going crazy," and it is important that therapists be able to teach the client about the divorce recovery process and what is likely to happen in the ensuing months. The therapist also needs to encourage clients to engage in those specific behaviors that research has shown to be beneficial. For example, clients frequently need to be encouraged to get socially involved, to develop creative uses of their time, to develop basic life skills, and so on. The professional must also be familiar with a specific body of knowledge on practical matters like household management, law, and finances.

3. The therapist also needs to maintain a balance between support and confrontation. Initially, intervention needs to be highly supportive, and relationship skills such as warmth, empathy, and unconditional positive regard cannot be underestimated. Divorcing people often feel deeply wounded, and the short-term goal is not so much "healing" as it is "sustaining." On the other hand, clients need eventually to be confronted with the fact that they are at least partially responsible for where they are at this point, and are totally responsible for where they go from here. In short, the therapist cannot afford to reinforce a "helpless victim" mentality. It is crucial that the professional help divorcing persons gain a sense of power and control over their own destiny. Only to the extent that they realize that they had something to do with their current predicament, can they also choose to do something about their future (Sprenkle and Cyrus 1983).

THERAPY DURING DIVORCE DECISION MAKING (STAGE I)

Existing divorce-therapy literature offers the least help in this area. As noted previously, therapy at this time can be frustrating because of potentially different agendas of husband, wife, and therapist. For this reason, it is often profitable to contract for "marital evaluation" as an alternative to either "divorce therapy" or "marriage therapy."

As Salts (1985) has pointed out, the couple can be helped to see that "divorce" itself is not their problem. Divorce is only one alternative solution to an unhappy marriage. Therefore, the goal of the evaluation contract is to ascertain whether the couple's needs can be met *within* the marriage (not necessarily *by* the marriage). She then goes on to identify an effective decision-making process during this time of marital evaluation:

1. Identification and definition of needs and problems of the individuals and couple
2. Development of alternative solutions to meet these needs and to solve the problems
3. Consideration of the possible outcome to each alternative solution
4. Choice of the best and most fair solutions
5. Implementation of the choices
6. Evaluation of the outcomes
7. Further identification of needs and problems if the evaluation is not satisfactory

Frankly, once the therapy has been framed as "marital evaluation" and the focus is on whether the couple's needs can be met within the marriage, a good deal of what the therapist does can be patterned after his or her typical marital therapy. The crucial difference is that this frame "joins" and is more respectful of the partner who is highly ambivalent about remaining in the marriage or who believes it is "hopeless." Pushing "marital" therapy on these reluctant partners will almost surely engender resistance and sabotage your work.

This author has found the framework for asking circular questions described by Fleuridas and colleagues (1986) to be an excellent way to proceed. The purpose of these questions is to ascertain from each member of the family his or her opinions and experiences of (a) the couple's major concerns, (b) the sequences of interaction related to these concerns, and (c) differences in their relationship over time. The goals of these questions are (1) to provide the couple and the therapist with a systemic frame that can (2) enable the therapist to generate hypotheses and design interventions to disrupt dysfunctional cycles and (3) challenge myths or beliefs that are detrimental to the relationship. While the first two call for a structural-strategic emphasis, the third leads this writer to do considerable family-of-origin work.

Therapists frequently find work during the time of decision making to be frustrating because of the ambivalence of the clients. There is often a "marital dance" (Whitaker 1970) during which time partners alternatively pursue and flee from each other, and there are frequently mixed messages. It is often very difficult for the therapist to know if he or she is doing marital or divorce therapy because of the persistence of attachment that endures even after the erosion of love in a relationship (Weiss 1975).

Rice and Rice (1986) believe that the most common therapeutic pitfall is for the therapist to become impatient or intolerant of the client's indecision. They believe that a period of six months to one year spent in exploration and decision making is often required for the client to feel some sense of cognitive and emotional closure. Impatience may result from the therapist's projecting his or her own values on the client and becoming overinvolved in what must remain the client's decision. Frequently therapists harbor prejudices either against or for divorce, or they develop irrational feelings about one of the spouses.

The therapist should also be aware that the actual decision to separate may produce a temporary state of relief and even mild euphoria, which may lead to a short-term renewal of the marriage. This has been called the "marital flip-flop" (Kressel 1980). It often does not stop until both parties recognize the pattern and the futility of the cycle of alternately pushing for and opposing divorce. Therapists must recognize, however, that this pattern often needs to be played out several times before partners are convinced of its futilities (Rice and Rice 1986).

When clients remain highly ambivalent, several techniques offered by Nathan Turner (1980, 1985) may be useful. Turner has drawn upon the social-psychological decision-making theories of Janis and Mann (1977) to make some sense out of the often bizarre decisional behavior of persons undergoing divorce—frequently marked by seeming irrationality, extraordinary ambivalence, regressive behaviors, decisional reversals, impulsive behavior, and the like.

The *grid balance sheet* described by Turner (1985) and adapted from the work of Janis (1983, p. 171) is a "left-brain" approach. Clients are handed a sheet of paper with two columns, one called "positive anticipations" and the other "negative anticipations." A grid is formed utilizing the following "rows": "tangible gains and losses for self," "tangible gains and losses for others," "self approval or disapproval," and "social approval or disapproval." A separate sheet is made out for each major alternative, such as "remaining married" or "trial separation." This method forces the client to investigate carefully all alternatives and systematically consider the major gains and risks.

A more "right-brain" approach is the *outcome psychodrama.* The client experiencing decisional conflict concerning divorce is asked to assume one side of the ambivalence: for example, "Let us say you have decided to get a divorce." As Turner (1985) describes the procedure:

The therapist leads the person through all of the consequences of that decision. "You are now telling your husband/children. What are you saying? How does that feel?" The client is led further. "You are now in the court. What are you feeling as you look over at your partner across the room? As you leave the courtroom as a newly single person?" The sequence progresses. "It is now six months after the divorce. What are you doing? What do you feel? How much support are you receiving?"

The process is then repeated taking the other polarity. You have decided to stay in your marriage. You are telling your husband of the decision. "What are you saying?" "How does that feel?"

By giving the client the freedom to fantasize about the consequences of both outcomes, there is the opportunity to clarify thoughts and feelings and to assess the emotional readiness for a given decision (pp. 35–36).

Ambivalent clients, therefore, are given the opportunity "to picture" or fantasize themselves acting out each decision, being aware of their feelings as they do so. Through this focused fantasy, they are encouraged to get in touch with affect, cognitions, and behaviors related to choosing both divorce and staying married (Sprenkle 1985).

A related technique is suggested by Evan Imber-Black (1986). Building on the work of the Milan group, she has couples enact a ritual where on the "odd days" of the week, they act "as if" they have made the decision to stay together; on the "even days" they proceed "as if" they had made the decision to divorce. One day per week is "free." The couple is encouraged to live out the various sides of their ambivalence, and this often moves them off dead center.

Clinicians fortunate enough to have the opportunity to work in a "team" format can use a "split" team opinion. Certain team members declare why a separation would be the most beneficial decision. Others take an opposite position, supporting a decision to continue the marriage. While the therapist can align with either opinion, he or she typically remains undecided or neutral and aligns with the clients after the stating of team opinions helps them break their impasse. Team "splits" can also be used as an opportunity to introduce a third alternative. The therapist empathizes with the distress caused by the ambivalence but reframes it as a "decision not to decide" rather than as a "failure to decide." This has the effect of validating the client's position and labeling it as a "choice" rather than as being "stuck." The client must then assess the merits of this choice in the context of other available choices (Adams and Sprenkle 1988).

What is common and essential to these interventions is the "no fault" component. These interventions are designed to help clients explore various options without implying that the clients are deficient in some way. The clients' ambivalence and decision alternatives are treated with respect.

The author generally favors conjoint treatment during the stage of divorce decision-making. Certainly the old practice of working individually with one spouse to the exclusion of the other at this time is often "an intervention in favor of divorce" (Whitaker and Miller 1971, p. 254). The children or parents of one or both spouses may be included in therapy at this time, depending upon the nature of the relationship issues and theoretical orientation of the therapist. Nonetheless, since the final decision regarding divorce is a couple issue rather than a family issue, the major emphasis should be on conjoint therapy with a low emphasis on both individual and family therapy (Storm and Sprenkle 1982). Once an irrevocable decision to divorce has been made, however, it is important to work with the couple around the important issue of informing the children. Dependent upon circumstances, they may or may not be present.

Another advantage of conjoint work is that it offers the therapist the opportunity to do what Kressel and Deutsch (1977) call "orchestrating the motivation to divorce" in the resistant spouse. If it is clear that the marriage cannot be restored, the therapist may need to inform the resistant party, "There is only one thing worse than a divorce you don't want—and that is being married to someone who doesn't want to be married to you."

Sometimes the process of challenging destructive or unrealistic expectations or beliefs about marriage, disrupting dysfunctional behavioral sequences and finding better ones, reframing relational patterns and creating new realities leads both partners to opt to stay in the marriage. In such cases, there can be a new contract for "marital therapy" that is satisfactory to all parties. If this does not occur, and both spouses become resigned to ending the marriage (or the therapist orchestrates the motive to divorce in the reluctant spouse), then a contract can be established for "divorce" therapy.

When the latter happens, this author attempts to achieve several often difficult tasks (which even if successful may carry over into the subsequent two stages of divorce therapy):

1. Each partner is encouraged to articulate his or her own contributions to the failure of the marriage.
2. Each is asked to express to the other an appreciation for what was good or positive in their shared life together.

3. Each spouse is encouraged to express forgiveness to the other for his or her contribution to the family hurt.

Realistically, these are difficult tasks, and often it is not possible to achieve results. Positive movement, however, significantly contributes to successful outcome in the subsequent two stages of divorce therapy. Couples can also be encouraged to devise a ritual as a means of saying "good-bye" to their relationship. There is considerable opportunity for therapist and client creativity here. Generally it is best to offer clients only general guidelines and let them work out the details of a ritual that will be meaningful for them (Imber-Black 1986). Kaslow (1981) also offers helpful suggestions on the role of rituals in divorce work (Kaslow and Schwartz 1987).

THERAPY FOR RESTRUCTURING (STAGE II)

Salts (1985) has indicated that if a couple's decision to divorce was facilitated by a therapist who created a mutually acceptable decision, and hence, toned down the intense emotions surrounding divorce, then the couple is more likely to restructure successfully. If the therapist was not involved with the couple during the decision-making phase, then reviewing this process with them may be important to assess the feelings each one has about the decision. The purpose of this intervention is not to change the decision to divorce, but to provide the opportunity for the couple to reaffirm that the decision is the best one for them or to move the unwilling spouse to the point of acceptance (Salts 1985).

The restructuring process entails the legal, emotional, financial, social, and parental arrangements necessary to make the shift from marriage to singlehood (Storm and Sprenkle 1982). This is a time of inordinate stress because of the multitude of changes that often occur—moving, lowered standard of living, shifting parental arrangements, changing social networks, and so forth. The degree of difficulty in this stage depends, in part, on the process used to arrive at the decision to divorce. If one spouse feels callously "dumped" and is desperately "holding on," restructuring will be more difficult (Sprenkle 1985).

Ideally, conjoint couple therapy with family therapy to deal with children's issues is preferable. It is interesting that conjoint work was once controversial here. In a study of the views of psychotherapists regarding divorce interventions, Kressel and Deutsch (1977) reported ". . . disinclination to see couples jointly after the divorce decision is correlated with the view that the therapist has no role to play in the mediation of divorce settlements" (p. 300). The current writer strongly disagrees with this view and believes that the therapist can play a significant role in the mediation of divorce settlements. A conjoint approach can be used not only to mediate custody, visitation, and financial arrangements, but also can facilitate the timing of separation, and can be used to facilitate the continuation of tasks delineated at the end of the section on divorce decision-making therapy. It provides a setting to continue dealing with the inevitable unresolved feelings that accompany divorce. If emotions of anger, disappointment, and hurt are not dealt with, they are often disguised in ongoing custody and visitation disputes. Individual therapy would be the treatment of choice only if there were a brief marriage, no children, no concerns about the settlement, and the couple already had an understanding of their relationship dynamics and their own contribution to the demise of their marriage. Of course, frequently people who have been "left" will initially seek help around the time of physical separation, and even the most engaging therapist will have difficulty getting the other spouse to participate (Salts 1985).

Including children at least at some point during this stage is crucial. Often children are neglected emotionally during this period because, as Wallerstein (1980) has noted, parents are overwhelmed by their own needs. Since there is compelling research evidence that children's postdivorce adjustment is directly related to the parents' own adjustment (Wallerstein and Kelly 1980), therapists may gain leverage by encouraging partners to continue working on their own emotional issues by informing them of the benefits their children will reap (Kaslow 1984, Salts 1985). Fortunately, there is a good variety of resources for the professional who wishes to learn more about working with children of divorce (Cantor and Drake 1984, Gardner 1976, Hetherington et al. 1981, Kurdek 1983, Nichols 1984, 1985, Stuart and Abt 1981, Wallerstein and Kelly 1980). There are also some good resources that therapists can share with parents to help them with their children (Francke 1983, Newman 1981, Oakland 1984). Finally, there are several excellent books written for children (Gardner 1971, 1978, 1982, Rofes 1982).

The time around the physical separation is typically the most stressful time for children of all ages. The therapeutic challenge is to help them deal with their feelings of loss as the separation occurs while at the same time working with the parents to minimize parental conflict and to encourage cooperation in parenting (Nichols 1985).

In sessions that include the children, this writer gives them the opportunity to express their feelings, to work through their grief, and to feel "parented." While all else seems to be crumbling, it is exceedingly important to maintain a psychological sense of family (Nichols 1985). This can be accomplished by facilitating the parents to demonstrate continued and consistent love. It can also be helpful to involve grandparents, or to mobilize other portions of the children's social/support network.

In private time with the parents, still focused on child issues, this writer uses whatever leverage can be employed to stress that they should compartmentalize their marital conflict from their ongoing role as parents. The temptation to triangulate the children is normalized, but the deleterious consequences of such action is driven home in whatever way the clients will accept. Couples are encouraged to provide as much continuity for the children as possible and to make it very clear that parenting is forever, even if marrying is not. Ex-spouses are encouraged to communicate directly with each other and not through their children and certainly not to "pump" the children for information about the other's activities. With highly inflammatory clients, the author has occasionally used the paradoxical directive, "If you wanted to be harmful to your children, how specifically would you go about doing it?"

The form of intervention most directly related to restructuring is divorce mediation. Because it is covered elsewhere in this volume, it will be dealt with only briefly here. Although mediation has been widely practiced in other aspects of life (for example, labor disputes), it has only recently been applied to divorce (Cohen 1985). Divorce mediation arose as a reaction against the destructive dimensions of the adversary legal system and was also facilitated by the widespread acceptance of no-fault divorce.

It is important to stress that mediation does not replace the legal system but attempts to circumvent its more negative aspects. When the current writer initiates mediation with a couple, he emphasizes that he can help them to prepare a "statement of intentions" about the terms of their dissolution, but an attorney or attorneys will be necessary to translate this statement into acceptable legal language.

The mediation process is typically present-centered and time-limited and focuses on the goals of reaching an agreement around such crucial issues as custody, visitation, and finances. A full discussion of the mediation process is beyond the scope of this chapter. Fortunately, therapists desiring to learn more about mediation have a variety of books to consult (Coogler 1978, Folberg and Milne 1988,

Haynes 1981, Irving 1980, Saposnek 1983, Shapiro and Kaplan 1983).

There is considerable debate as to the proper scope and direction of mediation (Cohen 1985). Many court-related mediating services have focused exclusively on the mediation of custody and visitation issues and have avoided mediating financial matters. Other mediators feel strongly that mediators should avoid dealing with psychological issues unless they can be dealt with very briefly and have an immediate bearing on the goal of reaching a settlement. Subscribers to this point of view are often mediators who begin meeting with couples only after a decision to mediate has been made following an irrevocable decision to divorce. The current author's mediation practice, however, is comprised mainly of couples with whom he has worked during the decision-making phase and whom he has also assisted through the acute separation portion of restructuring. More than once this author has mediated a settlement only to find that the process led to a recommitment to maintain the marriage.

> Ralph, an executive of a large company, became embroiled in a torrid affair with a younger coworker. Throughout the decision-making phase, he maintained his behavior was "caused" by his wife's frequent rejection, inability to share activities that he liked, such as golf, and her refusal to meet his sexual needs. Although he said he "thought through everything carefully" (perhaps a clue that he wasn't so committed to divorce), he insisted that divorce was nearly certain and that, in any event, the settlement must be mediated. In addition to this author, he consulted with a tax advisor about the intricacies of settling his complicated estate. After the mediation was completed, and after his wife had demonstrated a nonpunitive approach and sincere interest in his welfare, he reconsidered. We contracted for marital therapy and it was successfully completed. Four years later the couple reports "never having been happier."

Perhaps this case would have had a different outcome had the author not been sensitive to the psychological and interactional dynamics that were operating. The mediation seemed to serve as a kind of closure ritual on the "old" marriage and made it possible for a "new" relationship to be born. In short, there is a place for a form of mediation/therapy that some professionals might find uncomfortable. It seems clear that issues related to money, property, visitation, and child support are often inextricably intertwined with the marital drama and therefore cannot be readily separated.

THERAPY FOR POSTDIVORCE RECOVERY
(STAGE III)

Following restructuring, the therapist can begin to focus more on "individual" issues, such as coping with loneliness, regaining self-confidence, and rebuilding social relations. Unless there are continuing problems with parent-child relationships and custody/visitation issues, or unless remarriage issues are the focus, the individual is the unit of treatment during this stage (Storm and Sprenkle 1982).

The goals of divorce therapy at this stage are threefold:

1. Facilitate the remaining grief work the client needs to do to "let go" of the marriage. In his popular book for the lay person, Bruce Fisher (1981) offers a number of useful methods for dealing with emotional "leftovers," such as deliberately mourning over family pictures and then eventually setting them aside. Fisher's book describes a series of "rebuilding blocks" that the divorcing person must ascend on the way to recovery, and each chapter offers a useful self-quiz that serves as a mile marker along the way. This author typically uses this book as an aid on the road to recovery.

2. The client should be helped to revise self-destructive meanings attributed to the divorce. This author has previously identified (Sprenkle and Cyrus 1983) an unholy triad of interpretations that act as roadblocks for divorcing persons. These are "unworthiness," "meaninglessness," and "helplessness." Johnson (1977) demonstrates how rational-emotive methods can be used to attack these destructive beliefs. The writer finds even more refreshing the recent work of Marcia Brown (1985), who uses a structural-strategic approach to create "new realities" for the newly divorced. Brown builds upon clients' own language and perspective and gently reframes it to engender more hope. For example, if the client complains, "I can't concentrate at all," the therapist might query, "Did you drive yourself here today?" If the client responds affirmatively, the therapist might say, "So you are able to concentrate some, but not to the degree to which you would like" (p. 104).

3. The therapist should help the client to maximize resources so as to develop alternatives to the now defunct relationship. The second and third goals are interdependent, since as the client learns to develop his or her resources, it becomes easier for the client to attribute less destructive meaning to the divorce. Conversely, to the extent that the client stops making debilitating interpretations of the divorce, he or she will be more free to develop resources (Sprenkle and Cyrus 1983).

One needs to tap into resources that have been either under-utilized or outside the client's awareness, such as friends, family, children, community, work, and most importantly one's self. The author helps the client to identify his or her resources and strengthen those that seem most amenable to amplification. Obviously, resources vary from client to client. There is considerable empirical evidence that a support group of friends and social participation encourage divorce adjustment. Similarly, a job for which one is adequately compensated has been demonstrated to be highly related to adjustment (Kitson and Raschke 1981). Often men and women differ in the extent to which these resources need to be cultivated. Typically, men need less help in developing their vocational resources and more help in the friendship and social areas, whereas the reverse is often true for women (Johnson 1977, Sprenkle and Cyrus 1983).

Developing the "self" as a resource is the most challenging crucial task of the therapist. This typically includes:

1. The development of certain basic life skills. Men, for example, often need to learn to cook and sew, whereas women may need help with fiscal management and basic maintenance and repairs. (There are, of course, many exceptions to these stereotypical needs.)

2. Time-management skills. Clients frequently need to learn how to use their time in ways that maximize creativity. Frequently, clients can learn to come to terms with loneliness following a program of "loneliness tolerance training" (Johnson 1977), where clients are progressively introduced to longer periods of time alone.

3. Assessing inner strengths. Clients need help in learning how to use personal sources of strength and competence that have been useful in the past. For example, Kirsten and Robertiello (1978) describe a method of helping a client distinguish between his or her "Big You" and "Little You." The latter is the part of one's personality that represents his or her emotional and belief system as a frightened small child. Often the divorcing person feels overwhelmed, incompetent, frightened, and demanding, as a child might in a state of panic. The "Big You" represents that part of oneself that feels competent, confident, and capable of dealing with stress. Using the "empty chair" technique, this author frequently helps clients to utilize their "Big You" (strong part) as a resource to parent their "Little You" (weak part).

OTHER METHODS OF DIVORCE THERAPY

In this section, we briefly describe other methods of divorce therapy worthy of attention.

In the decision-making stage, structured separation is sometimes utilized for couples who do not appear to be benefiting from marriage counseling but are doubtful that divorce is the best alternative. Granvold (1983) is an excellent source describing different models of structured separation. Most require a written contract that specifies ground rules, including time limits (typically between six weeks to three months). Separation is structured in such a way as to maintain a balance between "absence makes the heart grow fonder" and "out of sight, out of mind" (Granvold 1983, p. 407). All these models mandate that couples attend therapy, typically once a week, and the therapist attempts to create a more rational environment for decision making (Sprenkle 1985). This author is cautious about structured separation, since follow-up studies suggest a high rate of marital termination (Green et al. 1973, Toomin 1972). It is certainly important to match the technique to the needs of the couple, and Granvold (1983) does offer some guidelines to assess if the technique is suitable.

In the restructuring phase, several authors have argued for the value of interdisciplinary teams composed of attorneys and therapists (Bernstein 1977, Kaslow and Steinberg 1981). They argue that therapists cannot keep up with the complex issues related to property, pension, taxes, support, and so forth, and that attorneys are not well trained to deal with the complex emotional issues surrounding divorce.

Since mediated divorces more often result in joint custody, therapists should be aware of Volgy and Everett's (1985) five criteria, which may be used to determine if couples are adaptative enough to make joint custody work. These authors stress that joint custody, like mediation, should not be seen as a panacea and therapists cannot be oblivious to contraindications to these approaches (Sprenkle 1985).

For the recovery stage, a great deal has been written about group and educational approaches. A variety of such programs and their goals are reviewed in Storm and colleagues (1985). Typically, groups are less expensive than individual therapy. The group experience also tends to normalize divorce and generates support and acceptance. Formats typically include short didactic educational emphases, skills training, group therapy, or combinations of these modalities (Storm et al. 1985).

The single-parent phase following divorce is often especially diffi-cult, and Weiss (1979) offers a text that is valuable both for the single parent and the mental health professional. Isaacs (1982) and Welt-ner (1982) offer structural family therapy models for dysfunctional single parents. Eno (1985) demonstrates how sibling relationships are affected by divorce and also how they can be used therapeutically to aid divorce adjustment in children.

RESEARCH EVALUATION OF DIVORCE THERAPY

Sprenkle and Storm (1983) offer a very thorough review of the em-pirical research in divorce therapy. Readers desiring more detail should consult this resource. Basically, they report that the only methodologically solid research has been done in the area of media-tion of child custody and visitation conflicts.

In direct comparisons between mediation and traditional adver-sary methods, mediation produced (a) considerably higher rates of pretrial stipulations or agreements than did control groups, (b) a significantly higher level of satisfaction with mediated agreements than with those imposed by the courts, (c) dramatic reduction in the amount of litigation following a final order, (d) an increase in joint custody arrangements, and (e) a decrease in public expenses, such as custody studies and court costs. One study (Pearson and Thoennes 1982), however, suggests that attorney fees may not be reduced by mediation. Controlled research of conciliation court counseling dem-onstrated a significantly greater number of reconciliations in experi-mental groups as opposed to no-treatment control groups, but only short-term results are reported.

Sprenkle and Storm (1983) conclude that the field of divorce intervention is still woefully empirically underdeveloped (p. 255). Aside from the conclusion that the mediation of custody and visita-tion disputes is preferable to the traditional adversary process, there is not a strong data base to conclude that any other form of divorce intervention is superior to no treatment. There is no controlled re-search whatsoever about what is probably the most widely practiced form of divorce therapy—namely individuals or couples who go to a therapist for help in getting through the trauma of divorce. There-fore, the most basic controlled research in the process and outcome of divorce has yet to be done.

None of the studies of divorce therapy have investigated effects of treatment on the children of divorce. Children have not been in-cluded as participants in the therapeutic experience, and such investigations are crucial for public policy as well as clinical reasons (Gurman et al. 1986). Moreover, there appears to be no research on interventions related to single-parent families or to remarriage, in spite of the excellent theoretical books in these areas. Divorce mediation research also needs to be broadened to include examining the mediation of child support and property settlements.

Finally, it is important that investigators compare various forms of treatment with one another. No one, for example, has examined the results of individual versus conjoint versus family treatment for divorcing people. Although, on theoretical grounds, Storm and Sprenkle (1982) argued that specific units for treatment (individual, conjoint, family, and group) are most appropriate for persons in various stages of the dissolution process, there has been no research to verify this speculation (Sprenkle and Piercy 1986).

CONCLUSION

The field of divorce intervention clearly remains in its infancy. We know much more about the phenomenon of divorce than we know about how to intervene effectively. Given the fact that only a minority of marriages being contracted will survive "till death do us part," it behooves family professionals to devote their creative time and energy to this significant, if highly challenging, field.

REFERENCES

Adams, J., and Sprenkle, D. H. (1988). Self-perception and personal commitment. Unpublished manuscript. Marriage and Family Therapy Program, Purdue University.

Ahrons, C., and Rogers, R. (1987). *Divorced Families: A Multidisciplinary Development View.* New York: W. W. Norton.

Bernstein, B. (1977). Lawyer and counselor as an interdisciplinary team: preparing the father for custody. *Journal of Marriage and Family Counseling,* 29–40.

Brown, E. M. (1976). Divorce counseling. In *Treating Relationships,* ed. D. H. Olson, pp. 399–429. Lake Mills, IA: Graphic.

Brown, M. D. (1985). Creating new realities for the newly divorced: a structural strategic approach for divorce therapy with an individual. In *Divorce Therapy,* ed. D. H. Sprenkle, pp. 101–120. New York: Haworth.

Cantor, D. W., and Drake, E. A. (1983). *Divorced Parents and Their Children: A Guide for Mental Health Professionals.* New York: Springer.

Cohen, S. N. (1985). Divorce mediation: an introduction. In *Divorce Therapy,* ed. D. H. Sprenkle, pp. 69–84. New York: Haworth.

Coogler, O. J. (1978). *Structural Mediation in Divorce Settlement.* Lexington, MA: Lexington Books.

Eno, M. M. (1985). Sibling relationships in families of divorce. In *Divorce Therapy,* ed. D. H. Sprenkle, pp. 139–156. New York: W. W. Norton.

Everett, C. A. (1987). *The Divorce Process: A Handbook for Clinicians.* New York: Haworth.

Fisher, B. (1981). *Rebuilding: When Your Relationship Ends.* San Luis Obispo, CA: Impact.

Fleuridas, C., Nelson, T. S., and Rosenthal, D. M. (1986). The evaluation of circular questions: training family therapists. *Journal of Marital and Family Therapy* 12:113–128.

Folberg, J., and Milne, A. (1988). *Divorce Mediation: Theory and Practice.* New York: Guilford.

Francke, L. B. (1983). *Growing Up Divorced.* New York: Linden.

Gardner, R. A. (1971). *The Boys and Girls Book about Divorce.* New York: Bantam.

——— (1978). *The Boys and Girls Book about One-Parent Families.* New York: Bantam.

Granvold, D. K. (1983). Structured separation for marital treatment and decision-making. *Journal of Marital and Family Therapy* 9:403–412.

Green, B. L., Lee, R. R., and Lustig, N. (1973). Transient structured distance as a maneuver in marital therapy. *Family Coordinator* 20:15–22.

Gurman, A. S., and Kniskern, D. P. (1981). Editor's note. In *Handbook of Family Therapy,* ed. A. S. Gurman and D. P. Kniskern, p. 694. New York: Brunner/Mazel.

Gurman, A., Kniskern, D., and Pinsof, W. (1986). Research on the process and outcome of marital and family therapy. In *Handbook of Psychotherapy and Behavior Change*, 3rd ed., ed. S. Garfield and A. Bergin, pp. 157–211. New York: Wiley.

Hansen, J. C., ed. (1982). *Therapy with Remarriage Families.* Rockville, MD: Aspen Systems.

Haynes, J. M. (1981). *Divorce Mediation: A Practical Guide for Therapists and Counselors.* New York: Springer Publications.

Hetherington, E. M., Cox, M., and Cox, R. (1981). The aftermath of divorce. In *Contemporary Readings in Child Psychology*, ed. E. M. Hetherington and R. D. Parke, pp. 234–249. New York: McGraw-Hill.

Imber-Black, E. (1986). Presentation at the Annual Meeting of the Indiana Association for Marital and Family Therapy, Indianapolis, Indiana.

Irving, H. H. (1980). *Divorce Mediation: A Rational Alternative to the Adversary System.* New York: Universe Books.

Isaacs, M. (1982). Helping mom fail: a case of a stalemated divorcing process. *Family Process* 21:225–234.

Isaacs, M., Montalvo, B., and Abelsohn, D. (1986). *The Difficult Divorce: Therapy with Children and Families.* New York: Basic Books.

Janis, I. L. (1983). *Short-term Counseling, Guidelines Based on Recent Research.* New Haven: Yale University Press.

Janis, I. L., and Mann, L. (1977). *Decision Making: A Psychological Analysis of Conflict, Choice, and Commitment.* New York: The Free Press.

Johnson, S. M. (1977). *First Person Singular.* New York: J. B. Lippincott.

Kaslow, F. W. (1981). Divorce and divorce therapy. In *Handbook of Family Therapy*, ed. A. S. Gurman and D. P. Kniskern. pp. 662–696. New York: Brunner/Mazel.

——— (1984). Divorce: an evolutionary process of change in the family system. *Journal of Divorce* 7:21–39.

Kaslow, F. W., and Schwartz, L. L. (1987). *The Dynamics of Divorce: A Life Cycle Perspective.* New York: Brunner/Mazel.

Kaslow, F. W., and Steinburg, J. (1981). Ethical divorce therapy and divorce proceedings: a psycho-legal perspective. In *Values, Ethics, Legalities, and the Family Therapist*, ed. L. L'Abate, pp. 63–74. Rockville, MD: Aspen Systems.

Kirsten, G., and Robertiello, R. (1978). *Big You, Little You.* New York: Pocket Books.

Kressel, K. (1980). Patterns of coping in divorce and some implications for the clinical practice. *Family Relations* 29:234–240.

Kressel, K., and Deutsch, M. (1977). Divorce therapy: an in-depth survey of therapists' views. *Family Process* 16:413–444.

Kurdek, L. A., ed. (1983). *New Directions for Child Development: Children and Divorce.* San Francisco: Jossey-Bass.

Newman, G. (1981). *101 Ways To Be a Long Distance Super-dad.* Mountain View, CA: Blossom Valley.

Nichols, W. C. (1984). Therapeutic needs of children in family system reorganization. *Journal of Divorce* 7:23–34.

——— (1985). Family therapy with children of divorce. In *Divorce Therapy*, ed. D. H. Sprenkle, pp. 55–68. New York: Haworth.

Oakland, T. (1984). *Divorced Fathers: Reconstructing a Quality of Life*. New York: Human Sciences.

Olson, D. H., Russell, C. S., and Sprenkle, D. H. (1980). Marital and family therapy: a decade review. *Journal of Marriage and the Family* 42: 973–993.

Pearson, J., and Thoennes, N. (1982). The benefits outweigh the costs. *The Family Advocate* 4:26–32.

Price-Bonham, S., and Balswick, J. O. (1980). The noninstitutions: divorce, desertion, and remarriage. *Journal of Marriage and the Family* 42:959–972.

Rice, J. M., and Rice, R. C. (1986). *Divorce Therapy*. New York: Norton.

Rofes, E., ed. (1982). *The Kids' Book of Divorce: By, For and About Kids*. New York: Vintage Books.

Sager, C. J., Brown, H. S., Crohn, H., Engel, T., Rodstein, E., and Walker, L. (1983). *Treating the Remarried Family*. New York: Brunner/Mazel.

Salts, C. J. (1979). Divorce process: integration of theory. *Journal of Divorce* 2:233–240.

——— (1985). Divorce stage theory and therapy: therapeutic implications throughout the divorcing process. In *Divorce Therapy*, ed. D. H. Sprenkle, pp. 13–23. New York: Haworth.

Saposnek, D. T. (1983). *Mediating Child Custody Disputes*. San Francisco: Jossey-Bass.

Shapiro, T. J., and Caplan, M. S. (1983). *Parting Sense: A Couple's Guide to Divorce Mediation*. Lutherville, MD: Greenspring.

Sprenkle, D. H. (1985). Introduction: divorce therapy. In *Divorce Therapy*, ed. D. H. Sprenkle, pp. 5–11. New York: Haworth.

Sprenkle, D. H., and Cyrus, C. (1983). Abandonment: the sudden stress of divorce. In *Stress and the Family*, vol. 2, ed. C. R. Figley and H. I. McCubbin, pp. 53–75. New York: Brunner/Mazel.

Sprenkle, D. H., and Piercy, F. P. (1986). Divorce therapy. In *Family Therapy Sourcebook*, ed. F. P. Piercy and D. H. Sprenkle, pp. 129–164. New York: Guilford.

Sprenkle, D. H., and Storm, C. L. (1983). Divorce therapy outcome research: a substantive and methodological review. *Journal of Marital and Family Therapy* 9:239–258.

Storm, C. L., and Sprenkle, D. H. (1982). Individual treatment in divorce therapy: a critique of an assumption. *Journal of Divorce* 5:87–97.

Storm, C. L., Sprenkle, D. H., and Williamson, W. (1985). Innovative divorce approaches developed by counselors, conciliators, mediators, and educators. In *Psychoeducational Approaches to Family Therapy*, ed. R. Levant, pp. 266–309. New York: Springer.

Stuart, I. R., and Abt, L. E. (1981). *Children of Separation and Divorce: Management and Treatment*. New York: Van Nostrand-Reinhold.

Sutton, P., and Sprenkle, D. (1985). Criteria for a constructive divorce:

theory and research to guide the practitioner. In *Divorce Therapy*, ed. D. H. Sprenkle, pp. 39–51. New York: Haworth.

Toomin, M. K. (1972). Structured separation with counseling: a therapeutic approach for couples in conflict. *Family Process* 11:299–310.

Turner, N. W. (1980). Divorce in mid-life: clinical implications and applications. In *Mid-life: Developmental and Clinical Issues*, ed. W. Norman and Scaramella, pp. 149–177. New York: Brunner/Mazel.

———— (1985). Divorce: dynamics of decision therapy. In *Divorce Therapy*, ed. D. H. Sprenkle, pp. 27–38. New York: Haworth.

Visher, E. B., and Visher, J. S. (1979). *Stepfamilies: A Guide to Working with Step-parents and Step-children*. New York: Brunner/Mazel.

Volgy, S. S., and Everett, C. A. (1985). Systemic assessment criteria for joint custody. In *Divorce Therapy*, ed. D. H. Sprenkle, pp. 85–98. New York: Haworth.

Wallerstein, J. S., and Kelly, J. B. (1980). *Surviving the Breakup: How Children and Parents Cope with Divorce*. New York: Basic Books.

Weiss, R. S. (1975). *Marital Separation*. New York: Basic Books.

———— (1979). *Going It Alone: The Family Life and Social Situation of the Single Parent*. New York: Basic Books.

Weltner, J. S. (1982). A structural approach to the single-parent family. *Family Process* 21:203–210.

Whitaker, C. (1970). Reply to: "The role of the psychiatrist in treating divorce cases." *American Journal of Psychiatry* 126:1328–1329.

Whitaker, C. A., and Miller, M. S. (1971). Evaluation of "psychiatric" help when divorce impends. In *Changing Families: A Family Therapy Reader*, ed. J. Haley, pp. 247–250. New York: Grune and Stratton.

10

POSTDIVORCE TREATMENT

Donald K. Granvold, Ph.D.

The increase in the divorce rate over the past 25 years has had a significant bearing on the meaning of divorce, the readiness of individuals to seek it as an option to marital distress, and the development of an available support network to guide those experiencing it. This increased divorce rate reflects a greater social acceptance of divorce; a change in economics, particularly with regard to women; a trend toward satisfaction of personal goals, interests and desires, and the ethic of self-realization identified by Weiss (1975); and a change in the view of marriage from the traditional belief in the intrinsic permanence of marriage to a "pragmatic" view, in which one's commitment to marriage is the product of internal and external reward-cost factors (Scanzoni 1972). While divorce has become more frequent, more widely accepted, and representative of a potentially healthy orientation to personal need satisfaction, the process of divorce is traumatic for most who experience it.

The treatment of postdivorce adjustment is difficult to address because of the complexity and nonuniversality of the divorce experience. Baker (1981) aptly states that it is a myth that "a divorce is a divorce is a divorce." The phenomenon of divorce has been identified as a highly complex series of processes, not an event (Sprenkle 1985). Divorce may be a unilateral decision, a shared decision, or an imposed condition. It is a crisis that has been rated as the second most severe form of stress one can undergo (Holmes and Rahe 1967).

While extremely stressful, the divorce experience has been found to include both positive and negative experiences (Buehler and Langenbrunner 1987, Chiriboga and Cutler 1977, Spanier and Thompson 1983, 1984). Divorce can be considered damaging, yet growth producing; fear provoking, yet self-assurance stimulating; dependency prompting while promoting independence; identity shattering, yet ego differentiation and individuation inducing; and relieving, yet distressing. Divorce, it appears, is a series of contravening processes involving personal, interpersonal, and environmental conditions producing cognitive, emotive, and behavioral change.

The literature reflects a variety of approaches to the treatment of divorce. Rice and Rice (1986a) provide an excellent review of the origins of divorce therapy covering the following areas: (1) marital and family therapy; (2) crisis intervention treatment; (3) grief and bereavement counseling; and (4) educational-supportive counseling. Treatment approach and unit of treatment (individual, couple, family, group) derive from the therapist's treatment philosophy, conceptualization of divorce therapy (process and goals), and conceptualization of therapist role. Intervention methodologies can be broadly organized under the categories of psychoanalytic, family systems, and social learning/cognitive approaches.

This chapter presents a cognitive-behavioral approach to the treatment of postdivorce adjustment. The challenges confronting the divorce therapist are highly contingent upon the client's stage of adjustment. The focus here is on the postdecision-making stage, when divorce is either a reality or is imminent. Attention will be limited to the divorced individual and his or her adjustment to single life. Parenting and child adjustment issues and family intervention will be excluded. The preferred orientation to divorce therapy is one that stresses "positive" crisis intervention and constructive, psychosocially adaptive adjustment to divorce (Rice and Rice 1986a,b, Sutton and Sprenkle 1985).

Postdivorce recovery obligates the individual to accommodate pervasive change. Against a backdrop of ambivalence and oscillating emotions, the individual is challenged to integrate: (1) the stress of wholesale change, (2) redefinition of self and object loss trauma, (3) role loss, disorientation, and restructuring, and (4) lifestyle adjustment. The process of postdivorce recovery is marked by circularity rather than linearity in which "affective, cognitive, and behavioral realities occur, change, convert and reoccur in a cyclical manner" (Crosby et al. 1983, p. 17). Demands from outside and within, personal preparation to accommodate change, and level of successful integration of change are in constant flux. The following section is a brief presentation of identity and attachment issues that are universal and central to the process of postdivorce recovery.

IDENTITY AND ATTACHMENT

Divorce is an identity crisis for all who experience it and, for many, the disruption to one's sense of self is extreme. From a cognitive-behavioral perspective, identity cannot be separated from the mechanisms of knowledge. The mind is characterized as a human knowing system functioning as "an active, constructive system capable of producing not only its output but also to a large extent the input it receives" (Guidano 1988, p. 309). Central to the conceptualization is the self-organizing capacity of the human system, out of which evolves "a full sense of self-identity with inherent feelings of uniqueness and historical continuity" (Guidano 1987, p. 3). Self-knowledge is considered to exist at both a conscious level and beyond awareness. Guidano and Liotti (1983) describe the two levels as "tacit knowledge, about which we cannot speak, and explicit knowledge, about which we can" (p. 9). Sager (1976) makes reference to these two levels of knowledge in terms of expectations, desires, and obligations held in relation to self and significant others. Based on the inextricable relationship of identity to mechanisms of knowledge, identity "is fundamentally an inferred theory of self, biased by one's own tacit self-knowledge" and functions as the basic structure of reference for monitoring and evaluating self in relation to ongoing experience (Guidano 1988, p. 317). This theory of self is comprised of the individual's beliefs, values, rules and expectations about self, the world, and his or her interaction in the world.

Disturbance to personal identity is the product of the perceived disparity between expectations and actual experience. Degree of maladjustment derives from an appraisal of disparity in terms of values (good—bad, comfortable—uncomfortable, right—wrong) and perceived ability to cope (self-efficacy). Divorce and the change demands of divorce recovery may thrust the individual into an extreme state of disequilibrium in which basic structures of self are threatened.

Attachment is considered to be a critical component to the normal development of identity. Processes of attachment are fundamentally interdependent with selfhood processes. Attachment behavior evolves from simple contact-seeking behavior to a complex cognitive and emotional bond. While the individual progresses through detachment from primary care-givers, the rewards of mature attachment become strongly cognitively fixed. Intimate relationships with significant others feel both "good" and "right." In essence, the individual becomes conditioned to develop and sustain attachment behavior. As in prior development stages, in adulthood the same interdependence develops between unique attachments and stability of selfhood (Guidano 1987). It is most understandable that the process of breaking a relationship with a primary attachment figure represents an extreme disruption emotionally and to one's sense of self. Furthermore, given the central role the attachment process plays in self-identity, it is little wonder that the divorcing individual experiences the persistence of attachment in light of an erosion of love as described by Weiss (1975).

ASSESSMENT

A primary ingredient in the treatment of postdivorce adjustment problems—or any clinical problem—is effective assessment. Consistent with Jacobson and Margolin's (1979) approach to assessing marital dysfunction, the purpose of assessment in divorce therapy is to: (1) identify problems in the individual's adjustment; (2) identify variables that control the problem behaviors; (3) select appropriate therapeutic interventions; and (4) determine when the intervention has been effective. A thorough assessment is to be comprehensive and specific, historic and contemporary, initial and ongoing, and therapy process oriented.

Identification of postdivorce adjustment problems requires a functional analysis of the client's target problematic behavior, including antecedents and consequences. Emphasis is placed on the interrelationship of thoughts, actions, and emotions. As the therapist gains an understanding of overt behavior and emotions in their environmental/situational context, assessment shifts to cognitive processes, including information processing and deep structure knowledge (beliefs, self-view, and rules).

The multiple aspects of postdivorce adjustment obligate the therapist to a comprehensive assessment. Although no consistent agreement exists regarding successful postdivorce adjustment, variables generally include emotional response, self-image, social role and life-style changes, interpersonal relationship modification, and practical changes. Although knowledge of the client's overall adjustment is important, it is only as the therapist identifies and analyzes specific target problems that intervention can be facilitated.

While a rationale can be built for the primary focus of assessment to address current cognitive functioning and behavioral excesses and deficits contributing to the individual's postdivorce maladjustment, gathering information on past history is advisable. Gaining an understanding and appraisal of the developmental bases of such phenomena as self-view, coping skills, chronic and situational emotional distress, cognitive distortions and behavior problems will provide valuable insight into: (1) patterns of dysfunction, (2) contextual variables, including antecedent conditions and extraneous controlling variables, and (3) historic frequency, magnitude, and duration of adjustment problems. This information, combined with current data, may expose repetitive, inflexible patterns of maladjustment reinforced over time. Haley (1976) asserts that the discovery of repetitive sequences of behavior that maintain dysfunctional behavior are potentially of greatest significance to the therapist.

Assessment that is ongoing satisfies the responsibilities of the therapist to: (1) track progress/change throughout treatment, rather than only pre- and posttherapy evaluation; (2) identify and appraise evolving adjustment dilemmas as they arise; and (3) plan the course of intervention efficaciously. Close monitoring of change in the target areas in which treatment goals have been set will provide therapist and client valuable feedback. Feedback on positive change is reinforcing to both client and therapist and may shape the development of the client's efficacy expectations. Data that fail to support constructive change serve to promote exploration of the barriers to effective treatment outcome. The complexity of postdivorce adjustment in terms of breadth of impact and the continuous and expansive adjustment demands placed on the individual by others and environmental circumstances make ongoing assessment imperative. It is highly unlikely that narrowly defined problem-focused intervention will satisfy the demands of postdivorce therapy. Hence, the treatment plan will require continuous modification.

In addition to identification of client problems and progress in relation to therapeutic efforts, it is important to assess the client's response to therapy and the therapist. Assessment includes appraising the openness of the client to express content and feelings in therapy; the client's active participation and collaboration with the therapist in various therapeutic operations (design, implementation, and evaluation of the change effort); willingness to complete homework, acceptance of explanation, interpretation, and feedback. The therapist should also assess the degree of client commitment to ongoing therapy process and goals as well as explication of evolving client-held expectations regarding the therapist's role.

A vital assessment responsibility of the therapist is to provide measurement of treatment efficacy. The clinical interview serves the therapist well in achieving other assessment reponsibilities, but is inadequate in performing outcome measurement requisite for practice accountability. There are a number of ways to measure client change, including behavioral observations, paper-pencil measures (standardized measures, self-anchored scales, and client logs), unobtrusive measures, and electromechanical measures. An array of standardized instruments exists to assess and measure emotion, self-concept, behavior, and cognitive variables including beliefs, satisfaction, and expectancy. The reader is directed to Corcoran and Fischer's (1987) *Measures for Clinical Practice: A Sourcebook* for a comprehensive compilation of measures and measurement device publishing sources.

EARLY STAGE OF THERAPY

Therapeutic objectives early in treatment are heavily biased toward data gathering/assessment, but also include intervention in terms of providing initial symptom relief (if possible), role structuring, including positive expectancy setting, and rapport/therapeutic alliance building. Through carefully strategized questions the therapist attempts to gather a developing view of the client's belief system (adaptive and maladaptive ideation), information processing errors, view of self, and the degree to which cognitive factors appear accountable for current maladjustment. An appraisal of behavioral excesses and deficits and environmental factors contributing to current adjustment problems should also be accomplished. In this manner, the therapist can begin to formulate a plan of intervention incorporating cognitive and behavioral intervention points and environmental modification. The following treatment procedures serve to engage the therapist and client in the initial stage of treatment:

1. *Assessment of the divorce events as viewed by the client.* Information gathered should include an identification of the primary causative factors; who initiated the divorce (not necessarily who filed); the level of conflict or amicability in the decision-making and initial postdivorce phases; dates of both the separation and finalization of the divorce; and the like. Particular attention should be paid to events corresponding to the development of marital distress, milestones leading to the divorce decision, and the event or events considered to ultimately prompt the divorce.

2. *Previous counseling experiences.* A determination of previous counseling experiences—marital, individual, and divorce—may provide valuable information regarding attempts to maintain the marriage, use of psychotherapy and treatment approaches with which the client is familiar.

3. *Current and past emotional consequences of the separation and divorce as experienced by the client.* Through careful questioning the therapist can solicit the emotional highs as well as the lows currently being experienced by the client. Encouraging the expression of emotion allows the client to become aware of feelings being denied and affords the therapist an opportunity to empathize with current feelings, a highly critical step in establishing an effective therapeutic alliance. Adequate history should be gathered to give the therapist a view of the emotional responses to the initial separation (Granvold 1983). Further objectives involve gaining a clear understanding of the client's emotional episodes including: (1) stimulus conditions; (2) specific maladaptive emotions (for example, depression, anxiety, guilt, regret, fear, hate, anger); (3) frequency, intensity, and duration of the episodes; (4) extraneous controlling variables, that is, what reinforcement from the environment might be strengthening the display of maladaptive emotions; (5) success the client may have had in controlling negative emotional episodes—methods used to stop or convert the emotions from negative to positive.

4. *Current view of self.* The marital relationship is an affectionate bond that plays a crucial role in the preservation of an individual's self-identity. Loss of self-esteem and instability of selfhood are inherently engendered in the divorce process (Guidano 1987, Rice and Rice 1986b, Weiss 1975). In exploring with the client his or her current view of self it is important to develop a historical understanding of the client's self-definition. Intervention with a client who has never had a positive self-image will require a different strategy than the treatment of a client whose current loss of self-esteem is primarily reactive to the divorce process. Investigating current self-image involves: (1) the identification of expectations of self the client considers representative of worthiness, (2) recurring self-statements (thoughts, self-talk) that contribute to current view (I'm a failure; I'm so stupid for having loved him or her; I'm nothing without him or her; and the like), and (3) environmental circumstances contributing to poor self-esteem (for example, underemployment, social inactivity, inadequate finances, and so on).

5. *Client expectation regarding control and self-change.* It is important that the therapist determine clients' sense of control

over their happiness and over the environment, the perception of their capacity to effect self-change. Several conceptualizations have been developed for an individual's sense of competency to act on his or her own world (execute a certain behavior pattern) and thereby promote a potentially positive effect on the course of personal development. The most prominent are self-efficacy (Bandura 1977, 1978a,b, Weiss 1984), learned helplessness (Maier and Seligman 1976, Seligman 1975), and locus of control (Rotter 1966). Postdivorce adjustment has been found to be associated with an internal locus of control orientation—a perception that an event is contingent upon one's own behavior (Bould 1977, Pais 1978, White 1985, Womack 1987). In making an appraisal of control and coping self-perceptions, the therapist should determine the extent to which the client: (1) views self as malleable and adaptable or unchangeable and destined to be subjected to punishing life experiences; (2) selects people, activities, and environments that promote success and personal well-being; (3) is disposed to an attitude of focused effort and sustained tenacity in adjusting to divorce. Gaining a sense of whether the client acts on his or her world—making constructive, self-actualizing, adaptive choices—or assumes a more passive, responsive stance in relation to the divorce and other life experiences and events will provide the therapist valuable information for strategizing the course of treatment. Modification of a client's sense of control over self and the world, sense of self-responsibility and view of his or her capacity to effect change become initial goals in therapy if deficiencies exist in these areas.

6. *Life-style changes.* The objective here is to determine the extent to which life-style changes have resulted from the divorce, and the client's view and emotive responses to the changes. It is well established that stress is a product of change in terms of the demands placed on the individual to accommodate such change. A change in living situation (geographic move), new job, initiating education or training, and altered financial conditions are examples of life-style changes placing demands on the client. Such changes typically thrust the client into new roles, creating temporary role disorientation. The meaning the client attaches to these changes, perception of choice in making change, and emotional reactions should be determined.

7. *Support system availability and usage.* The therapist should determine those significant others available in the client's environment and determine the frequency and manner of the contact. Those with support systems have been found to be better adjusted than those without (Granvold et al. 1979, Spanier and Casto

1979, Wallerstein and Kelly 1980). Socialization, sustained attachment, and emotional support may be sought through support network means. In contrast to the evidence noted above, Spanier and Hanson (1982) found support from and interaction with extended kin were either unrelated or negatively related to the adjustment to marital separation. The nature of the support (individual or group) should be assessed by the therapist to determine the extent to which contact is supportive of or detrimental to the client's adjustment.

8. *Fostering therapeutic expectations.* Early in therapy it is important to establish positive expectations with the client with regard to: (1) his or her capacity to become happier (less emotionally burdened) and more self-actualized, (2) the capability of the therapist to guide constructive change, and (3) the validity of psychotherapy as a forum for change. Frank (1961) notes that "part of the success of all forms of psychotherapy may be attributed to the therapist's ability to mobilize the patient's expectation of help" (pp. 70–71). Formidable barriers to the establishment of positive expectancies are a client's sense of futility, hopelessness, or despair; attribution of problems to fate, luck, the world, and others outside self; secondary gains associated with negative emotion, personal disability, and disadvantage; and resistance to change for such reasons as fear, self-punishment, and committed intractability. The therapist should conduct a careful assessment to expose beliefs, faulty information processing, and reinforcement properties related to the client's negative or apathetic stance. Caution should be exercised to avoid getting into a power struggle with the client regarding his or her dim expectations. Identification of modest change and therapist positive feedback regarding client success may erode the client's resistance to change. The reader is referred to Ellis (1985) for methods to treat resistance.

COGNITIVE-BEHAVIORAL TREATMENT

Cognitive-behavioral treatment of postdivorce problems is based on a mediational theory of human functioning in which cognitive processes, behavior, and emotion interrelate. Emotion and behavior are considered to be products of either a historical or current mediation in which the individual defines and interprets the meaning of a stimulus condition, appraises the event in the context of self-knowledge (structured knowledge of self and world), and selects a response consistent with learned or anticipated contingencies. The cognitive-behavioral perspective involves the use of a variety of approaches to change. The treatment strategy selected may seek: (1)

emotional or behavioral change through modification of thoughts, beliefs, expectations, or thought processing; (2) emotional or behavioral change through development of new verbal or behavioral skills, or the increased performance of adaptive verbal or behavioral skills infrequently used; (3) emotional or behavioral change through reduction of maladaptive behavioral excesses; and (4) environmental modification.

Each intervention methodology noted has a relevant role to fulfill in the comprehensive treatment of postdivorce adjustment. The author's approach to divorce therapy relies heavily on each methodology. The remainder of this chapter, however, will be primarily focused on the application of cognitive methods to treat postdivorce problems.

Cognitive Therapy Principles and Procedures

The implementation of a cognitive treatment strategy is built upon the following basic principles:

1. Inherent self-worth. All people have worth, value, and dignity regardless of behavior, status, or any other characteristic.
2. Self-acceptance. One must accept oneself as worthwhile but flawed, imperfect, and falliable by virtue of being human.
3. Behavior rating. One's performance, skill, and talent can be rated or judged, but rating is irrelevant with regard to self-worth. An honest rating of performance is not to be extended to a rating of self (Ellis 1971, Ellis and Bernard 1986).
4. Emotional disturbance is the product of thoughts, beliefs, attitudes, or expectations.
5. Emotions are the products of choice and are subject to self-control.
6. Each of us is ultimately responsible for our own emotions—blaming others for our feelings is faulty.
7. Thoughts, beliefs, and attitudes are subject to the same principles of learning as are overt behaviors (continuity assumption—Mahoney 1974). Essentially, it is possible to modify covert behavior just as one changes overt behavior.

It is important that the therapist instruct the client in these basic principles for cognitive intervention to be effective. Early goals of intervention may form around the creation of understanding and acceptance of each principle. Initial identification of the role of thought processes and belief systems in human emotional disturbance, behavioral dysfunction, and ineffective problem solving provides a shared theoretical base from which client and therapist can proceed. The next step is the application of this theoretical model to the client's presenting disturbance in a manner that promotes client and therapist collaboration. Consistent with Beck et al. (1979), the client is taught ". . . (1) to monitor his negative, automatic thoughts (cognitions); (2) to recognize the connections between cognition, affect, and behavior; (3) to examine the evidence for and against his distorted automatic thought; (4) to substitute more reality-oriented interpretations for these biased cognitions; and (5) to learn to identify and alter the dysfunctional beliefs which predispose him to distort his experiences" (p. 4). Together therapist and client identify cognitive processes potentially considered accountable for the client's current dysfunction, develop a monitoring system to track the cognitions, and test out hypotheses linking faulty cognitive operations with maladaptive emotional or behavioral functioning. The client is guided to systematically evaluate the validity of his silent assumptions and appraisals regarding self, others, and the world. Client and therapist actively collaborate to expand, shift, and modify the intervention effort based on outcome criteria previously explicitly delineated.

Cognitive intervention is conducted at two levels: superficial change and deep change (Arnkoff 1980, Guidano and Liotti 1983, Mahoney 1980). Superficial change involves a reorganization of the client's attitude toward reality (perceptual and information processing errors and distortions) without a revision of personal identity (Guidano 1988). Deep structure change involves the modification of basic beliefs, assumptions, rules, and expectations that govern the individual's identity and view of the world. While these two types of change are not mutually exclusive, according to Guidano (1988), deep change is contingent on superficial change.

Faulty Information Processing

The following information processing errors serve to distort the client's view of self, others, and the world. The result is a negative, pessimistic view that carries with it maladaptive emotion, negatively biased expectations of self, others, and life, and overt and verbal behaviors that promote negative responses from others.

Absolutistic, Dichotomous Thinking. The tendency to view experiences, objects, and situations in a polarized manner: good/bad, right/wrong, strong/weak.

Alice views herself as totally weak because she typically fails to "stand up" to her ex-husband when he violates preset agreements regarding the child visitation schedule. After avoiding opportunities to confront, she is extremely negatively self-critical and feels angry, guilty, disappointed, loathsome toward self, and depressed.

The intervention is focused on Alice's evaluation of her assertive abilities in degrees rather than dichotomously and identifying situations where she is assertive. Cognitive methods are joined with behavioral strategies to coach, rehearse, implement, and evaluate greater assertiveness with her ex-spouse.

Overgeneralization. Refers to the pattern of drawing a general rule or conclusion on the basis of one or more isolated incidents and applying the concept across the board to related and unrelated situations (Beck et al. 1979).

Donna's husband of twelve years filed for a divorce, having fallen in love with another woman during their marriage. Donna's view is that all men are no good, faithless, and uncaring when it comes to the feelings of women.

The intervention focused initially on the emotion associated with Donna's views. The hurt and anger she felt were refocused from men generally to her ex-spouse and his wrongdoing. Cognitive restructuring procedures (to be discussed later) were applied to those feelings. The validity of her generalized statement was tested out against her knowledge of men in her world whose behavior was incompatible with her generalization. She learned the dangers of generalization in terms of fostering negative expectations and perceptual errors.

Selective Abstraction. Typically a focus on the negative in a situation, ignoring other positive (sometimes more salient) features, and viewing the entire experience as negative based upon the selective view.

Arthur and his wife both wanted the divorce they had secured during 1987. Arthur viewed that year as a terrible, wasted year. He focused his appraisal of the year only on the divorce and did not consider the promotion he personally received, his daughter's successful graduation from college, and the birth of his first grandchild.

The therapist guided Arthur in seeing that screening out positive data and focusing on one or two negative factors (no matter what their magnitude might be) may be accountable for his strong sense of disregard emotionally. Arthur learned that, for him, selective abstraction was a rather pervasive cognitive error leading to faulty appraisals of himself, others, and life experiences. He found further that by changing this information processing error, he felt less emotionally burdened.

Arbitrary Inference. Reaching an arbitrary negative conclusion when there is no evidence to support the conclusion or there is evidence to the contrary. Freeman (1983) described two types of arbitrary inference as mind reading and negative prediction.

1. Mind reading—assuming that another has negative thoughts or feelings toward you, looking for vague, subtle cues to support your inferences, and failing to validate them. This creates a negative interaction pattern and promotes a negative view of self and others.
2. Negative prediction—imagining or anticipating that something bad or unpleasant is going to happen without adequate or realistic support for the prediction. The future, immediate and distant, is viewed with negativism, fatalism, and despair. "I'm going to grow old as a lonely, unloved person." "This date I'm going on is going to work out as badly as the last one."

Magnification and Minimization. Errors in evaluating the significance or magnitude of a behavior, condition, or event that are so extreme as to constitute a distortion. Imperfections in oneself and others are magnified while talents, knowledge, and skill are minimized. Magnification may result in becoming extremely emotional and critical over the misdeeds or human errors of others. Perceptual blinders may serve to filter the meaning of one's own and others' talents, positive qualities, and performances. To illustrate, after twelve years with the firm, Mary Ann became one of the 15 percent to achieve partnership. She believes and states that, "Anyone could have done it."

Personalization. The act of relating a negative event or situation to oneself without the adequate causal evidence to make the connection. This is a form of attribution, a process that will receive more attention later. There are two forms of personalization. In the first instance, an arbitrary conclusion is reached in which a negative event is viewed as caused by the subject. To illustrate, Mary, divorced for two years, is informed that her 6-year-old daughter behaved poorly in Sunday school. She thinks, "I'm really a poor mother." In the second form of personalization an arbitrary conclusion is reached in which one views himself or herself as the object of a negative event, and therefore causally connected. Kay encounters a traffic jam on the way to meet Roger for lunch and concludes, "If I didn't have a lunch date with Roger, there wouldn't be a traffic jam!" Kay failed to allow adequate time for the typically heavy midday traffic.

Negative Attribution. The view that a given behavior is produced out of a negative motivation. Mahoney (1974) defines attribution as implied causality. Attributions are often simplistic statements that are perceived as accountable for a given behavior. The tendency is to attribute singular causation to complex patterns of behavior. Negative attributions can take the form of blaming, "You make me so mad," in which the responsibility for the anger is displaced to the ex-mate. Hurvitz (1975) presents a form of negative attributions as "terminal hypotheses" in which behavior, meanings, or feelings are interpreted such that change cannot take place. Included are such determinants of behavior as psychological classifications ("You're a manic depressive"), pseudo-scientific labels ("You're a Virgo, that's why you act the way you do"), inappropriate generalizations about innate qualities or traits that cannot be changed ("He has no will-power, was born that way; that's why he's so fat"). Epstein (1982) identifies behavior changes that are attributed to coercion or impression management. "He treats my children extra kindly because he's afraid I won't make love with him if he doesn't." The implications are that: (1) the only reason behind the kindness is sexual desire and (2) being kind is actually misrepresentative of the individual's feelings and actual preferences in relation to the children. Another form of negative attributions is malevolent intent. "You took your secretary to lunch to make me jealous." Yet another negative attribution has ingredients of mind reading and inferential reasoning associated with it. "If my friend cared for me, she'd call me today." The failure of the friend to call is, by inference, motivated by a lack of caring. To restate the attribution, "My friend's lack of caring for me is causing her to be insensitive to what I want from her at this moment—a phone call." Such a thought pattern also qualifies as an unrealistic expectation.

Faulty Interpretation. The interpretation of a message inconsistent with the intention; a discrepancy between intent and impact (Gottman 1979). To illustrate, Joe and Mary negotiated an amicable divorce and have had minimal subsequent interactional problems. Mary informed Joe that she opened and is building a college fund for their child with a portion of each child support payment. Mary intended to merely keep Joe informed and to promote his view of her as a responsible parent with child support money. Joe thinks, "Mary doubts my commitment to paying for our child's education. She doesn't think I'll have the money when it's needed." Joe feels sad that Mary doesn't think more of him and feels some resentment regarding the account. He behaves coolly toward Mary in their next interaction.

The ease of making faulty interpretations is evident as one considers the variable meanings that can be attached to a given message. It is only as information is shared and clarification received that the discrepancy between intended and ascribed meaning can be minimized.

The procedure common to the treatment of all information processing errors is the identification of adequate, logical evidence to support the conclusions reached. It is for this reason that the process of "collaborative empiricism" is so important (Beck et al. 1979). For as the client and therapist begin to generate possible hypotheses related to the conclusions reached, the illogic in the thinking will surface with deliberate and focused guidance from the therapist. The initial lack of awareness of the self-sustained cognitive distortions and the emotional overlay associated with such thinking will evolve into the client's organized evaluation of the validity of the hypotheses that have heretofore operated automatically, invalidly in his thinking. As a result, change can be expected in the client's view of self and of significant others, and in the negative emotional episodes that have been associated with cognitive distortions.

Irrational Beliefs and Faulty Expectations

The cognitive distortions identified above may exist rather harmlessly at a low rate of performance in the nondistressed individual. Or perhaps an individual may be subject to "pocket" distortions that contribute to emotional disturbance and problematic interaction with others but exist as exceptions to typically logical thinking. Intervention focused on "blind spots" in the client's thought processes may produce relatively rapid change. In cases where the distortions are severe, extensive, and intractable, however, treatment requires an exploration of the individual's personal philosophy. Cognitive distortions emerge from and are governed by an underlying set of rules, including such elements as cognitive organization, structural causal theories, attitudes toward oneself and toward reality, and belief system. Terminology used to identify an individual's underlying set of rules varies as follows: personal constructs (Kelly 1955), irrational beliefs (Ellis 1973, 1977), automatic thoughts and schemas (Beck 1976, Beck et al. 1979), and paradigm (Guidano and Liotti 1983). The author will use the term *irrational beliefs* as representative of a personal philosophy that promotes a distortion in thought process and leads to emotional, behavioral, and interpersonal dysfunction.

There have been several initial efforts made to apply cognitive restructuring methods to the treatment of postdivorce adjustment (Broder 1985, Ellis 1986, Graff et al. 1986; Granvold and Welch 1977, 1979, Huber 1983, Johnson 1977, Walen and Bass 1986, Walen et al. 1980). Common among the procedures outlined by these authors is the identification of unrealistic, demanding expectations of self and others, specification of faulty attributions, and a deliberate effort on the part of the therapist to foster the client's disengagement from maladaptive beliefs and judgments. While attending to his clients, the therapist listens for evidence of their causal theories, basic assumptions, or irrational beliefs. These are framed as hypotheses and collaboratively the therapist and client proceed to disprove or confirm them through logical, empirical challenge.

Ellis (1962) has identified eleven irrational beliefs that serve as the basis for dysfunctional thinking and faulty expectations. These beliefs incorporate such imperatives as: (1) the demand (as opposed to the desire) for love and approval, perfection and control over one's world; (2) freedom from self-responsibility for one's own emotions; (3) extreme dependency on others; (4) irrefutable right to blame others for one's own and others' imperfections and shortcomings; and (5) the indelible effect of history on current behavior and emotions. Following is a discussion of these imperatives in relation to post-divorce adjustment.

Demandingness

Love and approval. It is not uncommon for the divorced individual to fail to detach his or her identity and sense of okayness from the ex-mate. Love and approval from the former spouse are considered imperative for a positive sense of self and overall worthiness. The negative view toward self has corresponding negative emotions such as depression, self-loathing, hurt, guilt, and despair. Often, there is a negative view of the ex-mate with corresponding negative feelings including anger, resentment, disappointment, disgust, and fear.

The belief that the love of another is a need rather than a desire or preference promotes prolonged emotional disturbance when the love is withdrawn. A shift in belief reflecting lost love as only a desire rather than a need contingent for survival with happiness is necessary for the divorced individual to develop or recapture a positive sense of self and constructively adjust to the divorce.

Irrational beliefs. "It is a dire necessity that I have the sustained love and approval of my chosen (ex) mate. I can't stand life without him (her) as my spouse. Her (his) rejection of me proves me unworthy—I'm no good." "I am nothing without him (her)." "I'll never be happy again." "She (He) is no good because she (he) divorced me."

Perfection and control. The failed marriage may represent imperfection and a lack of control over one's life and the world. The demand for perfection may translate into the view of divorce as the ultimate in marital "imperfection." The client's theology and personal philosophy regarding the permanence of marriage may be inherent in the demand for perfection and control. Sustained marriage becomes, in a sense, compliance with a higher-order law or rule, the violation of which leaves the individual feeling deeply flawed and powerless.

The demand for control may be an expression of narcissism and hedonism. Consistent with the views of Rice (1977), divorcing represents narcissistic injury. Furthermore, the rewards of controlling others and maintaining the order in one's world may be central to the expectation of extreme or total control. The divorce, then, becomes a threat to the individual's stability and pleasure in life.

The assumption of a central omnipotent position in the world produces demandingness. The client sets up artificial, self-declared imperatives that he considers necessary for his emotional wellbeing. Judgments regarding life's injustices, imperatives, and impositions made from a lofty, all-controlling position produce intolerance. The therapist should aid the client in the realization that, although he knows he is not the center of the universe, he is judging certain life experiences and conditions "as if" he were. The client's expectations require expansion to include tolerance and acceptance in light of personal dislike, disregard, and disapproval. Frustrated desires and marginal control over life's demands are to be considered properties inherent in the human social condition.

Irrational beliefs: "I should have prevented the divorce." "I am no good (imperfect) because I am divorced." "Life's a bitch."

It's Your Fault

The placement of responsibility for one's emotions on another is a denial that human emotions exist under one's self-control. While ex-spouses can be held responsible for their behavior (the activating event), the emotions one experiences in response to those actions are, in the last analysis, the responsibility of the individual. It is reasonable to expect the client to experience a "normal" expression of human emotion in relation to divorce recovery in which a fluctuation in mood is healthy and adaptive. However, extreme, highly consistent negative emotion viewed by the client as both the fault of the ex-spouse and as nonresponsive to self-control require cognitive restructuring. Acceptance or responsibility for one's own emotions and the development of the cognitive skill of emotional self-control represent appropriate treatment goals in response to blaming and a lack of emotional self-efficacy.

The client may further blame the ex-spouse for the divorce and the ensuing problems and accommodation demands. This placement of total responsibility on the ex-spouse is in violation of the collaborative view of couple interaction as set forth in social exchange theory (Homans 1958, 1974, Thibaut and Kelly 1959). Divorce is considered to result when one or both spouses find the relative "costs" of the relationship to be greater than the relative "rewards" available in either this relationship or outside the relationship. Each partner contributes to the exchange and, hence, any action or decision in the relationship cannot be logically considered to be purely unilateral. Such action or decision may, however, be directly contrary to the wishes or expectations of one party. Blaming the ex-spouse for past and current problems prevents the client from: (1) acknowledging his contribution to past and current problems, (2) accepting self-responsibility to cope and adjust to the current situation, (3) effective problem-solving, and (4) change.

Irrational beliefs: "It is his fault that I am having all this trouble with these children." "I can't be a father because of her." "I have been depressed for two years because of him."

I Need Another on Whom to Rely—Dependency

The strength of attachment to the ex-spouse may be so strong as to constitute a perceived "need" on the part of the client. Similar to the demand for love from the ex-spouse, the belief that one needs another on whom to rely for the satisfaction of practical and emotional demands is faulty. Such "needs" and dependency represent an erosion of the client's sense of self (lack of self-confidence, self-reliance) and prevent the client from developing and exercising mastery over his or her world.

It is highly likely that the client has not functioned totally dependently on the ex-spouse. Identification of long-standing skills of self-reliance and newly developed abilities to meet personal, interpersonal, and environmental demands may serve to begin restructuring the client's stance of extreme dependency. Graduated assignments promoting acts of independence may further enhance the client's recognition of the potential for greater independence.

Irrational beliefs: "I *need* another (ex-spouse) in my life to help me." "I am too insecure to make it alone." "I can't make decisions alone."

My Ex-spouse Deserves Punishment

The ex-spouse is often considered to be a villainous character with despicable qualities—one who has created disagreeable, offensive, and unhealthy attributes in the client. The ex-spouse is considered to deserve punishment for his or her unsavory behavior and "indelible" negative influence on the client. The client may be preoccupied with punishing thoughts and wishes or may actually be strategizing or implementing the administration of consequences hurtful to the ex-mate. Similar to placing responsibility for one's own emotions and problems on the ex-mate, the client holds the former spouse accountable for feelings of distrust, hate, coldness, vindictiveness, and the like. The negative ideation focused on the punishment of the former spouse typically has concomitant negative emotions—anger, resentment, hate. This preoccupation prevents the client from healthy, positive recovery efforts. The therapist should guide the client in shifting attention from the counterproductive irrational thoughts related to the ex-spouse to his or her own current goals, potential joys in life, and so forth.

Irrational beliefs: "He taught me how to hate." "I was kind and sweet before him (her)." "I'll never be able to trust again; she (he) took that with her (him)."

I Can't Change—This Is the Way I Am

While divorce presents an opportunity for pervasive change, many individuals consider themselves highly unchangeable. Beliefs, emotions, and behavior typical of the client's past functioning are considered to be all-important determiners of present behavior. Such committed intractability violates the learning potential in us all. The therapist is challenged to guide the client in the realization that change is a possibility, although not without commitment, hard work, and sustained effort. In uncovering the client's beliefs in his or her unchangeability, the therapist should also seek the identification of extraneous controlling variables that reinforce the client's beliefs and behaviors. The use of cognitive restructuring methods along with the assignment and completion of easily achievable tasks that invalidate the client's views, removal of environmental reinforcers, and strategic therapist encouragement and reinforcement can be expected to alter the client's view that he or she is unchangeable.

Irrational beliefs: "I'm shy and always will be." "I have always had a problem with anger, depression, worry." "I'm a failure—all divorced people are losers."

Even though a given belief is irrational, a client (or therapist, for that matter) may strongly believe it and suffer the concomitant emotional distress. It is the responsibility of the therapist, through the use of the Socratic method, to guide the client to: (1) a commitment to altering the belief on the basis that it is a destructive belief to hold, (2) test out the validity of the belief by looking for logical evidence to support or negate it, and (3) allow the strength of the belief to erode on the basis of the evidence—to repeatedly rate and rerate the *degree* to which the belief is held with an expectation of reduced commitment to the thought.

The following excerpt illustrates the initial application of cognitive restructuring methods to a client who irrationally believes that she will never be happy again without the love of Fred, her ex-husband.

Therapist: How do you feel when you think the thought that you'll never be happy without Fred's love?

Client: I feel terrible. . .sad, and I guess depressed.

Therapist: How do you act when you feel sad and depressed?

Client: I get tearful and I don't feel like doing anything.

Therapist: Do you do anything?

Client: No, not really. I just sit around the house. . .maybe talk on the phone, but I don't enjoy it.

Therapist: So that I make sure that I understand clearly, you feel sad and depressed when you think of not having Fred's love, and you cry and become inactive. And we could, perhaps, say that you don't enjoy what you might have enjoyed before—talking on the telephone.

Client: That's right.

Therapist: Do you *like* feeling and acting this way?

Client: Of course not.

Therapist: Of course not, I agree. That's good thinking—but not liking something and *doing* something about it are two different things. Do you *want* to change the way you feel and act?

Client: Certainly, that's why I'm here!

Therapist: And I'm pleased that you are here and that you want to change. You'll recall from our earlier discussions that I indicated that feelings come from thoughts or beliefs we hold. In this case, suppose we speculate together and say that the belief that you can't be happy without Fred's love is behind your sadness and depression.

Client: Okay.

Therapist: Now let's look for the evidence to support that view. Were you constantly unhappy before you met Fred?

Client: No, of course not. I've really been happy most of my life—until now.

Therapist: So you *have* been happy without Fred in your life. On the basis of that knowledge can you logically say that it is *impossible* to be happy without Fred's love?

Client: No, I guess I really can't—but I feel that way.

Therapist: I am certain that you do feel that way. But you see, your feelings in this situation appear to be based on a faulty belief—that you need Fred's love to be happy. Taking this one piece of evidence—that you have been happy before Fred—would it logically follow that you can once again be happy—without him?

Client: Yes, it would make sense all right.

Therapist: How would you revise your belief on the basis of this new evidence?

Client: I guess I'd say that it's possible to be happy again—without Fred—but it won't be easy.

Therapist: So the earlier belief you stated: "I'll never be happy without Fred's love," is really a false belief. You have revised it on the basis of logical evidence to, "It's possible to be happy again." How do you feel about this belief?

Client: At least there's some hope. But I still miss Fred.

Therapist: Do you feel as sad and depressed as before thinking this new thought, that you may become happy again in time?

Client: No, I don't think so, but it's hard to tell.

In this manner the client learns:

1. To judge her feelings and corresponding actions as unlikable (her personal value judgment).

2. To initially apply the view that feelings are the product of beliefs.
3. To practice testing out the validity of her belief.
4. To revise her original belief on the basis of logical evidence.
5. To achieve a preliminary change in feelings, including a slight reduction in sadness and depression and the important addition of hope. The client is cautioned that feelings are far slower to change than are thoughts, ideas, or beliefs. She is encouraged to be tolerant and sensitive to gradations in emotional change.

To avoid the untimely application of cognitive restructuring methods to postdivorce adjustment, the therapist must be sensitive to the adaptive aspects of negative emotion. It is incumbent upon the therapist to recognize the "normal" expression of human emotion and the process of recovery in which a fluctuation in mood is healthy, transitional, and adaptive. Cognitive restructuring is to be applied when negative emotions are considered abnormal on the basis of level of discomfort (frequency, intensity, and duration), interruption in the individual's active, adaptive participation in human interaction and mastery activities, and development of psychosomatic disorders with an emotional etiology.

OTHER COGNITIVE METHODS

Cognitive therapy techniques additional to those suggested may also be useful in modifying superficial cognitive processes and identifying belief systems. Meichenbaum's (1977) self-instruction training and stress-inoculation training; covert modeling, positive imagery, and other covert conditioning procedures (Cautela 1971, Mahoney 1974); systematic desensitization (Wolpe 1958); thought stopping (Wolpe 1958, 1969, Wolpe and Lazarus 1966); and problem solving (D'Zurilla 1988; D'Zurilla and Goldfried 1971) are procedures that have varying facility in helping people change beliefs, self-efficacy, emotion, and behavior.

BEHAVIORAL METHODS

An array of behavioral methods may be used in the treatment of postdivorce recovery problems. Stress management methods, including deep muscle relaxation, biofeedback, planned unstructured (leisure) time, and aerobic and "low demand" activities, are appropriate

at high stress periods and, ultimately, routinely. Behavioral problems may be addressed through:

1. Problem specification in which antecedent and reinforcing consequences are identified and modified
2. Skill training using therapist modeling, behavior rehearsal,
   graduated skill acquisition (shaping) and in-vivo assignments
3. Measurement and self-monitoring methods
4. Contingency contracting procedures
5. Increase in behavior competitive with targeted problem behaviors.

Where deficiencies in problem-solving abilities exist, the client may
benefit from problem-solving training (PST), a cognitive-affective-
behavioral process designed to promote coping and adaptation. Both
cognitive and behavioral methods are combined to identify, discover,
or invent effective or adaptive ways to cope with the demands of every-
day life (D'Zurilla 1988).

CONCLUSION

Cognitive-behavioral methods have been effectively applied to many
populations and problems. This chapter has focused on applications
to postdivorce adjustment problems. The limits of knowledge in the
treatment of postdivorce adjustment are most evident. The clinician
continues to be confronted with the demand to determine the unique
meaning of the divorcing client's pain and maladjustment and, further, to mobilize treatment strategies to effect healthy change. Gaining access to the private, inner meanings and processes of the
postdivorce experience is a first step. The therapist is then challenged
to select a clinically efficacious approach, to provide the treatment,
and to evaluate the application to the client's problems. Knowledge
and skill development in postdivorce treatment are dependent on this
process.

REFERENCES

Arnkoff, D. B. (1980). Psychotherapy from the perspective of cognitive theory. In *Psychotherapy Process*, ed. M. J. Mahoney. pp. 339–361 New York: Plenum.

Baker, L. (1981). The transition to divorce: discrepancies between husbands and wives. Unpublished doctoral dissertation, Purdue University.

Bandura, A. (1977). Self-efficacy: toward a unifying theory of behavior change. *Psychological Review* 84:191–215.

——— (1978a). Reflections on self-efficacy. In *Advances In Behaviour Research and Therapy*, vol. 1, ed. S. Rachman. London: Pergamon Press.

——— (1978b). The self system in reciprocal determinism. *American Psychologist* 33:344–358.

Beck, A. T. (1976). *Cognitive Therapy and the Emotional Disorders.* New York: International Universities Press.

Beck, A. T., Rush A. J., Shaw, B. F., and Emery, G. (1979). *Cognitive Therapy of Depression.* New York: Guilford.

Bould, S. (1977). Female-headed families: personal fate control and the provider role. *Journal of Marriage and the Family* 39:339–349.

Broder, M. S. (1985). Divorce and separation. In *Clinical Applications of Rational-Emotive Therapy*, ed. A. Ellis and M. E. Bernard, pp. 81–99. New York: Plenum.

Buehler, C., and Langenbrunner, M. (1987). Divorce-related stressors: occurrence, disruptiveness, and area of life change. *Journal of Divorce* 11: 25–50.

Cautela, J. R. (1971). Covert modeling. Paper presented to the Association for the Advancement of Behavior Therapy, Washington, DC.

Chiriboga, D. A., and Cutler L. (1977). Stress responses among divorcing men and women. *Journal of Divorce* 1:95–106.

Corcoran, K., and Fischer, J. (1987). *Measures For Clinical Practice: A Sourcebook.* New York: The Free Press.

Crosby, J. F., Gage, B. A., and Raymond, M. C. (1983). The grief resolution process in divorce. *Journal of Divorce* 7:3–18.

D'Zurilla, T. J. (1988). Problem-solving therapies. In *Handbook of Cognitive-Behavioral Therapies*, ed. K. S. Dobson, pp. 85–135. New York: Guilford.

D'Zurilla, T. J., and Goldfried, M. R. (1971). Problem solving and behavior modification. *Journal of Abnormal Psychology* 78:107–126.

Ellis, A. (1962). *Reason and Emotion in Psychotherapy.* New York: Lyle Stuart.

——— (1971). *Growth Through Reason: Verbatim Cases in Rational-Emotive Therapy.* Palo Alto, CA: Science and Behavior Books.

——— (1973). *Humanistic Psychotherapy.* New York: McGraw-Hill.

——— (1977). The basic clinical theory of rational-emotive therapy. In *Hand-*

book of Rational-Emotive Therapy, ed. A. Ellis and R. Grieger, pp. 3–34. New York: Springer.

—— (1985). Overcoming Resistance: Rational-Emotive Therapy With Difficult Clients. New York: Springer.

—— (1986). Application of rational-emotive therapy to love problems. In Handbook of Rational-Emotive Therapy, vol. 2, ed. A. Ellis and R. Grieger, pp. 162–182. New York: Springer.

Ellis, A., and Bernard, M. E. (1986). What is rational-emotive therapy (RET)? In Handbook of Rational-Emotive Therapy, vol. 2, ed. A. Ellis and R. Grieger, pp. 3–30. New York: Springer.

Epstein, N. (1982). Cognitive therapy with couples. The American Journal of Family Therapy 10:5–16.

Frank, J. D. (1961). Persuasion and Healing. Baltimore: Johns Hopkins Press.

Freeman, A. (1983). Cognitive therapy: an overview. In Cognitive Therapy with Couples and Groups., ed. A. Freeman, pp. 1–9. New York: Plenum.

Gottman, J. M. (1979). Marital Interaction. New York: Academic Press.

Graff, R. W., Whitehead, G. I., and Le Compte, M. (1986). Group treatment with divorced women using cognitive-behavioral and supportive-insight methods. Journal of Counseling Psychology 33:276–281.

Granvold, D. K. (1983). Structured separation for marital treatment and decision-making. Journal of Marital and Family Therapy 9:403–412.

Granvold, D. K., Pedler, L. M., and Schellie, S. G. (1979). A study of sex role expectancy and female postdivorce adjustment. Journal of Divorce 2: 383–393.

Granvold, D. K., and Welch, G. J. (1977). Intervention for postdivorce adjustment problems: the treatment seminar. Journal of Divorce 1:81–92.

—— (1979). Structured, short-term group treatment of postdivorce adjustment. International Journal of Group Psychotherapy 29:347–358.

Guidano, V. F. (1987). Complexity of Self. New York: Guilford.

—— (1988). A systems, process-oriented approach to cognitive therapy. In Handbook of Cognitive-Behavioral Therapies, ed. K. S. Dobson, pp. 307–354. New York: Guilford.

Guidano, V. F., and Liotti, G. (1983). Cognitive Processes and Emotional Disorders: A Structural Approach to Psychotherapy. New York: Guilford.

Haley, J. (1976). Problem-solving Therapy: New Strategies for Effective Family Therapy. San Francisco: Jossey-Bass.

Holmes, T. H., and Rahe, R. H. (1967). Social readjustment rating scale. Journal of Psychosomatic Research 11:213–218.

Homans, G. C. (1958). Social behavior as exchange. American Journal of Sociology 62:597–606.

—— (1974). Social Behavior: Its Elementary Forms. New York: Harcourt, Brace & Jovanovich.

Huber, C. H. (1983). Feelings of loss in response to divorce: assessment and intervention. Personnel and Guidance Journal 61:357–361.

Hurvitz, N. (1975). Interaction hypotheses in marriage counseling. In Cou-

ples in Conflict, ed. A. S. Gurman and D. G. Rice, pp. 225–240. New York: Jason Aronson.

Jacobson, N. S., and Margolin, G. (1979). *Marital Therapy: Strategies Based on Social Learning and Behavior Exchange Principles.* New York: Brunner/Mazel.

Johnson, S. M. (1977). *First Person Singular: Living the Good Life Alone.* New York: Signet.

Kelly, G. (1955). *The Psychology of Personal Constructs.* Vols. 1 and 2. New York: W. W. Norton.

Mahoney, M. J. (1974). *Cognition and Behavior Modification.* Cambridge, MA: Ballinger.

———— (1980). Psychotherapy and the structure of personal revolutions. In *Psychotherapy Process*, ed. M. J. Mahoney, pp. 157–180. New York: Plenum.

Maier, S. F., and Seligman, M. E. (1976). Learned helplessness: theory and evidence. *Journal of Experimental Psychology* 105:3–46.

Meichenbaum, D. (1977). *Cognitive-behavior Modification.* New York: Plenum.

Pais, J. S. (1978). Social-psychological predictions of adjustment for divorced mothers. Unpublished doctoral dissertation, University of Tennessee, Knoxville.

Rice, D. G. (1977). Psychotherapeutic treatment of narcissistic injury in marital separation and divorce. *Journal of Divorce* 1:119–128.

Rice, J. K., and Rice, D. G. (1986a). *Living Through Divorce: A Developmental Approach in Divorce Therapy.* New York: Guilford.

Rice, D. G., and Rice, J. K. (1986b). Separation and divorce therapy. In *Clinical Handbook of Marital Therapy*, ed. N. S. Jacobson and A. S. Gurman, pp. 279–299. New York: Guilford.

Rotter, J. B. (1966). Generalized expectancies for internal versus external control of reinforcement. *Psychological Monographs* 80:1, Whole No. 609.

Sager, C. J. (1976). *Marriage Contracts and Couple Therapy: Hidden Forces in Intimate Relationships.* New York: Brunner/Mazel.

Scanzoni, J. (1972). *Sexual Bargaining.* Englewood Cliffs, NJ: Prentice-Hall.

Seligman, M. E. P. (1975). *Helplessness: On Depression, Development and Death.* San Francisco: Freeman.

Spanier, G. B., and Casto, R. F. (1979). Adjustment to separation and divorce: an analysis of 50 case studies. *Journal of Divorce* 2:241–253.

Spanier, G. B., and Hanson, S. (1982). The role of extended kin in the adjustment to marital separation. *Journal of Divorce* 5:33–48.

Spanier, G. B., and Thompson, L. (1983). Relief and distress after marital separation. *Journal of Divorce* 7:31–49.

———— (1984). *Parting: The Aftermath of Separation and Divorce.* Beverly Hills: Sage.

Sprenkle, D. H. (1985). *Divorce Therapy.* New York: Haworth.

Sutton, P. M., and Sprenkle, D. H. (1985). Criteria for a constructive divorce: theory and research to guide the practitioner. In *Divorce Therapy*, ed. D. H. Sprenkle. New York: Haworth.

Thibaut, J. W., and Kelly, H. H. (1959). *The Social Psychology of Groups*. New York: Wiley.

Walen, S. R., and Bass, B. A. (1986). Rational divorce counseling. *Journal of Rational-Emotive Therapy* 4:95–109.

Walen, S. R., Giuseppe, R., and Wessler, R. L. (1980). *A Practitioner's Guide to Rational-Emotive Therapy*. New York: Oxford University Press.

Wallerstein, J. S., and Kelly, J. B. (1980). *Surviving the Breakup: How Children and Parents Cope with Divorce*. New York: Basic Books.

Weiss, R. L. (1984). Cognitive and strategic interventions in behavioral marital therapy. In *Marital Interaction: Analysis and Modification*, ed. K. Hahlweg and N. S. Jacobson, pp. 337–355. New York: Guilford.

Weiss, R. S. (1975). *Marital Separation*. New York: Basic Books.

White, J. J. (1985). The effect of locus of control on post-divorce adjustment. Unpublished master's thesis, University of Texas at Arlington.

Wolpe, J. (1958). *Psychotherapy by Reciprocal Inhibition*. Stanford: Stanford University Press.

—— (1969). *The Practice of Behavior Therapy*. New York: Pergamon.

Wolpe, J., and Lazarus, A. A. (1966). *Behavior Therapy Techniques*. New York: Pergamon Press.

Womack, C. D. (1987). The effects of locus of control and lawyer satisfaction on adjustment to divorce. Unpublished master's thesis, University of Texas at Arlington.

11

PSYCHOTHERAPY WITH CHILDREN OF DIVORCED FAMILIES

Carol Rotter Lowery, Ph.D.

Children in the aftermath of divorce have been a focus of clinical theory and intervention for over a decade (Gardner 1976, Tessman 1978). Much of the early work dealt primarily with individual therapy for the child and collateral contact with the custodial parent. These early works quite accurately identified the emotional issues for the child: denial, sadness, anger, blame, fear of abandonment, obstacles in psychosexual development. The process of therapy was construed primarily as the therapist's helping the child work through the various negative emotional states that often accompanied the process of divorce or states in which the child had become "stuck" subsequent to the divorce. Some attention was paid to the role and behavior of the parents, but the divorce was treated as a hazardous event that some children had not negotiated very well and consequently needed help in their recovery.

Another line of clinical literature has focused on the benefits of group therapy for children, largely in an education and prevention mode (Cantor 1977, Kalter et al. 1984, Pedro-Carroll and Cowen 1985, Rossiter 1988). Often the setting described was in the school, with the notion that putting a child with peers going through or recently having gone through similar experiences would reduce the sense of isolation and stigma, as well as provide the child with practical tips for handling awkward and novel situations that were likely to arise. A variety of educational materials, including game formats and films, have been developed for use in this area of intervention.

More recent theory has focused on divorce as a relatively long-term process beginning long before any papers are filed in the court (Weiss 1975) and often bringing with it a multitude of changes that put the child at risk for cumulative stress, a change in school or day care, a change in peer group, a decrease in financial resources, restructuring of immediate and extended family relationships. Approaching divorce from a family systems perspective, the process calls for a dramatic restructuring of the relationships in the immediate family, producing what Ahrons and Rodgers (1987) refer to as a binuclear family. This conceptual mode probably best captures the perspective and issues of children caught up in the dissolution of their parents' marriage.

Psychotherapy with children from divorced families needs to begin with a careful assessment of the role that living in a nonnuclear family structure plays in the development of the presenting problem. It is important to keep in mind that many children do not seem to develop any significant psychological, social, or academic symptoms during or after a divorce (Hess and Camara 1979, Raschke and Raschke 1979, Santrock 1975, Santrock and Warshak, 1979). This is not to say that the divorce has not been stressful for these children; it clearly has. But similar to many adults, they manage to cope with the stress and function effectively for all practical purposes. Such a child may develop other kinds of problems that do not seem to be the result of, or aggravated by, the circumstances of divorce.

> Edward had been struggling with an undetected learning disability since the first grade. Mom and Dad had divorced at that time, but with a minimum of acrimony and a commitment to cooperate on issues affecting their son's welfare. A careful look at Edward's school records, consultation with his teachers, and a comprehensive intellectual evaluation revealed evidence of a language-based learning disability. Appropriate school placement with remedial resources for the following year and consultation with Edward and his parents about the nature of his disability seemed to clear up his academic and behavior problems at school without further intervention.

It is important to communicate to parents and children that a divorce does not necessarily mean that the children are "damaged" or that they have to enter the world beyond their families with some handicap that must be overcome. Social science has historically done families a serious disservice by decrying the inevitable deleterious impact of divorce on children, when more careful research clearly indicates that this simply is not the case (Kurdek 1981, Kurdek and Sinclair in press a, b). As clinicians, it is important not to perpetuate the myth of inevitable damage. A divorce, well handled, does not seem to affect the subsequent development of children.

Obviously, the key here is the phrase, "well handled." When parents are able to bring their marital relationship to an end without excessive conflict, without putting the children in the middle of whatever conflicts exist, and with a commitment to cooperate on issues of the children's material, physical, educational, and emotional welfare, children seem to fare reasonably well in a divorce. This is an ideal standard that most parents meet only partially. An assessment of how far parents have deviated from this standard is usually a useful index of the extent to which a child's problems are related to unresolved issues from the divorce or are likely due to other factors.

Once it has been determined that the divorce was not well handled in some manner, a range of factors needs to be considered in trying to determine the best course of treatment. It is essential that the therapist remember that, from the child's point of view, there is no such thing as a single-parent family. Studies have documented in interviews and drawings that the noncustodial or nonresidential parent is very much a part of the child's sense of family, even years after a divorce and even when there has been minimal contact with the nonresident parent (Isaacs and Levin 1984, Lawton and Seechrest 1962). When there continues to be blatant hostility between the parents, it may not be advisable to include the nonresident parent in a conjoint interview, but contact with that parent is essential, whether by phone, letter, or separate interview.

WITHDRAWAL OF THE NONCUSTODIAL PARENT

A frequent issue for children, documented in the literature on child support and visitation (Berkman 1986, Hetherington et al. 1976, Koch and Lowery 1984, Wallerstein and Kelly 1980), is the withdrawal and disengagement of the nonresident parent from their lives, with consequent depression and low self-esteem or anger and acting out. Contact with the nonresident parent is virtually always useful in evaluating the feasibility of reconnecting that parent with the child as a goal for treatment and the changes that might need to occur for that to happen constructively. The contact is also often helpful in maintaining a balanced clinical perspective, given that the clinician is usually in closer contact with and relying on the report of the custodial parent.

A major factor in the disengagement of the nonresident parent is often the quality of the relationship between the parents postdivorce (Koch and Lowery 1984, Lowery and Settle 1985). When the child's problem behavior seems to stem from the lack of involvement of the nonresident parent, often the most effective course of therapy is working with the parents to establish a working relationship that allows them to cooperate more effectively around issues of visitation and child rearing. I have heard more than one noncustodial father say that as open conflict with his ex-wife continued to occur at the times of visitation, he became concerned that the arguing did more harm to the child than the visitation did good and consequently he stopped visiting. Although the accuracy of this line of reasoning may be open to question, its occurrence appears to be part of the reality of many noncustodial parents. Therapeutic intervention to help settle some of the issues or at least to get a commitment to some modifications of the structure of visitation, such as arranging for the noncustodial parent to pick up the child after school on Friday and return the child to school on Monday morning, often alleviates a major source of stress for the child. In one case, Timothy seemed to be quite angry about his father's gradual but obvious withdrawal from his life and seemed to be taking it out on peers, with chronic fights and altercations at school, and on his mother, with irritability and noncompliance at home. Efforts in sessions to resolve issues from the marriage and its ending didn't seem very productive; however, both parents could see the damage their quarreling was doing when it occurred in front of Tim when he was being picked up for or dropped off after visitation. Both agreed for visitation to begin with transportation from and to school. Although the adults continued to quarrel by phone fairly often, the change seemed to relieve Timothy of his burden of guilt about his visitation being the occasion for their quarrels and to reverse the trend of his father's withdrawal, that reversal apparently having a major impact in restoring Timothy's self-esteem.

THE CHILD'S DESIRE TO LIVE
WITH THE OTHER PARENT

Another common issue, usually some period after the divorce, is a child's normal curiosity about what it would be like to live with the other parent. In some instances, the child's desire takes the form of an unrealistic fantasy of how most of life's problems would disappear if only he or she lived with the other parent. And it is not unusual for this fantasy to become expressed as chronic blaming of and acting out against the custodial parent, especially if the dynamics are such that it is obvious that a simple request to go to live with the other parent would not be well received or discussed reasonably. I have seen more than one family where the child's subconscious (or conscious) strategy was to make the custodial parent so miserable that the parent would relent and let the child go. When this seems to be the scenario, it is obviously an extremely helpful intervention if the clinician can help clear away the camouflage of complaints and countercomplaints so that the child and parents can negotiate the real issue. If the child is to live for a period of time with the other parent, it is much more beneficial to all parties if this can be done in a cooperative and planful way. If the rationale for a change of custody is left on the basis of "Go live with your father and see if he can straighten you out," the chances of an extended game of Ping-Pong, with the child bouncing back and forth between the two households until the age of majority, is greatly increased. It is not so unusual for a child to change households after a divorce (Ihinger-Tallman 1985, Pasley 1988); the circumstances under which it occurs are critical.

Although at present this is only a clinical impression, it is my opinion that the child's desire to live with the other parent, at least for a while, is often not a condemnation of the custodial parent. Quite the opposite—particularly when the child can verbalize the desire to change households—his or her very request is a statement of the confidence and security of the custodial parent-child relationship. Often children are left with the fear of losing the custodial parent, once they have experienced the quasi-loss of the noncustodial parent. The occurrence of conflict and strain over living with the other parent is often testimony that children have recovered from that fear of loss and accept that the custodial parent is committed in their relationship with them. It is often helpful clinically to help the custodial parent understand this, in facilitating that parent's keeping an open mind in negotiating change. Ironically, the child is often in a painful relationship dilemma: he or she is sure of the custodial parent's commitment whether they live together or not, but feels the only way to have a meaningful relationship with the noncustodial parent is to live with him or her. Whenever there is some question of the noncustodial parent's commitment to the child, it is probably prudent to try to arrange things on a trial basis, where the child can return if things don't work out, with a minimum of legal and interpersonal conflict.

It should be noted that there are some cases where both custodial and noncustodial households are so chaotic and plagued with problems that the child may Ping-Pong back and forth in desperation, discovering that neither parent is able to offer much in the area of a stable and responsible commitment. Such was the case for Anthony. When problems related to his father's drinking reached a certain threshold, Anthony would flee across town and show up on his mother's doorstep. She would take him in, but her unemployment, the financial pressure on her, and chronic depression would eventually send him back to his father's home to see if things had improved over there. For Anthony, the availability of a stable relationship with a therapist seemed to be a lifeline that facilitated his connecting with other resource adults and pursuing meaningful goals for himself in spite of the lack of support in either household.

PARENTAL PARTICIPATION IN CHILD'S THERAPY

For the two issues discussed so far (withdrawal of the noncustodial parent, the child's desire to live with the other parent), the availability of the nonresident parent is very important. That parent's participation enables the resolution of the issues on a more realistic basis. When that parent does not agree to participate in the process of therapy, the clinician is faced with dealing with a "ghost." The prognosis generally is not as good if both parents do not participate. A more connected and cooperative reality seems to be more effective in facilitating a child's development than any coping methods for a deficient reality that may be constructed in therapy.

When the noncustodial parent has in fact withdrawn his or her emotional investment in the child, a combination of individual sessions with the child and joint sessions with the child and custodial parent (perhaps also with siblings) and individual sessions with the custodial parent usually are in order. Often the child has issues of guilt, self-blame, anger, and depression related to the loss of the relationship that often need to be dealt with separately with the therapist or in a group with other children from divorced families (Bankowski et al. 1985, Waldron et al. 1986). If the child could sort out these feelings by talking to the custodial parent, he or she probably would not have come in for treatment. Often custodial parents' inability to resolve feelings from the divorce and negative perceptions of the ex-spouse make it impossible for them to offer their children a receptive and reflective ear. Individual sessions with custodial parents are often helpful to them in moving beyond impasses they have reached in their own divorce recovery process. Helping the custodial parent be more available and empathic to the needs of the child provides some protection against relapse as the child needs to process again issues relating to the divorce at later points in his or her development. The joint sessions help clear out old disputes and provide a safe place for parent and child to practice new ways of talking about old issues.

INDIVIDUAL THERAPY WITH CHILDREN

Although it is somewhat unusual, there are instances when neither parent is available emotionally to the process of therapy; that is, neither parent is able or willing to participate in the treatment in a meaningful way. As was the case for Anthony, individual or group therapy with the child, without meaningful involvement of other family members, is sometimes the only option available. For these children, dealing with the negative feelings from the divorce plus the ongoing sense of emotional abandonment is no small task. In most cases, some combination of physical absence and physical or emotional disability account for the unavailability of the parents. When parents are not motivated to deal more effectively wth the disability or to change the physical absence, the clinician has few options except to work only with the child.

In some few cases, parental "absence" is due to their ongoing commitment to engage in conflict, legal or otherwise, with their ex-spouse. This situation is probably the most damaging set of circumstances for the child. Not only is neither parent emotionally available because of the preoccupation with seeking revenge or justification vis-à-vis the other parent, but also the child is often subjected to repeated appearances with attorneys, court officials, and perhaps well-meaning mental health professionals. Even if litigated issues don't directly involve custody or visitation (and they often do), the child cannot help but be aware of the continuing high intensity of conflict between the parents. Kressel and colleagues (1980) estimate that about 10 percent of divorcing couples become invested in a lifetime of conflict with their ex-spouses. Among those who have children, the stress for the children is severe. Again, individual and group therapy for the child is usually all that the parents will accept in the way of intervention, and the prognosis, even with long-term therapy as a support for the child, is not good.

However, some important things can be accomplished in individual therapy as long as the therapist has a good sense of the history of the family and an accurate sense of the child's perception of that history. As mentioned previously, most children have had intense, negative feelings about the divorce, including anger, sadness, anxiety, and guilt. After the therapist has established rapport, the specific context for each of these feelings can be explored and resolved. Often it is important to help the child understand that these feelings are normal and that they don't go away; any of them may be reactivated at a later point as the child proceeds through normal developmental stages, and the divorce acquires new meanings as the child accumulates new experiences. Techniques for resolving these feelings usually vary, depending on the maturity of the child. Older adolescents often do quite well with verbal interventions, such as the "empty chair" process or writing letters (that may or may not be mailed) to significant people. Younger children are usually more comfortable with enactment techniques, such as drawing, working with doll figures or puppets, or telling stories in turn with the therapist, often with thinly veiled identities for the characters that provide the safety of third-person distance for troublesome feelings.

Children's Cognitions and Perceptions

In addition, the child's cognitions and perceptions also need to be explored. Children's natural egocentricity often contributes to major distortions of and faulty explanations of parents' and siblings' behavior. Particularly with very young children, it may not be possible to facilitate a sophisticated understanding of events around the divorce, since the complexities may simply be beyond the child's experience. But the process of introducing alternative explanations, scaled to the child's level of understanding, may itself be important in helping the child not to get locked into age-determined explanations that, if embraced with certainty and rigidity, may interfere with later integration of the events. The therapeutic task is often facilitating the child's comfort with uncertainty, so that a "childish" explanation of or set of beliefs about the divorce that oversimplify the circumstances are not so rigidly embraced that they interfere with later integration as the child becomes developmentally more mature and better able to understand what happened. This task is often complicated by influence, direct or indirect, from the belief system of the custodial parent. The therapist needs to be sensitive not to put the child at odds with the primary caretaker, or to contribute to an obstacle to contact with the noncustodial parent. Here the therapist is often most vulnerable to countertransference issues. It is important that I be aware of my own beliefs about marriage, divorce, and gender roles so that they do not interfere with my perception of the child and the history of the child's family. Techniques for sorting out the child's beliefs usually vary by age, and the same approaches for dealing with feelings are also useful here.

Matt was an 11-year-old boy who seemed to be struggling to deal with issues related to his parents' recent divorce. Dad was in the foreign service, with a temporary assignment overseas. Mom was quite clear in her choice not to participate in sessions. It was fine for me to work with Matt, but she was not about to discuss her own adjustment to or perceptions of the divorce, except in a very limited and guarded way. I worked with Matt for about six months. Together we read a couple of children's books about divorce, written for his age level. Reading about other children's experience of divorce seemed to free him to discuss his own feelings about what had happened, especially his anger at his father for being so completely unavailable at this time of crisis and his fear that his father would be lost to him forever. He was also able to identify a sense of not being a "good enough" son, for surely if he were, Dad would not have left the country so soon after the divorce. Mom was able to confirm that, in fact, Dad's decision to go was not without a great deal of struggle and distress on his part. In her view, he had rationalized that the assignment was temporary, that he would be back in "only" two years, and that accepting the assignment was essential to his career. The fact that he had not shared any of his soul-searching with his son and had presented Matt with the product—his decision to go—but not with the process had left Matt to wrestle and agonize with his 11-year-old point of view. Individual therapy with Matt seemed to help resolve some of his most painful feelings and provide a place to explore some alternative perceptions that probably fit the reality better and put the events in a less painful context. Matt still missed his father, but he no longer blamed himself for his father's absence.

DIVORCE-RELATED PROBLEMS
AFTER REMARRIAGE

Although intervention with remarried families will be discussed later in other chapters, there are a few areas in which it is helpful to sort out whether the major clinical issues are primarily related to the divorce rather than to the more complex structure resulting from one or both parents' remarriage. Two sets of circumstances present obvious examples in which the issues are more divorce related that stepfamily related: when a parent quickly remarries (within the first year of the divorce, often subsequent to outside involvement during the marriage) and when a parent marries a "defender," that is, a new spouse whose primary role is to protect and defend the parent from the ex-spouse.

Although I have not seen research-based estimates, a fair number of divorces occur in the context of an ongoing extramarital relationship involving one of the parties. (In some instances, both adults may be involved in intimate relationships outside the marriage). In many cases, the outside relationship begins to flounder after the divorce is final. Although the majority of adults under age 50 do remarry after a divorce, usually within three to five years (Glick 1957, Roberts and Price 1985), they usually do not marry the first person with whom they have a serious relationship. More typically each parent has a period of dating, which has its ups and downs, before they settle into another marriage. This seems to be the normal developmental pattern after a divorce. Exceptions to this pattern warrant somewhat closer attention, since they often have clinical relevance.

When one of the parents marries the partner to an affair that went on during the marriage, it usually seems to precipitate some special issues for the children. It is often difficult for children to accept a stepparent under any circumstances. The history of how a person becomes a stepparent often creates a pull for distance in the relationships with the children; children often need time to work out issues of conflicting loyalties to the biological parent, as well as issues around the authority and commitment this new adult has toward them. When the stepparent was involved with a parent prior to the divorce, these issues are intensified, and an additional issue of morality or integrity is often raised. If the child is too young at the time of the remarriage to be aware of the moral or ethical issues of an extramarital relationship, these issues will likely emerge when the child is older, as the history of the family remains very much alive. School-age children often need someone to blame in a divorce, and this type of stepparent is an obvious target. It becomes easy to forget the conflict and tensions between the parents that may have been more accurately the source of the divorce when it is simpler to blame the new spouse: "If she hadn't been around, none of this would have happened," when in fact the divorce very likely would have happened anyway.

I listened to Margaret plan and plot gleeful revenge against her new stepmother for several sessions, everything from simple pranks like hiding her car keys to malicious efforts to sabotage friendships and relationships in the extended family. Margaret seemed to have no remorse and felt justified, given "all this woman had done" to her. In the meantime, the stepmother could not understand Margaret's aloofness and lack of response to her overtures of outings, clothes, and favorite foods. Only when Margaret was able to voice her pain and fear of the last year of the marriage, as she watched her parents angrily pushing each other away, was she able to begin to perceive her stepmother as a person rather than as an ogre who had intruded into and destroyed her family. Fortunately the stepmother was a reasonably sensitive person and was able to perceive more accurately Margaret's point of view; she backed off on her overtures to give Margaret more space and time to work out her feelings. Although Margaret was never totally able to give up her resentment, she and her stepmother were able to work out a smoother relationship that they both could accept. One important key was the biological mother's ability to give up her role as the aggrieved and innocent party in the divorce and establish a satisfying life for herself after the divorce. Although the mother continued to harbor a thinly veiled contempt for the stepmother, as the mother lost interest in the latest word of how poorly things were going for the father in his new marriage, Margaret was able to drop her role as informant with an eye for every weakness and failure of her father's new spouse. Her father was able to back off from trying to convince Margaret that his new spouse was as good as, if not better than, his old one. Not all situations improve in this fashion. All three adults were able to make changes that benefited Margaret.

In the case of Shawn, no one had told him that his father had been involved with Amy, his stepmother, for at least three years before his parents divorced. Shawn had been four years old at the time of the divorce, and his father had been fairly discreet in having the affair. At age 11, a trip to visit maternal grandparents had been disastrous. His grandmother had alluded to the affair and when Shawn inquired, had filled him in on the details as she knew them. Shawn returned from the trip a changed boy. His grades dropped; he became sullen and irritable on visits with his father and Amy, and he totally dropped a series of activities he had come to enjoy and share with his stepmother. Although his mother and Amy were not on the best of terms, all three adults were able to agree that something was wrong and that some professional consultation might be helpful. A couple of awkward and tense sessions with the adults fairly quickly revealed the "secret" they had all agreed to keep. With some encouragement and direction, his father agreed to talk to Shawn about what happened, with an understanding that his mother would give her side of the story after his father took the initiative. Only then did the story, and the feelings, of his grand-mother's revelation come pouring out. The fact that both parents were willing to present their versions as just that, different sides of the story, without an exclusive claim to what "really" happened, greatly helped Shawn in coming to terms with this new version of how the divorce had occurred. He was able to reestablish what had been a relatively close and important relationship with Amy.

The case of Angie did not have such a fortunate outcome. Coopera-tion in the treatment by all of the adults is often crucial. Angie had pretty well figured out that Catherine was more than the book-keeper for her father's plumbing supply business. Even during the marriage, her father had taken Angie along at times when he "had" to go to Catherine's house to drop off receipts or consult about tax preparation. At age 9, she had noticed that these occasions of stop-ping by at Catherine's turned into fairly lengthy visits, during which she was often ushered into another room to watch cartoon videos or encouraged to play the Atari. Although she had no recollec-tion of their disappearing into the bedroom together, their conver-sations were obviously warm and emotional and certainly not strictly business. She was not very surprised when her father an-nounced his intention to marry Catherine within weeks of the di-vorce. Her mother, however, was surprised and furious. There soon followed a series of four or five phone calls in which her mother let Catherine know exactly what she thought of her. An unlisted phone number put a stop to the calls, and three months later the mother sent Catherine a letter, apologizing for her behavior. Cather-ine never responded. When Angie somewhat suddenly became in-volved in a negative peer group and started skipping school, her mother sought conseling in the hope of avoiding the juvenile court system. Both parents were willing to participate in sessions. When invited, Catherine refused to come under any circumstances on the ground that she wasn't "going to have anything to do with that woman." The father's participation was less than whole-hearted, given that he felt he put his second marriage at risk every time he came for a session. He reported that Catherine questioned him at length after each session, more with an ear for what had been said about her rather than for what steps would be helpful to Angie. The parents' decision to enroll Angie in a different school, with Angie participating in the selection of the school, seemed to help the peer influence problem. Some individual sessions with the mother, whose suspicions of Catherine's character had been reactivated by her refusal to participate, seemed to help her accept her lack of control in the situation and to keep a more open mind about a woman she knew little about. However, I had reservations that these were, at best, stopgap measures and that I might well hear from the family again in a couple of years.

The Role of the New Spouse

Probably the most difficult challenge is presented by the family in which one or both parents have quickly remarried and have selected a partner who is equally or even more angry at the ex-spouse than the parent is. Again, here the issues often have more to do with the divorce than with the more typical kinds of issues that arise in the more complex structure of forming a stepfamily.

The case of Joey was one of the more striking examples of this divorce-related problem I have seen. The court had requested a consultation on resolving some disagreements that had arisen over Joey's visitation with his father. The history revealed a period of about four years since the divorce that witnessed a series of restraining orders, counterrestraining orders, changed phone numbers, motions to deny out-of-state trips, allegations and counterallegations of abuse and neglect, subpoenas to neighbors to testify regarding a variety of parental misconduct.

The session with the parents revealed a father who was somewhat quiet and inhibited and a mother who was somewhat more assertive but modest in her concerns and also somewhat restrained in her expression of emotion. The sessions with each parent with their new spouses gave a totally different picture. The father had remarried within six months of the separation; the mother had remarried within eight. The original divorce had moved through the courts quite rapidly, within three months of the separation, since the parties had disagreed about very little in the final settlement. In fact, it was somewhat difficult to pin down the reasons for their separating in the first place.

The father had married a woman whose brother was a state trooper; his new wife seemed to feel that the solution to any misunderstanding or disagreement was to call up "the law" and its agents. The mother had discovered, to her embarrassment, that if she were 30 minutes late dropping Joey off for visitation, she might well find a trooper in her driveway offering to escort her to the father's house.

The mother's new husband was an outspoken, opinionated guy who had decided that his wife "didn't have to put up with this—." He had a well-established relationship with his attorney and was fond of filing complaints of harrassment and whatever other court action could be construed to fit the circumstances. A relatively wealthy man, the stepfather was also quite willing to foot the bill for these actions that he took to "protect" his wife. Joey seemed to have got quite lost in the process and seemed to feel (quite accurately) that none of the adults were paying much attention or putting much energy into what he wanted or needed. It was particularly difficult for him because his biological parents were obviously such "nice," mild-mannered people. He had no idea how this war had gotten started or why it continued. Therapy sessions with each of the couples produced some progress in both households in getting the stepparents to back off and allow the biological parent primary responsibility for decisions about Joey and about how to "handle" Joey's other parent. This effort was somewhat more successful with the mother and stepfather, as the latter began to channel his financial resources into other methods of showing his wife how much he loved her and wanted to make life easier for her. The stepmother had a great deal of difficulty in backing off since, in her view, women always knew more than men did about what was good for children. She finally did agree to consult with her brother, who joined us for a session, about whether a phone call to the state police (or other law enforcement agency) was appropriate under whatever circumstances arose. Fortunately, her brother had already been concerned about her repeated calls to involve the police and agreed to serve in this function. During the period of the sessions, the stepmother was never quite able to let go of her fear that her husband would abandon her and return to the mother of his son. Joey had been showing some minor and sporadic symptoms of stress—occasional nightmares, some nighttime enuresis, and fears of entering new situations. These cleared up as therapy progressed. He had a warm and sheltering haven at his paternal grandparents' that seemed to help him through his parents' battles. He was also a resilient kid who seemed to have a lot going for him; he was bright, attractive, and well liked by his peers.

Jeff was not so lucky. Although only one of Jeff's parents had recruited a "protector" after the divorce, she had done so in spades. About ten months after the divorce, his mother had married an attorney who practiced criminal law. Dan, her new husband, seemed to expect and suspect the worst of people on a routine basis and seemed to feel that "whatever the law will allow" was a good rule of thumb in interpersonal relationships. The picture was complicated by the fact that Dan acknowledged that he had never had much interest in children, never planned to have any of his own, and seemed very ill at ease with his new 10-year-old stepson. He seemed to tolerate Jeff as one might tolerate a room-mate's pet cat; Jeff was acceptable as an adjunct to his new wife.

Jeff's dad, a successful building contractor, seemed intimidated by Dan's professional status but determined not to be "defeated" in the legal arena. Just about everything that could be litigated had been. Dan acknowledged that he considered Jeff's dad a good father but maintained that his wife was entitled to every legal consideration available. Several sessions with the adults, in varying combinations, seemed to make little difference. Dan's lack of knowledge, compounded by his lack of interest in learning about children's needs, continued to be a substantial obstacle as he politely described his role as legal advisor to his wife. The mother was unable to be more assertive on Jeff's behalf and always acceded to her new husband's advice. Fairly long-term therapy would probably be necessary to untangle the father's history of not living up to his own father's expectations and his feelings about Jeff's stepfather. Jeff's behavior at school, along with his grades, continued to deteriorate. The family left therapy when Jeff began shoplifting and got involved with the juvenile court system. It was almost as though he had decided to give Dan something he could really sink his teeth into, to distract him from his efforts in domestic law.

CONCLUSION

To sum up, psychotherapy with children of divorce is not an easy matter. Careful assessment and history are necessary to determine the relative contribution of the divorce to the child's presenting distress. Once it has been determined that features of the divorce or its sequelae are major factors, eliciting the cooperation of the needed parties is often a difficult clinical task requiring judgment and diplomacy, but usually well worth the effort. Individual therapy with the child is often a necessary component of the treatment plan, but seldom the most efficient or effective part. Involvement of the significant adults in the child's life in the treatment is probably the best prognostic indicator.

REFERENCES

Ahrons, C. R., and Rodgers, R. H. (1987). *Divorced Families*. New York: W. W. Norton.

Berkman, B. G. (1986). Father involvement and regularity of child support in post-divorce families. *Journal of Divorce* 9:67–74.

Bonkowski, S. E., Boomhower, S. J., and Bequette, S. Q. (1985). What you don't know can hurt you: unexpressed fears and feelings of children from divorcing families. *Journal of Divorce* 9:33–45.

Cantor, D. (1977). School-based groups for children of divorce. *Journal of Divorce* 1:183–187.

Gardner, R. M. (1976). *Psychotherapy with Children of Divorce*. New York: Jason Aronson.

Glick, P. C. (1957). *American Families*. New York: Wiley.

Hess, R. D., and Camara, K. A. (1979). Post-divorce family relationships as mediating factors in the consequences of divorce for children. *Journal of Social Issues* 35:79–96.

Hetherington, E. M., Cox, M., and Cox, R. (1976). Divorced fathers. *The Family Coordinator* 25:417–428.

Ihinger-Tallman, M. (1985). Perspective on change of custody among step-siblings. Paper presented at the annual meeting of the National Council on Family Relations, Dallas, November.

Isaacs, M. B., and Levin, I. R. (1984). Who's in my family? A longitudinal study of drawings of children of divorce. *Journal of Divorce* 7:1–21.

Kalter, N., Pickar, J., and Lesowitz, M. (1984). School-based developmental facilitation of groups for children of divorce: a preventive intervention. *American Journal of Orthopsychiatry* 54:613–623.

Koch, M. A., and Lowery, C. R. (1984). Visitation and the noncustodial father. *Journal of Divorce* 8:47–65.

Kressel, K., Jaffe, N., Tuchman, B., Watson, C., and Deutsch, M. (1980). A typology of divorcing couples: implications for mediation and the divorce process. *Family Process* 19:101–116.

Kurdek, L. A. (1981). An integrative perspective on children's divorce adjustment. *American Psychologist* 36:856–866.

Kurdek, L. A., and Sinclair, R. J. (in press a). The adjustment of young adolescents in two-parent nuclear, stepfather, and mother-custody families. *Journal of Consulting and Clinical Psychology*.

——— (in press b). The relation of eighth graders' family structure, gender, and family environment with academic performance and school behavior. *Journal of Education Psychology*.

Lawton, M., and Seechrest, L. (1962). Family drawings by young boys from father-present and father-absent homes. *Journal of Clinical Psychology* 18:304–305.

Lowery, C. R., and Settle, S. A. (1985). Effects of divorce on children: differential impact of custody and visitation patterns. *Family Relations* 34: 455–463.

Pasley, K. (1988). Contributing to a field of investigation. *Journal of Family Psychology* 1:452–456.

Pedro-Carroll, J., and Cowen, E. (1985). The children of divorce intervention project: an investigation of the efficacy of a school-based prevention program. *Journal of Consulting and Clinical Psychology* 53:603–611.

Raschke, H. J., and Raschke, V. J. (1979). Family conflict and children's self-concepts: a comparison of intact and single-parent families. *Journal of Marriage and the Family* 41:367–374.

Roberts, T. W., and Price, S. J. (1985). A systems analysis of the remarriage process: implications for the clinician. *Journal of Divorce* 9:1–25.

Rossiter, A. B. (1988). A model for group intervention with preschool children experiencing separation and divorce. *American Journal of Orthopsychiatry* 58:387–396.

Santrock, J. W. (1975). Father absence, perceived maternal behavior, and moral development in boys. *Child Development* 46:753–757.

Santrock, J. W., and Warshak, R. A. (1979). Father custody and social development in boys and girls. *Journal of Social Issues* 35:112–125.

Tessman, L. H. (1978). *Children of Parting Parents.* New York: Jason Aronson.

Thomes, M. M. (1968). Children with absent fathers. *Journal of Marriage and the Family* 30:89–96.

Waldron, J. A., Ching, J. W., and Fair, P. H. (1986). A children's divorce clinic: analysis of 200 cases in Hawaii. *Journal of Divorce* 9:111–121.

Wallerstein, J. S., and Kelly, J. B. (1980). *Surviving the Breakup.* New York: Basic Books.

Weiss, R. S. (1975). *Marital Separation.* New York: Basic Books.

12

SCHOOL
INTERVENTIONS

Janine M. Bernard, Ph.D.

Any parent who has greeted a grumpy child returning from school can attest that school life and home life often interact. Similarly, the teacher who observes a child becoming increasingly distracted or irritable in the classroom often assumes that the stimulus for such behavior is in the home. For better or for worse, the days are over for school and family life to be treated as separate entities. Although schools differ in their comfort level when confronted with home-related problems, most concede that they have little choice but to react to them.

In the past decade, nothing has done more to accelerate the process of school and family interinvolvement than the high incidence of divorce. The effects of divorce on children as determined by school performance (as well as other measures) have received much attention in the professional literature. Consequently, schools have been challenged to react to the changing demographics of the family both administratively and functionally. As schools have groped with the effects of divorce on the educational and developmental process, they have found themselves evolving in their understanding both of divorce and the types of interventions available to them in assisting children of divorce. Family therapists also have contributed to this evolution by introducing to the helping professions the concept of systems and systemic interventions. As a result, the range of school interventions for children of divorce include those that are systemic as well as those that are intrapsychic, those that are preventive as well as those that are remedial.

This chapter reviews briefly the research reporting differential effects of divorce on children, effects that often have been determined by school performance. Second, preventive interventions are described, most of which are intrapsychic and school-based. Next, remedial interventions are reviewed, especially those that attempt to consider the systemic and/or ecosystemic reality of the child. Finally, the challenges to the family therapist who wishes to work with school systems are presented.

CHILDREN OF DIVORCE: HOW HAVE THEY FARED?

Lowery and Settle (1985) have produced an excellent review of the research concerning the differential effects of divorce on children. Their discriminating critique found most studies that attempted to determine a *causal link* between divorce and disruptive behavior to be wanting. Rather, the authors reported that more recent studies seem to favor one of two models: (1) the *cumulative stress* model, which assumes that a series of stressful events that happen close together can cause problems for children of divorce; and (2) the *family systems* model, which assumes that family relationships do not end as a result of divorce and that a child's behavior can be understood only in the context of continuing relationships among family members. All three models, however, have produced empirical studies that are flawed methodologically (Lowery and Settle 1985). In fact, since most designs must compromise internal validity for external validity, much of what we view as reliable trends in the divorce literature are viewed as such because of the accumulation of flawed studies producing the same results. We must, therefore, continue to view all research results on the effects of divorce on children with caution.

It also is important to remember that the majority of children of divorce do not differ from children from intact families *to any significant degree* on a variety of adjustment criteria. Rather, it is a significant minority of children of divorce who are a cause of concern. According to a study recently conducted by Isaacs and colleagues (1986), however, a dichotomy between children of divorce who are coping well and those who are not is an overly simplistic position. They evaluated divorcing families, using several instruments, and attempted to contrast those who had requested counseling with those who had not. What they found was that both groups differed significantly from both normal and clinical standardized samples. In other words, the groups used in this study, whether they requested counseling or not, were more distressed than a random normal population, but were less dysfunctional than a typical clinical population. Another finding of this study relevant to our purposes here was that " . . .20 percent of the children fell within the clinical range for both behavior problems and social competence, and about 8 percent fell within the clinical range for the school score" (p. 113). The importance of this study is twofold: (1) It supports attempts by schools to reach all children of divorce, assuming that these children fall in some middle ground between coping well and not coping. A sound preventive program might make a difference for many of these children. (2) It cautions against treating all children of divorce as a clinical population.

As was stated earlier, although the research is far from flawless, there are certain trends regarding children of divorce that are worth reporting:

1. Boys tend to fare less well than girls (Hetherington et al. 1985).
2. Younger children are more vulnerable than older children to the negative consequences of divorce. However, children in later latency (9 and 10) tend to show a greater disruption in school performance than do children at other age levels (Kanoy and Cunningham 1984, Wallerstein and Kelly 1980, Tedder et al. 1987).
3. Continued parental conflict is correlated with poorer adjustment for children (Chess et al. 1983, Ellison 1983, Guidubaldi et al. 1986, Kurdek and Siessky 1980, Wallerstein 1985).
4. Postdivorce stability (financial and geographic) is correlated with better adjustment for children (Hodges et al. 1979, Koch 1982, Lowery and Settle 1985, Scherman and Lepak 1986).
5. Mental health of the custodial parent is correlated with better adjustment in children (Wallerstein and Kelly 1980).
6. A continuing relationship with the noncustodial parent is correlated with positive adjustment in children (Wallerstein and Kelly 1980).

It is the belief of many professionals in the field that the latter four variables can be instrumental in determining whether boys or latency age children will have difficulty as a result of divorce. In other words, no specific demographics per se seem to put children in jeopardy. Rather, certain demographics in combination with negative familial patterns should be cause for concern. For example, most boys are in the custody of their mothers. This alone is perhaps no problem. If, however, maternal custody is paired with a disinterested or absent father, the lack of a male role model may be detrimental to the child and he may be added to the statistics of troubled children of divorce. Or perhaps an unstable financial situation causes home life to be insecure, and this along with father absence accumulates to be more stress than the child can handle. My point is that each child brings to us a variety of variables that will interplay with his or her status as a child of divorce—variables that will enhance or detract from the adjustment process.

PREVENTIVE INTERVENTIONS

Schools have struggled to arrive at their appropriate role with regard to divorce and its effect on children and the educational process. Until fairly recently, children of divorce were viewed as individuals who either were adjusted or who needed some remedial attention as a result of their parents' divorce. With the number of children of divorce increasing substantially, and an accumulation of experience with children of divorce, the schools seem to agree with Isaac and colleagues' (1986) assertion that these children fall somewhere between coping and not coping. This realization has spawned a preventive approach to divorce that also fits well with the educational goals of school. Therefore, although remedial efforts in the schools continue, the call to be preventive has been embraced by many school systems.

Rationale for Preventive Approaches

As long as divorce was seen as a "problem," schools stayed relatively clear of it. In the past two decades, research on the effect of divorce on children, coupled with soaring divorce statistics, have made divorce more approachable as a topic for school personnel. In addition, the large numbers of students who have coped relatively well with the divorce of their parents have contributed to a view that divorce poses substantial challenges for children but does not, in and of itself, damage children psychologically. The educational challenge, therefore, is to identify those conditions that are helpful to children and incorporate them into the school. Said in another way, the preventive model assumes that if the child is assisted in an appropriate, timely fashion, the incidence of negative reactions to parental divorce can be reduced.

Another reason for schools to get involved arises out of the realization of the centrality of the school to the child. As Pfeifer and

Abrams (1984) have stated: "It might be argued that in light of the disruptive influence that divorce has upon our culture's most fundamental institution, the family, the significance of school to the child is increased, and it is particularly important that some sort of compensatory resources be available there" (p. 23).

The School's Response

Schools have responded in a variety of ways to the challenge generated by divorce (Bernard 1984). Administratively, they have reviewed their procedures to protect the rights of both custodial and noncustodial parents (Aiello and Humes 1987) and to diminish the potential of children and their teachers being caught in the middle of warring parents. Teachers have received in-service training (Cantrell 1986) to inform them of relevant information regarding children of divorce and to help them arrive at strategies for dealing with a variety of divorce-related situations. School functions that involve parents have been reviewed to increase sensitivity to different family structures. In short, schools have become more articulate about divorce and less reactive to the complications caused by divorce. As a result, children of divorce can have greater confidence that the school will not exacerbate an already difficult home situation.

The second major thrust of preventive efforts by schools is the amplitude of programs offered by school counselors, school psychologists, and social workers that are targeted specifically at children of divorce (Cantrell 1986, Coffman and Roark 1988, Freeman and Couchman 1985, Holzman 1984, Kalter et al. 1984, Omizo and Omizo 1987, Pedro-Carroll and Cowen 1985, Pfeifer and Abrams 1984, Reid 1984, Robson 1987, Roseby and Deutsch 1985, Tedder et al. 1987). Although each makes a specific contribution, the goals of these programs are relatively similar, as is the group counseling format. Although there are group programs that have been successful in working with adolescents (for example, Coffman and Roark 1988), most programs are found in elementary schools. Research has targeted elementary school children as the largest group of children of divorce, and 9 to 10-year-olds as most vulnerable to the negative effects of divorce; therefore, programs seem to focus upon these ages. Among the goals espoused by such preventive programs are to:

1. Help shore up those children who were functioning marginally *before* the divorce and, therefore, are in a weakened position to handle the stress of divorce.

2. Alter children's negative attitudes and expectations about divorce, thereby normalizing divorce.
3. Increase children's coping skills.
4. Ease the burden of parents.
5. Validate children's experiences and feelings.
6. Impart information and clarify misperceptions.
7. Help children master developmental issues complicated by the divorce.
8. Identify children in need of additional, remedial help.
9. Teach specific skills (problem-solving, communication skills, anger control).

All the programs cited in the literature report gains, either subjective or objective, for the children involved. It seems that goals relating directly to the divorce were more often attained than more nebulous goals. That is, normalizing divorce was an easier goal to achieve than decreasing depression, for example. Some programs offered support groups for parents that ran simultaneously to the children's groups. When this was the case, children often made more substantial gains, reinforcing a more systemic view of divorce. Finally, recruitment and selection for membership in the group was important if a positive outcome were to occur. It was essential that children not be coerced into being a member of a group and that groups represent a fairly broad range of divorce adjustment and circumstance. As several authors noted, it was helpful to have children who were coping very well in groups with children who were having some difficulty in order to offer appropriate role models to the latter.

Assumptions of Preventive Programs

Preventive school-based programs appear to offer children a valuable service. There does not seem to be any question that they have contributed to some positive outcomes for children of divorce. Most such programs, however, are conducted by persons who have not received training in systems thinking and view divorce as having an intrapsychic and/or developmental effect on the child. Interactional models are underrepresented in these programs. If one adheres to a systemic view of dysfunction, some of the activity of these preventive programs would seem to miss the point. In fact, no study has been reported to date to determine whether or not the actual incidence of dysfunction is decreased in a given school system based on the impact of a preventive program. One could speculate that these programs are most advantageous for children whose families already are functioning adequately. This alone would make them worth offering, but may not meet their intended goal of reducing the incidence of dysfunction.

Another assumption of preventive programs should be mentioned. By definition, prevention requires that there is some ill that one is trying to avoid. Most preventive programs for children of divorce have a negative overtone concerning divorce and its effect on children. By focusing on divorce per se, these programs tend to ascribe inordinate power to an event or series of events, rather than to a process that began before divorce and will continue afterwards.

The Role of the Family Therapist in Prevention

The role of the family therapist in the prevention of school problems is most likely to occur through his or her work with the family outside of the school. As part of divorce therapy, each parent's involvement with the child's school should be addressed. Key concerns to be raised are each parent's motives for involvement and the hostility between the divorcing couple (Bernard 1984). For example, it is not unheard of for a parent to be involved in the child's school life for competitive, rather than supportive, reasons. By the same token, some parents choose to remain uninvolved rather than put the child in a difficult situation. To sidestep such issues often leaves children in the position of not only negotiating between the school and family systems, but also between their parents. Of course, conducting effective systemic therapy with the divorcing family also will help to prevent school problems, if one adheres to the belief that a child's symptomatic behavior is an ill-advised attempt to stabilize the family system.

Finally, and with somewhat growing frequency, the family therapist will be a consultant to the school, conducting in-service training on divorce to teachers, administrators, and counseling personnel. In fact, school systems are becoming increasingly influenced by family therapy and systemic thinking, as we shall see in the remainder of this chapter.

REMEDIAL INTERVENTIONS

By the time remedial interventions are needed, divorce has typically been relegated to the background and it is the child's specific symptom that constitutes the foreground. In other words, a teacher might assume that a recent divorce is the "cause" of a child's disruptive classroom behavior, but it is the behavior, not divorce adjustment, that will be the primary target of an intervention. Therefore, most school interventions that are remedial, as mentioned in the literature, do not specify children of divorce as their specific target.

The teacher is usually the first person to encounter a school problem. Teachers have been trained in classroom management and, therefore, will most likely employ traditional techniques in response to a child's inappropriate behavior. Or, if the child seems despondent or in emotional crisis, the teacher will refer the child to the school counselor or psychologist, and/or will attempt to relate to the child in a more personal and understanding manner. Often, such approaches are fruitful, especially if parental separation, divorce, or remarriage has been recent and the young person simply needs to be grounded in new circumstances. Most such interventions are either intrapsychic or behavioral, assuming either that the child is struggling internally with the meaning of divorce events, or that the child's environment needs to be manipulated to reinforce some activities and extinguish others. When such interventions do not work, the school may continue with "more of the same" solutions (Watzlawick et al. 1974) or may initiate contact with the family. At this time, an outside therapist might be approached to offer assistance to the child, the family, or the school system. As the reader can presume, this is a critical point of decision for both the family and the school as they determine what must be done to correct what has evolved into a substantial problem.

Some schools have outside therapists or agencies to which they routinely refer students and their families for emotional or behavioral problems. If outside therapists adhere to linear models of therapy, they will work separately with the child or, perhaps, the family. They will most likely not try to intervene in the school except to let the school know that therapy is in progress or, perhaps, to suggest a behavioral intervention. Systemic family therapists, however, typically will work differently with a school-related problem, including those stimulated by a divorce. The remainder of the chapter focuses on systemic interventions. Specifically, the following are considered:

1. How and when a family therapist should become involved with the school.
2. The school as a system.
3. Systemic and ecosystemic interventions with children of divorce.
4. The emergence of the systemically trained school professional.

Family Therapist Involvement in School Problems

DiCocco (1986) offers an excellent set of guidelines for the family therapist to consider when a student's problem involves two systems, that is, when a child's reaction to any part of the divorce process spills over into his or her school behavior. DiCocco presents what she refers to as four phases, each phase representing an escalation of the school problem.

In Phase I, the school problem is mild and occurs infrequently. DiCocco observes that resources are usually available within the school structure for solutions to Phase I problems. Examples of the kind of problems that fall into this category are failure to turn in homework assignments or fighting on the school grounds. Because of the school's capacity to handle these situations, the family therapist would be unwise to attempt to become involved in a Phase I issue. In fact, should the therapist attempt to intervene, the intervention will most likely be rejected by the school. If the family is concerned about the school problem, the family therapist should work to make the family more comfortable with the school's solution.

Phase II problems are more serious and more frequent. They are the type of problems that usually result in the school's contacting the parents, a symbol that responsibility for resolution of the problem is, at the very least, being shared with the family. DiCocco points out that when problems become more serious, schools have fewer options. This, in turn, provides an opportunity for the school system to make its boundaries more permeable and to consider advice and help from the outside. Excessive absenteeism or extreme social withdrawal are examples of problems that DiCocco would place in Phase II. Should a family therapist be asked to intervene at this phase, he or she could implement interventions that target the family alone, the school alone, or both systems.

Phase III represents a critical situation that has evolved into dysfunctional cycles. "Generally, the school has exhausted all its avenues except that of making an alternative placement of the child elsewhere in the community or outside of the community" (DiCocco 1986, p. 57). Phase III problems would include severe truancy, phobias, or serious substance abuse. The school and the family may be deteriorating into a mutual blaming posture, or both systems may be blaming the child. DiCocco is firm that interventions at this phase must be ecosystemic, involving both school and family into one adult organization. When an intervention is ecosystemic, it sees the world through the child's eyes, with the family and the school becoming subsystems of one larger reality. The external family therapist is, perhaps, most needed in this situation in that it would be difficult for a member of either subsystem to choreograph an intervention for the entire ecosystem.

Phase IV is present when existing systems have failed and the child is referred to a new context, a foster home, a residential treatment center, or the like. Once there is a new set of subsystems, Phase III interventions might again be considered.

DiCocco's contribution is significant on several counts. First, she cautions the family therapist not to react too quickly to family invitations to become involved with the school. Given the fact that divorce has the power to cause heightened reactions from parents, a school flare-up might stimulate a request for the therapist to help the parents nip a problem in the bud. Although it is totally legitimate for the therapist to work with either or both parents around the issue, it would be unwise for the therapist to mandate a school intervention. DiCocco also differentiates between the appropriateness of using systemic versus ecosystemic interventions. Although it is not implied that ecosystemic interventions would be "overkill" for Phase II problems, there is a clear assertion that they are essential for Phase III issues. We will discuss both levels of intervention in greater detail later in this chapter. Before this, however, we should consider the implications of the school as a system.

The School as a System

In recent years, various authors have begun to concede that although the family is the primary system for the child, it is not the child's sole system (Campion 1984, Green and Fine 1980, Lusterman 1985, Molnar 1985; Okun 1984, Pfeiffer and Tittler 1983, Wendt and Zake 1984). Formerly, practitioners working with the family have been reluctant to recognize the occasional necessity of coordinating efforts with a school when a child's behavior is the target of intervention. Schools, on the other hand, have always acknowledged the family's influence on the child, but have been reluctant to bring the two systems together to effect change, especially if there was any implication that the school might have to change as well as the family. Only more recently have both school systems and family therapists inched toward the "explicit acknowledgment that the two systems, school and family, are intimately interrelated and reciprocally influential" (Pfeiffer and Tittler 1983, p. 168).

From the family therapist's perspective, acknowledging the school as a system and understanding that system are two different matters. As Molnar (1985) has stated, schools are complex organizations that cannot as yet be explained completely by using systemic concepts from family therapy. Therefore, Molnar suggests that family therapists, when attempting to work with a school system, approach both the task and the organizational structure with few assumptions. Lusterman (1985) underscores this point by noting that a first attempt to bring the family and school systems together might threaten school personnel and might result in an interaction laden with covert messages. For example:

> Information pertaining to a decision about a student may be volunteered prematurely by a teacher in an open meeting, which may cause the principal to become defensive. The principal may likewise perceive him- or herself to be in a battle for hierarchical position with the therapist or the parents. . . .The therapist may leave such a meeting believing that s/he has become an agent of change in a larger system, but be unaware that a defensive position has developed. Thus, in fact, the meeting's agreed-upon goals may be subverted by the hidden agendas of the school system. [p. 23]

A built-in complication in working with schools is that the person most invested in change (usually the teacher) is not the person who holds power in the system (the principal). Both Chapman (1988) and Molnar (1985) have stressed the importance of obtaining the principal's support for any extended therapeutic work within a school system. In addition, the counseling personnel in the school will most assuredly be involved and their roles, especially in elementary schools, may be ambiguous. For example, when there are a school counselor, a school psychologist, and a social worker attached to the school, should all be involved? What is the distinct function of each professional (Humes and Hohenshil 1987)? And more important, what is the role of each in maintaining the system as it exists? Some simple guidelines for the outside therapist would include the following. Although they are particularly relevant for the elementary school, they should be kept in mind for the middle and high school as well.

1. If the school has made the referral either directly or through family, make your initial contact with the person making the referral. If this person is *not* the principal, ask if the principal is aware of the referral and what involvement he or she has had thus far. Set up a first meeting with the referral person, the principal, and any other relevant school personnel. By all

means, this meeting should include the child's teacher or, if the young person is in a higher grade, the teacher most connected to the adolescent.

2. If the family has made the contact independent of the school, the therapist should contact the principal to determine what the school's awareness of and reaction to the problem is at this time. It should be noted that an attempt to become involved in the school at the parents' request without the interest of the school is usually doomed for reasons outlined by DiCocco (1986). If, however, the school's frustration is equal to the parents', the school may welcome the involvement of an outside therapist. Lusterman's (1985) approach of acting as a buffer between the school and family is discussed further on.

3. Do not assume that schools are the same, even within the same school system. Systems evolve over time, greatly influenced by the persons that make up the system. Boundaries, rules, power, and the like will be either slightly or vastly different among schools. A modified circular questioning technique might help you to understand the system within which you hope to intervene.

4. Assume a competent, involved group of school personnel who want to be of help to you. Schools are an easy target and have been battered over the years by parents, the media, higher education, and state departments of education. As a result, they are naturally defensive when approached by an outside professional, *even if they have initiated the contact.* The gentle art of reframing may be all that the therapist needs to arrive at a common perception of the problem. However, some resistance should be expected and accepted. In fact, no resistance may mean trouble down the road.

5. Remember that both subsystems (family and school) must feel empowered if any intervention is to work. An intervention that aligns with one subsystem only is not sound ecosystemically. Ecosystemic interventions are more difficult to implement than systemic interventions, because the power within each subsystem must be addressed as well as the messages between subsystems. Furthermore, when the school is one of the two subsystems, and a divorce has taken place in the family, the therapist must remember that he or she will be negotiating with several parental figures, including parents, stepparents, teachers, counselors, and administrators.

6. Keep your options open. An ecosystemic intervention may not be desirable once you have a better understanding of the problem. It may make more sense to work with one of the subsystems exclusively. It is possible to become overly committed to a

certain level of intervention, thus compromising outcome for process.

7. Finally, remember that families and schools have different purposes for existing. One of the family's primary purposes is to provide psychological safety to its members; the school's primary purpose is to enhance competence in its members. These essentially different goals must each be respected even while the therapist appreciates their interconnectedness.

Whether a therapist decides to intervene within the school or not, it is helpful to keep the above suggestions in mind. Next, we consider the therapist's actual options for intervention.

Three Levels of Intervention

Assuming once more the perspective of the family therapist outside the school system, the following gives greater detail concerning the three ways in which the therapist can affect a youngster's school behavior.

A Family System Intervention

This most common "school" intervention requires that the family therapist work with the family exclusively (or with tangential contact with the school) regarding a school problem. The assumption when one is using this approach is that the problem rests within the family and that school difficulties are only an extension of family issues.

Dorothy was in fourth grade, a bright student who had been doing very well until her parents divorced last fall. Soon after the divorce her father was transferred to another location 800 miles away. Dorothy's relationship with both her parents was strong. When Dorothy's grades began to plummet, her teacher called her mother to tell her that there was some danger that Dorothy would be left back if things did not improve. She described Dorothy as daydreaming most of the day. When asked by the therapist what she was thinking about, Dorothy said that she was worrying about how her father was doing in his new environment. Of course, as things worsened, Dorothy's father called more frequently and made a trip back to her home to have a special conference with the teacher.

The therapist attempted a paradoxical intervention that was

successful. The father was requested to call on a regular schedule basis regardless of Dorothy's school work. Both parents were to praise Dorothy for her love and concern of her father, and she was encouraged to spend as much time thinking about him as she liked, even if it meant that her school work suffered. They noted that, although school work was very important and she might be held back, love for her father was more important. The teacher's involvement was secondary; she agreed not to scold Dorothy for daydreaming but to tell her that she should do as her parents wished. Within two weeks, Dorothy's school work had improved markedly.

A School System Intervention

Molnar and Lindquist (1985) have worked extensively with school systems using principles from family therapy. They note that a child's disruptive behavior can be a message from home to the school, but it can also be a message from teacher to teacher, from teacher to school administration, and so on. In other words, and this is especially true when a divorce is involved, it can sometimes be too easy to scapegoat the family situation for a problem that is systemic within the school. Even if the student's problems originated during the family crisis, the school's reaction to the student might overshadow the original issue. Or as Watzlawick and colleagues (1974) have suggested, the solution may have become the problem. This commonly occurs with ethnic minorities when they bring different cultural rules to the classroom. In response to school problems, Molnar and Lindquist work closely with school systems to use the concepts of reframing, positive connotation, paradoxical intention, and punctuation to understand the systemic nature of a child's behavior. An intervention at this level is appropriate when the problem seems to be predominately school-based.

An adolescent boy, living with his mother, is reacting negatively to a male teacher. Because of his negative reaction, he is avoiding the work assigned in this class and is in danger of flunking the course. This teacher has some traits similar to the boy's father, who keeps only sporadic contact with the boy. Although the problem is divorced-related, the problem can be defined as a school problem if the mother reports no problems at home and the father is absent. A family therapist attached to the school might give the teacher some suggestions as to how he might handle the boy when specific situations arise, or the boy might be seen in counseling to help him differentiate from his father and, therefore, to react less reflexively to someone who reminds him of his father. Of course, if the school problem can be resolved, there is always hope that such a resolution will somehow enhance the boy's familial life. However, this would be seen as a by-product of the intervention, not its goal.

Ecosystemic Interventions

Both in practice and in theory, ecosystemic interventions are the most efficient; at the same time, however, they are the most difficult to realize, especially when the parents are separated or divorced. However, building on some of the earlier thinking of Aponte (1976), several authors report having engaged successfully in ecosystemic solutions to family/school problems (for example, Chapman 1988, DiCocco 1986, Fine and Holt 1983, Lusterman 1985, Okun 1984). From a systemic frame of reference, it was only a matter of time before it was recognized that the child personified an interface of two systems (Bernard 1984) and that his or her behavior could be grounded in either or both systems. Just as family therapy was the only option for the therapist who made the paradigm shift from linear to systemic case analysis, ecosystemic interventions often appear to be the only alternative for the child who is floundering both at home and at school.

The following example is taken from Okun (1984).[1] It describes a case where the therapist worked with the entire ecosystem of the child:

Ralph, age 7, was referred to a family therapist by the school psychologist because of his underachievement, inattention in class, poor peer relationships, and inappropriate talking during lessons. The school psychologist and Ralph's mother were at loggerheads; the former blaming the latter for poor home discipline, which she believed carried over into the classroom, and Ralph's mother believing that school personnel were unfairly picking on her son.

The family therapist's first meeting with Ralph and his divorced parents provided important family information. Ralph had been in treatment at a local guidance clinic since his parents' divorce four years earlier; this "patient" role kept his parents in constant communication with each other, preventing their emotional separation, and resulted in triangulation over discipline

---

[1] From B. F. Okun (1984). Family therapy and the schools. In *Family Therapy with School Related Problems*, ed. J. C. Hansen and B. K. Okun. Reprinted with permission of Aspen Publishers, Inc.

issues with Ralph at the apex of one triangle involving his parents and another involving his mother and the school. Because Ralph spent every weekend with his father in a downtown high-rise apartment, he missed necessary peer socializing experience; thus his peer relationship skills were underdeveloped. As the sole focus of each parent's attention, he was accustomed to getting his own way most of the time, and he felt more comfortable with attentive adults than with other children. He had developed effective manipulative strategies to manage his parents, and he was puzzled as to why these strategies did not work as well with his teacher at school.

A visit to Ralph's classroom revealed other significant data. As the family therapist entered the school building, she was met by the principal and the school psychologist, who carried a very thick file about Ralph. The principal's first comment was "Oh, I'm so glad you've come. Ralph is the most disturbed boy in this school, and we all worry so much about him." Already, Ralph's role as the school system's identified patient was evident.

The family therapist observed in the classroom that Ralph was indeed singled out for discipline more frequently than other boys whose behavior was even more disruptive. Later discussion with the classroom teacher indicated that the observed behavior was typical and further emphasized the teacher's enmeshment with Ralph and her determination to keep him in the identified patient role. The therapist also found out that the teacher was in the process of a painful divorce herself and that she was experiencing enormous anxiety about the effects of her divorce on her 7-year-old son. She expressed fear that her son would end up "disturbed like Ralph."

Thus, the family therapist learned that both the school psychologist and Ralph's parents were right. Home discipline *was* inconsistent, and Ralph *was* picked on unfairly in the classroom. The therapist's major goals were to relieve Ralph of his learned patient role and to teach him more effective peer relationship and teacher relationship skills. This was accomplished by (1) working with the parents to provide more consistent discipline and management at home, as well as clearer boundaries and (2) working with the school psychologist and classroom teacher to provide similarly consistent discipline and management at school and to restructure the classroom boundaries. Simultaneously, the family therapist was able to establish a trusting rapport with the classroom teacher and refer her for divorce counseling. Ralph's mother and teacher developed a working alliance that improved congruency between home and school operating rules, and Ralph was helped to differentiate his relationship with each of his parents in separate father-son and mother-son sessions. The therapist served as a coordinator and consultant. Ralph's immediate behavior improvements reinforced the cooperation of the family and school system. [pp. 9–11]

It should be noted, as indicated by this example, that in a divorce situation, the child's ecosystem usually includes two households in addition to the school. In addition, as more school personnel are themselves divorced, there may be several divorces involved in any one case (especially if either of the parents have remarried and their new spouses are divorced). Therefore, ecosystemic interventions can be particularly cumbersome for the therapist, especially if the parents and/or stepparents are not willing to cooperate with each other.

Lusterman (1985) observed that by the time a family therapist is involved in a case, the school and the family may be at odds following several unsuccessful attempts to correct the problem. Therefore, his model begins with total disengagement between the school and the family, with the therapist acting as the go-between. During this time, the therapist is attempting to work with the child within each subsystem, but especially within the family. Both school and family agree to call the therapist, not each other, in case of difficulty. Once the therapist sees improvement with the child at home, he or she gradually reintroduces parent-school involvement. Finally, the therapist begins to disengage as the family and the school are able to work together more productively.

Chapman (1988) describes a three-year pilot program based on an ecosystemic model that was viewed as highly successful within an elementary school. The intent of the Teacher/Family Consultation program was to prevent some youngsters from being referred for consideration in special education for behavioral reasons, or, in the case of special education students, from being referred for more elaborate services. The program provided for four consultations with the child's ecosystem, three of which were directed by a family therapist, whenever the child was considered to be in danger of placement into a more restrictive (and more costly) educational environment. Therefore, it was assumed by the school system that the program would not only be therapeutically successful, but cost-effective. Although the program did not target children of divorce, Chapman notes that a significant majority of the children referred to the program were from divorced families.

Once a child was identified as having some severe difficulty in school, an in-house team met to discuss the situation. This team included the school counselor, school psychologist, social worker, and the classroom teacher. If it was decided to go further, another meeting was scheduled with the team, the child, the parents, and siblings. At this time, it was decided whether the services of a family therapist were needed. Note, however, that the school staff had already intervened ecosystemically prior to the introduction of family therapy. If therapy was called for, three sessions were offered in the school (and at the school's expense) with the entire ecosystem of the child present. At the conclusion of these sessions, the problem was either resolved or the family was referred for additional therapy. Chapman asserts that for the majority of cases, the family concerns overshadowed school issues and family therapy was the vital determinant of the child's adjustment. However, involvement of school personnel increased everyone's motivation to help the child and kept everyone accountable. Among her other observations:

1. Teachers, though reluctant at first to become involved in family problems, were enthusiastic about the program. They realized that they *were* involved in the family's problems while perpetuating the myth of uninvolvement.
2. An ecosystemic approach *will not work* if the school-based team does not enjoy strong collegial relationships. Role conflicts and/or territoriality among team members will sabotage the program.
3. Items 1 and 2 notwithstanding, the support of the principal is most important for the success of an ecosystemic approach. A staff should not proceed until they have gained such support.
4. Schools have a tremendous amount of power with families, and parents will come to the school if beckoned. This is true for divorced parents as well. Chapman also advocates the inclusion of stepparents.
5. Although Chapman believes the program met all its goals, including cost-effectiveness, she concedes that the procurement of an outside family therapist can be expensive. Therefore, she advocates the training of school personnel to work from a systemic perspective and to conduct limited family therapy when necessary.

School Personnel as Systemic Interventionists

As was alluded to earlier, a slowly growing trend is for school counselors, school psychologists, and/or social workers to work directly with the family, or with the family and the school, using systemic interventions (Campion 1983, Chapman 1988, Fine and Holt 1983, Green and Fine 1980, Pfeiffer and Tittler 1983, Wendt and Zake

1984, Williams and Weeks 1984). School personnel have arrived at their interest in systemic family theory by necessity. They have been increasingly frustrated with their inability to effect change with the child when working with him or her individually. Furthermore, parents tend not to accept referrals to outside therapists when this is the only intervention the school makes. Campion (1983) notes that there exists a sizable percentage of parents who are quite satisfied with the *status quo* of their families, even when their children seemed to be having difficulty. "These parents, well-meaning as they often were, either saw no problem, or saw problems as existing largely outside the family—in school, in other children, in the community. Such parents seem unlikely to seek help of their own accord" (p. 60). However, once these parents were requested to receive family therapy in the school, outcome was good *if* parental cooperation was forthcoming at the first session. Also of interest, of the seventy-two children whose families were involved in family therapy over two and one-half years, more than half were from divorcing families.

Systemic interventions performed by school personnel are similar to those choreographed by an external therapist. However, there are certain distinct issues that arise for the school counselor or psychologist wishing to intervene systemically:

1. Working with the family system will be easier than working with the school system or with the child's entire ecosystem. This is because membership in the school system will interfere with one's role as systemic therapist.
2. Because of the homeostatic quality of sytems, there might be resistance to the counselor or psychologist's taking on a new role in the school system, one that seems juxtaposed to how this person was perceived previously (Fine and Holt 1983).
3. A systemic orientation is a challenging one that takes a considerable amount of training and supervision. With programs in school counseling, school psychology, and social work increasing in their requirements, it is unlikely that the trainee will opt for this additional training, or that faculty in these programs will be able to offer it. Training as a family therapist is not yet appreciated by school districts or state departments of education. Therefore, incentives are low to receive additional training.
4. Even more central than item 3, most training programs in school counseling or school psychology adhere to theoretical positions that are linear. It must be questioned whether a functional melding of orientations and roles can be accomplished by one person.

The Role of the Family Therapist

Because of the problems listed above, it is unlikely that school personnel with systemic intervention skills will be forthcoming in great numbers. However, the belief that family problems can become school problems is unlikely to be reversed. Therefore, schools will most likely be more and more open to soliciting the services of family therapists as trainers, consultants, or in-house therapists. In order to meet this opportunity, family therapists must become cognizant of the systemic properties and internal logic of school systems.

CONCLUSION

The rising rate of divorce has had a tremendous impact on schools and schooling. It seems that we are beyond the crisis of recognizing that a change has occurred, and have begun to creatively tackle the situation with approaches that are either preventive, remedial, or both. In the process, we have learned more about how families and schools operate and how all children dance between the two.

The purpose of this chapter is to aid the family therapist or school counseling personnel in their attempts to make divorce less treacherous for children. It is important in reviewing the material in this chapter to determine when prevention or remediation are called for. Often we turn to therapy when education or guidance are the alternatives of choice. If remedial work is necessary, the therapist must be patient enough to learn about both systems, family and school, before choosing the level of his or her intervention. The literature cited in this chapter provides many useful concepts and guidelines.

School behavior and performance will continue to be an obvious barometer for the adjustment of children of divorce. Therefore, family therapists can count on increased contact with the schools, and if prepared for the contact, can find a new domain for the use and study of systemic principles.

REFERENCES

Aiello, H., and Humes, C. W. (1987). Counselor contact of the noncustodial parent: a point of law. *Elementary School Guidance and Counseling* 21:177–182.

Aponte, H. J. (1976). The family-school interview: an eco-structural approach. *Family Process* 15:303–311.

Bernard, J. M. (1984). Divorced families and the schools: an interface of systems. In *Family Therapy with School Related Problems*, ed. J. C. Hansen and B. F. Okun, pp. 91–102. Rockville, MD: Aspen Systems Corporation.

Campion, J. (1984). Psychological services for children: using family therapy in the setting of a school psychological service. *Journal of Family Therapy* 6:47–62.

Cantrell, R. G. (1986). Adjustment to divorce: three components to assist children. *Elementary School Guidance and Counseling* 20:163–173.

Chapman, H. (1988). Family therapy in the schools: are we ready? Paper presented at the American Association for Counseling and Development Annual Conference, Chicago, IL, March.

Chess, S., Thomas, A., Korn, S., Mittleman, M., and Cohen, J. (1983). Early parental attitudes, divorce and separation and adult outcomes: findings of a longitudinal study. *Journal of American Academy of Child Psychiatry* 22:47–51.

Coffman, S. G., and Roark, A. E. (1988). Likely candidates for group counseling: adolescents with divorced parents. *The School Counselor* 35:246–252.

DiCocco, B. E. (1986). A guide to family/school interventions for the family therapist. *Contemporary Family Therapy* 8:50–61.

Ellison, E. S. (1983). Issues concerning parental harmony and children's psychosocial adjustment. *American Journal of Orthopsychiatry* 53:73–80.

Fine, M. J., and Holt, P. (1983). Intervening with school problems: a family systems perspective. *Psychology in the Schools* 20:59–66.

Freeman, R., and Couchman, B. (1985). Coping with family change: a model for therapeutic group counseling with children and adolescents. *School Guidance Worker* 40:44–50.

Green, K., and Fine, M. J. (1980). Family therapy: a case for training for school psychologists. *Psychology in the Schools* 17:241–248.

Guidubaldi, J., Cleminshaw, H. K., Perry, J. D., Nastasi, B. K., and Lightel, J. (1986). The role of selected family environment factors in children's post-divorce adjustment. *Family Relations* 38:141–151.

Hetherington, E. M., Cox, M., and Cox, R. (1985). Long term effects of divorce and remarriage on the adjustment of children. *Journal of American Academy of Child Psychiatry* 24:518–530.

Hodges, W. F., Wechsler, R. C., and Ballentine, C. (1979). Divorce and the preschool child: cumulative stress. *Journal of Divorce* 3:55–69.

Holzman, T. (1984). Schools can provide help for the children of divorce. *The American School Board Journal* 171:46–47.

Humes, C. W., and Hoenshil, T. H. (1987). Elementary counselors, school psychologists, school social workers: who does what? *Elementary School Guidance and Counseling* 22:37–45..

Isaacs, M. B., Leon, G., and Donohue, A. M. (1986). Who are the "normal" children of divorce: on the need to specify population. *Journal of Divorce* 10:107–118.

Kalter, N., Pickar, J., and Lesowitz, M. (1984). School-based developmental facilitation groups for children of divorce: a preventive intervention. *American Journal of Orthopsychiatry* 54:613–623.

Kanoy, K. W., and Cunningham, J. L. (1984). Consensus of confusion in research on children and divorce: conceptual and methodological issues. *Journal of Divorce* 7:45–71.

Koch, M. P. (1982). The visitation experience on divorced noncustodial fathers. Unpublished doctoral disseration, University of Kentucky.

Kurdek, L. A., and Siesky, A. E., Jr. (1980). Effects of divorce on children: the relationship between parent and child perspectives. *Journal of Divorce* 4:85–99.

Lowery, C. R., and Settle, S. A. (1985). Effects of divorce on children: differential impact of custody and visitation patterns. *Family Relations* 34: 455–463.

Lusterman, D. D. (1985). An ecosystemic approach to family-school problems. *American Journal of Family Therapy* 13:22–30.

Molnar, A. (1985). Home-school intervention: a systemic approach to helping families with school-related problems. Paper presented at the American Association for Marriage and Family Therapy Annual Conference, New York, October.

Molnar, A., and Lindquist, B. (1985). A systemic approach to increasing school effectiveness. Unpublished manuscript.

Okun, B. F. (1984). Family therapy and the schools. In *Family Therapy with School Related Problems*, ed. J. C. Hansen and B. K. Okun, pp. 1–12. Rockville, MD: Aspen Systems Corporation.

Omizo, M. M., and Omizo, S. A. (1987). Group counseling with children of divorce: new findings. *Elementary School Guidance and Counseling* 22:46–52.

Pedro-Carroll, J. L., and Cowen, E. L. (1985). The children of divorce intervention program: an investigation of the efficacy of a school-based prevention program. *Journal of Consulting and Clinical Psychology* 53:603–611.

Pfeifer, G., and Abrams, L. (1984). School-based discussion groups for children of divorce: a pilot program. *Group* 8:22–28.

Pfeiffer, S. I., and Tittler, B. I. (1983). Utilizing the multi-disciplinary team to facilitate a school-family systems orientation. *School Psychology Review* 12:168–173.

Reid, M. (1984). Divorced children. *Canadian Journal of Public Health* 75:99–102.

Robson, B. E. (1987). Changing family patterns: developmental impacts on children. *Counseling and Human Development* 19:1–12.

Roseby, V., and Deutsch, R. (1985). Children of separation and divorce: effects of a social role-taking group intervention on fourth and fifth graders. *Journal of Clinical Child Psychology* 14:55–60.

Scherman, A., and Lepak, L., Jr. (1986). Children's perceptions of the divorce process. *Elementary School Guidance and Counseling* 21:29–36.

Tedder, S. L., Scherman, A., and Wantz, R. A. (1987). Effectiveness of a support group for children of divorce. *Elementary School Guidance and Counseling* 22:102–109.

Wallerstein, J. S. (1985). The overburdened child: some long-term consequences of divorce. *Social Work* 30:116–123.

Wallerstein, J. S., and Kelly, J. B. (1980). *Surviving the Break-up.* New York: Basic Books.

Watzlawick, P., Weakland, J., and Fisch, R. (1974). *Change.* New York: Norton.

Wendt, R. N., and Zake, J. (1984). Family systems theory and school psychology: implications for training and practice. *Psychology in the Schools* 21:204–210.

Williams, J. M., and Weeks, G. R. (1984). The use of paradox techniques in a school setting. *American Journal of Family Therapy* 12:42–47.

13

GROUP INTERVENTION FOR CHILDREN OF DIVORCED FAMILIES

David M. Young, Ph.D.

It is customary to begin articles on children of divorce with at least one or two citations predicting trends in divorce rates, statistics displaying the number of children to be affected before the end of the decade, or the impact that the rupture of a marriage has on young people, recounting the incidence of particular forms of psychopathology in this at risk group.

The students and professionals reading this chapter are most likely familiar with the figures. Thus, we will leave to others the task of cataloging the incidence and general impact of a problem we can accept as the single best predicting variable (Felner et al. 1975) (along with death of a parent) of eventual mental health referral for school-age children. Practitioners, even those not working with children, can trace many roots of adult problems to experiences related to parental separation. Wallerstein (1985, p. 840) summarizes well when she notes, " . . .the entire pattern of conscious and unconscious psychological needs, wishes, and expectations that parents and children bring to each other is profoundly altered under the impact of marital rupture." The task of this chapter, then, is not to document the monumental impact that the family breakup has upon the child, but to speak of healing via group treatment, especially the type of intervention a community can provide its youth prior to the development of pathology after the rupture of the family. Specifically, we are interested in what a general group approach can do for *all* children who experience their parents' divorces, not just those children who exhibit observable pathology, or those children whose primary caretakers are invested in obtaining professional assistance in preparing their children for the vicissitudes of being a child of divorce. An even greater remedy available to children is the possibility of true primary prevention in groups. I shall speak of primary prevention as a relatively radical idea, that is, assisting children from intact families in understanding the nature of family ruptures. A special section of this chapter is devoted to this topic.

A group is indeed the appropriate setting for children to learn about divorce and their reactions and feelings to their parents' separation. Even without outside intervention, the group is the natural healing location for children to discuss and process their reactions to the family breakup. As aptly pointed out by Schaefer and colleagues (1982), children possess a "social hunger, an instinctive, affective need for human association—which can be gratified only through communion with other individuals, preferably with peers" (p. 1). At a time in which the familial group resources appear to be crumbling, the peer group, or even the artificially created peer group created for therapeutic experience, can be a lifesaver. Similarly, children also experience many of their more difficult emotional reactions to divorce in groups. For example, feelings of peer ridicule and avoidance of other children are processes very much related to many children's reactions to divorce. Children learn in groups: in the classroom, on the playground, and in the family unit; children grow in the group setting. In a way, groups are also safe, less threatening, and sometimes more comforting and reassuring that traditional individual therapy. Even in learning about an impending divorce, experts such as Gardner and Wallerstein advise parents to share such announcements with all children present, regardless of age differences. Wallerstein and others have found a group buffering effect when three or more children are present in a family of divorce. Perhaps with three children, the chances of having sufficient psychological resources to offer support to one another reaches a kind of critical mass, or perhaps simply outnumbering the parents provides enough reassurance for the group.

COURT-MANDATED GROUP INTERVENTION
FOR ADOLESCENTS AND CHILDREN

Throughout childhood, much energy is invested in formal and informal training on the importance and the procedures of pairing.

Young children play house; high school health classes often focus on how to prepare financially and emotionally for married life; even children in grade schools rehearse the business of "going with each other," even if such brief commitments involve only an announcement to peers and an occasional phone call. Divorce is commonplace to children, and most young children receive greater exposure to marital rupture than they do to most childhood diseases, yet most children who experience a divorce are unable to understand, predict, and cope with common child and parent reactions to the experience. They may be able to explain chicken pox or measles, but they may be horrified at their own experience of self-blame for their parents' divorce or confused by their feelings related to fear of abandonment. This section of our chapter, then, is devoted to presenting our programs of court-mandated early group intervention designed to prepare latency age children and adolescents whose parents had filed for divorce and were awaiting final disposition by the court. In addition, our work in outpatient groups and as group consultants to organizations such as Parents Without Partners are shared as appropriate to relevant sections of this chapter. Some related resources from the recent literature are reviewed.

We must stress the point that even informal preparation for these children is often lacking. Traditionally, adults have expected that the child will "adapt himself promptly and without preparation to radical changes in the environment" (Mahler and Rabinovitch 1956, p. 53). Part of this avoidance, for both child and adult populations, of any routine education or preparation for divorce stems from the cultural emphasis on pairing mentioned above. Parents, too, retreat from discussing the process of divorce with their children because they are preoccupied with their own pain (Toomin 1974) or because they simply want to protect the child from having to face any "unnecessary" problems. Most clinicians active in this field can recount numerous children reporting, "Daddy just packed his bags on Saturday morning." In our surveys of the general population experiencing divorce, it is a rare child indeed who reports discussing the divorce with both parents. In fact, at the time of separation, only 38 percent of latency age children in our court-mandated groups report that both parents discussed the divorce with them (Young 1981). This paradox presented by the avoidance of learning about divorce is similar to that posed by the slowly eroding taboo on teaching about death and dying: statistically there is undeniable relevance, but the content is simply psychologically unacceptable.

Futhermore, we may be calling on parents at a most inopportune time to teach, understand, and nurture their children. In our study of recently divorced custodial parents and their children, only in the areas of academic performance and conduct problems at school were parents' perceptions significantly related to their children's (Young 1983). As one of our parents in our sample commented in a debriefing interview, "How can I 'read' my kids when I can hardly focus on the morning newspaper?" Explaining or even announcing an impending change in family structure beyond the child's control creates a negative emotional climate (Beier and Young 1984).

OTHER RESOURCES FOR STRUCTURED EXERCISES AND GROUP APPROACHES

Since Kurdek (1981) has recommended the use of support systems for children of divorcing families, a variety of structured and semistructured approaches to group work with children have been publicized. The following does not represent an exhaustive list of possibilities, but rather a representative sampling of the types of programs available through the literature. A treatment manual of cognitive-behavioral approaches for latency age children has been developed by Bornstein and colleagues (1985). The group experience appears designed to facilitate communication between parent and child. Epstein and Borduin (1985) have developed a game that can be used for children of divorce (or by those whose parents have separated) in group treatment. The game "Could This Happen?" consists of hypothetical situations that children rate as to their probability of occurrence. Children earn points for guessing the most common response to a situation, for presenting evidence to support their choice of whether the hypothetical situation could occur or not, and for talking about their feelings. We have found this game an excellent way of encouraging children (and possibly even adults) to discuss openly feelings and experiences of the separation, divorce, or postdivorce situation.

In response to the needs of children experiencing acute reaction syndromes, Titkin and Cobb (1983) have developed dual group strategies for parents and children. The model consists of a parent-child assessment program, a structured set of group exercises, and concurrent integrative parent sessions. The special feature of this system is, of course, the parent-child assessment function.

Homework, long a trademark of the more behavioral approaches to treatment, is a noted ingredient of the multimodal group approach developed by Barbara Green (1978). After-group assignments for children include tasks such as reading *Dr. G.* (Richard

Gardner's book for children), expression (for example, assign each child the task to tell themselves and another person how they feel as least once a day), dealing with peers (for example, sharing the divorce experience with a friend and reporting back to the group about it).

School-based groups (for example, Pedro-Carroll and Cowen 1985), bibliotherapy (Martin et al. 1983), church-related programs (Vogelsand 1982), and groups for low-income, ethnic minority children (Kaminsky 1986) are also well represented in the current literature. Of these approaches, those most commonly found are the school-based programs. Usually, the programs are of a voluntary nature, time limited, and preventively oriented. The program developed and evaluated by Pedro-Carroll and Cowen (1985) represents a model of an effective and well-documented school-based program. After sending recruitment letters to the parents of fourth-grade through sixth-grade pupils, the ten-session program began with the first three sessions serving as the focal affective component. Skits, role plays, and filmstrips depicting divorce and the feelings it predisposes were presented and discussed. Sessions four through six of the program consisted of the program's cognitive skill-building component. Working on self-statements and specific skills for resolving interpersonal problems were included in these sessions. Sessions seven through nine were designed to deal specifically with anger control. In these sessions children discussed their angry feelings and the appropriate and inappropriate ways of expressing anger and the consequences of such expressions. The last session was devoted to evaluating the group experience. Outcome data for this program following seventy-two children in demographically matched groups indicated that the experimental group improved significantly on teacher ratings of problem behavior and competence, parent ratings of adjustment, and self-reports of anxiety as compared to a delayed intervention (control) group.

Before we leave this section on special programs and group techniques, it is important to note that most of the programs described in this section are designed for relatively intact youth who may be experiencing adjustment reactions to the rupture in the family. While there appears to be a paucity in the literature of empirically evaluated programs designed to treat very troubled youth in this category, some note should be made. Therapy for psychotic children in groups usually involves focused activity groups that provide highly structured activities. The assumption here is that through being productive and learning to socialize within the structure of a group, the children will develop greater self-esteem and overall emotional growth. Thus, the

case could be made that applying a highly structured divorce adjustment program to psychotic children could have sound benefits. Alternatively, Haaken and Davis (1975) present the point of view that a less
structured, more spontaneous type of group, where free expression
and direct communication, rather than communication through materials or format, is encouraged. Here, the point is that a narrow or
topical approach would be counterproductive. Future research is
clearly needed to assist us in determining effective group strategy for
more disturbed children of divorce.

TREATING CHILDREN
IN COURT-MANDATED GROUPS

Whenever one of our research group is invited to speak about research on the effects of divorce on children, we usually speak about
prevention—in all of its various forms. Agreeable head nods are
almost always forthcoming when we speak of the higher levels of
prevention. Discussions of school personnel referring children of
divorce who appear at risk because they are showing signs of acting-
out behavior meet with approval. Offering school-based programs
for children of divorce is acceptable. Even requiring "educational"
groups for parents and children of parents who file for divorce meets
with understanding. However, what we would define as true primary
prevention via group work is almost never accepted—it appears as
incredibly threatening to most audience members.

As noted in the previous section, divorce is an unpleasant and
frightening topic and is frequently avoided as part of traditional
social education. Additionally, we have found that the natural resistance of some parents would preclude many of the children from
attending group. Here the mechanism of denial appears as the major
factor to the resistance. Through our experience with self-selected
group therapy programs, we have found that most of the children
have had prior discussions with parents about many important topics. This is not to say that parents who "volunteer" their children are
not accurately perceiving a need. In fact many of these parents have
children who are noticeably acting out problems related to their
parents' marital hostility.

The children themselves, notably adolescent members, are often
highly resistant to participation during the initial phases of group
work. The initial reactions to required group work were primarily
negative. In fact, in one study of 46 adolescents required by the
court to attend group meetings (Young 1980), a total of 37 percent

reported that they felt "bad" or "very bad" about having to attend group. A total of 45.7 percent reported that they maintained a neutral feeling concerning the workshop. The strongest predictive variable of how adolescents feel about coming to their first group session appears to be their own perception of how their parents feel about the program. A fairly strong correlation [$r(46) = 0.47$, $p < 0.001$] revealed that adolescents who held positive attitudes toward the workshop reported that their parents were pleased that their children were attending. Similarly, teenagers who held initially negative attitudes toward the program reported that their parents were displeased with their children's having to attend. Age was also a good predictor of how the adolescents would react toward having to come to group. As expected, the older adolescents in this 12–17-year-old age group expressed more negative feelings while describing their initial reactions to the program than did the younger adolescents [$r(46) = -0.36$, $p < 0.01$]. The older adolescents, involved in naturally obtaining distance from their families, appear even more prone to the detachment, strategic withdrawal, and denial that are often discussed as typical adolescent coping responses to family stresses such as divorce (Anthony 1974, Gardner 1971, Tessman 1978, Toomin 1974, Wallerstein and Kelly 1974).

One final thought remains when we consider such measures as court-required or "forced" therapy. That is that the child *in almost any setting* is essentially an involuntary patient. Accordingly, the involuntary child referred by the court differs little from the involuntary child brought to us by a parent. Thus, these children do not present a problem in treatability, but rather a case where the child's awareness of needing help has not been established. Group therapists should be sensitive to this distinction.

Adolescent Group Procedures

Groups for adolescent children of divorcing parents, whether developed for long-term therapy approaches or short-term educational intervention, work smoothly and assist in overcoming the sometimes considerable initial resistance toward the group if structured introductory, warm-up, and educational procedures are adhered to, especially in the early sessions. Of course, when the group shifts into more advanced phases, where less structure is in fact desirable, the traditional modes of group process are involved (see section, "Guidelines for Intervention," this chapter). However, the group therapist is cautioned to remember that no matter how interested he or she is in group process, or how many wonderful opportunities for spontaneous exploration seem to be occurring, it is important not to increase resistance or drive group members "under cover" by a too rapid departure from a structured predictable experience, especially during the early phases of the group. As in other therapeutic modalities, the rule of thumb is that therapeutic opportunities will not be missed. As problems are thematic, they will surface again in the group in similar forms.

The use of male and female cotherapists for groups of children of divorce is frequently reported in the literature (for example, Borenstein et al. 1985, Guerney and Jordan 1979). The opportunities for positive parental role-modeling, identification, and transference are enhanced, along with the possibilities for observation of interaction, when two therapists of different sexes are used.

In the case of adolescent or latency age groups, we ask that siblings not attend the same group, even if they are close in age and all of the children wish to attend. If we separate family members, the full benefit of the group can be achieved. Members can learn to interact in exploratory ways. They can be daring and take a variety of risks in testing each other and themselves, as there are only limited consequences to this behavior. There are no fears that group members will punish or inform if they do explore new modes of behavior, a fear that unfortunately is quite relevant in the family setting.

Therapists officially open initial sessions by asking each participant to make an identification tag. Then the group leaders introduce themselves and offer a short summary of the group activities and goals. At this initial phase of the workshop, the group leaders make a special point of acknowledging that the workshop is required and that many of the participants probably do not want to be there. In discussing resistance feelings, the therapists cite several examples of participants who did not want to attend, and stress that this reaction is "normal," and that she or he understands it, but hopes that each participant will enjoy the meetings and learn something important. As a warm-up exercise, therapists ask participants to introduce themselves, tell their ages, identify their schools, and talk for a minute about what they like to do for fun. Before calling on the group members to respond, the therapists model (via self-disclosure) an appropriate response to the task. After each participant responds, the group leader always provides follow-up questions related to the adolescent's interest designed to provide encouragement to disclose and interact.

We then ask our therapists to present three additional questions to the group for general discussion: (1) Why do you think you are here? (2) What do you think a divorce is? (3) How do families and people within families change when there is a divorce? During the discussion that follows, the therapists are careful not to call on any participant who does not indicate a desire to respond. Hiding needs to be permitted in this group, especially with such a captive audience. Therapists support discussion and raise issues and examples for clarification. After the discussion of the three major questions is complete, the therapists move on to the next phase of the group, the stimulus film.

The therapists briefly introduce the stimulus film to the participants. The group members are prepared for discussing emotional reactions to divorce when they are informed that although the film is only 15 minutes long, it usually evokes strong feelings in the audience. The therapist provides further reassurance for the group members by assuring participants that these feelings are normal and that it is important to discuss these reactions when the film is over. A film or video (such as *Family Matters—What Is a Family?* from the Agency for Instructional Television, Bloomington, Indiana, 1975) is then shown to the group. The films selected usually focus on the conflicts and problem-solving strategies of an adolescent or latency age child whose parents are divorced. In one film used in the court project, for example, the adolescent daughter wrestles with her reunification fantasies by inviting both of her parents (unbeknownst to each other) to attend an athletic competition. Films that are successful display the tensions common to children in varying phases of adjustment to their parents' separation. Essentially, the film serves as a shared experience and a starting point from which the group members can identify and communicate their own concerns about divorce, without having to directly take responsibility or "own" the emotions discussed. The discussion of a hypothetical case appears to provide enough safety for the adolescents to disclose and discuss more personal concerns. Of course, therapists should be equipped with somewhat structured probes to present to the group, should resistance provide too great an inhibition to the emotional climate of the group. This rarely occurs, however.

After discussing the stimulus film (approximately 20 minutes), we schedule a 10-minute break. In fact, regardless of whether we are conducting a one-day "divorce workshop" or an ongoing psychotherapy group for adolescents of divorcing parents, we schedule a break and refreshments. The importance of this break and the significance of serving refreshments should be briefly discussed. The "break" itself provides the children with a time to experiment socially with other children who share a common and often uncomfortable role. As we have learned through many years of evaluation data, one of the major positive feelings reported by children attending our groups is "I'm not the only one who feels this way, and there are others who feel this way too—and it is normal to have these reactions." One of the more striking findings that we consistently obtain when running divorce groups is the uniformly large number of children, even older adolescents, who experience shame and embarrassment at being a child whose parents are divorced or divorcing. The Peer Ridicule and Avoidance (PRA) scale of Children's Attitudes Toward Parental Separation Inventory (CAPSI) provides a good measure of this problem with a fairly straightforward Yes-No approach (Berg 1979). Although it may sound like window dressing or an unnecessary frill for a serious therapy group, providing refreshments, or at least something to drink, is a significant event for divorce therapy groups designed for children. On the surface level, providing refreshments for the children serves to normalize or socialize the awkward experience of having to interact in a way that most of these youngsters have probably rarely encountered. On a deeper level, the children whose parents are going through a divorce strongly welcome the "nourishing" efforts of caring adults. The group feeds the children in many ways. We have conducted group therapy for latency age and older children in a variety of settings; however, we have never seen children who are literally hungrier than children of divorce.

After the break, when the group reconvenes, the therapists begin a presentation on the variety of emotional reactions to parental separation and divorce. Although the presentations begin in primarily didactic form, questions and discussion from group members are encouraged. Whenever a particular emotion, reaction, or coping strategy is presented, we find it important that one of the group leaders process the information in three ways: first, she or he points out that this feeling (anger, sadness, blaming) is a common experience for young adults, children, and parents; second, the group leader attempts to create a positive emotional climate in the group by indicating that the particular feeling being discussed is natural, justifiable, and "OK" to experience; finally, the group leader repeatedly speaks about the importance of talking about the ways of sharing the particular feeling under discussion. Most of the specific feelings or reaction patterns presented to the adolescents are adapted from *The Boy's and Girl's Book about Divorce* (Gardner 1971). The eight primary emotions or reaction patterns that we try to present to each group at least once are (1) experiencing the loss of control over parents' behavior, (2) feeling sadness, (3) being disappointed in parents, (4) feeling ashamed, (5) feeling that parents will stop loving you, (6) being angry, (7) feeling guilty (self-blame), (8) blaming one parent.

Guidance for Intervention

When the review of the variety of emotional experience is completed, the groups move into their less structured or didactic phase of work. We believe it is important for therapists to use their own strengths, stylistic features, and theoretical orientation. Thus, for example, we would be perfectly comfortable having a Rogerian therapist, a rational emotive therapist, a psychodynamic therapist, or a cognitive behaviorist lead our groups provided that each could reasonably get across the didactic material and could be sensitive to group interaction and communication styles. We have adapted the following five guidelines for intervention with groups from Beier and Young (1984).

1. The therapist intervenes when a member uses blaming behavior or says or implies that *someone or something else must change* to solve a problem. Children of divorce are great users of blaming. Our previous research has demonstrated that they blame parents (especially fathers!), themselves, and the unfairness of the world that would permit their lives to be so shaken. Initially, blaming may provide the child with some welcome, perhaps even necessary relief; however, when it is indulged in to the point that growth is precluded, the relief function fails, and stress is maintained. When the child of divorce who is failing in school says, "If only my dad would stop this business with his new girl friend," he or she is using this responsibility shifting device. Here, it is the therapist's responsibility to engage the group member to assess his or her own contribution to the problem that is being presented. The positive implication of this intervention in group is that the patient has more power and more control over her or his environment than he or she believes. The negative implication is that the patient is to blame. The therapist must carefully guard against using this intervention to merely shift blame to the patient, for, as we know, self-blame is also a place to hide, even in group.

2. The therapist intervenes when any member of the group makes a statement that is *designed to maintain the status quo*. A child in group recently remarked, "My mother wants me to be more aggressive and speak up to Dad when I need to, but I am what I am, I can't help it. . . ." Here, the therapist responded to this communication device with "You are saying, 'I am the way I am. I am not willing to accept the possibility of making changes in myself.'" The thera-

pist attempts to create some uncertainty and flexibility in the patient by questioning his or her favorite hiding place, represented by the "I am what I am" statement. Historical remarks ("My mother never loved me." or "Dad never had time for me.") should be regarded as just another means of holding onto the past. Here the therapist can cautiously work to teach that the patient is using blame as an alibi.

3. The therapist intervenes when a member constricts communication in the group by asking loaded questions or by conveying messages of which the member may not be aware. These techniques require confrontation with caring. If the therapist observes a child heavily pressuring another group member to "open up" or to "defend himself" and is achieving the expected result of even greater silence, the therapist intervenes: "I know you want Robert to act more directly. You constantly remind him about this, yet you haven't been successful." The group member responds, "I'm not sure what else to do." The therapist gets up and shakes the group member's hand. "I have to congratulate you; we're off to a new start." It should be noted that in such situations the therapist analyzes the communication patterns in the group and does not take sides. The therapist must take great care not to be viewed as supercritical.

4. The therapist must make a *distinction between motivation* (that is, the way a group member interprets an act) *and procedure* (the way the group member tries to reach for the goal). In effect, this procedure helps the group member to reevaluate his or her own motivation. The thought processes here are as follows: "If I am desiring to have a good relationship with my father on visitation, but I am also using procedures to make him angry and disturb him, then perhaps my interpretation of my motivation is wrong. Perhaps I do not really want a good relationship with Dad—or perhaps I should change my procedures."

5. The therapist must *maintain balance* within the group over the course of the session. Throughout the session, especially if the group is under an hour and a half in length, the therapist must be alert not to be engaged in conversation with the more responsive group members. Equally important, the therapist must be careful not to "chase" the silent member. That a silent group member has less of a therapeutic experience in the group than a talking member has never been demonstrated. Why, then, do so many therapists assume that the child must speak in order to have a therapeutic experience? We believe that silent members make therapists (and other group members) feel uncomfortable. Therefore, therapists and group members make special efforts to get the silent members to

talk. However, we believe that this is a therapeutic error and that such efforts are reinforcing of special stylistic strategies. Instead, the therapist should respond to the silent member in the same fashion used with the more talkative children, indicating that the therapist understands the subtle information. By treating the silent child as an equal, the therapist gives the children the message that they are in a beneficial environment and that they cannot fall into disfavor because they behave differently from other group members. This acceptance is most likely a better guarantee of restraint-free interaction than rejection of the silence—or the silent member.

The Use of Research Data in Group Treatment

Our research on group members of latency age, adolescence, and adulthood has attempted to isolate variables related to consumer satisfaction, common themes representing the most concern, and factors related to perceived adjustment difficulty. We have found thematic presentation or at least emphasis on special problems to be stimulating and therapeutic at all three levels. A set of key findings we discuss with all three groups includes the parental- and self-blaming styles of children. We have found repeatedly in our research that children and adolescents are quite open when asked anonymously (via questionnaire or individual interview) about their feelings of blaming parents and themselves (Young 1983). However, in the group context, especially in the early phase of the work, the children are much less apt to disclose their feelings, so we take the lead and do it for them. Often we share the results of our previous studies and remind the children that the data from their group probably looks a lot like the results we have gathered over the years. It should be noted that we always collect data from the children prior to starting a new group. Not only does this supply information for future research questions, but it sets the stage for the children to begin to work on important cognitive issues that have been established as significantly related to their development.

We usually start with the concept of self-blame and then move on to discussions about parents and blame. Our data from several studies (for example, Young 1980, Young 1983, Young and Bodie 1984) reveal that about 50 percent of the children attending our groups initially report experiencing at least some blame for their parents' breakup. Many of that group actually see themselves as a primary cause of the separation. Even though the "no-fault" system of divorce has replaced the adversary system of fault-finding, children observing the negative life events associated with a divorce are prone to make attributions about the cause of such events (Zautra et al. 1981).

We explain to the children, of course depending on their age and level of comprehension, that blaming the self (or one parent to the extreme) may actually serve the child's need to maintain a feeling of control or predictability in the face of an environmental or perceived intrapsychic threat. By attributing causality for negative events via blaming to an external source ("Dad is the bad one," or "Mom's boy-friend is the evil one—it's all his fault,") or to a relatively static per-sonal characteristic ("If I weren't such a wild kid, they could still love me and stay together"), a child may be able to escape difficult changes in habitual patterns of thought and behavior. In the ex-treme, a need to maintain a belief in a "just world" (Lerner and Miller 1978) can even lead children to blame or denigrate an individual (self, sibling, or parent) that most related outside observers would consider a victim. Thus, the relief function of blame is discussed and assessed within the group. Blaming the self or parents can provide relief and a perception or feeling of control. The negative effects of blame, of course, are also explored. The ideas of delayed growth in relationship with parents, lowering of self-esteem, and increases in anxiety and adjustment difficulty are also explored. However, it is important that the group see blame as a natural reaction to divorce and not purely as a problem or a sign of pathology. If the group is permitted to develop the relatively restrictive emotional climate that blame is a sign of "big problems," none of the children will be able to honestly work through and understand the function that blame serves for them.

In the same way, the positive and negative functions of parent blaming are presented to the children in our groups. Again, sharing the findings from our previous research, we show how the typical pattern of blaming the noncustodial parent (usually the father—for adolescents, 43.8 percent; for latency age children, 35.7 percent) relates to anticipating an "easier adjustment." Our findings gener-ally indicate that children who blame either the mother or both parents anticipated significantly greater difficulty in adjusting to the divorce, while those who blamed either the father or neither parent expected fewer problems. In exploring these findings with the children, we note that the great majority (over 90 percent) of our sample was living with the mother as the custodial parent. Perhaps those children who blamed their father felt secure about their coali-tion with their mothers (the custodial parent), while those who blamed their mothers were less secure about the safety of their home base. Fathers may also make convenient targets for blame, given their general unavailability to members of the household after the initial separation. Discussing the data we have obtained from past groups often provides the distance necessary to stimulate disclosure of personal blame issues and a working through via group processes.

A third area of research we chose to process with our groups includes an understanding of the ways in which parents are not always capable of accurately perceiving and appropriately responding to the needs of their children, especially when the separation has been relatively recent (Young 1983, Young and Bodie 1984). We certainly do not want the children to form the full impression that they are on their own, that Mom and Dad are simply going to be psychologically unavailable until the dust clears and wounds heal. In fact, many divorced parents tend to overestimate the magnitude of their children's distress. The major finding, however, is that at a time of crisis and change, parents are unable to accurately perceive their children's needs; they are out of synch with their children. Methods of coping with this almost universally found problem are presented and processed in the group. We explore how to clearly make needs known, how to identify other adult resources to assist in problem solving, and even how to make use of professional help when parents are unavailable. For example, traditional traps sometimes involved in attempting to cope with the unavailable parent include discussion of problematic strategies such as becoming a "hypermature" child or special parental surrogate.

CONCLUSION

To the casual reader, it may appear that most of our group work is didactic, or at least fully a topical approach. To permit such a conclusion to remain at the termination of this chapter would indeed be an error. More than teacher, provider of information, confidant, and the like, we feel the leader of the therapy group for children of divorce is a communication analyst. The group leader is not just another group member (as some human potential group leaders wish to proclaim). Just as a father cannot be a child's "pal" without betraying the parental trust when responsibility for and authority over the child must be taken, a group leader would be hypocritical to proclaim that she or he is just a group member. As a communications specialist or analyst, the therapist serves neither as a group member nor as a direct participant. The therapist on occasion will interpret the emotional climate of the group, assist individual members in their bid for clarification, process the engagement maneuvers of individual members, and raise relevant thematic material.

A closing note on the nature and partial dangers of "theme" groups is in order. A major portion of what occurs in group depends upon how that group is introduced and defined to its members. What happens in group depends fairly heavily on what group members are led to believe. For example, if children in a divorce group are introduced to their status in group as "victims" rather than as active participants in creating their own psychological environment, they will tend to view all distress that they experience as a result of their status, which, of course, they are powerless to change. Thus, the therapist must be cautious in preventing the group members from hiding behind the victim or any other label. At the same time, however, the therapist should permit the group to experience the support that comes from having a common bond. As we have heard time and time again at the termination of our groups, the children are able to articulate that one of the most positive aspects of their therapy has been learning that "We are not alone."

We define primary prevention as preparing all children, especially children from intact families, for the eventual changes in form and function that families take. At first glance this philosophy of teaching children from intact families about divorce—how it affects families, how children and parents can develop successful coping models—appears unnecessary, perhaps even cruel. However, we believe that the cruelty lies in the common situation of taking children who are largely unprepared for their parents' separation and simply expecting them to adjust. Similarly, we are also simply expecting children to adjust without preparation to changes in the families of peers, teachers, extended family members, and others within the social sphere. Stolberg and Garrison (1985) speak of primary prevention as offering a voluntary program for those families who have recently separated and have not received formal mental health treatment. The problems of self-selection appear as an issue here. Of even greater concern is thinking of education about divorce—after the fact—as primary prevention. Would you call a drug administered after an infection has taken hold a vaccine?

REFERENCES

Anthony, E. J. (1974). Children at risk from divorce: a review. In *The Child in His Family: Children at Psychiatric Risk*, ed. E. J. Anthony and C. Koupernik. New York: Wiley.

Beier, E. G., and Young, D. M. (1984). *Silent Language of Psychotherapy*. 2nd ed. New York: Aldine.

Berg, B. (1979). *Children's Attitudes Toward Parental Separation Inventory*. Dayton, Ohio: University of Dayton Press.

Bornstein, M. T., Bornstein, P. H., and Walters, H. A. (1985). Children of divorce: a group treatment manual for research and application. *Journal of Child and Adolescent Psychotherapy* 2: 267–273.

Epstein, Y. M., and Borduin, C. M. (1985). Could this happen? a game for children of divorce. *Psychotherapy* 22:770–773.

Felner, R. D., Stolberg, A., and Cowen, E. L. (1975). Crisis events and school mental health referral problems of young children. *Journal of Consulting and Clinical Psychology* 43:305–310.

Gardner, R. (1971). *The Boy's and Girl's Book About Divorce*. New York: Bantam.

Green, B. J. (1978). Helping children of divorce. a multimodal approach. *Elementary School Guidance and Counseling* 12:31–45.

Guerney, L., and Jordan, L. (1979). Children of divorce—a community support group. *Journal of Divorce* 2:283–294.

Haaken, J. K., and Davis, F. B. (1975). Group therapy with latency age psychotic children. *Child Welfare* 54:703–710.

Kaminsky, H. (1986). The divorce adjustment education and support group for children. *Conciliation Courts Review* 24:45–49.

Kurdek, L. A. (1981). An integrative perspective on children's divorce adjustment. *American Psychologist* 36:856–866.

Lerner, M. J., and Miller, D. T. (1978). Just world research and the attributional process: looking back and ahead. *Psychological Bulletin* 85: 1030–1051.

Mahler, M. S., and Rabinovitch, R. (1956). The effects of marital conflict on child development. In *Neurotic Interaction in Marriage*, ed. V. S. Eisenstein. New York: Basic Books.

Martin, M., Martin, D., and Porter, J. (1983). Breaking up is hard to do. *The School Counselor*, 30:315–319.

Pedro-Carroll, J. L., and Cowen, E. L. (1985). The children of divorce intervention program: an investigation of the efficacy of a school-based prevention program. *Journal of Consulting and Clinical Psychology* 53:603–612.

Schaefer, C. E., Johnson, L., and Wherry, J. N. (1982). *Group Therapies for Children and Youth*. San Francisco: Jossey-Bass.

Stolberg, A. L., and Garrison, K. M. (1985). Evaluating a primary prevention program for children of divorce. *American Journal of Community Psychology* 13:111–124.

Tessman, L. H. (1978). *Children of Parting Parents.* New York: Jason Aronson.

Titkin, E. A., and Cobb, C. (1983). Treating post-divorce adjustment in latency age children: a focused group paradigm. *Social Work with Groups* 6:53–66.

Toomin, M. K. (1974). The child of divorce. In *Therapeutic Needs of the Family,* ed. R. E. Hardy and J. G. Cull. Springfield, IL: Charles C Thomas.

Vogelsang, J. D. (1982). Working with the divorced and separated. *Journal of Religion and Health* 21:325–330.

Wallerstein, J. S. (1985). Children of divorce: emerging trends. *Psychiatric Clinics of North America* 8:837–855.

Wallerstein, J. C., and Kelly, J. B. (1974). The effects of parental divorce: the adolescent experience. In *The Child in His Family: Children at Psychiatric Risk,* ed. E. J. Anthony and C. Koupernik. New York: Wiley.

Young, D. M. (1980). A court-mandated workshop for adolescent children of divorcing parents: a program evaluation. *Adolescence* 15:763–774.

——— (1983). Two studies of children of divorce. In *Children and Divorce,* ed. L. A. Kurdek, pp. 61–69. San Francisco: Jossey-Bass.

Young, D. M., and Bodie, G. L. (1984). The accuracy of parents' perceptions of children of divorce. *Early Child Development and Care* 13:309–320.

Zautra, A., Young, D. M., and Guenther, R. T. (1981). Blaming—a sign of psychosocial tensions in the community: findings from two surveys. *American Journal of Community Psychology* 9:209–224.

14

GROUP THERAPY FOR DIVORCED ADULTS

Connie J. Salts, Ph.D.

During the recovery stage of the divorce process, therapy focusing on individual issues, such as coping with loneliness, regaining self-confidence, and rebuilding social relationships is indicated as the most legitimate form of divorce treatment for adults (Storm and Sprenkle 1982). In discussing the role of rituals in easing the transition for divorcing individuals, Lewis (1983) suggests ritualizing the divorce adjustment group as a means of educating formerly marrieds about the process they are experiencing and of supporting them during that time.

Divorce adjustment/therapy groups are directed toward helping the individual adjust to the status and roles of singlehood. This adjustment involves personal growth and changes in attitudes, feelings, and behavior toward themselves, the ex-spouse, children, relatives, friends, sex and dating, marriage, work, hobbies, and life as a whole. The counseling group also provides the divorced adult with the opportunity to achieve autonomy, to gain increased understanding of self and others, and to acquire an enhanced ability to handle problems that may arise in the future.

In this chapter we give an overview of the various clinical approaches to adult divorce groups and review the current research evaluating the effectiveness of various approaches. An example of a specific approach to an adult divorce group is also provided.

CLINICAL APPROACHES TO DIVORCE GROUPS

Various short-term models have been proposed for group counseling of divorced adults. Agreement is found among the designers of divorce groups that the group experience provides the divorced person with emotional support, companionship, a vehicle for ventilating feelings, and the realization of commonalties present among those who have had partnership breakdowns. Two major differences exist: (1) the degree to which the groups should be structured or unstructured and (2) the degree to which the groups should be educational groups or therapy groups.

In the unstructured therapy-style groups, the therapist does not initiate topics, but follows the conversation and feeling tone of the group (Levine 1975, Morris and Prescott 1975). Discussions center on the understanding and expression of feelings, with a focus on the skills of listening and the importance of self-knowledge. Occasionally the therapist intervenes to clarify specific points or to deal with special problems. Due to the rapidity of movement from topic to topic in some sessions, the therapist may also intervene to assure that concerns are adequately discussed before the group moves on to another topic. The therapist's assessment of group or individual needs at the time guides these interventions, the aim of which is to provide some of the ingredients necessary to the therapeutic growth process. Group therapy literature has identified several aspects of group dynamics that provide the mechanisms for growth and personal change. Some of these include the expression of intense personal feelings, self-disclosure, receiving information about one's behavior, experiencing strong emotions, and self-insight. Other experiences include the capacity to experience unity with the group, being helpful to others, learning from being in situations where others are having critical emotional experiences, the discovery of similarity between one's own and others' problems, receiving advice on how to deal with important life issues, and modeling behavior or styles of problem solving observed in the group (Yalom 1975).

Other postdivorce group models (Fisher 1974, Granvold and Welch 1977, Hassall and Madar 1980, Hoopes 1978, Kessler 1977a,b) propose that divorced persons need and want more structure. Thus, they utilize such techniques as time-limited task-oriented sessions, leader-led discussions, and prearranged role playing. Fisher's (1974) and Kessler's (1977a,b) groups fall on the educational side of the continuum. Hassall and Madar (1980) employ a crisis model, while Granvold and Welch (1977) employ a cognitive-behavioral treatment approach. The Hoopes (1978) model focuses on use of supportive behaviors and problem solving.

Fisher (1974) assumes that many divorced persons either do not need or want major reorganization of their personality, but are seeking something to ease their pain and confusion. Therefore, she focuses on healthy growth, on personal and social adjustment, and on improved attitudes and skills in human relationships. During the first session of the structured counseling-education groups, specific topics are selected by the group from a list of relevant topics presented by the members and the counselor. The group sessions can shift from a seminar-type format to a more personal level of discussion; however, topics are kept within the range of the subject originally introduced. Fisher offers concurrent individual therapy for group members.

Kessler's (1977a,b) model employs an unstructured portion to provide members the opportunity to raise specific concerns. The group then moves to a lecturette, psychodrama, skill-building exercise, or film designed to portray potential problem areas in divorce and to elicit discussion and skill-building exercises. Specific goals of this model are to provide support, identity, and open sharing to persons separating or divorcing; to strengthen self-definition and autonomy of the participants; and to learn specific tools to deal with several divorce issues. These issues include:

1. Communicating with one's former spouse
2. Letting go
3. Training friends to deal with the divorce appropriately
4. Working through anger
5. Confronting assumptions about divorce
6. Reviewing personal values about marriage, divorce, and children
7. Helping children express their feelings
8. Coping with intense emotions
9. Giving up guilt
10. Setting new goals, including new vocational directions
11. Resurrecting rusty dating skills
12. Recognizing needs for one's next intimate relationship.

Granvold and Welch's (1977, 1979) cognitive behavioral approach employs a seven-week, structured treatment, seminar format. The topics are predetermined, and various techniques such as group discussion, role reversal, modeling, problem solving, and homework assignments are utilized. They provide a detailed outline of the didactic content covered during the seminar. Major topic areas include the emotional impact of separation/divorce, the continuing relationship with the ex-spouse, the impact of separation on family and friends, the impact of separation on relationships with children, dating and interpersonal relationship formation, sexual adjustment as a single adult, and marriage as a positive institution.

Hassall and Madar (1980) utilize a crisis model to structure their divorce groups. Eight steps to crisis resolution are used to structure the group, and the goal of the therapist is to move each member of the group through the substeps of the model.

Hoopes (1978) utilizes an eight-week Divorce Adjustment Treatment with three phases. Phase 1 (week 1) consists of development of support among group members and commitment to the group process. The purpose of phase 2 (weeks 2–5) is to assist individuals in acquiring problem-solving skills. During phase 3 (weeks 6–8), members gain an increased awareness of their own personal strengths and capabilities through introspection and information given by other group members.

This brief overview of divorce therapy groups provides a look at the variety of models that have been developed. The important element common to all of them is the reliance on the group process as an effective means of helping individual adults adjust to divorce. The theoretical orientation of the developer, as well as the setting in which divorce groups are provided, greatly influences the structure, content, and tone of the groups.

Critiques of short-term group models for divorced adults also reflect differences in orientation. Brown (1985) questions the ability of short-term divorce groups to address underlying issues of the individuals choosing the groups rather than other forms of therapy. She indicates that a more useful approach is to offer ongoing therapy groups and a series of educational seminars for the separated and divorced. She also questions use of divorce groups that are limited to women only or to men only, stating that it becomes too easy for the participants to blame the opposite sex and avoid the painful work of self-examination.

In contrast, Carter (1977) states that the most important characteristic for divorced women to learn is autonomy. She believes individual counseling reinforces a deference model and women's dependence. Thus, she suggests that a women's group is preferable to a mixed-sex group, as it provides women the opportunity to learn new ways of relating to other women. The clinical experience of Langelier and Deckert (1980) also supports the use of an all-female therapy group for the late divorced female. Tedder and colleagues (1984), in developing group sessions for single, custodial fathers, indicated that participation in a group with individuals who are in a similar situation is an effective way to get support and learn to cope with problems that arise in that situation.

Gettleman and Markowitz (1974) specifically criticize Fisher's (1974) particular approach for utilizing a "grief" model. They suggest that a negative bias is reflected by Fisher and that there is no evidence that divorce is a mistake or that persons who divorce are immature adults now expected to mature emotionally.

EFFECTIVENESS OF DIVORCE GROUPS

In an effort to answer the question regarding whether or not adult divorce groups are an effective means of helping individuals adjust to divorce, researchers have conducted evaluation studies for specific group therapy models. Studies comparing different group models with one another and studies comparing group therapy to other treatment approaches, however, have been limited.

A review of the research revealed that overall divorce adjustment and self-concept were the variables most frequently used to measure the effectiveness of short-term divorce counseling groups. The Postdivorce Problems and Stress Scale (Raschke 1974) was used in several studies (Barlow 1982, Campbell 1983, Farenhorst 1982, Goff 1983, Salts and Zongker 1983). It is a 60-item Likert-type summated rating scale that was developed to measure current postseparation and postdivorce adjustment. The Fisher Divorce Adjustment Scale (Fisher 1976) has also been used as a measure in evaluating the effectiveness of divorce groups (Broder 1981, Fisher 1976, Henry 1981, Tedder et al. 1984). The Tennessee Self-Concept Scale (Fitts 1965) was the most frequently used measure of self-concept (Fisher 1976, Henry 1981, Kessler 1977c, Salts and Zongker 1983, Goff 1983, Campbell 1983).

Fisher (1976) conducted divorce adjustment seminars for the purpose of partially meeting the social and emotional needs of people who were working through the divorce process. He found that participants in the ten-week divorce adjustment seminar had more growth in self-acceptance of divorce, disentanglement of the love relationship, rebuilding of social relationships, and total divorce process as measured by the Fisher Divorce Adjustment Scale than the control group. The group participants had more growth in rebuilding self-concept as measured by the Tennessee Self-Concept Scale. There was not, however, a significant decrease in symptoms of grief.

Henry (1981), in comparing participants of an eight-week unstructured group with a no-treatment control, confirmed the effectiveness of small-group counseling in facilitating divorce adjustment. Those who had attended the group counseling showed reduced levels of depression, increased feelings of self-worth, more disentanglement from the love relationship, decreased feelings of anger toward spouse, decreased symptoms of grief, and increased social trust. There was also a strong trend toward increased self-concept.

Broder (1981) conducted an all-day eight-hour workshop with a three-hour follow-up group four weeks later. The participants met in same-sex leaderless groups on a weekly basis between the sessions. Participants in this program showed improvement as measured by Fisher's Divorce Adjustment Scale.

A research study by Kessler (1977c) compared a structured group, an unstructured group, and a control group receiving no treatment. The treatment groups met for eight weeks, two hours per week. Findings of this posttest-only design showed that members in both the structured and the unstructured group were more successful than members of the control group in attaining the goals of regaining their sense of confidence and emotional autonomy and in learning a better sense of self-mastery. The structured group was also more effective than the unstructured group as assessed by the Tennessee Self-Concept Scale and the Self-Description Inventory (Ghiselli 1971). An explanation given for this difference was that the structured experience may have provided a modeling order and security that made the floundering feelings, which many persons tend to experience during divorce, more manageable.

In other research studies using a group format similar to that of Kessler, additional support was found for the effectiveness of short-term structured group treatment models to facilitate divorce adjustment as measured by the Postdivorce Problems and Stress Scale (Barlow 1982, Campbell 1983, Farenhorst 1982, Goff 1983, and Salts and Zongker 1983).

Vogel-Moline (1979) and Hoopes and colleagues (1979) compared depression and self-esteem in individuals attending the structured eight-week, two-hours-per-session divorce group with individuals in a no-treatment control group. They found decreased levels of depression as measured by the Depression Adjective Check List and increased levels of self-esteem as measured by social worth and social competence factors of the Modified Osgood Semantic Differential in individuals who had attended the Divorce Adjustment Treatment (Hoopes 1978).

In Gillen's (1976) study of the effects of paraprofessionally conducted group therapy on the self-concept of divorced or separated persons, no significant effects were found. These groups were conducted for a period of only four weeks for two and a half hours per week. Gillen suggested that the time period was too short for therapeutic change to occur. Goff (1983) found that the participants of an eight-week professionally directed structured group experienced greater improvement in divorce adjustment than did participants of the self-directed structured group and the minimal contact group. Members of a self-directed structured group experienced some improvement in divorce adjustment over the control group. Both the professionally directed and the self-directed group participants showed improved self-concept over the control group..

Tedder and colleagues (1984) offered a structured group for custodial fathers that provided information addressing the issues of single parents plus an opportunity for discussion of concerns by the participants. Their results indicated greater positive changes in divorce adjustment, loneliness, and self-concept for those men who attended the groups than for those who did not attend.

Farenhorst (1982) compared a structured group treatment with a structured individual treatment and found participants in both treatments showed greater improvement in divorce adjustment than a minimal-contact control. There were no significant differences in adjustment between participants in the group treatment and the individual treatment.

Thus, research supports the use of short-term group counseling as a means of assisting the divorcing individual to make adjustments. Although the unstructured group has been shown to be effective in improving divorce adjustment over a control group (Henry 1981, Kessler 1977c), comparison studies imply that participants in structured counseling groups show greater improvement than those in unstructured counseling groups (Kessler 1977c, Salts and Zongker 1983). The eight-week, two-hours-per-session, counseling group was the format most frequently used in the various studies that showed the structured counseling group to be effective in improving divorce adjustment (Barlow 1982, Campbell 1983, Farenhorst 1982, Goff 1983, Kessler 1977c, Salts and Zongker 1983, Vogel-Moline 1979). There is also research that indicates professionally directed groups may be more effective than self-help groups (Goff 1983). Structured group counseling was also shown to be as equally effective as a structured individual therapy (Farenhorst 1982).

Since group counseling is recognized as not being suitable for all people, the question of who will be effectively served by a divorce group has been raised. Note should be made that many of the research reports do indicate a greater proportion of female participants than male participants, thus possibly adding a limiting factor to the findings. Other research suggests additional limitations for the use of divorce adjustment groups.

In a group of females who received group counseling and had been separated for at least three months, Mackeen and Herman (1974) found a significant change in their level of self-esteem. However, in a group that had only been recently separated, no positive changes in self-esteem were realized. Barlow's (1982) research raised the question of the adequacy of group treatment alone to meet the needs of moderately to severely depressed, poorly adjusted persons who experience divorce.

Henry (1981), reporting data from subjects who left treatment before the end of the eight weeks, indicated that group counseling may be most appropriate for persons who are past the shock and denial stage of divorce adjustment and have entered into the grief and mourning stage. In evaluating the data of individuals who discontinued the group counseling and dropped out of the research project, Salts (1983) found divorce adjustment scores of the dropouts indicated a poorer adjustment to divorce, while their average length of separation from spouses was longer than for those who completed the counseling. A greater percentage of the dropouts had children as well as very low incomes. It was determined that since the primary objective of the divorce adjustment group was to promote self-understanding and personal growth, the immediate basic survival needs of these individuals were not being met, resulting in the decision to discontinue the group. The inherent danger of this premature termination is that the individual may be discouraged from seeking additional needed assistance.

To reduce casualties within the divorce counseling groups, Salts (1983) recommends that the screening process for member selection take into consideration the goals of the group, the stage of divorce an individual is in, and the prognosis for the individual to be able to move from that stage into another during the time period of the group. Individuals struggling to fulfill needs not addressed by the group might view themselves as not benefiting from the group participation and end their membership.

Individuals who have been separated for more than nine months and who are still unable to cope with "breaking old habits" or who are in an economic panic are potential casualties in a divorce counseling group. If effective assistance is to be provided, it is imperative that the counselor be aware of the client's position in the divorce process. Further, a knowledge of what each stage of divorce requires on·the part of both the counselor and the client is necessary (Salts 1979). Data from Salts's (1984) research indicating that the group counseling may have been more beneficial for individuals whose spouse suggested the divorce further supports the contention that divorce therapy groups must be flexible in order to meet the varying needs of all group members.

Thus we have an overview of the majority of the printed information available on group therapy/counseling for divorced adults. Unfortunately there is not information available to determine how frequently the group approach is employed by clinicians or how responsive specific segments of the divorced population have been to its use. Nearly all the research studies have been conducted in university-based programs, with many of the groups being offered for the purpose of research rather than as part of an ongoing community program. Thus, there is little information regarding the success of such programs in meeting the mental health/social service needs of a community. Verbal reports from individual participants do, however, indicate that the groups are very helpful for the divorced individual.

Throughout this chapter the terms *divorce therapy groups, divorce counseling groups,* and *divorce adjustment groups/programs* have been used interchangeably, and are partially addressed through the issue of structured vs. unstructured and therapy vs. education. The most appropriate and most effective group format will ultimately depend on the individual client and to some extent on the orientation of the professional providing the service. The provision of a group treatment designed to fit the needs, budget, and expectations of a majority of the individuals experiencing divorce in a particular population segment will meet with success as evaluated by the participants. The challenge to the provider is to create such a program. The next section offers the reader a look at an approach to providing a divorce adjustment group that combines group techniques with aspects of strategic family therapy.

DESCRIPTION OF A DIVORCE GROUP

Before we describe the content and process components of the program, we note issues that have an impact on the success of the groups. Although no longer a part of a university research project, these groups are provided free of charge to the participants as part of a university training program in marriage and family therapy. Thus, these groups are available to participants who, due to financial limitations, may not have other forms of professional help available to them. Second, approximately 80 percent of the participants become aware of the groups through newspaper and other public media exposure rather than referral from other professionals in the helping fields. The announcements do not use the terms *therapy* or *counseling,* but describe the groups as being designed to provide a supportive environment conducive to the sharing of strengths and explorations of concern for those struggling to adjust to being separated or divorced from their spouses. Thus, many of the participants may not deem themselves in need of professional counseling, but are open to the idea of an adjustment group.

Although the groups are not called therapy groups, individuals must participate in an intake session before beginning a group. The purposes for the intakes are to explain specifics about the program and the group experience, and to determine the individual's suitability for participation in a divorce adjustment group, by using standard group counseling guidelines and the guidelines noted earlier in this chapter by Salts (1983).

From a clinical viewpoint, most of the divorce adjustment groups seem to function best with five or six members. As the group increases in size, less and less time is available for each individual to deal with his or her issues. More dropouts are noted with larger groups. The groups generally meet one evening per week for eight weeks for approximately two and a half hours. Each group varies in actual length per week, and sometimes members request an additional week or two in order to complete any unfinished group work.

Structured techniques are used during the first group session to help the participants ease into becoming active group members. We begin with an icebreaker, such as having the group members pair up and share information, which can be used to introduce one another to the group. Once all the introductions are complete, the leader sets the stage for the group work by discussing expectations and ground rules, with emphasis placed on active participation in the sessions and completion of homework assignments by all group members.

With these housekeeping tasks complete, the leader distributes and discusses an Obstacle Check List adapted from Kessler (1977b). It contains these thirty obstacles that many individuals experiencing divorce must overcome:

1. Letting go of former spouse
2. Making new friends
3. Forgiving former spouse
4. Self-blame

5. Communicating divorce to children
6. Vocational choice
7. Feeling uncomfortable around other sex
8. Dealing with parents over divorce issues
9. Feeling depressed
10. Feeling as if children are deprived in a single-parent home
11. Feeling anxious much of the time
12. Breaking habits that are now self-defeating
13. Saying "no" to former spouse
14. Disciplining children
15. Budgeting money
16. Drinking too much
17. Sleeplessness
18. Eating too much or too little
19. Mood swings
20. Concerns over sexual involvement
21. Difficulty in taking new risks
22. Expressing pent-up anger
23. Curtailing or giving up bitterness
24. Worry about being judged by friends, family
25. Afraid of intimacy in new relationships
26. Feeling guilty over initiating divorce
27. Feelings of rejection
28. Confused about feelings, thoughts, intentions, limitations
29. Inability to assert feelings, thought, and wishes
30. Other

Members individually rate each obstacle as either a major, moderate, or slight problem, or a nonproblem. The remainder of the first session is spent with the group members sharing at least one obstacle that is a problem for them. The leader helps each group member clarify in behavioral terms how the obstacle is a problem for him or her and, if time permits, what has been done to attempt to solve the problem. Using a problem-focused approach, the leader begins modeling problem solving rather than advice giving as a group norm. For homework, group members are requested to list on paper four or five obstacles they want to work on during the group and to think about how each obstacle is a problem for them. They are encouraged to rank these obstacles, listing at the top the obstacles they believe will be the least difficult to overcome. Group members are also encouraged to begin making use of the lending library, which contains books and articles about divorce and various self-help techniques.

During the second session, group work begins with the members sharing their list of four or five obstacles. The leader writes these lists on the board in order to observe similarities and differences among the group members. The group then begins the process of helping each member to clarify in behavioral terms how the obstacle is currently a problem, to review what solutions have been attempted, and to creatively design new solutions to fit each situation. From there the group moves to helping each member set goals that are small, realistic, concrete, behavioral and "measureable." It is emphasized, however, that the recommended solutions must remain individualized to fit each member's particular needs. During this process, the leader uses such techniques as reframing the problem, establishing new behaviors, encouraging the setting of self-reinforcement schedules, suggesting the use of pretending as a way to practice desired behaviors, and assignment of individualized homework tasks. The intent is for the members to begin to focus on small changes and to experience success in making these changes. The overall approach of the leader reflects a theoretical integration of various proponents of the brief strategic models of family therapy (deShazer 1982, Fisch et al. 1982, Haley 1987, L'Abate et al. 1986, Madanes 1981, 1984).

In the remaining six sessions, the problem-solving approach continues with the checking on homework tasks, the practicing of tasks in session, and the continued development of individualized homework that is designed to address the obstacles the members designated as problems. This task-oriented approach is also accompanied by the fostering in the group of an atmosphere of positiveness, affirmation, respect, and building on strengths. Thus, using the curative factors of group dynamics and adapting the techniques of change from family therapy, we have created a model for a divorce adjustment group that fits both the needs of the group members and the theoretical position of the leader, and has been evaluated by the participants as successful.

CONCLUSION

This chapter has provided an overview of the majority of published information available on group therapy/counseling for divorced adults. Unfortunately there is no information available to determine how frequently the group approach is employed by clinicians or how responsive specific segments of the divorced population have been to its use. Nearly all the research studies have been conducted in university-based programs, with many of the groups being offered for the purpose of research rather than as part of an ongoing community program. Thus, there is little information regarding the success of such programs in meeting the mental health/social service needs of a community. Verbal reports from individual participants do, however, indicate that such groups are very helpful for the divorced individual.

Throughout this chapter the terms *divorce therapy groups, divorce counseling groups,* and *divorce adjustment groups/programs* have been used interchangeably, and they are delineated through the issues of structured vs. unstructured and therapy vs. education. The most appropriate and most effective group format will ultimately depend on the individual client and, to some extent, the orientation of the professional providing the service. Providing group treatment designed to fit the needs, budget, and expectations of a majority of the individuals in a particular population segment experiencing divorce will meet with success as evaluated by the participants. The challenge to the provider is to create such a program.

REFERENCES

Barlow, L. O. (1982). A Comparison of the Effectiveness of Group Therapy on Divorce Adjustment and Depression for Separated and Divorced Persons. Unpublished doctoral dissertation, Florida State University.

Broder, M. S. (1981). A Descriptive Study of a Program Designed to Help Participants to Deal with Issues Related to Divorce and Separation from Long-term Relationships. Unpublished doctoral dissertation, Temple University.

Brown, E. M. (1985). The comprehensive divorce treatment center: the divorce and marital stress clinic model. *Journal of Psychotherapy and the Family* 1:159–169.

Campbell, M. S. (1983). Extra-Group Socializing Instructions and Outcome of Divorce Adjustment Counseling. Unpublished doctoral dissertation, Florida State University.

Carter, D. K. (1977). Counseling divorced women. *Personnel and Guidance Journal* 55: 537–541.

deShazer, S. (1982). *Patterns of Brief Family Therapy: An Ecosystemic Approach.* New York: Guilford.

Farenhorst, D. (1982). The Comparative Effectiveness of Individual and Group Counseling Modalities for Postdivorce Adjustment and Self-esteem. Unpublished doctoral dissertation, Florida State University.

Fisch, R., Weakland, J. H., and Segal, L. (1982). *The Tactics of Change: Doing Therapy Briefly.* San Francisco: Jossey-Bass.

Fisher, B. F. (1976). Identifying and Meeting Needs of Formerly Married People through a Divorce Adjustment Seminar. Unpublished doctoral dissertation, University of Northern Colorado.

Fisher, E. O. (1974). *Divorce: the New Freedom. A Guide to Divorcing and Divorce Counseling.* New York: Harpers.

Fitts, W. H. (1965). *Manual: Tennessee Self-Concept Scale.* Nashville, TN: Counselor Recordings and Tests.

Gettleman, S., and Markowitz, J. (1974) *The Courage to Divorce.* New York: Simon and Schuster.

Ghiselli, E. E. (1971). *Explorations in Managerial Talent.* Pacific Palisades, CA: Goodyear Publishing Company, 1971.

Gillen, F. C. (1976). A Study of the Effects of Paraprofessionally Conducted Group Therapy on the Self-Concept of Divorced or Separated Persons. Unpublished doctoral dissertation, University of South Dakota.

Goff, D. R. (1983). The Effectiveness of Professional- and Self-directed Group Treatments for Divorce Adjustment and Self-Esteem. Unpublished doctoral dissertation, Florida State University.

Granvold, D. K., and Welch, G. J. (1977). Intervention for postdivorce adjustment problems: the treatment seminar. *Journal of Divorce* 1:81–92.

———— (1979). Structured, short-term group treatment of postdivorce adjustment. *International Journal of Group Psychotherapy* 29:347–358.

Haley, J. (1976). *Problem-solving Therapy*. San Francisco: Jossey-Bass.

Hassall, E., and Madar, D. (1980). Crisis group therapy with the separated and divorced. *Family Relations* 29:591–597.

Henry, C. J. (1981). The Effects of a Structured Group Treatment on Self-esteem and Depression of Divorced/Separated Persons. Unpublished doctoral dissertation, University of Washington.

Hoopes, M. H. (1978). Structured Group Treatment for Divorced Persons. Unpublished outline, Brigham Young University.

Hoopes, M. H., Moline, M. V., and Stanfield-Packard, K. (1979). Structured Group Treatment for Divorce Adjustment. Unpublished manuscript, Brigham Young University.

Kessler, S. (1977a). *Beyond Divorce: Leader's Guide*. Atlanta, GA: National Institute for Professional Training.

———— (1977b). *Beyond Divorce: Participant's Guide*. Atlanta, GA: National Institute for Professional Training.

———— (1977c). *Structured vs. Unstructured Divorce Adjustment Groups*. Unpublished manuscript.

L'Abate, L., Ganahl, G., and Hansen, J. (1986). *Methods of Family Therapy*. Englewood Cliffs, NJ: Prentice Hall.

Langelier, R., and Decker, P. (1980). Divorce counseling guideline for the late divorced female. *Journal of Divorce* 3:403–411.

Levin, E. (1975). Development of a family life education program in a community social service agency. *Family Coordinator* 24:343–349.

Lewis, P. H. (1983) Innovative divorce rituals: their psycho-social functions. *Journal of Divorce* 6:71–81.

Mackeen, B. A., and Herman, A. (1974). Effects of group counseling on self-esteem. *Journal of Counseling Psychology* 21:210–214.

Madanes, C. (1981). *Strategic Family Therapy*. San Francisco: Jossey-Bass.

———— (1984). *Behind the One-Way Mirror*. San Francisco: Jossey-Bass.

Morris, J. D., and Prescott, M. R. (1975). Transition groups: an approach to dealing with post partnership anguish. *Family Coordinator* 24:325–330.

Raschke, H. J. (1974). Social and Psychological Factors in Voluntary Post-marital Dissolution Adjustment. Unpublished doctoral dissertation, University of Minnesota.

Salts, C. J. (1979). Divorce process: integration of theory. *Journal of Divorce* 2:233–240.

———— (1983). Divorce adjustment groups are not for all divorcees. *The Personnel and Guidance Journal*, September:37–39.

———— (1984). Who suggested the divorce: how it affects the success of divorce counseling groups. *Conciliation Courts Review* 22:49–51.

Salts, C. J., and Zongker, C. E. (1983). Effects of divorce counseling groups on adjustment and self concept. *Journal of Divorce* 6:55–67.

Storm, C. L., and Sprenkle, D. H. (1982). Individual treatment in divorce therapy: a critique of an assumption. *Journal of Divorce* 6:87–97.

Tedder, S. L., Scherman, A., and Sheridan, K. M. (1984). Impact of group support on adjustment to divorce by single, custodial fathers. *American Mental Health Counselors Association Journal* 6:180–189.

Vogel-Moline, M. E. (1979). The Effects of a Structured Group Treatment on Self-esteem and Depression of Divorced/separated Persons. Unpublished doctoral dissertation, Brigham Young University.

Yalom, I. D. (1975). *The Theory and Practice of Group Psychotherapy.* 2nd ed. New York: Basic Books.

Part III

NEW FAMILY SYSTEMS

15

SINGLE-PARENT FAMILIES

Nancy J. Warren, Ph. D.
Judy T. Konanc, Ph. D.

When society defines a "family" as two parents and a child or children, single-parent families formed due to divorce are typically regarded as an anomaly, labeled as "broken," disintegrated, and presumed to promote maladjustment in their members (Brandwein et al. 1974, Leahey 1984). Even when families of divorce are not stigmatized, the single-parent family is often regarded as a transitory variation in family structure preceding remarriage (Crosbie-Burnett and Ahrons 1985, Morawetz and Walker 1984). Although most divorced adults in the United States remarry within five years after divorce (Furstenberg et al. 1983), the significance of family members' lives within the single-parent unit should not be slighted. Recent census projections suggest that up to 40 percent of children under 18 may spend a part of their childhood in a single-parent household (Norton and Glick 1986). Ahrons (1979) has proposed the welcome nomenclature of "binuclear families," wherein two separate nuclear households of single parents sequentially share children. This term appears best suited to those families of divorce where both parents remain involved in child care. Single-parent families after divorce may actually be binuclear or solo-parent.

Understanding the single-parent family of divorce has been further complicated by earlier studies that loosely categorized all father-absent children together, regardless of the reason for the fathers' uninvolvement. Single-parent families formed by out-of-wedlock births, poverty, or death were combined statistically with those of divorce. The resulting studies of such mixed groups, often with questionable measures of child maladjustment, led to the inevitable conclusion that future research must be more carefully done (Blechman 1982). Single-parent families of divorce cannot be considered equivalent to other types of single-parent households. In contrast, enthusiastic uncritical praise of single-parent families, extolling the consistency or attentiveness of one parent versus two, for instance, reflects how polarized the views of the single-parent family of divorce have become (Burden 1980, Schultz-Brooks 1983).

Given the differences in conceptualization and attitude, the single-parent family of divorce has been a relatively neglected focus for study or intervention. In their recent book on brief therapy with single-parent families, Morawetz and Walker (1984) noted that such families were easy to find; they were the large group at the bottom of their agency's waiting list!

For purposes of this chapter, single-parent families of divorce will be identified as single-parent family 1 (the solo parent with total child-rearing responsibility after divorce) or single-parent family 2 (the binuclear structure with both parents involved to varying degrees). A two-part focus on single-parent families will provide description of what challenges these families face, and what interventions have been developed and studied when problems arise. Interventions to be reviewed will be limited to specific techniques that center directly on improving parent-child and family functioning. Interventions that may indirectly affect family functioning through enhancing individual adult or child functioning are considered beyond the scope of this chapter.

WHO ARE SINGLE-PARENT FAMILIES?

Divorce occurs in all parts of the country, in every socioeconomic class, and across all ethnic and religious groups. Demographically, single-parent families consist primarily of a female parent and more than one child, reflecting the routine granting of custody to the mother in the past. Recent estimates note that 90 percent of single-parent families are headed by women, and only 10 percent by men (Hetherington 1979). As joint custody has become a respected alternative, the incidence of father-headed single-parent families has slowly increased. Thirty states now authorize joint custody, with several states presuming that joint custody is the best alternative for the children unless demonstrated otherwise (Melli 1986). Whether or not single-parent families are really solo-parent (single-parent families 1) or shared care by ex-spouses (single-parent families 2) cannot be determined from census figures. Interestingly, studies of single-parent families that highlight problems typically assume single-parent family 1 status, while therapies for single-parent families usually assume involvement of both parents, as in single-parent families 2.

CHALLENGES

Economic Challenges

Economic circumstances of single-parent families are more than challenging. Such families, especially single-parent 1 households headed by women, are often financially distressed. A California study found that after a year divorced men's income increased 42 percent, while divorced women's income fell 73 percent (National Women's Law Center 1983). For women with children, regular child support is awarded to only 59 percent, routinely sent to 35 percent of those eligible, and averages $150 per month (Morawetz and Walker 1984). Weiss (1984) reported that the average income of his sample of divorced families remained about half the income of married families over a five-year period. Obviously, the chances are quite high that a divorced mother and her child or children may be impoverished.

The job options for single parents, particularly women, may not lead to substantial relief of economic pressures. Working women in America now earn 59 cents for every dollar men make (Coalition of Women and the Budget 1983). Although the proportion of women in higher-paying professions and skilled technical jobs has risen, the vast majority of working women and mothers are employed in low-paying semi-skilled, clerical or service occupations (Morawetz and Walker 1984).

Prospects for more highly paid work are also limited, due to the life circumstances of the average single-parent mother. She is in her late 20s or early 30s, has children age 6 or younger, and was married for seven or fewer years (Camara et al. 1980, Morawetz and Walker 1984). Thus she may have attended high school or college but not have graduated or pursued advanced degrees. She has also been involved in the time-consuming demanding care of preschool children. While her skills as a homemaker and parent have developed, her paid work experience and training have likely been limited and low-level.

Within the United States the complications of welfare support for dependent children have been well documented. In essence, poor single mothers receive marginally adequate supplements and may lose aid if they assume full-time employment or if ex-spouses or new male friends help them financially. Moving off welfare and out of poverty remains difficult.

There are families whose economic circumstances may improve after divorce. When the absent parent's addictions, compulsive spending, or poor job performance have formerly consumed much of a family's economic resources, the single-parent household may flourish under more stable norms. When grandparents on one or both sides of the family contribute money and/or time, finances may improve. If both parents now work for reasonable wages or child support payments are generous, economic hardship may not occur.

As a rule however, most single-parent 1 families are economically distressed, particularly in the immediate aftermath of divorce. Single-parent 2 families vary in prosperity, with the primary custodial parent likely more disadvantaged.

Legal Challenges

The single-parent family must also work within the legal system, one which is generally structured to handle conflicts between strangers. The adversarial system is often not able to meet the needs of the divorcing family or of the children (Elkin 1982). Divorcing spouses are frequently far from ready to handle the complex negotiations required to resolve financial and child-related matters (Kressel 1985). Families may reach an impasse in negotiations due to factors in three areas: preexisting individual pathology, interactional problems, or conflicts in the extended network of family/helpers (Johnston et al. 1985). Lawyers' different styles may also strongly influence the experience of the family (Kressel 1985). Proposed alternatives to traditional legal proceedings have been discussed in other chapters of this book.

Social Challenges

The societal assumption that nuclear families are the norm has influenced how most social organizations are designed and run. The workplace, the school system, and the neighborhood presume that two spouses in the same household cooperatively parent together. Until the movement of more women into the work force, mothers were presumed available to meet situational or seasonal child-rearing demands. Preschool and after-school care, health and illness checkups, school-scheduled conferences or holidays, and transportation problems were traditionally part of mothers' schedules.

Single parents quickly learn how burdensome the demands are for job performance coupled with total child care. Despite the need for available and affordable quality day care, neither U.S. governmental agencies nor employers have provided sufficient centers. Care for school-age children is also necessary outside of school hours. When youngsters become sick, care and transportation problems are intensified. Thus, the first social challenge for single-parent families becomes one of combining employment with the physical and emotional demands of child care, often single-handedly.

An added challenge is to establish and maintain a variety of social relationships, including a network of friends and helpers. Since single-parent 1 and 2 families often move during the divorce process (Weiss 1979a), familiar friends and neighbors may be more distant. Association with former friends may be harder due to financial burdens, added time pressures, and uncertainty about how a single parent now fits in. The single-parent family must simultaneously juggle taking care of itself and connecting with others who may both befriend and help.

Intrafamily Functioning Challenges

While economic, legal, and social pressures help determine how single-parent families function, both single-parent 1 and single-parent 2 families also require reorganization as systems. New boundaries are formed that define subsystem membership, rules for communication and cooperation, and roles and responsibilities. Depending upon the custodial arrangement, boundaries may be permeable and flexible to facilitate coparenting (Ahrons 1985) or solidified to avert conflict. Intergenerational relationships must be worked out anew. Former in-law connections become complicated; grandparents are always grandparents, but no longer are related by marriage to the one ex-spouse. Ferriero et al. (1986) recommend constructing a family map to characterize relationships.

Family reorganization also occurs within a time frame of change; divorce is a process with a series of stages (Salts 1979, 1985). The seemingly urgent demands of the early postdivorce phase may give way to a less frantic pace as time passes. As the single-parent family system gains confidence in its functioning, boundaries and rules may shift once again, allowing new relationships and changing old routines.

Mental health and educational interventions characteristically have been targeted to help single-parent family reorganization. All single-parent family systems do not function poorly, however, and the following descriptions present only potential structural problems.

Membership Issues

Who belongs to the single-parent family of divorce has been contested both by families themselves and by theorists. The single-parent family may include all former members and relatives, without overlap between the ex-spouses' respective families. Family therapists assert that divorce does not exclude either parent from the family system (Goldman and Coane 1977, Goldsmith 1979, Isaacs et al. 1986, Morawetz and Walker 1984, Pais and White 1978). Yet even if both ex-spouses are still considered members of the family, routines and ordinary functioning change.

Problems may arise when the single-parent subsystem includes new parental substitutes. Grandparents may do more than help or coparent; they may become the true functioning parent, relegating the biological parent to a less adult role (Isaacs et al. 1986, Kaplan 1977). Helping professionals may inadvertently find themselves replacing a missing ex-spouse or directing a baffled solo parent. A temporary helping alliance may become transformed into a seemingly long-term dependency (Morawetz and Walker 1984).

Relationship Issues

Numerous writers have noted that parent-child relationships change after divorce, often evolving to a greater closeness and sharing of family responsibilities (Weiss 1979b). In single-parent 2 families, fathers especially may come to know their child or children better; visitation time may promote more contact than was experienced during marriage.

Difficulties occur when a child, usually the eldest or most responsible one, becomes a "parental child," that is, a youngster functioning beyond his or her chronological age and carrying many adult responsibilities (Hajal and Rosenberg 1978). Such a child both loses a part of childhood and is caught between the parental subsystem and the sibling subsystem.

A second complication develops when a single parent is overwhelmed by the demands of parenthood and assumes peer-like relationships with his or her children (Glenwick and Mowrey 1986). With no one in charge, tasks may go undone. When seeking help, this problematic family may first look to the mental health professional to take over the parental role (Hajal and Rosenberg 1978).

Just as responsibilities can color and shape relationships, so too may ex-spousal conflict. Rather than cooperatively accepting each other's child-rearing routines, single-parent 2 households may feud through the child or children. Suspicious interest and inquiry, message-carrying, and battles over rules of visitation and conduct may create loyalty conflicts for youngsters, placing them more in the role of arbitrator than child.

For single-parent 1 families with an absent parent, one child may be scapegoated due to one parent's continuing negative feelings or denied grief about the other (Fulmer 1983). Perhaps chosen on the basis of like gender, appearance, or behavior, or simply available for projection of a parent's hostility, the scapegoated child experiences anger and rejection that he or she neither earned nor can easily dispel.

For intrafamily functioning the major issues of membership and relationship are boundary problems, according to the structural terminology of Minuchin (1974). Diagrams of the single-parent family system readily illustrate the range of problems. Professionals who see single-parent families may find that diagramming the system is both a useful summary of problems and a diagnostic marker for future interventions.

INTERVENTIONS

The rising frequency of divorce and the increasing awareness of the stresses inherent in single parenting have led to the development of a variety of intervention programs. The majority of interventions have been developed from work with clinical single-parent families, where one or more symptomatic family members sought help at a mental health facility, be it a school counselor's office, community clinic, or family institute. More recently, preventive educational programs for nonclinical divorcing families without overt symptoms have been developed, supported in part by the National Institute of Mental Health's interest in preventive projects. Several three-year studies were supported in 1981; others were designed and implemented. The creation of the *Journal of Divorce* in 1977 has also provided a forum for ideas and findings.

In this section, individual, group, and family interventions for both clinical and nonclinical single-parent families are reviewed, methods whose effectiveness has been empirically studied being emphasized. Specific examples of structured interventions developed by the authors, with illustrative case vignettes, are detailed. A list of diagnostic questions is proposed, to help the clinician or educator decide how to assess and help any specific single-parent family.

Individual Interventions

As the forerunner of later studies of divorce, Wallerstein and Kelly's (1980) descriptive research with sixty northern California families combined elements of prevention and therapy for a middle-class population of nonclinical families. Clinical vignettes illustrate the range and severity of family members' problems. Longitudinal contacts with those families have provided a rich source of information about adaptation to divorce over time.

As Wallerstein and Kelly noted, one of their three interventions was "child-centered," designed to enable the ex-spouses to parent better. Advice about communication, discipline, household routines, and visitation was directly given to parents. Phone calls and follow-up contacts permitted continuing input over time. Family contact was flexible, including interviewing with the children during play and speaking to the parents alone or together. The actual intervention seemed directed at the parents, however, on an individual basis. Short-term clinical intervention (as in diagnosis and recommendations) perhaps best characterizes their early, very individualized approach.

Lewis (1981) outlined efforts by Wallerstein and associates to incorporate standardized assessment and intervention into their work. Evaluation included several adult symptom scales (for example, the Beck Depression Scale), a newly developed Divorce TAT, and a behavioral drawing task. The intervention consisted of six sessions over six weeks, with children and parents seen together and separately. Comparisons were to be made with group therapy intervention for some parents. No results have yet been published.

McKinnon and Wallerstein (1986, 1988) described a similar approach for single-parent 2 families seeking joint-custody arrangements for their young children. In response to parental request, a monthly parent group was added. Although standardized assessment has been included, no outcome data have been reported. Future research reports should augment the striking clinical vignettes and developmental descriptions.

Other individual programs for single-parent families do exist, but many of these are highly individualized and may or may not deal with issues pertinent to the parent-child relationship (Storm and Sprenkle 1982).

Group Interventions

Group interventions for single-parent families have been character-ized as falling into one or more of the following types: education, support, skill building or self-help (U.S. Department of Health and Human Services 1980). Group programs may also be targeted pri-marily for nonclinical or for clinical single-parent families. Only a small number of such programs are truly family focused in that the family unit or parent-child interactional unit is the major target of the intervention, rather than the children or the divorcing adult. While some adult-oriented groups may have one or two sessions pertaining to children's concerns and adjustment (Barnes and Cop-lon 1980, Granvold and Welch 1977, Weiss 1976), most do not di-rectly address the parent-child relationship.

Group interventions with a family focus enable the clinician to work with the parent within a family perspective, and facilitate re-structuring the single-parent family into a functional unit. Cebollero and colleagues (1986) describe a program consisting of twenty-session concurrent mother and child groups. The groups appear to be therapy groups in content and process, focusing on mutual sup-port, sharing about coping and life stresses, and feedback from group members. Unfortunately, the literature on other group ap-proaches to clinical single-parent families is sparse and limited meth-odologically (Coche and Goldman 1979, Hassell and Madar 1980). As Sprenkle and Storm (1983) have concluded, more research is needed to assess the usefulness of clinical group interventions for single parents.

By contrast, many group interventions have been designed pri-marily for nonclinical single parents. Because the groups are simi-lar in content and structure, only three representative and well-researched programs will be reviewed here (Stolberg and Garrison 1985, Warren and Amara 1984, Wolchik et al. 1988). Two of the three programs (Stolberg and Garrison 1985, Warren et al. 1984) have outcome data. The third is a new but very promising group based on research findings of other prevention studies (Wolchik et al. 1988). Themes and content of other parent-child focused groups reviewed (Barnett et al. 1980, Cantor and Drake 1983, Rugel and Seracki 1981, Young 1978, Miyares 1980) are reflected in the pro-grams detailed.

The Single Parent Support Group or SPSG (Stolberg and Garrison 1985, Garrison et al. 1982) is a twelve-week support and skills-building group for single parents. Groups were offered as part of a larger prevention program for nonclinical single parents and their children (the Divorce Adjustment Project), which also included school-based children's support groups and a no-treatment control group. Group procedures have been well articulated in a program manual with session-by-session materials and sample videotapes of sessions available from the authors. Group procedures were intended to focus equally on parenting skills and individual development of the single parents. Participants selected topics from a list of 20 options provided by group leaders (for example, "The Social Me," and "Communicating with My Former Spouse about the Children"). However, according to Stolberg (1988), parents tended to choose material that emphasized the development of the adult to the exclusion of parenting issues. In analysis of program effectiveness, Stolberg reported more changes in parent's social and emotional adjustment than in parenting skills and parent-child relationships. He concluded that groups should focus specifically on parenting skills if a program goal is to affect the adjustment of the children in the single-parent home.

The Parenting After Divorce (PAD) programs were developed by Warren and colleagues (Konanc 1983, Warren et al. 1983, 1984, 1986, Warren and Ilgen 1987). Two different interventions were designed as part of a study to evaluate prevention programs for nonclinical single-parent families: a parent education group and a family intervention program. These programs were compared to a self-study control group. Families who had children between 7 and 12 and who had filed for divorce within three months were eligible to participate in the programs. Families were recruited by the use of court records of divorce filings. This method was used to obtain a nonclinical sample of single-parent families, more like the population of divorcing families at large. Sixty-five families were randomly assigned to the programs and completed posttesting after the intervention. Families were tested four times: before participating in a program, two to six weeks later, one year later, and five years later. Multiple measures assessed child and parent adjustment as well as family functioning.

Results of program impact showed that two to four weeks after the interventions, parents of both the parent program and the family program were significantly more improved than parents in the self-study control group. Children in all three programs were not significantly different. At one-year follow-up, parents and children in all groups were significantly improved, with no group differences remaining. At five-year follow-up, however, analysis revealed that children who had participated directly in the family program, or whose parents had attended the parent group, had significantly fewer behavior problems than those in the self-study control group, as reported by the parents on the Eyberg Child Behavior Inventory. Thus, like Bloom and his colleagues (1985) the PAD researchers found that significant long-term improvement occurred for those who participated in active programs. Apparently, family and parent-child focused programs have lasting utility for nonclinical single-parent families.

Finally, a new program has recently been reported by Wolchik et al. (1988). The intervention group consists of ten group and two individual sessions focusing on parent-child and family issues. The sessions were designed on the basis of the empirical research on divorce of the last 15 years and the research on interventions, such as the above studies. Research results are not yet available on group effectiveness, but these investigators will have a sample of over 100 families by the end of 1988.

In sum, a number of very promising, parent-child focused, group models exist for single-parent families. Of the group models reviewed, the programs for nonclinical single parents have been the best articulated and researched. This specificity allows for the replication of such groups in other settings and with other populations of single-parent families. There remains a need for more research on group interventions with clinical single-parent families.

Family Interventions

The development of explicit family interventions for single-parent families have been relatively new. Kaslow (1981) observed that family treatment seemed well suited to divorce, although there were then few published studies of method or results.

Family interventions for single-parent families share a systemic perspective in which ". . . issues are seen in the context of family structure and process" (Nichols 1985). The aims of actual intervention vary widely, from counseling the single parent alone to conjoint coparent therapy to education of the solo parent and children together. Both clinical and nonclinical families may be seen, and descriptions of treatment are more prevalent than outcome evaluations.

The content discussed during interventions includes many of the problems inherent in reorganization of the single-parent family. For example, strengthening the parental functioning of the new single parent may be the general goal, and any aspect of parenting may be open for specific discussion, for example, discipline, limit-setting, communication. Other common concerns include building coparental cooperation in single-parent 2 families or helping single-parent 1 families relate smoothly to older generations of relatives.

The earliest descriptions of family therapy for divorced families focused on clinical cases with much conflict between coparents or generations (Kaplan 1977, Weisfeld and Laser 1977, Goldman and Coane 1977). Interventions included both parents, their children, and sometimes their families of origin in structural family therapy.

Other clinically derived methods emphasized the stress-related problems of family reorganization after divorce. Typical problems of newly single parents were described, accompanied by a variety of suggested interventions (Weltner 1982). Educational sessions for parents and children together were recommended (Henning and Oldham 1977) or gradual observation-participation of a single parent in a child's play therapy was encouraged (Hajal and Rosenberg 1978, Rosenthal 1979). Unfortunately, some of these earliest efforts described as family therapy were not systemic in orientation, so children might be absent or ex-spouses ignored.

The best detailed and researched family interventions have appeared more recently. Morawetz and Walker (1984) described their work with 30 families in a three-year study at the Ackerman Institute in New York City. Their sample was part of a clinical population that included some single-parent families due to reasons other than divorce. They reviewed assumptions that family members commonly bring to therapy and provided hints for getting families started in treatment. The actual therapeutic approach used strategic and structural techniques with an underlying three-generational perspective. The clinicians skillfully provided family therapy to single-parent families, recognizing the membership or relationship issues of each family, appreciating the special stresses experienced, and adapting to the stage of the divorce process the family occupied. Detailed case studies illustrate the process of therapy for readers less familiar with family work.

Isaacs and colleagues (1986) reported a similar approach to family therapy with 103 families one to three years after divorce. Their Philadelphia sample was a mix of symptomatic clinical families who requested help and volunteer families who responded to advertisement. Aid was not limited to single-parent families and was extended to remarried, blended families as well. Paradoxical interventions were readily used to circumvent resistance, especially during "controlled encounters" of the parents. Crisis induction was also employed to help improve parenting. How family therapists decide when to employ specific techniques is reflected in enlightening verbatim write-ups, accompanied by the therapists' immediate impressions and decisions.

Unlike purely clinical studies, Isaacs and colleagues also collected pre- and postintervention data on both adults and children. Differences between nonclinical and clinical participants were not specified, and presumably were a matter of degree of severity or frequency of problems. They reported that adults improved within one year and children within three years after divorce. Yet the children of clinical families were still less improved than those of their volunteer sample. However, detailed statistical results from their work have not been published. Despite such measurement efforts, Isaacs and her colleagues' work best represents sophisticated family therapy with clinical families.

Campbell and Johnston (1986) and Johnston and colleagues (1985) highlighted interventions with litigious, highly conflicted parents who cannot agree on custody. Adults in almost 95 percent of the 80 families seen met criteria for psychiatric diagnosis; most were also economically distressed. Although not labeled as a clinical sample, the couples seem very like the hard-to-treat portion of a clinical population. Interventions were intended to enhance parental functioning and avert further legal battles.

The authors usefully attributed conflicts to "the divorce transition impasse," viewed systematically as due to convergence of external (kin, attorneys), interactional, and intrapsychic factors. Their ten-week intervention, labeled Impasse-Directed Mediation, contained many elements of strategic family therapy as well as careful mediation. Campbell and Johnston saw half their families in individual family work, with each parent and child or children seen separately and conjointly "when ready." Eighty percent of such families reached agreements postintervention, with 70 percent staying out of court for six months. The authors noted that small group mediation with similar families was as effective and more cost-efficient. Both the blend of counseling and mediation and the comprehensive systems view of impasses should prove useful to other professionals seeing conflict-laden divorced families.

Volunteer single-parent families have typically been seen in preventive family interventions. Neither parent nor children are currently in therapy; indeed, many have never sought counseling. Preventive approaches aim to blend clinical acumen with the experimental rigor of representative or random samples, multimethod assessment, pre- and postintervention as well as follow-up data collection, statistically understandable and tested differences, and replicable interventions. The complexity of that undertaking may explain why only two such preventive family interventions have been developed and described.

Taylor and colleagues (1984) conducted a three-year study of weekend workshops for largely volunteer families of divorce in Topeka, Kansas. Participants were single-parent families with at least one child aged 7 to 11. The one-and-a-half-day workshop emphasized parent-child communication about divorce, the quality of the parent-child relationship, and the resolution of coparental conflict. While families were together initially and at the conclusion, separate parents' groups were run concurrently with children's groups. Group discussions, lectures, and videotapes provided divorce-related information to all. Though the primary means of intervention was via groups, the focus and participants were families. The children's groups developed creative or playful ways to share feelings, while the small groups of parents applied the new information about divorce to their own family situations.

Unfortunately, the combination of clinical judgment (psychiatrists rated families' "degree of messiness," for example) and complex statistical path analysis did not produce readily generalizable results. Until further publications, the Topeka workshops provide primarily a ready-made educational intervention that participants rate as very satisfying.

The Parenting After Divorce (PAD) project of Warren and colleagues (1984) in semirural North Carolina was described above, under group interventions. Follow-up data one year and five years after active group or family intervention showed lasting improvement among family participants. The Family Intervention (Konanc 1983) was originally intended to aid in the crisis aspects of divorce, but was redesigned to address the needs of nonclinical families. Rather than immediate help with problems, affirmation and information were typically sought by participating single-parent families.

The actual structure and outline of the PAD Family Intervention is presented in detail below. Unlike the interventions for clinical families, the PAD Family Intervention represents a replicable, structured, educational intervention that can be carried out by family clinicians of a variety of backgrounds.

In sum, family approaches to single-parent families are well articulated. The literature is outstanding in its explication of technique for work with clinical single-parent families. Like most therapy models, however, there continues to be a need for more research to document the efficacy of family approaches.

SAMPLE INTERVENTION OUTLINES

The group and the family intervention developed by the authors will next be outlined. Suggestions for implementation and clinical vignettes illustrating frequent issues accompany each outline.

Structured Group Format

The PAD Group was a five-session group designed to strengthen parenting skills and parent-child communication. The groups provided information about children's reactions to divorce, skill-training in active listening, direct communication with the child or children and more effective limit-setting, and discussion and guidance about ways to improve communication with the noncustodial parent. Each group was led by male and female co-leaders, and where possible both male and female custodial parents were included in the groups. Child care was provided free of charge. An outline of the groups follows:

Session 1

The primary goals are introductions, setting of group rules, and presentation and discussion of the effects of divorce on children. Emphasis is placed on the normal reactions of children over time and children's cognitive understanding of divorce events. Time is allowed for questions and answers for individual parents.

Session 2

The focus is on the parenting skills of active listening and direct expression of feelings, "I" messages, and congruency of words and feelings. After a structured presentation, parents practice listening for their children's feelings, using vignettes; leaders model accurate listening, empathy, and nondefensive responses. The second half of the session is devoted to discussion and role play, to help parents feel more comfortable talking to their children and answering their questions truthfully.

Session 3

The emphases are on the parenting skills of limit-setting, clear and consistent expectations, use of praise, specific rather than general feedback, and negotiation. Divorce-related disruptions in parenting and expectations for children are discussed. Discussion, role play, and leader feedback are used to teach skills.

Session 4

The group focuses on the relationship between divorced parents. Discussion of anger and anger management, development of a "business relationship" (Ricci 1980), and keeping children out of parental conflicts are the main topics.

Session 5

The final session sums up the previous meetings, helps parents set specific goals for future work, and assesses stress management strategies. Superparent expectations are addressed, and positive support of coping is given.

Parent satisfaction for the PAD parent group program was high, and parents with more needs reported gaining the most (Warren and Amara 1984). However, leaders commented that the groups were too short to cover all the material, and that a program of eight to ten sessions would allow more time for skill training and integration.

Group Implementation Issues

Recruitment and Screening of Group Members

Recruitment and screening procedures vary, depending upon the type of setting (psychiatric clinic, mental health center, court, school, church) and whether the group is to be clinical or nonclinical in nature. Little is known about screening for the suitability of members for clinical group interventions specific to divorce. Readers should be aware of the literature pertinent to group therapy screening. Screening for groups of nonclinical single parents should exclude those parents who are severely depressed, suicidal, psychotic, or those who are locked in angry impasses two or more years after the divorce.

Composition of Groups

While many of the published group programs are described for women or mothers only, it was helpful to have at least one man in each PAD group as well as the male co-leader. Group members reported that the inclusion of fathers was helpful to bring in the perspective of custodial fathers and to avoid stereotyping "all men." The PAD groups were primarily for custodial parents. Groups that include both custodial and noncustodial parents together would need to be structured differently, since the issues are somewhat different for the two types of parents.

Timing

An optimal time for parent-child focused groups is six months to a year after parental separation. At the time of separation the issues of grief, loss, self-esteem, and coping are paramount. Material about parenting is sought and accepted later in the transition process after the initial crisis. While parents expressed the desire for groups earlier in the divorce process, they clearly had different needs earlier.

Group Structure and Format

Groups are most helpful when they are educational and skill-building rather than merely supportive. Parents report benefiting most from concrete suggestions and skills taught in sessions. Structured rather than unstructured groups are perceived as most useful.

Skills Required

Leaders should be skilled in a variety of educational techniques, such as brainstorming, role play, skill training, and lecture/discussion. Leaders need to be willing to be active and structure experiences as well as give practical, concrete suggestions. Mastery of the material on parenting skills, effects of divorce on children and families, and coparental relationships is extremely important. It is helpful if one co-leader is a parent as well.

Clinical Vignettes From Group Interventions

Superparent

Occasionally, parents are so concerned about the effects of divorce on their children that they overfunction, robbing the child of age-appropriate responsibilities, here called "superparent" expectations. Group feedback was especially helpful in the following case.

Mrs. R. was a black woman who worked as a public school teacher and lived with her son, B., aged 11. A very conscientious and strong woman, she tried to be both mother and father to her son, to make sure that he would "grow up right" and not "suffer from the effects of not having a father." She felt she had to make up for the absence of the father, who visited seldom. Mrs. R. and B. had a warm and close relationship; during the family interaction observation, they enjoyed a game of Chinese checkers immensely, competing spiritedly and laughing when the other would make a particularly good move. Mrs. R. had not dated since her separation 14 months before; "I want to get things straight with my son and my job, then I'll think about meeting someone new."

In the group Mrs. R. reached out easily and received much support for her efforts. The group noted that she was doing all the chores around the house, leading to her feeling depleted at all times. Group members suggested age-appropriate chores that B. could pitch in with and noted that she could not be B.'s father— she was his mother. The group also recommended that Mrs. R. go out more, and spend time with friends. At follow-up, Mrs. R. stated that the group feedback about trying to be "superparent" was the most helpful aspect of the group. "I enjoyed B. a lot more, and did not resent him when I relaxed a little bit," she noted. At five-year follow-up, B. was preparing to attend a state college "to study engineering," Mrs. R. reported proudly.

The Indulgent Parent

Not uncommon to single-parent families is the feeling that the parent should not set limits for the children. "They have suffered enough" is a frequent theme, placing parents in the dilemma of not feeling able to discipline or set limits because it would cause further unhappiness for their children. Parents may also feel competitive with the former spouse and fear losing the love of their children if they set limits. Finally, indulgence may be a problem for a parent who never set limits for the children, letting the other parent play the role of the disciplinarian during the marriage.

The following two vignettes illustrate the difference in parents' abilities to deal with this issue in a brief educational format.

Mrs. A. was a young mother of three boys aged 5–8 who was acutely tuned to her sons' suffering about the divorce. She had read that "Parents should not talk bad about ex-spouses" and struggled to put that into practice even when the father disappointed the children. "I just don't have the heart to argue with them about chores and school when I know how they are hurting right now." She seemed surprised when the group pointed out that the boys needed structure and would feel relieved if she stepped in "to show she cared." Later, she thanked the group and proudly noted how well her boys were responding to the new structure in the household.

Mrs. B., by contrast, was a passive, dependent, and depressed woman who had never set limits for her son C. or asserted herself in the marriage. She missed several appointments, stating, "I couldn't get C. to come." Later she revealed that he hit and kicked her at times when he did not get his way. During group time, C. wrecked the child-care room and teased the other children in a sexually provocative manner. When therapy was recommended, she sighed, "He will never come." At a five-year follow-up, she reported that C. had become unmanageable, and had gone to live with his father. Clearly, the group support and education about discipline and limit setting was not sufficient for Mrs. B.; she needed a more extensive clinical intervention.

The Quiet Child

A frequent complaint of parents is that they do not know what their children are feeling. Parent groups provide an excellent, supportive atmosphere to explore this problem and to teach parents how to listen for feelings. Mrs. H. complained that she could not be sure how her children were reacting to the divorce; they never said what they were feeling. Attempts to "sit down and talk about how you feel" led to long stony silences and much discomfort. Group exercises were aimed at teaching parents to listen for feelings in commonplace conversation such as comments made about school, friends, or upcoming plans. Parents role-played these situations and learned to listen for feelings. They noted how defensive they became when the "child" expressed anger, sadness, or discomfort. As Mrs. H. remarked after doing listening "homework" between sessions, "I never knew how much she was feeling; I just had to 'cool' my feelings and reactions so I could hear her." Other parents noted how they "put themselves on a back burner" to listen to their children—not reacting immediately and defensively.

Structured Family Intervention

The PAD Family Intervention consisted of six sessions of seventy minutes each. Families were seen individually by two co-leaders; all children and the primary residential parent were the unit of focus. With parental permission, a separate individual session for assessment and education was available for the other (nonresidential) parent. Structured materials, handouts, games, and play materials were used to facilitate sharing of information and to improve family communication. Refreshments were served at each session's end. Prescribed topics were modified to the functioning of each family, as follows.

Sessions 1 and 2

Interview and play assessment of children, parent and family functioning, and establishment of rapport occurred in these two sessions. Developmental information about the divorce process was shared via handouts and discussion. Parents and children were seen separately and then together.

Session 3

This session facilitated family communication about divorce through viewing and critique of a short film.

Session 4

In this session semi-structured play, via puppets or a board game for families, opened up communication of feelings and relationship issues.

Session 5

Family problem-solving of hard and easy routines occurred, designed to strengthen the single parent's functioning.

Session 6

The family focused on a review of the meetings and future plans. Specific and general feedback was provided for each family. Award ribbons were given to the children and good-byes, often tearful, were said.

Goals of the intervention were to provide information; to increase communication, especially of feelings; to help families play and problem solve; and to acknowledge the competence of the single parent.

While the PAD family intervention helped single-parent families polish their functioning, some participants lamented the loss of peer contact that groups provide. The combination of general information and specific advice fitted to the relationship, role, or communication needs of any given family requires some familiarity with structural and behavioral family therapy, plus willing and cooperative participants. The sample selection did not exclude clinical families who might have earlier or later therapy, and fortunately the family intervention was readily adaptable to most such participants. Both single-parent 1 and 2 families were seen.

Family Implementation Issues

Recruitment and Screening of Families

Families are more likely to be referred by attorneys, the court, or the school system than to participate in voluntary family intervention. Single parents welcome the peer contact available in group interventions and may in fact yearn for a break from child care. Thus most families seen for family work will probably have symptomatic members or marked difficulties in functioning. Interventions targeted toward conflicted couples caught at an impasse should continue to be in demand.

Assessment

Routine standardized assessment of families has yet to be established. Semi-structured interviews and behavioral observations are often the primary means of evaluation. Without adequate preintervention measurement, outcome studies are few.

Skills Required

A systemic view is essential to whole-family intervention. Family interventions depend upon astute use of all the major methods of family work. Given the anger and resistance aroused in families during divorce, strategic interventions are especially important. Comfort in short-term work is also a plus.

Special Considerations

The professional's sensitivity to the economic and social situation of single-parent families will be appreciated and help families continue treatment. Transportation to sessions and parking, low or no fees, schedules respectful of work, school, and day-care commitments, and refreshments and play for children should be considered as interventions are planned. Additionally, affirmation is most welcome to all single-parent families. Their courage and persistence in making a better life are admirable, and family functioning may be at its best ever.

Clinical Vignettes from Family Interventions

The Emotionally Fused Child

For families with young children in elementary school, it was not unusual to find that single parents assumed that a child felt exactly what an adult did. Puppet play activities were especially useful in helping parents differentiate whose feelings were whose.

> Mrs. C., a spunky young mother of son D., aged 8, spoke easily of how much better and more predictable their life together was since her divorce. D.'s dad was an impulsive, angry man with an erratic work history; he had wrecked their former home. She lengthily detailed her own work opportunities and enjoyed a teasing, playful relationship with D. D. was largely nonverbal in initial sessions and responded to words with aggressive noises or faces. During puppet play he struggled to speak in sentences and was able with time and quiet attention from Mrs. C. (versus her usual jovial interruptions) to describe how scared he had been when his father left. D. both feared and longed for increased contact with his dad. By the end of six sessions, mother and son were able to communicate with words, and Mrs. C. was appreciative of how her son was "at a different place" emotionally.

The Anger-As-Solution Family

The process of divorce extends over time and may coincide with numerous other stresses in family members' lives. Sometimes, animosity toward the former spouse or displaced hostility serves to maintain a familiar equilibrium when too much change is required.

> Mrs. Y. was about to remarry, but she dismissed any need for her future husband to be involved in the family intervention. Her only stated problem was her 10-year-old son W.'s behavior. She complained of the complications of "unnecessary" visitation between W. and his father, whom she bitterly disparaged. W. was pseudomature and anxious, but rose to verbal combat with his mother, arguing like a peer. Mrs. Y. recollected with dismay that she and W. were once close, until his sister had died. Mrs. Y. appeared

angry at most men and seemed stuck in her beleaguered role. The effect of other events in her life was denied. The preventive family intervention failed to have much effect on W., and Mrs. Y moved on in her hurt quest.

The Happy Family

Any professional or educator who sees nonclinical families after divorce can expect to encounter happy single-parent families. These families serve as helpful reminders that divorce is an opportunity and that stress can lead to greater strength and happiness.

The M. family cordially and eagerly came to "help out" in the study of divorcing families. Mrs. M. and her three children were attractive and well-spoken. Twenty-year-old A., off at college, agreeably made time to attend a session. Twelve-year-old S., poised on the brink of adolescence, soberly bantered with her mom. Her reportedly stormy anger around the actual divorce of her parents had subsided. Nine-year old N. was acutely shy, but both Mrs. M. and N.'s siblings were quietly encouraging. Mrs. M. glowed with the luster of newly earned self-respect. She referred positively to prior counseling that had helped her gain the courage to leave her domineering, verbally abusive husband. Despite his periodic threats, Mrs. M. and youngsters were confident that their solidarity and mutual respect would continue.

GUIDELINES FOR INTERVENTION

General guidelines may aid in the selection of the most appropriate treatment modality from the numerous varied interventions. Table 15-1 offers questions to help decide if a single-parent family is clinical or nonclinical in its needs.

Although additional questions might be included, those in Table 15-1 combine information about symptoms, timing, and external and internal family pressures. The overlap between clinical and nonclinical families is obvious, and it may be easy to view nonclinical families as less healthy than they are. The timing of the divorce, the structural alterations in the family system, and the adjustment of the parents seem to be the essential differences between clinical and nonclinical status. Educational approaches may help both types of families, but clinical single-parent families are likely to require therapeutic treatment interventions also. Whether or not a single-parent family is type 1 or 2 says much about predictable economic and

Table 15-1   Diagnostic Questions for the Single-Parent Family

	Clinical	Nonclinical
1. Are one or more family members symptomatic?	yes	yes
2. Are the children symptomatic, but the single parent/s reasonably well adjusted?	no	yes
3. Has the divorce occurred within the last two years?	yes	yes
4. Have crisis-precipitating events recently happened, for instance, an anniversary of the separation or remarriage of the noncustodial parent?	yes	yes
5. Do economic or social problems account for the family's difficulties?	no	yes
6. Does the family have major boundary problems of membership or relationship?	yes	no
7. Did the divorce occur more than two years ago?	yes (usually)	no
8. Do both ex-spouses continue to have intense ongoing hostility involving the children?	yes	no
9. For single-parent 2 families, is there a stable pattern of visitation months after the divorce?	no	yes

emotional pressures, but little about the kinds of intervention it may need.

CONCLUSION

Single-parent families must face and overcome a wide variety of challenges, including economic deprivation, social and legal challenges, and family system restructuring. Single-parent families also vary in their ability to handle these situations; while many families can cope on their own, some may need help to do so. Interventions reviewed here focused on the family system or parent-child system as a target for treatment, and included individual, group, and family-based interventions for both clinical and nonclinical single-parent families. Although for some single-parent families, the stage of single parenthood is only one phase in a progression from divorce to remarriage, for others it is a stable and permanent family system. Thus, it is important to respect the single-parent family as a viable family form deserving of understanding, support, and acceptance.

REFERENCES

Ahrons, C. R. (1979). The binuclear family: two households, one family. *Alternative Lifestyles* 2:499–515.

——— (1985). Divorce stage theory and therapy: therapist's implications throughout the divorcing process. In *Divorce Therapy*, ed. D. H. Sprenkle, pp. 13–23. New York: Haworth.

Barnes, B. C., and Coplon, J. K. (1980). *The Single Parent Experience*. Boston: Resource Communications.

Barnett, P., Gaudio, C. P., and Sumner, M. G. (1980). *Parenting Children of Divorce*. New York: Family Service Association of America.

Blechman, E. A. (1982). Are children with one parent at psychological risk? A methodological review. *Journal of Marriage and the Family* 44:179–195.

Bloom, B. L., Hodges, W. F., Kern, M. B., and McFaddin, S. C. (1985). A preventive intervention program for the newly separated: final evaluations. *American Journal of Orthopsychiatry* 55:9–26.

Brandwein, R. A., Brown, C. A., and Fox, E. M. (1974). Women and children last: the social situation of divorced mothers and their families. *Journal of Marriage and the Family* 36:498–514.

Burden, D. (1980). Women as single parents: alternative services for a neglected population. In *Alternative Social Services for Women*, ed. N. Gottlieb, pp. 255–279. New York: Columbia University Press.

Camara, K. A., Baker, O., and Dayton, C. (1980). Impact of separation and divorce on youths and families. In *Environmental Variables and the Prevention of Mental Illness*, ed. P. M. Insel, pp. 69–136. Lexington, MA: Lexington Books, D. C. Heath.

Campbell, L. E. G., and Johnston, J. R. (1986). Impasse-directed mediation with high conflict families in custody disputes. *Behavioral Science and the Law* 4:217–241.

Cantor, D. W., and Drake, E. A. (1983). *Divorced Parents and Their Children: A Guide for Mental Health Professionals*. New York: Springer.

Cebollero, A. M., Cruise, K., and Stollack, G. (1986). The long-term effects of divorce: mothers and children in concurrent support groups. *Journal of Divorce* 10:219–228.

Coalition of Women and the Budget (1983). *Inequality of Sacrifice: The Impact of the Reagan Budget on Women*. Washington, DC: Women's National Law Center.

Coche, J., and Goldman, J. (1979). Brief group psychotherapy for women after divorce: planning a focused experience. *Journal of Divorce* 3:153–160.

Crosbie-Burnett, M., and Ahrons, C. R. (1985). From divorce to remarriage: implications for therapy with families in transition. In *Divorce Therapy*, ed. D. H. Sprenkle, pp. 121–137. New York: Haworth.

Elkin, M. (1982). The missing link in divorce law: a redefinition of process and practice. *Journal of Divorce* 6:37–63.

Ferriero, B. W., Warren, N. J., and Konanc, J. T. (1986). ADAP: a divorce assessment proposal. *Family Relations* 35:439–449.

Fulmer, R. H. (1983). A structural approach to unresolved mourning in single-parent family systems. *Journal of Marital and Family Therapy* 9:259–269.

Furstenberg, F. F., Nord, C. W., Peterson, J. L., and Zill, N. (1983). The life course of children of divorce: marital disruption and parental contact. *American Sociological Review* 48:656–668.

Garrison, K. M., Stolberg, A. L., Mallonee, D., Carpenter, J., and Antrim, Z. (1982). *The Single Parents' Support Group: A Procedures Manual.* Unpublished manual, Virginia Commonwealth University, Richmond, Department of Psychology, Divorce Adjustment Project.

Glenwick, D. S., and Mowrey, J. D. (1986). When parent becomes peer: loss of intergenerational boundaries in single parent families. *Family Relations* 35:57–62.

Goldman, J., and Coane, J. (1977). Family therapy after the divorce: developing a strategy. *Family Process* 16:357–362.

Goldsmith, J. (1979). The postdivorce family system. In *Divorce and Separation-Context, Causes, and Consequences,* ed. G. Levinger and O. C. Moles, pp. 297–330. New York: Basic Books.

Granvold, D. K., and Welch, G. J.. (1977). Intervention for post-divorce adjustment problems: the treatment seminar. *Journal of Divorce* 1:81–91.

Hajal, F., and Rosenberg, E. B. (1978). Working with the one-parent family in family therapy. *Journal of Divorce* 1:259–269.

Hassall, E., and Madar, D. (1980). Crisis group therapy with the separated and divorced. *Family Relations* 29:591–597.

Henning, J. S., and Oldham, J. T. (1977). Children of divorce: legal and psychological crises. *Journal of Clinical Child Psychology* 6:55–59.

Hetherington, E. M. (1979). Divorce: a child's perspective. *American Psychologist* 34:851–858.

Isaacs, M. B., and Leon, G. H. (1986). Social networks, divorce, and adjustment: a tale of three generations. *Journal of Divorce* 9:1–16.

Isaacs, M. B., Montalvo, B., and Abelsohn, D. (1986). *The Difficult Divorce.* New York: Basic Books.

Johnston, J. R., Campbell, L. E. G., and Tall, M. C. (1985). Impasses to the resolution of custody and visitation disputes. *American Journal of Orthopsychiatry* 55:112–129.

Kaplan, S. L. (1977). Structural family therapy for children of divorce: case reports. *Family Process* 16:75–83.

Kaslow, F. W. (1981). Divorce and divorce therapy. In *Handbook of Family Therapy,* ed. A. S. Gurman and D. P. Kniskern, pp. 662–696. New York: Brunner/Mazel.

Konanc, J. T. (1983). Crisis and preventive interventions for the new family system. Paper presented at the American Psychological Association Meetings, Anaheim, CA, August.

Kressel, K. (1985). *The Process of Divorce*. New York: Basic Books.

Leahey, M. (1984). Findings from research on divorce: implications for professionals' skill development. *American Journal of Orthopsychiatry* 54:298–317.

Lewis, J. (1981). Interventions with Families in Divorce. Paper presented at The American Psychological Association Meetings, Los Angeles, CA, August.

McKinnon, R., and Wallerstein, J. (1986). Joint custody and the preschool child. *Behavioral Science and the Law* 4:169–183.

———— (1988). A preventive intervention program for parents and young children in joint custody arrangements. *American Journal of Orthopsychiatry* 58:168–178.

Melli, M. S. (1986). The changing legal status of the single parent. *Family Relations* 35:31–35.

Minuchin, S. (1974). *Families and Family Therapy*. Cambridge, MA: Harvard University Press.

Miyares, K. (1980). Center for children in family crisis. In *Helping Youth and Families of Separation, Divorce, and Remarriage*, U. S. DHHS Monograph, pp. 225–242. DHHS no. 80-32010, Washington, DC.

Morawetz, A., and Walker, G. (1984). *Brief Therapy with Single-Parent Families*. New York: Brunner/Mazel.

National Women's Law Center (1983). *Testimony on the economic equity act, H. R. 2090. Title V, H. R. 2374: Child support enforcement act before the Committee on Ways and Means*. Washington, DC: Public Assistance Sub-Committee, House of Representatives.

Nichols, W. C. (1985). Family therapy with children of divorce. In *Divorce Therapy*, ed. D. H. Sprenkle, pp. 55–68. New York: Haworth.

Norton, A. J., and Glick, P. C. (1986). One parent families: a social and economic profile. *Family Relations* 35:9–17.

Pais, J., and White, P. (1978). Family redefinition: a review of the literature toward a model of divorce adjustment. *Journal of Divorce* 1:271–281.

Ricci, I. (1980). *Mom's House, Dad's House: Making Shared Custody Work*. New York: MacMillan.

Rosenthal, P. A. (1979). Sudden disappearance of one parent with separation and divorce: the grief and treatment of preschool children. *Journal of Divorce* 3:43–54.

Rugel, R. P., and Sieracki, S. (1981). The single parent workshop: an approach to the problem of divorce. *Journal of Clinical Child Psychology* Fall:159–160.

Salts, C. J. (1979). Divorce process: integration of theory. *Journal of Divorce* 2:233–240.

———— (1985). Divorce stage theory and therapy: therapeutic implications throughout the divorcing process. In *Divorce therapy*, ed. D. H. Sprenkle, pp. 13–23. New York: Haworth.

Schultz-Brooks, T. (1983). Single mothers—the strongest women in America. *Redbook*, November, pp. 87–89, 188, 190.

Sprenkle, D. H., and Storm, C. L. (1983). Divorce therapy outcome research: a substantive and methodological review. *Journal of Marital and Family Therapy* 9:239–258.

Stolberg, A. L. (1988). Prevention programs for divorcing families. In *Families in Transition: Primary Prevention Programs That Work*, ed. L. A. Bond and B. M. Wagner, pp. 225–251. Newberry Park: Sage.

Stolberg, A. L., and Garrison, K. M. (1985). Evaluating a primary prevention program for children of divorce: the divorce adjustment project. *American Journal of Community Psychology* 13:111–124.

Storm, C. L., and Sprenkle, D. H. (1982). Individual treatment in divorce therapy: a critique of an assumption. *Journal of Divorce* 6:87–97.

Taylor, J. B., Green, A., and Frager, C. (1984). Divorce Related Pathology: A Study in Preventive Intervention. Paper Presented at the National Institute of Mental Health's Workshop on the Impact of Divorce on Children, Washington, DC., June 14–15.

U. S. Department of Health and Human Services (1980). *Helping Youth and Families of Separation, Divorce and Remarriage*. Publication No. 80–32010. Washington, DC: DHHS.

Wallerstein, J. S., and Kelly, J. B. (1980). *Surviving the Breakup—How Children and Parents Cope with Divorce*. New York: Basic Books.

Warren, N. J., and Amara, I. A. (1984). Educational groups for single parents: the Parenting After Divorce programs. *Journal of Divorce* 8:79–96.

Warren, N. J., Grew, R. S., Ilgen, E. R., Konanc, J. T., Van Bourgondien, M. E., and Amara, I. A. (1984). Parenting after Divorce: Preventive Programs for Divorcing Families. Paper presented at The National Institute of Mental Health's Workshop on the Impact of Divorce on Children, Washington, DC, June 14–15.

Warren, N. J., Grew, R. S., and Konanc, J. T. (1983). Parenting after Divorce: A Look at Participating Families and Programs. Paper presented at the American Psychological Association Meetings, Anaheim, CA, August 26.

Warren, N. J., and Ilgen, E. R. (1987). Long Term Follow-up of Prevention Programs for Divorcing Families. Paper presented at the American Psychological Association Meetings, New York, August 30.

Warren, N. J., Ilgen, E. R., Van Bourgondien, M. E., Konanc, J. T., Grew, R. S., and Amara, I. A. (1986). Children of divorce: the question of clinically significant problems. *Journal of Divorce* 10:87–106.

Weisfeld, D., and Laser, M. S. (1977). Divorced parents in family therapy in a residential treatment setting. *Family Process* 16:229–236.

Weiss, R. S. (1976). Transition states and other stressful situations: their nature and programs for their management. In *Support Systems and Mutual Help: Multidisciplinary Explorations*, ed. G. Caplan and M. Killilea, pp. 213–232. New York: Grune and Stratton.

—— (1979a). *Going It Alone: The Family Life and Social Situation of the Single Parent*. New York: Basic Books.

—— (1979b). Growing up a little faster. *Journal of Social Issues* 35: 97–111.

———— (1984). The impact of marital dissolution on income and consumption of single parent households. *Journal of Marriage and the Family* 46: 115–127.

Weltner, J. (1982). A structural approach to the single-parent family. *Family Process* 21:203–210.

Wolchik, S. A., Westover, S., Sandler, I. N., and Balls, P. (1988). Translating Empirical Findings into Interventions for Parents and Children of Divorce. Paper presented at the American Psychological Association Meetings, Atlanta, GA, August.

Young, D. M. (1978). The divorce experience workshop: a consumer evaluation. *Journal of Divorce* 2:37–47.

16

THE STEPFAMILY

Patricia Kain Knaub, Ph.D.

Launching a stepfamily, it has been suggested, is somewhat like a Cecil B. DeMille production with a cast of thousands (Westoff 1977). Both the numbers of people who may be involved in stepfamilies and the subsequent myriad relationships that are created contribute to the complexity of this family form. In fact, *complex* is the term most often used to describe the family of remarriage. This description has resulted in much of the research concerning stepfamilies being directed toward describing, defining, and analyzing the conflicts and problems inherent in this more complicated, diverse lifestyle. More recently researchers have given attention to factors that contribute to stepfamily strength (Hanna and Knaub 1981, Ganong and Coleman 1983, Knaub et al. 1984). Therefore, this chapter explores not only the complexities of the stepfamily structure and some of the problems associated with it, but also the factors that contribute to its success.

STEPFAMILY STRUCTURE

With the exception that the persons involved have experienced marriage before, a remarriage between two previously married, childless adults in most ways resembles a first marriage. Divorce between childless couples most often occurs between younger individuals and relatively early in the marriage (National Center for Health Statistics 1985). Likewise, the probability of remarriage is high and the interaction with the former spouse tends to be minimal. Though by no means a painless task, for most, new relationships gradually replace former ones and a new, differentiated life is built. It is another matter if the remarriage results in creating a stepfamily.

The joining together of family members made up of parts having participated in disparate and usually unhappy family experiences is an inherently difficult task. The result of blending two family groups in which the children are biologically related to only one parent is a complicated structure in which normal family conflicts and tensions are intensified with the new, unique problems created (Ahrons and Rogers 1987, Duberman 1975, Goldstein 1974, Schulman 1972).

Perhaps the development of a stepfamily can best be understood as the final phase of a process that begins with the termination of a former marriage. Ahrons and Rodgers (1987) have advanced the argument that rather than viewing divorce as pathology and remarriage as deviance, each would more adequately be defined as social institutions that are guided by normative expectations. Although well-developed norms concerning the various stages involved or about how divorced or remarried families ought to deal with each other are not yet well defined, societal attitudes toward normalization are developing.

Take, for instance, the couple who recently announced their divorce by hosting a "Denouncement" celebration for their friends and business associates complete with attendants and gifts. The party featured traditional wedding rituals, only in reverse. For example, during the "divorce" dance, the recently divorced woman appeared with dollar bills attached to her all black but gala clothing and invited the male guests to dance with her. Each guest could claim a dollar for himself as he completed his turn. The party was received well and assumed to be all in good fun, though everyone there knew it was a serious event. The couple explained that they were attempting to announce to their world that the marriage was over, that they, individually, were okay, having survived with their sense of humor intact, and that they were ready to begin a new phase of their lives. One could argue with the appropriateness of their particular celebration but not with their intent.

Though it is difficult to eliminate the notion of pathology, gradually researchers and therapists are focusing on the transitional processes involved in producing positive outcomes. As a result, the factors associated with healthy functioning are being identified. One important factor is the definition individuals, families, and the culture ascribe to the stepfamily structure itself.

Much of stepfamily research is based on a "deficit-comparison" approach in which variations from the intact nuclear family are regarded as dysfunctional, problematic, and inadequate (Coleman and Ganong 1984). The model assumes that the nontraditional family structure is of lesser quality and more problematic than the intact, nuclear ideal. Beginning with nursery stories such as *Cinderella*, popular literature has also taken this problem-oriented, deficit approach (Pasley and Ihinger-Tallman 1985). Imagine the composite effect on children as first being defined as coming from a "broken home" and then living in a stepfamily with a "wicked stepparent." On the other hand, consider the more positive, hopeful approach contained within the concept of the binuclear family.

Constance Ahrons (1987) suggests that the nuclear family undergoes a reorganization through the divorce process resulting in two interrelated households, maternal and paternal. From the nuclei of the child's family of orientation, two households are formed into one system—the binuclear family. Whether or not they have equal importance in the child's life, the resultant family is made up of a system containing two nuclear households.

Conceptualizing the divorced family as binuclear is particularly useful in the important task of terminating a marital relationship while simultaneously continuing to parent. Whereas the public image may be that ex-spouses terminate all aspects of their relationship, in reality they must find a way to end the marriage while facilitating the parenting role. By thinking of their family in its new two-household dimension, it is possible for family members, adults and children alike, to redefine their family in terms not of its deficiencies, but of its new structure.

Relationship Styles of Former Spouses

Considerable variation exists in the ability of families to reorganize themselves positively. For one thing, the relationship style of former spouses will determine how the instrumental and emotional functions of the family are carried on. Ahrons and Rodgers (1987) have identified the major styles of ex-spousal relationships:

Perfect Pals. Ex-spouses see each other and are frequently seen together at family and school events. They share a common purpose of effecting joint parenting. Their divorce is amiable;

their binuclear family system tends to blur between the two households.

Cooperative Colleagues. The tendency is for one household to be primary and the other secondary, with the child's time divided and arrangements more formally defined. While anger and hostility may occur, the parents' main objective is doing what is best for the child.

Angry Associates. "Coparenting" is less applicable, for it is more of a "parallel" approach. There is need for explicit negotiation and specification of arrangements with little flexibility. Old antagonisms rooted in the marriage arise frequently. Children feel less free in their relationships with one or both parents.

Fiery Foes. The potential for hostility is consistent, even at major family events such as birthdays, graduations, and weddings. Characteristics of attack and counterattack with overlapping boundaries in the system are likely. This family form is highly vulnerable and contains a high level of stress.

Dissolved Duos. There is no personal contact between the exspouses. Many in this group could be accurately labeled "singleparent families."

Ahrons and Rodgers (1987) using the event of a high school graduation, illustrate the functional properties of ex-spousal styles:

> The perfect pals would plan festivities to celebrate the graduation together as a family unit. They might plan a lunch or dinner together, sit together at the graduation, and perhaps even give their son or daughter one gift. The cooperative colleagues would be less likely to plan the festivities together, but both would attend them. Perhaps mother would plan a dinner and invite father to join them. They might sit together at graduation, but interactions would be more strained and formal.
>
> The angry associates would celebrate separately with the child, perhaps one taking the child to dinner the evening before and one having lunch after the ceremonies. They would sit separately at the ceremonies and avoid contact with each other as much as possible. It is very likely that in the fiery foes one parent would be excluded from the celebrations surrounding the event and not even be invited to the graduation. The excluded parent would be aware of the event and feel angry and hurt to be left out. In the dissolved duos the noncustodial parent would probably not even be aware that his or her child was graduating and, if he or she were aware, would not acknowledge it in any way. [p. 130]

The research from which the ex-spousal styles were developed suggests that about 50 percent of the couples fall into the first two categories. However, as the researcher suggests, the sample most likely underrepresented is the very hostile divorcees. Perhaps more importantly, the styles allow the categorization of families in terms of their "functional" and "dysfunctional" properties as related to the reorganization after divorce. The constructive or "functional" divorce minimizes the psychic damage to the children involved, because a continuing relationship with both parents is protected. The first two styles result in functional binuclear family reorganization and the last three in dysfunctional systems (Ahrons and Rodgers 1987).

Whichever of the ex-spousal styles emerges in the divorce reorganization, functional or dysfunctional, the binuclear family must reorganize itself when a new stepfamily is formed. The weaknesses and strengths of the existing system will be taken into the stepfamily and, as such, will become a part of the new, expanded system.

Cohabitation Before Remarriage

One approach to minimizing the difficulties assumed to be present in forming a stepfamily has been cohabitation. The incidence of cohabitation is higher among the formerly married than among the never married, accounting for about half of all those who cohabit (Ihinger-Tallman and Pasley 1987). But is cohabitation associated with later success in remarriage?

In a study of 80 stepfamilies of which 40 had cohabited and 40 had not, my colleague Sharon Hanna and I (1981) corroborated earlier research (Macklin 1978, Newcomb and Bentler 1980) that found differences in background variables between those who do and do not cohabit are few. However, from our investigations, it would appear that among the previously divorced it is, perhaps, the age of the oldest child involved that is pivotal to the decision to cohabit. As the age of the oldest child approached adolescence, the incidence of cohabitation was less. With regard to the perception of success in their remarriage, the cohabitors perceived their adjustment to be significantly higher than the noncohabitators. Likewise, four of the seven components used to measure family strength emerged significantly higher among the cohabitators (perceptions of positive communication, closeness, promoting the other's welfare, and happiness with the remarriage). Cohabitation could be especially important because of the intense pressure to succeed. On the other hand, Pasley and Ihinger-Tallman (1987) reported that they found no significant relationship between cohabitation and marital happiness for 784 remarried husbands and wives.

In a subsequent study of the adolescent children within the 80 stepfamilies whose adults were surveyed earlier (Knaub and Hanna 1984), we found that children whose families had not cohabited scored significantly higher on the family strength measure. It could be that because the formerly divorced may be particularly anxious about succeeding in a subsequent remarriage, they enter the cohabitation experience with a serious agenda. The children involved may not have the same commitment; indeed, they may stringently oppose the new association and resist the living-together arrangement, both of which could negatively affect later perceptions of their stepfamily strengths. Again, whatever the perceptions of the experience, for those who cohabit, the outcome will become a factor in the subsequent stepfamily formation.

Family Reorganization After Remarriage

The formation of a stepfamily means the binuclear family must reorganize itself once again. If the remarriage occurs before the binuclear family has had the opportunity to stabilize itself, the potential for dysfunction is high (Ahrons and Rodgers 1987). Each of the subsystems must be redefined in addition to expanding the binuclear family, often substantially. As an example, consider the Peterson-Marshall-Barth stepfamily:

> Dan Peterson, newly divorced from Elaine and with custody of his two sons, had recently moved from Chicago to Columbia, Missouri, to establish a new business in the community where he had attended college. There he met Nancy, also recently divorced from her husband, Doug Marshall. She, with her two daughters, had moved to Columbia so that Nancy could return to school after living in Cincinnati for 12 years. Although Dan and Nancy were in familiar surroundings, they had few friends in Columbia and were each drawn to attend Parents Without Partners, where they eventually met.
>
> Dan and Nancy's relationship developed though they were both skeptical about marriage, as it had been only slightly over two years since their divorces. Neither of them felt their lives or families were really settled yet, and they simply did not want to take the chance of being hurt again. However, after seeing each other for 10 months and cohabiting for a time, they married. Their new stepfamily was formed.
>
> Since both had custody of their children, Nancy's daughters

aged 10 and 13 and Dan's sons aged 13 and 15 immediately had stepsiblings. Scott remained the eldest child but Terry, Nancy's daughter, had to relinquish being oldest child in the family and, in addition, she had another sibling, Mark, her same age and grade in school. Jennifer remained the youngest; however, being the youngest of four was quite different from having one older sister.

Additionally, each binuclear family (Dan, Scott, and Mark; Nancy, Terry, and Jennifer) had functioned independently for three years. Both Nancy and Dan felt their respective families had operated as a "pretty good team" while they were going it alone. In addition, expressive of the growth in independence and competence Nancy experienced in returning to school, she had her maiden name, Barth, restored and retained it after remarriage.

All the children's grandparents were living, so they now had four sets plus a great-grandmother. Aunts, uncles, and cousins also were married. Within the first year, Doug Marshall, the girls' father, had married Marcey, and Elaine Peterson, the boys' mother, had married Marvin. Although there were no new stepsiblings, the number of grandparents, aunts, uncles, and cousins who now were a part of the four children's families again increased. It is easy to see why, as there are more and more stepfamilies, a society's composition changes from families with many children to families with many adults and few children, certainly a characteristic of this stepfamily. Within two years of the remarriage, the four children were involved in a family system consisting of three households residing in three states, and had acquired the involvement of 18 adults—six parents and 12 grandparents.

Charting the relationship course within such a complex structure is a primary challenge for stepfamilies. One of the perplexing issues, especially for children, is to define who is and who is not part of their family system. It truly does seem big, cumbersome, and complex. Furthermore, we have a deficient language with which to define current and past relationships (for example, "my ex," stepsibling, "my father's new wife"). One tool that can readily be used by families and those working with them is to diagram the binuclear family (Ahrons and Rodgers 1987). Using the Peterson-Barth-Marshall stepfamily, consider how much easier conceptualizing the structure would be if it were in diagram form (see Figure 16-1).

PROBLEMS OF STEPFAMILIES

One theme predominates in the stepfamily literature: those embarking on this family style should be prepared for problems. The chal-

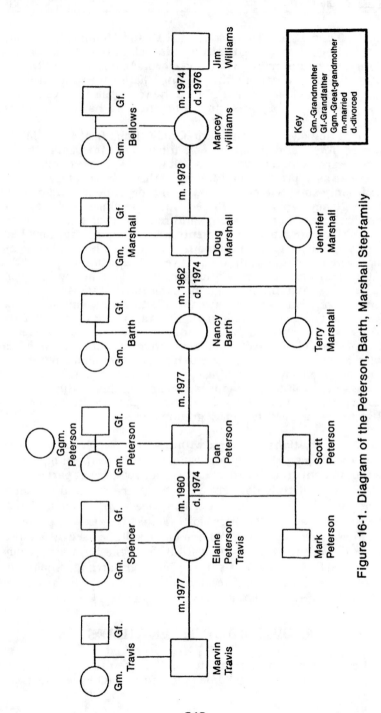

Figure 16-1. Diagram of the Peterson, Barth, Marshall Stepfamily

lenges associated with stepfamily living primarily center around the complexity of the family structure and on the need to reformulate existing relationships while simultaneously defining and forming new ones. The primary task is the integration and expansion of two previously established part-families, which will inevitably be a stressful process. This joining of two family groups in which the children are biologically related to only one parent and some siblings has been described as intensifying the normal family conflicts and tensions as well as creating some new ones (Duberman 1975). Further complicating the process of adjustment is the fact that stepfamilies, although a common occurrence in society, are still plagued with a lack of established norms, guidelines, and defined roles. In addition, a negative connotation may accompany the new role designation, as in the case of stepmother or stepfather (Cox 1981).

Other concurrent themes in the literature are that stepfamilies are surrounded by culturally accepted and fostered myths and that they are besieged with unrealistic expectations. Both parents and children have been described as being susceptible to fantasies of perfect relationships and instant love and happiness (Duberman 1975, Schulman 1972). Yet counter to these expectations is the image of the wicked stepparent. Such myths and unrealistic expectations may exacerbate familial problems and contribute to disappointment. Of specific concern have been controversies relating to the children and discipline, finances, and the noncustodial parent(s). Often, the conflicts occurring within these areas have been complicated by the lack of norms and clear role definitions as well as by unrealistic societal and personal expectations.

In the sample of 80 stepfamilies mentioned earlier, my colleagues and I, in an open-ended format, asked the husbands and wives to identify the most troublesome areas of conflict within the stepfamily (Knaub et al. 1984). The husbands and wives most often mentioned discipline and handling of the children (35 percent) followed by financial difficulties (31 percent) and various interpersonal concerns (23 percent). In a subsequent study (Knaub and Hanna 1984), when asked about discipline the predominant theme from the children was for the stepparent to proceed gradually and carefully. One child suggested, "New stepparents should observe for a long time before inflicting their principles of life on the child. It's easy to observe from the outside when walking into a family, but tension only results when the new parent tries to change everything immediately." Some described their stepparent in an undesirable, dogmatic manner such as, "The worst thing about my stepfamily is that my stepfather thinks he's always right and we're always wrong—what he says goes." These comments illustrate one problem common to most stepfamilies—relationships with the children.

Unlike first marriages, stepfamilies begin with the parent-child subsystem predating the spousal subsystem and, for the children, an additional parent-child subsystem existing in another household. Thus, children may be participating members of more than one household with more than one stepparent. Defining and maintaining boundaries between two households, therefore, becomes a major task within the binuclear family.

The members of a stepfamily system have all sustained loss of a primary relationship and are, most likely, in different phases of grieving. The formation of a new stepfamily may also mean moving from a familiar house, neighborhood, and/or school and, perhaps, significant travel between two households. Returning to the Peterson-Barth-Marshall stepfamily as an illustration, consider the changes all the members sustained, but particularly the four children:

> As they approached their marriage, Dan Peterson and Nancy Barth decided to purchase a new home, which would comfortably house their new family of six and have no previous memories for any family member. Although the move was only to another area of the city, it meant that all of the children changed schools, and thus they also lost contact with many of their former friends. Because both Nancy and Dan had moved following their divorce, the children's other biological parent and household were in another state. In addition, Doug Marshall moved to distant Oregon following his remarriage only a year after his children entered the Peterson-Barth stepfamily. When Elaine Peterson remarried, she remained in the same state but moved to a different city. The particular custody arrangements allowed for generous visitation during school holidays and the summer months; hence, the children experienced significant travel and absence from their primary household and school friends. Consider the logistics with which this family must deal, the additional financial burdens associated with visitations, the disruption to each of the households when children move in and out, and the potential discrepancy in family values, parenting styles, and household functioning to which the children and families must adjust.

Stepfathers

Due to the greater frequency with which mothers are awarded custody of their children in divorce settlements, the most common stepfamily form involves the biological mother, her children, and a stepfather. The stepfather role is ambiguous at best. Stepfathers rate themselves as less successful than natural fathers, which likely perpetuates a negative image of themselves in that role (Bohannan 1975). This uncertainty seems to be related to a variety of issues, including: the lack of a legal relationship with the child while at least sharing financial responsibility; questions concerning the degree of authority they have in the father role, particularly in relationship to discipline and enforcement of rules related to the stepchildren; guilt over having children from a previous family for which they also have financial and emotional responsibility; loyalty conflicts; money conflicts; affectional questions; sexual conflicts (Robinson 1984). The need to define the role by both parent and child is illustrated by a participant in the study of 80 stepfamilies:

> At first Michelle [his stepdaughter] wanted me to be a father as opposed to a stepfather. About the time Linda and I were married a custody suit was filed (the two events were related; the suit rushed our marriage plans). I came to feel that it was a mistake for her to think of me as a father in that it seemed to lead to emotional confusion on her part. The development of our relationship came through this understanding. She is 10 years old now and beginning to be very social, so I am not so close to her as I was but probably very close as stepparent/stepchild relationships go (stepfather, age 38).

Stepmothers

The research literature is explicit in concluding that being a stepmother is a difficult role (Bowerman and Irish 1962, Collins and Ingoldsby 1982, Ihinger-Tallman and Pasley 1987). Pervasive myths and stereotypes concerning "the wicked stepmother" abound and serve only to hinder the stepchild/stepmother adjustment.

As with stepfathers, stepmothers may acquire stepchildren who reside in the household on a permanent basis. She may or may not have biological children of her own residing in her household as well. However, more frequently the pattern is that she will function in the stepmother role on a part-time basis; that is, her stepchildren are irregularly a part of her household. She may have children of her own who reside in the household, and the stepchildren may join them on a temporary basis. If either or both stepparents have joint custody of their children, considerable moving back and forth between households will be a significant factor in the stepfamily adjustment. Not insignificant is the fact that any of these arrangements are subject to change. A child who has been residing with the biological mother may join the biological father's household, or vice versa. Finally, one or more of the parent/stepparent couples may have a mutual child, adding yet another factor to consider. Each of these situations presents a different challenge for the household members, especially stepmothers.

The wife/mother role in any household remains central, particularly as related to establishing rituals and routines in all aspects of family functioning from cleaning the house to holiday celebrations to standards of behavior and religious observations. This establishment and subsequently passing on of each family's "culture" continues to be highly influenced by the female head of the household. Many conflicts between stepmothers and stepchildren, especially with older stepchildren, are likely to involve conflicts over "how to do things." For example:

Alice, single at age 35 and a successful executive, met Tim at their company's annual meeting. Tim lived in a distant city and had a top-level management position that involved a lot of travel. Their relationship developed over the course of two years, mostly through meeting in cities where their respective business assignments took them. When they married, Alice moved to Tim's home location and assumed a new assignment in the company. However, a few months after they were married, Tim's two teenaged daughters joined their household on a permanent basis and Alice became a full-time stepmother. The girls' mother was bitter and angry about the divorce, and she felt Tim had not carried his load for parenting while they were married. It was her turn now for education and some freedom from the responsibility of parenting. The girls had also suffered with the divorce and it was an angry, bitter ordeal. Consequently, they had begun acting out and became difficult for their mother to handle. Alice, being in her first marriage and first marital household had, along with Tim, begun to establish the internal culture of their family. Tim's daughters, already teens, were well socialized into their mother's family culture. Tim's job now, as in his former marriage, frequently kept him out of town, so Alice and the girls were on their own much of the time. Predictably this stepfamily had serious conflict.

During a stepfamily workshop Alice shared, "I try very hard not to press my expectations, but the girls have grown up with a very different approach to everything. I feel our home just isn't our own; we can't live the way we would like to."

Obviously, the above situation involves more than conflicts about how to do things; in fact, these conflicts may be masking other, more basic difficulties imbedded in the divorce and stepfamily transitions.

Stepchildren

Following an extensive literature review, it was concluded that it is simplistic and inaccurate to think of divorce as having uniform consequences for children. However, family conflict has been found to contribute to many problems, including those related to social development, emotional stability, cognitive skills, low self-esteem, increased anxiety, a loss of self-control, and reduction of the child's attractiveness to the parents. It appears that parental separation is more beneficial for children than continued conflict (Demo and Acock 1988). Therefore, for any particular child, the context of the separation, divorce, binuclear family, and stepfamily transitions is crucial. Those situations that are fraught with unresolved conflict are dysfunctional for the well-being of children and adults alike.

The basic difficulties incurred by children in stepfamilies have been identified as dealing with loss, divided loyalties, confusion in terms of belonging, membership in two households, unreasonable expectations, fantasies of natural parents' reuniting, guilt over causing the divorce, and identity and sexuality issues among adolescents (Visher and Visher 1979). One particular problematic area can be the relationship with the absent parent. Children may be plagued with divided loyalties and may feel guilty receiving love from one parent for fear this would imply disloyalty to the absent parent. It appears that those children who are encouraged to develop full relationships with both parents adjust better following a divorce (Ahrons and Rodgers 1987, Kelly and Wallerstein 1976).

Ties to the family of origin affect children directly as the relationship with the stepparent develops. Not surprisingly, the conflict of loyalty with attendant guilt over the new attachment with the stepparent may occur. Children often view cooperation with their stepfamily as disloyalty to their biological family (Hunter and Schuman 1980). One of the more difficult problems for children in stepfamilies to handle is the attachment-detachment with the absent biological parent and attachment to the new stepparent. "For the children an attachment to the stepparent means an inherent disloyalty to the natural parent . . ." (Whiteside and Auerbach 1978, p. 278).

Remarriage may have more disturbing effects on school-age children and teenagers than on younger children. Although research on personal adjustment suggests that young children, particularly boys, suffer temporary deleterious effects when their parents divorce

(Demo and Acock 1988), they adapt more readily to a stepfamily because they have fewer memories and conflicting loyalties and are less likely to have been scarred by the trauma of a previous marriage (Schlesinger 1968). School-aged children appear to be especially vulnerable to the remarriage of a custodial parent (Wallerstein and Kelly 1980) and girls have more difficulty in their relationship with stepparents than do boys (Clingempeel and Segal 1986). Teens especially tend to be wary of stepparents and are more likely to test the limits of discipline (Rosenbaum and Rosenbaum 1977).

Another issue of general concern to children in stepfamilies, but potentially of greater importance to teens, is the issue of "turfs," that is, feelings of ownership of a space or material possession, or of a right to another person (Espinoza and Newman 1979). "My room" may become "our room" and "my mother" is not "your mother"; similarly, "You are not my real father; you cannot tell me what to do." Consider the following 13-year-old's response to the question, "What advice would you give another young person who was about to become a stepchild?"

> Be on guard because your natural parent will give their new husband/wife a lot of attention . . . you will feel neglected probably, but in time more attention will come back to you. Don't complain . . . mostly stick up for your rights in the family . . . let them know (in a calm way) that you need and want their attention.

Though concerns for the well-being of the children involved in a stepfamily must be a high priority, it is important for stepparents to remember that the divorce rate is higher in remarriages with stepchildren (Cherlin 1978, White and Booth 1985). Children may not have much to say about the remarriage, but they do have the power to break it up (Ihinger-Tallman and Pasley 1987). The spousal pair must be mindful of the difference between their marriage and the stepfamily. Particularly for a man, the preeminent relationship in remarried families is the spousal relationship, and he is little affected by the problems in his wife's relationship with his children, though he is aware of them (Hobart 1988).

STEPFAMILY STRENGTHS

A relatively recent approach to studying the family is to give attention to the factors that contribute to family strength. Instead of focusing on familial problems and deficiencies, researchers and therapists have emphasized strengths. Building on earlier work by Otto (1962), six characteristics have emerged as being descriptive of family strength: expression of appreciation to each other, willingness to spend time together and participate in activities together, good communication patterns, commitment, religious orientation, and ability to deal with stress in a positive manner (Stinnett 1979). In the study of 80 stepfamilies mentioned earlier (husbands, wives, and the children residing in the household), my colleagues and I found that although these stepfamilies did not deny they had difficulties, especially as related to the children, their scores on the family strength, marital satisfaction, and perceptions of family adjustment measures were high (Hanna and Knaub 1981, Knaub et al. 1984, Knaub and Hanna 1984).

In analyzing the factors that were thought to potentially affect the family strength score, we found that those husbands and wives who perceived the attitudinal environment (defined as the degree of positive support by family, friends, and society) as the most supportive scored highest. In a similar analysis of the children's responses, the children who perceived their family's adjustment to be positive and those whose families had not cohabited scored the highest on the family strength measure. It would appear, for both spouses and children, that a positive definition of their family situation together with a perception of support from friends, relatives, and the community enhance adjustment and the development of stepfamily strengths. Both findings underscore the need to discontinue the use of the deficiency model in describing and working with stepfamilies, especially as related to the children. Divorce and remarriage need not sever parenting; therefore, the children involved do not necessarily lose their parent, though they may not live in a household containing both biological parents. In addition, the children may gain stepparents who love and respect them. In response to the question, "What do you think has contributed the most to making your relationship with your stepchildren strong?" a stepmother said, "Love and patience. I really liked my stepchildren from the beginning and I'm sure they liked me."

The families were asked, "What do you consider to be the most important strength of your stepfamily?" Various components of love or intimacy (that is, caring, affection, acceptance, understanding, closeness) constituted 69 percent of the replies. Family unity, described as working together, sharing goals, values, and activities were cited by 33 percent, and 30 percent regarded positive patterns of communication (honesty, openness, receptiveness, sense of humor) as strengthening factors. To illustrate, a participant stated,

"The fact that my husband and I are each other's best friends, that we have essentially the same value system in life, that we are in agreement as to obligations to his children, and probably that he puts up with my weaknesses. Also, we work very hard to make our family situation a workable one." Seemingly recognizing the positive aspects of the binuclear family, another stated that a strengthening factor was "My children's understanding that they have two families who love and accept them." And in a heartening note, one of the children, when asked about the positive aspects of her stepfamily, replied, "You get to love more people you know!"

CONCLUSION

The material presented in this chapter illustrates the very real differences between remarried and once-married families. Establishing and maintaining a functional stepfamily is no task for the faint-hearted. Even so, any suggestion that the stepfamily denotes a broken, weak, inferior, or pathological family model would appear to be dysfunctional to successful stepfamily adjustment. Therefore, it is crucial that those in the helping professions, as well as the larger community, be aware of the stepfamily's unique characteristics and potential problems, as well as their positive features. Being aware of the differences without interpreting the differences as weaknesses, combined with continued positive support, would seem to be essential contributions to the development of success among stepfamilies.

REFERENCES

Ahrons, C. R., and Rodgers, R. H. (1987). *Divorced Families: A Multidisciplinary Developmental View.* New York: W.W. Norton.

Bohannan, P. (1975). *Stepfathers and the Mental Health of Their Children.* Washington, DC: National Institute of Mental Health.

Bowerman, D. E., and Irish, D. P. (1962). Some relationships of stepchildren to their parents. *Marriage and Family Living* 24:113–121.

Cherlin, A. (1978). Remarriage as an incomplete institution. *American Journal of Sociology* 84:634–650.

Clingempeel, W. S., and Segal, S. (1986). Stepparent–stepchild relationships and the psychological adjustment of children in stepmother and stepfather families. *Child Development* 57:474–484.

Coleman, M., and Ganong, L. H. (1984). Effect of family structure on family attitudes and expectations. *Family Relations* 33:425–432.

Coleman, M., Ganong, L. H., and Gingrich, R. (1985). Stepfamily strengths: a review of popular literature. *Family Relations* 34:583–589.

Collins, L. J., and Ingoldsby, B. B. (1982). Living in step: a look at the reconstituted family. *Family Perspectives* 16:23–31.

Cox, F. D. (1981). *Human Intimacy: Marriage, the Family and its Meaning.* St. Paul, MN: West.

Demo, D. H., and Acock, A. C. (1988). The impact of divorce on children. *Journal of Marriage and the Family* 50:619–648.

Duberman, L. (1975). *The Reconstituted Family.* Chicago: Nelson-Hall.

Espinoza, R., and Newman, Y. (1979). *Stepparenting.* Rockville, MD: Department of Health, Education and Welfare.

Ganong, L. H., and Coleman, M. (1983). Stepparent: a pejorative term. *Psychological Reports* 52:919–922.

Glick, P. C. (1979). Children of divorced parents in demographic perspective. *Journal of Social Issues* 35:170–182.

——— (1980). Remarriage: some recent changes and variations. *Journal of Family Issues* 1:455–478.

——— (1984). Marriage, divorce and living arrangements. *Journal of Family Issues* 5:7–26.

Goldstein, H. S. (1974). Reconstituted families: the second marriage and its children. *Psychiatric Quarterly* 48:433–440.

Hanna, S. L., and Knaub, P. K. (1981). Cohabitation before remarriage: its relationship to family strengths. *Alternative Lifestyles* 4:507–522.

Hobart, C. (1988). The family system in remarriage: an exploratory study. *Journal of Marriage and the Family* 50:649–661.

Hunter, J. E., and Schuman, N. (1980). Chronic constitution as a family style. *Social Work* 25:446–451.

Ihinger-Tallman, M., and Pasley, K. (1987). *Remarriage.* Newbury Park, CA: Sage.

Kelly, J., and Wallerstein, J. (1976). The effects of parental divorce: experience of the child in early latency. *American Journal of Orthopsychiatry* 46:20–42.

Knaub, P. K., and Hanna, S. L. (1984). Children of remarriage: perceptions of family strengths. *Journal of Divorce* 7:73–90.

Knaub, P. K., Hanna, S. L., and Stinnett, N. (1984). Strengths of remarried families. *Journal of Divorce* 7:41–55.

Knox, D. (1989) Trends in marriage and the family—the 1980s. *Family Relations* 39:145–150.

Macklin, E. D. (1978). Review of research on nonmarital cohabitation in the United States. In *Exploring Intimate Lifestyles*, ed. B. I. Murstein, pp. 197–243. New York: Springer.

National Center for Health Statistics (1985). *Vital Statistics of the United States, 1981, Vol. III, Marriage and Divorce.* DHHH Pub. No. (PHS) 85-1121. Washington, DC: U. S. Printing Office.

Newcomb, M. D., and Bentler, P. M. (1980). Cohabitation before marriage. *Alternative Lifestyles* 3:65–68.

Otto, H. A. (1962). What is a strong family? *Marriage and Family Living* 24:77–80.

Pasley, K., and Ihinger-Tallman, M. (1985). Portraits of stepfamily life in popular literature: 1940–1980. *Family Relations* 34:527–534.

Prosem, S. S., and Farmer, J. H. (1982). Understanding stepfamilies: issues and implications for counselors. *Personnel and Guidance Journal* 60: 393–397.

Robinson, B. E. (1984). The contemporary American stepfather. *Family Relations* 33:381–388.

Rosenbaum, J., and Rosenbaum, J. (1977). *Stepparenting.* Corte Madera, CA: Chandler and Sharp.

Schlesinger, B. (1968). Remarriage—an inventory of findings. *Family Coordinator* 17:248–250.

Schulman, G. L. (1972). Myths that intrude on the adaptation of the stepfamily. *Social Casework* 53:131–139.

Stinnett, N. (1979). In search of strong families. In *Building Family Strengths: Blueprints for Action*, ed. N. Stinnett, B. Chesser, and J. DeFrain, pp. 23–37. Lincoln, NE: University of Nebraska Press.

Visher, E. B., and Visher, J. S. (1979). *Stepfamilies: A Guide to Working with Stepparents and Stepchildren.* New York: Brunner/Mazel.

Wallerstein, J. S., and Kelly, J. B. (1980). *Surviving the Break-up: How Children and Parents Cope with Divorce.* New York: Basic Books.

Westoff, L. A. (1977). *The Second Time Around.* New York: Viking.

White, L. K., and Booth, A. (1985). The quality and stability of remarriages: the role of the stepchildren. *American Sociological Review* 50:689–698.

Whiteside, M., and Auerbach, L. (1978). Can the daughter of my father's new wife be my sister? Families of remarriage in family therapy. *Journal of Divorce* 1:271–283.

17

TREATMENT OF THE REMARRIED FAMILY

Clifford J. Sager, M.D.

Most couples in second marriages (remarried families—Rem—or stepfamilies) who seek help are conscious of a previously failed marriage and fear that this marriage will turn into the nightmare of another divorce experience. This creates a vulnerability that can leave members reluctant to admit problems and to ask for help, or to sustain treatment once it is begun.

In this article we address treatment of the remarried family that has children from a previous marriage who are "residential" or "visiting" with a parent. It is their family we refer to as the *remarried* (rem) *family*. As Pasley and Ihinger-Tallman's (1982) research indicates, second marriages in which neither spouse has previously had children do not have the complex structure and problems of those who bring children into the second marriage.

Adults and children in remarried family situations have to accept that they are and will be living out their lives in what had been a minority form of family structure for the past century and only very recently has come close to equaling the number of nuclear families in our population. It is now commonplace for children and adults to live out their life cycle in two or more separate households with each of their biological parents, either one of whom may have a new spouse.

A reasonable dividing line is 1975, when an escalation of clinical and research work on remarriage began to reach publication (Walker et al. 1979, Sager et al. 1980). Clearly, most special aspects of treatment that differ between first married nuclear and remarried couples and families relate to the family structural differences (Messinger et al. 1978, Sager et al. 1981, 1983, Visher and Visher 1987, McGoldrick and Carter 1980, 1988).

There are many aspects of preparation for becoming remarried and the significance of the Rem family structures that cannot be discussed here.[1] This article speaks to those factors that are unique to Rem families. It is important for the reader to keep in mind that these families and the individuals therein are also subject to the same stresses as are those in nuclear families. Not only is the need to triangulate, to scapegoat, and to hide out in pseudomutuality prominent in Rem families, but also this more complex family system makes it easier to fall into these destructive maneuvers, as well as those that are ignited by guilt and conflicting loyalties.

The suprafamily system (Sager et al. 1981, 1983) is composed of the households of the two biological parents, the children of their union, the new Rem couple(s) and their household. Grandparents and anyone else who impact on the system in a significant fashion may be included.

In Figure 17-1 the suprafamily system consists of the members of the above labeled three families of origin that Mary, Joe, and, more recently, Barbara came from. Mary and Joe were married first. They begot Abner and Sally. Mary and Joe divorced, and Joe remarried Barbara. The immediate reason for seeking help was because Abner, previously an excellent student, was doing poorly at school and seemed to be depressed.

From the genogram we see that Abner and Sally lived with their mother and maternal grandmother, Mrs. Hill (solid line encircles these four). The children regularly visit their father (Joe) and stepmother (Barbara). It was these two subsystems that we invited to the first meeting. The school system (teacher and guidance counselor) was also seen in a school visit and is a part of the suprasystem. The Olsen and Davidson grandparents did not have significant input in regard to the immediate problem and were not seen during the course of treatment, but Grandmother Hill played an overdetermining role in the divorce and current problems and was seen as a member of her daughter's household and for two individual sessions.

Preparation for remarriage begins with the quality of the separa-

---

[1]See the references in the preceding paragraph as well as the preceding chapter in this volume by P. K. Knaub, "The Stepfamily."

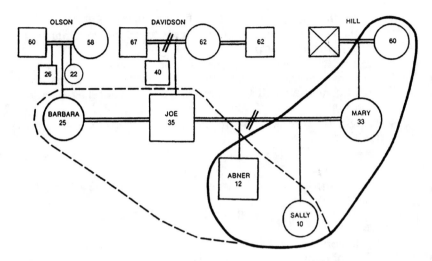

Figure 17-1.   Olson-Davidson-Hill Family at Time of Remarriage

tion and divorce each has had from his or her first spouse. Those
who have effectively prepared their children for the divorce, who
have maintained a presence and availability to the children, who
have not denigrated the other parent to the children, who have not
used money or the children as weapons in their struggle, and who
continued as coparents for the children are ahead of the game—for
all concerned (Sager et al. 1983). Similarly, participants in a negotiated divorce that treats the divorcing spouses fairly and encourages
the responsibility and respect of the parting spouses towards each
other and the children, are much more likely to move on to a better
second marriage than they would if attorneys are allowed to argue
from "killer" adversarial positions. The nonadversarial result is
much less traumatic for the children. They continue to feel love and
support from both parents and tend to arrive at better relationships with stepparents.

A second marriage is severely handicapped if one is still in love
with his or her former spouse. This love is often evidenced by the
remaining intensity of anger at injustice and/or betrayal perpetuated
by the former mate. Others may continue to carry a brightly burning
torch. Excessive guilt towards a former spouse will interfere with the
new marriage, causing spasmodic acts of repentant overconcern or
anger.

Goldrick and Carter (1988) have outlined a number of predictors
of difficulty in making the transition to remarriage:

1. A wide discrepancy between the family-life cycles of the families.
2. Denial of prior loss and/or a short interval between marriages (2–3-year minimum).
3. Failure to resolve the intense relationship issues of the first families—for example, if family members still feel intense anger or bitterness about the divorce or if there are still legal actions pending.
4. Lack of awareness of the emotional difficulties of remarriage for children.
5. The inability to give up the ideal of the intact first family and to move to a new conceptual mold of family.
6. Efforts to draw firm boundaries around the new household membership and push for primary loyalty and cohesiveness in the new family (through excluding all other members of the family).
7. Exclusion of natural parents or grandparents or combating their influence.
8. Denial of difference and difficulties and acting "as if" this is just an ordinary household.
9. Shift in custody of children near the time of remarriage.

I would add a tenth parameter—the possibility of anger, envy, or fear surrounding any discrepancy in available income to either of the two biological parents' households.

We also have to deal with different levels of subsystems that are likely to be significant etiologically in the malfunction of the remarried family system. These can be summed up as systems, cycles, and psyche:

1. *System frames.* These may include the Rem family system, the other biological parent's family system, the family of origin system of biological parents and stepparents. The court system, schools, work, and religion may be other systems that play a significant role.
2. *Psyche frames.* System therapists are now beginning to appreciate the role of intrapsychic factors as they affect the system. Conversely, "insight therapists" are increasingly learning to utilize system approaches. Understanding of both often leads to therapeutic synergism.
3. *Societal frame.* This includes cultural, socioeconomic, religious, and ethnic factors, gender roles, and the impact of the ecosystem.

4. *Biological frame.* This includes genetic, biochemical, and medical factors, as well as substance abuse.
5. *Life-cycle frame*
   a. The life-cycle needs of the Rem suprasystem.
   b. The life-cycle needs of the different subsystems: for example, the Rem family, the Rem couple, the bioparents, the single-parent family, the sibling-stepsibling unit, and so on.
   c. The life-cycle needs of the individuals. The spouse life-cycle needs are often conflictual. For example, the Rem life-cycle may require concerned age-appropriate parenting for a child. The parent or stepparent may be unable or unwilling to fullfill this need because he or she may perceive his or her own life-cycle needs to be free of child-care responsibilities.

During the course of treatment the therapist may place therapeutic efforts on one or more of these five sets of framework. However, in assessment all five must be considered.

In this chapter we try to indicate how we translate these constructs into practice, starting with the first telephone call, which begins the engagement and evaluation process. Goals are then established and a treatment plan is formulated. After engagement the treatment plan flows into the middle and termination phases of therapy.

INVOLVING THE REM FAMILY AND SIGNIFICANT MEMBERS OF ITS SUPRASYSTEM

Our optimal goal is to include the Rem family and all the relevant suprafamily members from the beginning. If one ignores significant suprasystem members, for instance, a bioparent or grandparent who currently has input into the presenting problem, then sooner or later either that "significant other" will try to sabotage treatment or there will be a failure to resolve the problems in the Rem subsystem. Once therapy has begun, it is more difficult to include members, for instance, a former spouse, since the therapist is likely to be identified as being partisan to the Rem family and viewed with suspicion or hostility by others in the suprasystem.

These principles are applied flexibly and with sensitivity. It is wise to avoid battles with family members, and we settle graciously for less than the optimal; otherwise we will lose the family. It is wise to cast as wide a net as necessary, but don't lose the person who has made the call for help, or there may not be another opportunity. We do not, however, give up easily. We use our ingenuity, time, and energy to work toward arranging for everyone to be seen at least once during this evaluation phase.

The First Telephone Call

Treatment begins with the first telephone call. Goals for this stage vary, depending on the nature of the presenting problem or symptoms and the nature of the Rem suprasystem. If the call comes from a Rem couple and they are requesting marital therapy for themselves, we make the appointment for both spouses and finish the call. Where a child is identified as "the problem," our optimal goal is to have all of the parenting adults, whether they be bioparents, stepparents, grandparents, or stepgrandparents, as well as the other children, present for the first meeting. We achieve this by introducing the caller to the concept of the Rem suprasystem—not using the term, of course! We find out who is in the overall family, who and where each bioparent is, and how much contact the child has with each. We remind the caller that the child has two bioparents and that each is important and needed by the child. We ask about others in the Rem suprasystem, including visiting and living-in children, stepchildren, half-siblings, grandparents, and significant others. We ask if the bioparents and stepparents have discussed with one another the child's problems, and who knows of this call. We may do a thumbnail genogram for ourselves at this point so that we can order the information.

With this early understanding of the composition and nature of the Rem suprasystem and its problem, we then proceed to introduce the caller to the idea of including all the parental figures as well as the children in the evaluation. We often get a negative response. However, once it is explained, clients are often willing to cooperate. Where there is hesitation and there clearly continues to be much dissension in the Rem suprasystem, especially between the two household subsystems, we listen to the concern and try to point out that since the child is in the middle and lives in both families, it is in the best interests of the child for the adults to work together. Here we may underscore that it will be the parenting and stepparenting issues that will be addressed in the first session, not the former spouses' old or current complaints against each other.

When our caller is opposed to the inclusion of others, has not told the other parent of the interest in treatment, or identifies the other bioparent as "anti-therapy," we try to move them away from a blaming, critical approach to one that emphasizes cooperation. We rehearse with our caller what he or she can say and how it might be said. Most often when individuals have been guided in this way they can, despite their anxiety, follow through, or can then see that they really do not want to include the other parent.

If the caller is unsuccessful in getting the former spouse to agree to come in, we may then ask permission to call directly. We explain why we are calling, our concern for their child, and why we consider his or her presence invaluable. Our goal is to bypass the anger, hostility, and fear of the spouse at this time. We do not wish to lose the case and will start work with whatever segments of the suprasystem that will come in.

First Meetings

Evaluation may constitute three to six sessions in which we assess the Rem and other subsystems and establish goals of therapy. Patterns of interaction are observed; unconscious behavior and the effects of symptoms are noted. How to achieve reasonable, agreed-upon goals for subsystems and individuals is mapped out.

Prior to the meeting, the therapist makes sure that there are enough chairs and sufficient space for everyone. For the children there are two or three sets of family puppet dolls, enough to include the possible combinations of bioparents, stepparents, and children. Also available are age-appropriate play material, paper, crayons, dolls, hand puppets, trucks, cars, soldiers, and the like.

The task of the therapist in this initial meeting is to help the family members feel welcome, to begin to develop a working alliance with each, and to begin the process of establishing a safe, facilitating therapeutic environment. Family members are helped to express their feelings about being present and are asked what they see as the problems, both for themselves and for their families. Where there is a scapegoated child, the therapist may relabel the behavior by directing the attention to the positive purpose and function the child's behavior may be serving in the Rem suprasystem. At the same time the therapist is thinking diagnostically and formulating a tentative hypothesis about the purpose of the presenting problem(s) for the Rem suprasystem, the subsystems, and the individual. Also, life-cycle and intrapsychic aspects are being considered for every member.

If evaluation is successful, we shall have achieved our immediate goals and have moved on to establish intermediate and long-range goals. Each individual and subsystem is helped to define achievable goals. For example, when a child says, "I want my parents to live with me," it's clear that this goal is not achievable. We then try to help the child mourn (within his or her ability) the loss and irretrievability of his nuclear family, experiencing the anger and sadness that lead to acceptance. At the same time, we work with both biological parents for them to reassure the child of their continued love, commitment, physical presence in the child's life, and being there for him. We take means to minimize loyalty conflicts between bioparent and ipsolateral stepparent.

All goals must be agreed upon. Goals and contracts are under constant evaluation and review as treatment progresses. This work forms the essence of the middle phase of the therapeutic process.

Some goals that surface frequently are:

1. To consolidate the Rem couple as a unit and establish their authority in the system.
2. To consolidate the bioparental authority in the suprasystem among bioparents and stepparents with the formulation of an effective coparenting team that leaves room for the stepparent(s).
3. As a corollary to item 2, to help children deal with and minimize the continuance and exacerbation of loyalty bonds.
4. To facilitate mourning of the nuclear family, former spouse, old neighborhood, friends, and way of life.
5. To be certain there is a secure place for the child's development through optimal utilization of the suprafamily system.
6. To help family members accept and tolerate their differences from their idealized intact family model. Some such new differences may be lack of complete control of money allocation and in child rearing; differences in feelings for and of the bioparent and stepparent; differences in rules, cultures, values, and expectations in the two households; different intensity of bonding in Rem and earlier households.

Therapy is structured to achieve goals in as orderly a progression as possible, accented by a strong dash of the serendipitous. Rarely have I formulated a treatment plan that did not have to be revised. For example:

Presenting complaint was of a child's recent poor functioning in school. Evaluation indicated that the child was living in a chaotic suprafamily system in which none of the adults took responsibility for setting limits with him.

This situation began after his mother's remarriage. In his Rem family household there was role confusion between mother and her spouse—each expecting the other to parent the child.

Biofather abdicated his parental role, too. He communicated hastily and perfunctorily with his son's mother about the child. When with his son, the father focused on entertaining him and giving him whatever he wanted. Mother and stepfather were frustrated because the child's needs seemed to interfere constantly with the fulfillment of their own romantic needs for each other.

The immediate goal was to help all the adults—biomother, biofather, and stepfather—form a collaborative parenting team and begin to clarify their parenting expectations, both with one another and the child. Once this was accomplished, the chaos diminished and the child's functioning in school was restored. The Rem couple then requested further help in consolidating their relationship with each other, which becomes a new treatment goal for them.

Biofather worked through his feelings about the loss of his former wife and family, which had been stirred anew by the remarriage and which he could now see had been interfering with his capacity to function optimally as a single parent.

Goals of the two bioparental systems may be mutually exclusive, as may be those of any subsystem or individual vis-à-vis another. These goal differences must be clearly delineated to determine if they are real or only apparent. If real, can they be reconciled or negotiated in some fashion? Some are so pervasive and mutually exclusive that family members and therapist may have to accept that a particular system is not viable.

TREATMENT

Common treatment issues may include the inability to consolidate into a viable marital unit, meeting the love needs of the adults, and yet allowing them to carry on with parenting and other appropriate family life–cycle needs. Often there are bonds and priorities as powerful, or more powerful, elsewhere, which can produce crisis, confusion, and jealousy in the current couple relationship. Such factors may lead to concomitant failure to resolve pivotal marital issues of intimacy, power, exclusion-inclusion of others, and failure to negotiate and resolve their individual and joint marital contracts (Sager 1976, 1979).

These failures may have come about through a variety of circumstances. Parents often experience guilt or confusion between loyalty to their children of a former spouse and to a current spouse. The parent, not the child or new spouse, must take prime responsibility for confronting and resolving this dilemma. One partner may have failed to appropriately work through and accept the loss of his or her former spouse. Other couples may be involved in a bond of pseudo-mutuality (Wynne 1958). This bond inevitably intrudes destructively into the relationship. Conversely, the former spouse may have refused to accept termination of the marital relationship, and may constantly intrude himself or herself into the current pairing, at times using the children for this purpose. The remarried partner may covertly condone this intrusion out of his or her own guilt over the end of their marriage.

Some parents develop an overly close bond to a child during the dual single-parent household phase. Later, neither the parent nor the child is able to alter the quality and intensity of this bond in order to make room for the entry and/or inclusion of the new marital partner into the system. It is a process that usually takes time and patience. The new marital partner may have been unable or unwilling to help his mate separate from the child and move into a closer couple pairing without arousing defensiveness and drawing hostility onto himself. The difficulty in keeping the adult-pairing love separate from the parent-child love reappears as a common problem of new Rem families.

We cannot deal here in further detail with the process of the middle phase of therapy. It is necessary to normalize the remarriage situation and to live one's life out cognizant of the past marriage and its influence on the present. Let me touch on a few of the issues that come up frequently that are not present when one is dealing with first marriages.

Incomplete Emotional Divorce

Continued hatred and anger toward the former spouse that is as fresh as the day of separation is an important sign of overattachment. An equally reliable sign of overattachment is the ex-spouse who still carries a torch, extols the virtues of the divorced spouse, and makes invidious comparisons to the present spouse.

The therapist's first step is to attempt to get through the defensive denial of the continuing overattachment. After accumulating a few examples with the help of the current spouse, if there is no true recognition of the problem, I sometimes see the overattached partner a few times alone. Often without the presence of the current spouse it is easier for someone to be in better touch with feelings and be more ready to deal with them.

A man was excessively generous with his former wife because she would "get upset" if he did not give her sizable sums of money beyond their agreement for "emergencies." He couldn't stand the idea that she would be angry with him. He had left her for his current wife and felt guilty that the latter and he had a much better relationship. His present wife was upset over the attention and extra money he gave to his first wife. His wife mentioned how recent photographs of her husband's former wife and him had been taken by their son (her stepson) on a recent visit and sent to him by his former wife with a note replete with some loving comments. He had made no mention of these pictures but had placed them in an open envelope in a drawer that he and his wife both used. The husband grudgingly began to perceive how provocative his actions might have been. He recognized that although he had made the decision to leave his former marriage, he blamed his present wife for this because he loved her and she had refused to have an affair with him unless he left his marriage. His uncon-·scious attachment and guilt toward his former wife and his blaming of his current mate led to his provocative behavior.

His behavior had been preconscious and was readily seen by him with a little help after two individual sessions. We then resumed conjoint sessions, which ended shortly thereafter. Altogether there were twelve sessions. He now had completed his emotional divorce and was more fully able to accept his wife, and she her stepparent role.

Children of a Previous Marriage

This most common situation can be a source of friction between two adults. A good starting therapeutic approach is to try to normalize the situation with all its attendant difficulties for the bioparent and stepparent as well as the child. The therapist should help to define the problem and get it out in the open; he or she should explore superego factors related to guilt of the bioparent and relieve them if it is appropriate to do so. For example, the therapist can help to change an overly cathected mother-child relationship that served useful functions during the single-parent phase but must be careful not to blame the parent for its understandable origin. The therapist should elicit the plausible positive effect the Rem situation can now offer to all concerned. He or she can help the bioparent to allow the child and stepparent to develop their own relationship. The bioparent is not to ask the stepparent to intervene or discipline the child and then interfere by undermining his or her efforts. The bioparent is to allow the stepparent slowly to take on a more disciplinary role as the relationship, role definition, and trust grow. Stepparents cannot expect instant love or obedience from a child. Stepparents must accept that the child has a father or mother in another household.

The therapist should help the couple minimize the child's potential for loyalty conflict by not forcing choices and by respecting the child's need and feeling for her or his other bioparent.

> A stepmother vented her anger in a conjoint session about her stepdaughter and her husband; she felt rejected by the child. After having spent a delightful day, later at the dinner table, the child suddenly withdrew, refused to eat, and asked when she could go home. I wondered out loud if the child had suddenly thought about her biomother and felt guilty because she had experienced such a good time with her stepmother. The stepmother thought it was a good possibility. We then discussed ways in which she could be alert to situations like this. I suggested that she tell the child that it's O.K. if she likes her stepmother too, but of course her mother is someone very special whom she has special love for, and so on.

Spouses' Life-Cycle Positions

Spouses may be in different life-cycle positions. Conflict arises, for example, when a woman embarks on a career at the time her husband has already had success in his. He now wants a companion, lover, and playmate, and he finds it difficult to accept the time and preoccupation his wife may put into her career instead of him. On the average, remarried couples have a greater age spread than do first marrieds and are therefore more likely to have different life-cycle and family-cycle needs and desires (McGoldrick and Carter 1988).

Life-cycle and marital-cycle needs may be consonant for the two partners, but the stepparent may not accept or be able to fulfill family-cycle roles. This is particularly so in regard to coparenting and its attendant responsibilities. An awareness of where the problem lies and bringing the problem to full awareness of both spouses is a prerequisite step for resolution. The therapist in these situations often has to help the bioparent accept that his or her spouse will not share the responsibility for child care as fully as he or she wishes.

Sexual Abuse

A number of factors make the likelihood of household sex abuse greater in Rem families than in intact families. Certainly the abuse ("incest") barrier between stepfather-stepdaughter and stepsiblings is appreciably lower than in consanguinous relationships.[2] Parents and stepparents should be alert to these possibilities. It is particularly important for bioparents to take seriously any attempt on their child's part to discuss possible abuse with them, be it heterosexual or homosexual.

Finances

Men who remarry are often not in a position to finance the endeavor, or can do so only marginally, or the couple may not be able to make peace with relying on the wife's contribution. If there is not full disclosure of income and obligations by both partners before marriage, the marriage may have been founded on false premises. The therapist may have to play a mediating role in such situations and help the couple explore motivations for marriage and whether they feel duped, exploited, or taken advantage of in other ways as well.

Young couples starting out in marriage most often accumulate together. In remarriage there is more of a tendency to try to hold on to and control the assets each has brought to the marriage. Those who have children often wish to protect the financial future or inheritance of their children. And, having been divorced once, a woman or man may fear a financial debacle the second time. These questions have led to the common practice of prenuptial agreements, which at times can be very destructive, though they often have a positive effect. With an awareness of the frailty of marriage, many prenuptial agreements that start out severely limiting or excluding inheritance rights to the new spouse may also include increasing amounts of more equitable distribution after incremental years of continued marriage. It is important that mates-to-be discuss financial matters in advance. Not to do so can effectively and rapidly destroy Cupid's work.

Those who remarry are obviously older than they were the first time around. They have obligations to children and/or former spouses. They literally bring with them the baggage of former marriages and homes in terms of life-styles, furniture, and customs to which they have been committed. It is necessary to accept that life with someone else they love will be different from what it had been previously. Having mates reverse positions in role-playing and the use of quid pro quos and compromise can be effective therapeutic

---

[2]Household sexual abuse in related families is discussed more fully in Perlmutter et al. (1982).

techniques when the spouses have a reasonable measure of affection and caring for each other upon which to build.

TREATMENT MODALITIES

Starting with a good working knowledge of family systems theory and conviction regarding the correctness of the concept of multiple genetic and environmental inputs to all individuals and family systems, we can approach working with the Rem family. We keep in mind family structure and individual needs and function, values, and intrapsychic needs and defenses. Some issues are specific to Rem families; some emotional and interactional family system dynamics are more generalized. Both for evaluation and treatment, it is important that the therapist conceptualize the problems in terms of the suprafamily system while keeping in mind the needs of the individual members and the two bioparent systems.

Our primary therapeutic process is to refocus and redefine the problem with the family in terms of the whole system and its subsequent needs and responsibilities. In Rem, the therapist helps the family understand the expanded system: its differences from a nuclear family, the appropriate significance and role of any of the suprafamily nonhousehold members, and how they all may affect one another. This process facilitates de-scapegoating children, who often are blamed for the Rem family's troubles. Insight methods are utilized if and when the therapist views them applicable. When tasks are used, we are concerned with any resistance to carrying them out as well as with the feelings evoked. The reasons and feelings surfaced by an incompleted task are often of great therapeutic import. The therapist should choose tasks that are designed to produce a specifically predicted behavioral and/or attitudinal change.

There are no hard and fast rules, and sensitive timing is of the essence. Familiarity and ease in working with a variety of modalities is helpful. It is easier to begin immediately with everyone involved in the problem and then work down, breaking into subunits, than it is to begin with the microsystem (for instance, the child), and try to include others later.

If the Rem couple's relationship is the presenting problem, other family members need to be seen. When there is clearly unfinished business with a prior partner, then a few couple-sessions with the divorced pair, or individual sessions with that Rem partner may be held to focus on further completion of the emotional divorce, while at the same time moving into couples work with the current partners. It is not necessary to include all suprafamily or Rem members in every session. However, one should keep in mind the different subsystems and how the present parts fit into the entire dynamic mosaic. The capacity for both flexibility and activity on the part of the therapist is crucial; successful treatment depends on the therapist's comfort with moving in and out of the different parts of the system while utilizing different modalities, including family, couple, individual, and child, as indicated. Since emotions in Rem families often run high, the therapist must be comfortable in being active and able to take charge of the sessions. These abilities are particularly necessary when: (1) the session includes the former spouse, (2) there is a psychotic individual, (3) members are manipulative or form an alliance to defeat the therapist, or (4) the family's underlying feelings of hopelessness and despair are rampant.

I try not to use cotherapists, unless absolutely necessary (when there is strong conflict between one subunit and another). Cotherapy is sometimes prohibitively expensive. A solo therapist can achieve similar results through separate appointments with different subsystems of the suprafamily—for instance, with the Rem system and with the single parent system—prior to meeting with the entire system. Another excellent way is to split a session, seeing one subsystem for part of the session, the second subsystem for another part of the session, and then all together.

The Use of Groups

Couples groups often are the treatment of choice for many Rem couples. My experience and that of my colleagues demonstrates that this modality best addresses several important problem sources in the Rem system, notably, the lack of consolidation of the couple, ill-defined mourning of the lost relationship and spouse, and guilt and conflict about children or former spouse. The group can provide a structure for the couples, separate from their children and stepchildren. It provides time and privacy for them to work on their mutual contracts with each other, experiencing support from others who are struggling with similar issues. In groups one has the opportunity to be "reparented" in a corrective emotional experience with the therapist and one another. Family meetings separate from the group can be held periodically, for the purpose of both helping the couple integrate their changes into the system and facilitating the children's integration into the Rem family.

We have tried multiple family therapy groups (MFT) (Lacquer 1972) of unselected Rem families, but we do not recommend this modality for families who are very chaotic and needy. Further, MFT makes it more difficult to include former spouses and other suprafamily members, because to include these makes the group unwieldy and is disruptive of ongoing processes, as many suprafamily members need be only transiently engaged in treatment. Adolescents, though, have found MFT to be most beneficial. We currently advocate couples groups and separate groups for children of Rem, particularly for adolescents, who often feel like "orphans" in their Rem families and isolated from their peers.

We are also experimenting with including children in their own and in the couples group for some sessions, after the couples have been successful at consolidating themselves and are then ready to address the parenting issues directly, within the supportive framework of the group. We will return to the use of MFT with better consolidated Rem couples, whose situations are not so chaotic as were those in our earlier experiences.

THE THERAPIST

The therapist working with remarriage situations is subjected to constant confrontation with his or her own emotions and value systems. The first area of emotional assault on the therapist has to do with male/female relatedness and systems of loyalty and consanguinity. The therapist may have values markedly different from those that have allowed Rem adults to divorce and remarry, live with someone, or break up a marriage. Actions and feelings of various Rem family members touch off emotional reactions based on experiences the therapist has had, has feared will happen, or has not dared to bring about in his or her own life because of guilt, anxiety, superego constraints, or cultural considerations. True countertransferential reactions may also occur wherein patients and/or their system enmesh the therapist, and he or she reacts in the way individuals or the system unconsciously set him or her up to react.

The complexities of the Rem system, the sense of despair, hopelessness, and loss, and the chaos and crisis that are at work may spill over into the therapists' personal lives. At first we found ourselves putting our personal relationships on hold and avoiding decisions about making or ending commitments to others. Depression and despair were common reactions without clarity about the source of these feelings.

These reactions can best be dealt with through the use of a trusted and supportive group of peers. Consultation, supervision, and the use of the group to help individual therapists recognize and address personal reactions mitigate some of the anxiety and pain that seems built into work with Rem systems. Specific areas of vulnerability for the therapists working with Rem system have been elaborated upon elsewhere (Sager et al. 1981, 1983, Sager 1986).

CONCLUSION

The approach to treating remarried or suprafamilies described in this chapter is not the final word by any means. It is a flexible approach that provides a theoretical system and methodology that allows a great deal of individual initiative for therapists to follow their own choices of theoretical and technique proclivities. It is a system of therapy that usually calls for one therapist. As in all therapy, however, therapists require the support of their colleagues in some form of supervision in a peer group. The more diverse the professional, theoretical, and experiential backgrounds of the group, the more likely it is that therapists will constantly review their work and continue to improve the quality of their endeavors.

REFERENCES

Carter, B., and McGoldrick, M. (1988). *The Changing Family Life Cycle*, p. 409. New York: Gardner.

Lacquer, A. P. (1972). Mechanics of change in multiple family therapy. In *Progress in Group and Family Therapy*, ed. C. J. Sager and H. S. Kaplan. New York: Brunner/Mazel.

Messinger, L., Walker, K. N., and Freeman, S. J. (1978). Preparation for re-marriage following divorce. *American Journal of Orthopsychiatry* 48: 263–272.

Pasley, K., and Ihinger-Tallman, M. (1982). Remarried family life supports and constraints. In *Family Strengths, Vol. 4, Positive Support Systems*, ed. N. Stinnett et al. Lincoln, NE: University of Nebraska Press.

Perlmutter, L. H., Engel, T., and Sager, C. J. (1982). The incest taboo: loos-ened sexual boundaries in remarried families. *Journal of Sex and Marital Therapy* 6:83–106.

Sager, C. J. (1976). *Marriage Contracts and Couple Therapy*. New York: Brunner/Mazel.

——— (1981). Couples therapy and marriage contracts. In *Handbook of Family Therapy*, ed. A. S. Gurman and D. P. Kniskern. New York: Brunner/Mazel.

——— (1986). Therapy with remarried couples. In *Clinical Handbook of Marital Therapy*, ed. N. S. Jackson and Alan S. Garman. New York: Guilford.

Sager, C. J., Brown, H. S., Crohn, H., Engel, T., Rodstein, E., and Walker, L. (1983). *Treating the Remarried Family*. New York: Brunner/Mazel.

Sager, C. J., Brown, H. S., Crohn, H. M., Rodstein, E., and Walker, E. (1980). Remarriage revisited. *Family and Child Mental Health Journal* 6:19–25.

——— (1981). Improving functioning of the remarried family system. *Journal of Marital and Family Therapy* 7:1–13.

Visher, E., and Visher, J. (1987). *Old Loyalties, New Ties: Therapeutic Strategies with Stepfamilies*. New York: Brunner/Mazel.

Walker, L., Brown, H. S., Crohn, H., Rodstein, E., Zeisel, E., and Sager, C. J. (1979). Annotated bibliography of the remarried, the living together and their children. *Family Process* 18:193–212.

INDEX

COMMENTARY

"Textor's *Divorce and Divorce Therapy Handbook* is comprehensive and contemporary in its coverage. The wide-ranging chapters cover all major aspects of the dynamics and process of divorce and remarriage, summarizing what has transpired in the past few decades and adding critical insights. There are practical suggestions for assessing and intervening with the troubled individuals, couples, and families who seek therapeutic services around issues ostensibly emanating from these life cycle events."

—Florence W. Kaslow, Ph.D.

"Professor Textor has produced an eminently readable and highly practical volume for all mental health practitioners. Its territory of coverage is broad, necessarily so, since the clinician needs to know about a variety of different content domains to successfully deal with divorce and its aftermath. Textor's book will last. Well done!"

—Howard Liddle, Ed.D.

"The chapters collectively offer the reader a wealth of information about divorce, separation, parent–child issues, and remarriage, culled from a broad base of research studies and the manifold clinical experiences of seasoned practitioners. Of significant clinical value are those chapters offering step-by-step precise approaches to divorce mediation and counseling. The serious student of human relations, as well as the sophisticated layman, will find this clearly written and well-organized volume a valuable contribution."

—Bert L. Kaplan, Ed.D.